People, Population Change and Policies

European Studies of Population

Volume 16/2

The book series *European Studies of Population (ESPO)* aims at disseminating population and family research, with special relevance for Europe. It may analyse past, present and/or future trends, as well as their determinants and consequences. The character of the series is multidisciplinary, including formal demographic analyses, as well as social, economic and/or historical population and family studies. The following types of studies are of primary importance: (a) internationally relevant studies, (b) European comparative studies, (c) innovative theoretical and methodological studies, and (d) policy-relevant scientific studies. The series may include monographs, edited volumes and reference works.

The book series is published under the auspices of the *European Association for Population Studies (EAPS)*.

Charlotte Höhn · Dragana Avramov ·
Irena E. Kotowska

Editors

People, Population Change and Policies

Lessons from the Population Policy
Acceptance Study Vol. 2: Demographic
Knowledge – Gender – Ageing

 Springer

Editors

Charlotte Höhn
Federal Institute for Population Research
Wiesbaden
Germany

Dragana Avramov
Population and Social Policy Consultants (PSPC)
Brussels
Belgium

Irena E. Kotowska
Warsaw School of Economics
Warsaw
Poland

ISBN: 978-1-4020-6610-8   e-ISBN: 978-1-4020-6611-5

Library of Congress Control Number: 2007938400

Printed on acid-free paper.

9 8 7 6 5 4 3 2 1

springer.com

Acknowledgement

The two volumes of the work "People, Population Change and Policies: Lessons from Population Policy Acceptance Study" are the final outcome of the DIALOG project. This project was funded by European Commission for three years in the 5th Framework Programme.

Contents

Contributors

Anita Abramowska
Institute of Statistics and Demography, Warsaw School of Economics, Poland
aabram@sgh.waw.pl

Dragana Avramov
Population and Social Policy Consultants (PSPC), Brussels, Belgium
avramov@avramov.org

Alfred Bertschinger
Sociological Institute of the University of Zurich, Zurich, Switzerland
a.bertschinger@freesurf.ch

Marc Callens
Research Centre of the Flemish Government (SVR), Brussels, Belgium
marc.callens@dar.vlaanderen.be

Robert Cliquet
Population and Social Policy Consultants (PSPC), Brussels, Belgium
robert.cliquet@avramov.org

Piero Dell'Anno
Istituto di ricerche sulla Popolazione e le Politiche Sociali, Consiglio Nazionale delle Ricerche, Rome, Italy

Jürgen Dorbritz
Federal Institute for Population Research, Wiesbaden, Germany
juergen.dorbritz@destatis.de

Charlotte Höhn
Federal Institute for Population Research, Wiesbaden, Germany
charlotte.hoehn@destatis.de

Janina Jóźwiak
Institute of Statistics and Demography, Warsaw School of Economics,
Warsaw, Poland
ninaj@sgh.waw.pl

Osmo Kontula
The Population Research Institute, Family Federation of Finland, Helsinki, Finland
osmo.kontula@vaestoliitto.fi

Irena E. Kotowska
Institute of Statistics and Demography, Warsaw School of Economics,
Warsaw, Poland
iekoto@sgh.waw.pl

Ralf Mai
Federal Institute for Population Research, Wiesbaden, Germany
ralf.mai@destatis.de

Beatrice Elena Manea
Faculty of Social Studies, Masaryk University, Brno, Czech Republic
manea@fss.muni.cz

Adele Menniti
Istituto di ricerche sulla Popolazione e le Politiche Sociali, Consiglio Nazionale
delle Ricerche, Rome, Italy
a.menniti@irpps.cnr.it

Maura Misiti
Istituto di ricerche sulla Popolazione e le Politiche Sociali, Consiglio Nazionale
delle Ricerche, Rome, Italy
m.misiti@irpps.cnr.it

Robert Naderi
Federal Institute for Population Research, Wiesbaden, Germany
robert.naderi@destatis.de

Rossella Palomba
Istituto di ricerche sulla Popolazione e le Politiche Sociali, Consiglio Nazionale
delle Ricerche, Rome, Italy
r.palomba@irpps.cnr.it

Dimiter Philipov Österreichische Akademie der Wissenschaften – Institut für
Demographie, Vienna, Austria
dimiter.philipov@oeaw.ac.at

Ladislav Rabušic
Faculty of Social Studies, Masaryk University, Brno, Czech Republic
rabu@fss.muni.cz

Kerstin Ruckdeschel
Federal Institute for Population Research, Wiesbaden, Germany
kerstin.ruckdeschel@destatis.de

Peter Schimany
Federal Office for Migration and Refugees, Nuremberg, Germany
peter.schimany@bamf.bund.de

Ronald C. Schoenmaeckers
Studiedienst Vlaamse Regering, Brussels, Belgium
ronald.schoenmaeckers@dar.vlaanderen.be

Ismo Söderling
The Population Research Institute, Family Federation of Finland, Helsinki, Finland
ismo.soderling@vaestoliitto.fi

Lieve Vanderleyden
Studiedienst Vlaamse Regering, Brussels, Belgium
lieve.vanderleyden@dar.vlaanderen.be

Lucie Vidovićová
Faculty of Social Studies, Masaryk University, Brno, Czech Republic
lucie.vidovic@seznam.cz

Part I
Demographic Trends, Population Related Policies and General Attitudes

Chapter 1
Demographic Change and Family Policy Regimes

Osmo Kontula and Ismo Söderling

Abstract The DIALOG countries are experiencing long-term downward trends in fertility, leading to demographic ageing. Natural population growth rates are entering periods of declining growth or outright decrease. There are a great number of societal problems that arise from this demographic transition. Up to date, it has been disputable whether public policies have had any impact on population trends.

This article groups DIALOG countries into four family policy regimes based firstly on the generousness of the public support they provided to families, and secondly on their variant emphasis on the socio-economic and gender equity issues in their societies. In addition, the associations between the family policy types and the socio-economic clusters and demographic change and public opinion are presented.

Family policy regimes were found to have considerable overlaps with the clusters that were formulated on the basis of demographic, economic, social policy, employment and educational indicators of the same countries. Societies form their family policies in great part according to the monetary resources that are available in their countries. As an exception to this, some countries limit their public support to means-tested benefits for poor families, and they also pay less attention to gender equity issues at home and in the labour force.

These choices have been associated with demographic changes in these countries. Countries relying on the "Labour market" regime in their family policy had the highest fertility rates. In contrast, "Imposed home care" countries had cut down their income transfers and benefits to their citizenships. This transition was associated with very low fertility. DIALOG countries that had applied family policy approaches that were in harmony with the population's family values had higher fertility rates than the other countries. This finding has policy implications for population policies.

Keywords: Demographic change · Family policy regimes · Fertility · Public opinion

O. Kontula
The Population Research Institute, Family Federation of Finland, Helsinki, Finland
e-mail: osmo.kontula@vaestoliitto.fi

C. Höhn et al. (eds.), *People, Population Change and Policies: Vol. 2: Demographic Knowledge – Gender – Ageing*, © Springer Science+Business Media B.V. 2008

1.1 Introduction

European countries, including the DIALOG countries, have faced a major demographic change and transition in the last thirty years. They are experiencing long-term downward trends in fertility, leading to demographic ageing. Fertility rates are now below replacement level in nearly all countries. As a result, natural population growth rates are starting to decline, or population sizes are falling outright. At the same time, the proportion of elderly dependants continues to grow while the working-age population declines in absolute and relative terms (see Kontula and Miettinen 2005). Moreover, net immigration, which potentially could offset declines in working-age population, remains generally low in most European countries (Grant et al. 2004).

There are a great number of societal problems that arise from this demographic transition. The International Monetary Fund (2004) argues that the impact of upcoming demographic changes on economical growth could be substantial. The historic association between demographic and macro-economic variables suggests that the projected increase in elderly dependency ratios and the projected decline in the share of the working-age population could result in slower per capita GDP growth, and lower saving and investment (IMF 2004, 147). For example, the estimates suggest that demographic change could reduce annual real per capita GDP growth in advanced countries by an average of $1/2\%$ point by 2050, i.e., growth would be $1/2\%$ point lower than if the demographic structure had remained the same as in 2000 (IMF 2004, 147).

Demographic change in Europe has stimulated demographers. The concept of the "Second Demographic Transition" was undoubtedly the theory of the 1990s. It describes and explains the substantial, unprecedented growth of cohabitation, lone parenthood, extramarital childbearing and low fertility observed in many countries since the 1960s (Coleman 2005, 11). The concept was developed actively during the 1990s (Lesthaeghe and Surkyn 2004): Post-materialist demography has now evolved further into "post-modern" demography (van de Kaa 2001).

To date, it has been disputable whether public policies have had any impact on population trends. Fertility is a key component for future demographic trends, and it would be most helpful if research could find some evidence of how public policies could make a difference to the declining trends in fertility, or indeed reverse these trends. As yet, only in France and Sweden have new approaches and efforts carried out in family policies been shown to have provided a boost to total fertility rates (Hoem 2000; NIDI 2005; Courbage 2003). At the same time, the rapid economic and social transition in the former communist countries has undoubtedly caused the collapse in fertility rates. The policies applied in these countries in the past ten years are a kind of antithesis to successful population policy.

This chapter aims to look for possible associations between the applied family policies and fertility trends in the DIALOG countries. For this purpose, we use the family policy typology of Kontula and Miettinen (2005) and the clusters of DIALOG countries based on their demographic and socio-economic characteristics, i.e. so called contextual macro indicators (see also IMF 2004).

The chapter also presents a brief overview of population growth in the DIALOG countries from 1990 to 2002, based on demographic statistics. This presentation continues with preferences regarding population growth formulated by the populations under study. Attitudes towards population and family issues (public opinion) are compared to family policy regimes. To that end, people's attitudes have been used towards population growth, marriage and children, as well as opinions on family policy measures and about possible impacts of institutional childcare for children's development.

The chapter is an outcome of studies carried out under DIALOG Work Package 4, coordinated by the Population Research Institute (PRI), Family Federation of Finland. Work Package 4 aimed to collect and analyse contextual data on the social and demographic situation in the participating countries, as well as on recent developments in the respective policy fields, especially focusing on policies related to family and ageing, and to relate this to the PPAS data.

1.2 Concepts and Measurement

The information dealt with in this chapter is very largely derived from the country reports that experts from 15 DIALOG countries contributed in 2004 under the guidelines provided by the Population Research Institute (PRI) in Finland (Söderling and Laitalainen 2005). The national reports described socio-demographic and socio-political situation in the DIALOG countries during the period 1990–2002. The final versions of the reports were sent to PRI in summer 2004. They were called "15 parsimonious National Studies Based on Contextual Data and Analysis of General Attitudes". This information is supplemented by public opinion on demographic change studied by the results of the PPAS data.

The detailed information on social and family policies in each DIALOG country report was used by Kontula and Miettinen (2005) to classify countries in four groups (typology of family policy regimes). Countries were divided into four regimes: "Day care service" countries, "Income transfer" countries, "Labour market" countries, and "Imposed home care" countries. These family policy types are applied to analyse demographic and socio-economic contexts and public opinions towards population change and family policies in these countries.

Country variations in socio-economic contexts are studied by using 18 contextual macroindicators which refer to population, the economy and social policies, employment and education. Our aim is to examine whether the clusters based on these 18 contextual macroindicators are in any way related to the family policy regimes existing in these countries (for the actual indicators and figures, see the Appendix). Next, interrelationships between population growth and its basic components (natural increase and migration) and family policy regimes are analysed. And finally, people's attitudes towards marriage and children, as well as opinions on family policy measures and about possible impacts of institutional childcare for children's development, are analysed by family policy regimes to reveal some characteristic "opinion profiles".

1.3 Population Growth and Attitudes Towards it

The growth rate has been very moderate in the DIALOG countries, and in some cases even negative (Table 1.1). The population increased in ten out of the 15 countries during the period 1996–2002, and in six out of these ten countries positive net migration contributed considerably to that change. The highest population growth was found in Cyprus, Switzerland and the Netherlands. These countries also have the highest rates of net migration.

A negative natural increase has been characteristic of many Eastern and Central European countries. In Estonia, Lithuania and Romania, a negative natural increase has also been combined with negative net migration, leading to a relatively large population decrease (especially in Estonia and Lithuania).

Taking into account the main component of population growth (either natural increase or migration) and changes in the population size during the period 1996–2002, the DIALOG countries can be divided into three groups:

1. **Population growth with a marked natural increase:** Belgium, Cyprus, Netherlands, Switzerland and Finland
2. **Population growth based mainly on positive net migration:** Austria, Germany and Italy
3. **No population growth or population decrease:** the Czech Republic, Estonia, Hungary, Lithuania, Poland, Romania and Slovenia

In most of the DIALOG countries belonging to cluster 3, the notable majority of respondents (three-quarters) preferred the population to increase in the future (Table 1.2).

The exceptions are the Czech Republic and Poland. Slightly more than one-half of respondents preferred an increase in the former, but a remarkable share also preferred the population size to remain stable. In contrast, in the latter respondents more frequently preferred stability than an increase in the population size.

In countries where population growth is largely based either on natural increase or on net migration, the majority of respondents were satisfied with the population size as it was at the time of the survey (between 2000 and 2003). This finding was the most marked in the Netherlands, a country which was also exceptional due to a larger proportion of respondents who were in favour of decreasing than of increasing the population size. Another exception is Cyprus, where respondents were strongly in favour of increasing the population size, even though the growth rate was already quite high in 1996–2002.

Based on these findings, one can conclude that a stable population size was mostly preferred in countries which experienced population growth, while strong preferences for increases in the population size were expressed in other countries. However, several exceptions show that public opinion on population growth is not always related to the actual population change in the country. It can be presumed that the public debate on population issues could have a major impact on preferences towards population growth.

Table 1.1 Average population growth rate (per 1,000) during 1990–1995 and 1996–2002 in the DIALOG countries

Countries	Average growth rate 1990–1995	Rate of natural increase 1990–1995	Rate of net migration 1990–1995	Average growth rate 1996–2002	Rate of natural increase 1996–2002	Rate of net migration 1996–2002
Belgium	3.2	1.6	1.6	3.0	1.0	2.0
Switzerland	9.4	3.3	6.3	5.1	2.2	2.9
Czech R.	0.3	−0.4	0.7	−0.9	−1.9	0.9
Germany	5.6	−1.0	6.6	1.3	−1.0	2.2
Estonia	−16.2	−2.4	−13.8	−7.1	−4.3	−2.8
Italy	1.9	−0.0	1.9	2.0	−0.5	2.4
Cyprus	16.8	9.1	7.8	10.3	5.2	5.1
Lithuania	−3.6	1.7	−5.3	−6.2	−1.6	−4.6
Hungary	−0.9	−2.6	1.8	−2.5	−3.9	1.4
Netherlands	6.6	4.2	2.4	6.3	3.8	2.5
Austria	6.6	1.3	5.3	2.0	0.4	1.7
Poland	2.5	2.9	−0.4	0.1	0.5	−0.4
Romania	−4.0	0.1	−4.2	−2.1	−1.8	−0.3
Slovenia	−0.5	0.6	−1.1	0.3	−0.4	0.8
Finland	4.7	3.1	1.6	2.5	1.6	0.8

Source: Kontula and Miettinen 2005

Table 1.2 Preferences regarding future population growth around 2000 by clusters (percentage of respondents), DIALOG countries

Clusters	Population increase	No change	Population decrease	Total
Growth with natural increase				
Netherlands	9	62	29	100
Belgium (Fl)	35	49	16	100
Finland	40	58	2	100
Cyprus	75	23	2	100
Growth with net migration				
Italy	42	51	7	100
Slovenia	62	35	3	100
No growth or decrease				
Estonia	77	22	1	100
Lithuania	73	26	2	101
Hungary	76	22	2	100
Romania	73	22	5	100
Czech Republic	55	40	5	100
Poland	39	51	10	100

Notes: No data are available for Germany or Austria
Source: IPPAS

1.4 Remarks on Population and Family Policies in Europe

There has been a call for targeted population policies in response to population changes in Europe. Population policy may be defined as deliberately constructed or modified institutional arrangements and/or specific programs, through which governments influence demographic change directly or indirectly (Encyclopaedia of Population 2003). Population policy covers explicit measures instituted by a government to influence the population size and its distribution.

Population policy has been neither a widely used governmental approach towards population issues in Europe, nor a popular concept among policy makers. In their country reports, the national DIALOG experts did not find much evidence of active population policies in their homelands. In some CEE countries there had been pronatal policies in the era of communist rule – this had disappeared in the 1990s along with the new political rule. Governments were found to be quite passive in their population policies (Söderling and Laitalainen 2005; NIDI 2005).

The term "family policy" is used to describe what the government does to and for families. It refers to those public policies that are explicitly designed to affect the situation of families with children or individuals in their family roles, as well as to those that have clear consequences for children and their families, even though the impact may not have been intended. The family may be both an object and a vehicle of social policy, for example, policies may be designed to compensate families for the costs of children or to encourage parents to have more children (Kamerman et al. 2003).

Governments in the EU Member States have sought to meet three main family policy objectives, reflecting the different rationales underlying their welfare regimes: income (re)distribution, pronatalism, and equal opportunities. Some Member States have pursued all three objectives simultaneously. All governments have implemented measures through taxation and benefits that redistribute resources, either horizontally between families from those who have no children to those who do, or vertically from wealthier to poorer families. Concern about population decline has served to justify the promotion of family policy measures to stem the decline in fertility (Hantrais 2004).

With regard to the CEE countries, economic transfers to families in terms of social benefits and family allowances (including large families, lone-parent families, etc.) and services were an essential part of their family policies prior to 1989. Only France and the Nordic countries have always enjoyed benefits comparable with those in the former communist countries. These countries have undergone a general erosion in the support and services provided to families with children due to a decline in government expenditure and with the introduction of substantial user fees after the economic reforms started. The real value of social transfers has been eroded for all social groups (O'Reilly 1996).

1.5 Family Policy Regimes and Their Interrelations with Demographic Change

There have been a number of models for clustering European welfare states. Family policy has been an important element in these attempts to group countries according to the specified criteria. Lewin-Epstein et al. (2000) have grouped countries with their family policies into Traditional, In-between and Generous. Ostner and Lewis (1995) have classified several European countries according to the strength of the male-breadwinner norm as manifested in national tax and social security systems, the level of public childcare provision, and the nature of female labour force participation.

Social and family policy regimes have also been divided into three groups labelled as "Etatism" (services, financial incentives), "Familialism" (financial incentives, pronatal) and "Individualism" (weak financial incentives, hardly any services) (Fux 2002, 2004). Under the "Etatism" regime, important values are equality and equal opportunities. These opportunities are promoted with redistributive policies. The "Familialism" regime makes security in society and solidarity inside the family system the important values. The policy is based on financial incentives.

Liberal values such as independence and freedom of choice prevail in the "Individualism" regime. The basis of social policy is subsidiary assistance targeting the poor population.

Referring to the data available that have been collected in the DIALOG studies, a typology of family policy regimes has been proposed (Kontula and Miettinen 2005). It is a combination of different aspects of family policy and welfare, focussing on the generosity of the State in its policies towards families and their allocation of support via incomes and services. The DIALOG countries have been divided into four family policy groups:

1. **Day care service model:** Finland and Slovenia
2. **Income-transfer model:** Belgium (Flanders), Germany, Austria and Italy
3. **Labour market model:** the Netherlands, Switzerland and Cyprus
4. **Imposed home care model:** the Czech Republic, Estonia, Hungary, Poland, Romania and Lithuania

More generous support is generally provided to families in countries belonging to the "Day care service" and "Income transfer" models. In the "Day care service" model, support is channelled more into services intended to reconcile work and family. Part-time work is rare. These countries share some features of "Etatism" as defined by Fux (2004).

The "Income transfer" countries rely more on income transfers than on public services. They encourage either the male-breadwinner model or reconciliation of work and family by use of female part-time work and support of relatives. These countries have some of the features of Western European "Familialism" (Fux 2004).

Less generous support is provided to families in countries included in the "Labour market" and "Imposed home care" models. Countries of the "Labour market" model rely mostly on a well-functioning labour market that offers (young) women good opportunities to work part-time. Day care services are available only locally, also organised by employers. These countries represent "Individualism" as defined by Fux (2004).

Countries belonging to the "Imposed home care" model face economic hardship and have high unemployment. They cannot afford to provide many income transfers and public services to families. Home care without public support is imposed in these countries. State support is increasingly channelled to poor families (means-tested allowances and benefits). These countries have some of the features of Central and Eastern European (imposed) "Familialism" (Fux, 2004).

Similarities and differences between the DIALOG countries included in these four family policy types will be analysed by use of 18 aggregated contextual macroindicators (Table 1.3), based on country-specific figures presented in the Appendix. In general, the greatest differences exist between "Imposed home care" countries and other countries representing the remaining three family policy types.

Economic hardship (low per capita GDP) in "Imposed home care" countries has created a number of implications for citizens' socio-economic conditions. These include a low level of social expenditure in terms of GDP, a high poverty rate and high unemployment rates, especially among young people. Differences in the population indicators between that group and the other groups of countries result mostly from different life patterns, traditions and mortality developments, and in former

Table 1.3 Values of contextual macroindicators in four DIALOG family policy types

Contextual domains	Day care	Income transfer	Labour market	Imposed home care	Total
Population					
Life expectancy at birth, females	81.0	81.8	81.6	77.3	79.8
Mean age of women at first marriage	27.9	27.7	27.6	24.7	26.5
Mean age of women at first birth	27.1	27.6	28.0	24.5	26.4
Live births out of wedlock	38.3	20.9	21.9	29.0	26.7
Proportion of foreign citizenship	2.1	7.1	9.3	4.1	5.6
Economy and social policy					
Per capita GDP (in PPS) EU-25 = 100	94.2	113.9	109.9	47.9	84.1
Human development index	0.94	0.93	0.91	0.84	0.89
Social expenditure, (% of GDP)	26.2	28.5	21.1	15.3	21.4
Expenditure on families and children (% of GDP)	2.7	2.5	1.1	1.0	1.6
Poverty rate after social transfers	11.0	14.2	12	14.5	13.5
Employment					
Economically active people (30–34)	86.5	73.8	80.7	75.2	77.4
Female full-time employment rate (20–39)	61.0	33.0	31.6	48.5	42.6
Female part time employment rate (20–39)	12.4	26.8	41.6	9.2	20.8
Unemployment rate, females (20–64)	7.6	8.0	3.3	11.0	8.2
Youth unemployment rate (under 25 years of age)	18.2	15.6	7.5	22.5	17.1
Ratio of female to male earned income	66.0	45.8	50.0	60.8	55.3
Education and public opinion					
Female in tertiary education	82.0	56.3	39.7	55.0	55.9
Early school leavers (18–24)	5.3	13.4	11.5	11.4	11.1

Source: The means of the percentages after summing up the country figures from Appendix

communists countries compared to other European countries. These include low mean ages at first marriage and at birth of first child, as well as low life expectancy at birth in Central and Eastern European countries.

"Day care service" countries have made considerable investments in social welfare and gender equality. Social expenditure, as well as expenditure on families and children, are high while the poverty rate and the proportion of early school leavers are low. The female full-time employment rate and female enrolment in tertiary education are very high. Also the ratio of female-to-male earned income is high. First births take place relatively late, and are frequently extramarital. The general policy approach emphasises the promotion of equality among citizens.

"Income transfer" model countries have plentiful economic resources in terms of high per capita GDP and social expenditure. However, redistribution of income does not promote equality, and these countries have a relatively high poverty rate. The proportion of early school leavers is also high. Gender equality is not an equally important goal. The female full-time employment rate is low. There is a considerable gender gap when it comes to earned income.

"Labour market" model countries also have plentiful economic resources, measured in terms of per capita GDP, while their public investments in families and children are relatively low – figures related to social expenditure and expenditure on families and children are well below the levels found for two of the models discussed above. Low female and youth unemployment rates are combined with high part-time female employment. Parallel to that, female enrolment in tertiary education is relatively low. The ratio of female-to-male earned income signals a wide gender gap when it comes to earnings. Female part-time employment and support provided by relatives determine childcare provision. "Labour market" countries have much in common with the so-called male breadwinner welfare regime, in which men work full-time and women either work part-time or stay at home.

Country-specific information on the 18 contextual macroindicators was used to cluster the DIALOG countries by Ward's method (Fig. 1.1). Despite the fact that only one indicator, namely the share of expenditure on families and children in terms of GDP, is directly related to family policies, the four clusters which were obtained resemble the country grouping according to the four family policy types presented above (see also Table 1.5).

One cluster covers Finland and Slovenia, two countries belonging to the "Day care service" model. Even though GDP is not as high in Slovenia as in Finland, similarities in socio-economic context and social policy led to these countries being clustered together in spite of differences in demographic and labour market indicators.

The second cluster consists of four countries of the "Income transfer" model (Belgium, Germany, Austria and Italy) plus the Netherlands and Switzerland, which represent the "Labour market" policy regime. This clustering demonstrates the fact that these two countries differ from the first four countries basically only as a result of their less generous income transfers to families.

The third cluster includes Lithuania, Poland, Estonia and Romania, four similar countries of the "Imposed home care" model. Poland and Lithuania seem to have very much in common – the national economy and social policy are not highly

Dendrogram using Ward Method

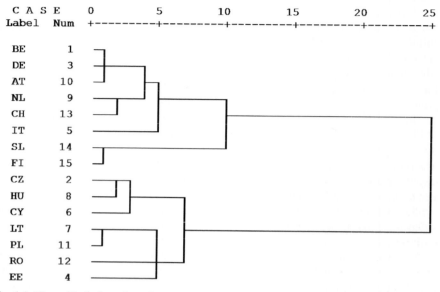

Rescaled Distance Cluster Combine

Fig. 1.1 Hierarchical clustering of the DIALOG countries based on 18 standardised contextual macro indicators

developed in these countries. Among the original "Imposed home care" countries, the Czech Republic and Hungary stepped out to the fourth cluster due to their somewhat better socio-economic conditions. Cyprus joined them from the "Labour market" countries. Cyprus is economically more advanced than the two other countries, but they have much in common in terms of their low level of investment in social policy.

1.6 Family Policy Types and Population Growth

The family policy regimes reveal some associations with the population change which has taken place in the DIALOG countries (Table 1.4). The "Labour market" countries had the highest natural increase rate, and the rate of net migration was also high. Cyprus kept these rates high both in the first part of the 1990s, as well as in the period 1996–2002. Cyprus and the Netherlands are distinct among the DIALOG countries due to the highest rate of natural increase. The "Labour market" policy regime seems to be associated with higher population growth. These statistics are in line with the population growth trend in the U.S., a country which also applies the "Labour market" model in social and family policies. Economic conditions attract

Table 1.4 Family policy types and population growth in the DIALOG countries

Family policy types	Net migration rate	Natural increase rate	Population growth rate
Day care	0.80	0.60	1.40
Income transfer	2.08	−0.03	2.08
Labour market	3.50	3.73	7.23
Imposed home care	−0.97	−2.17	−3.11
Total	0.97	−0.05	0.94

Source: Means of the rates after summing up the country figures from Kontula and Miettinen 2005

immigration in "Labour market" countries, thus contributing to population growth, also due to the fact that migrants' fertility is usually higher.

"Income transfer" countries, especially Germany and Austria, had high net migration rates in the early 1990s, but these rates dropped considerably in the period 1996–2002. As a consequence, the population growth rate decreased but still was positive.

Finland and Slovenia, the "Day care service" countries, represent different stages of family and fertility transformations. They had different population growth rates, mostly due to fertility differences since the net migration rate became positive in Slovenia in the period 1996–2002. Only "Labour market" countries had higher fertility than Finland, while Slovenia belonged to the lowest-low fertility countries.

Most of the "Imposed home care" countries had negative population growth rates in the early 1990s, and this trend was even more pronounced in the period 1996–2002. This was due to both the negative natural increase (low fertility), and to the negative net migration. The highest negative rates of net migration were observed in Lithuania and Estonia, while Hungary and Estonia experienced the most negative natural increases. Only Poland managed to keep the natural increase positive until 2001, despite its steady decline.

Besides possible interrelationships between family policy regimes and population growth and its components, it seems to be interesting to take a look at whether there are any associations between some contextual macroindicators and population growth. Even when accounting for the fact that there are a number of intervening macro- and microcomponents that have their complex impacts on population growth, as well as on fertility in each country, a correlation analysis as given in Table 1.5 supplements our discussion of the population growth referred to in this context.

Per capita GDP and the human development index have a quite strongly positive correlation with population growth, natural increase and net migration. Female unemployment is negatively correlated with population growth and net migration. The natural increase was higher in countries in which more part-time jobs were available for women. Interestingly, expenditure on families and children as a percentage of GDP was not linked to population growth.

Table 1.5 Correlation between selected contextual macroindicators and population growth

Contextual macro indicators	Growth rate	Natural increase	Net migration
Per capita GDP	.69	.59	−.66
Human development index	.54		.50
Unemployment rate, females	−.50		−.60
Female part-time employment rate (20–39)		.52	
Expenditure on families and children	.11	.11	.09

Source: See Appendix (variables 6, 7, 14, 13, 9)
Note: The empty cells are correlations which are not statistically significant

1.7 Family Policy Regimes and Public Opinion

Family policy types reflect the governmental approach to the provision of public support for families. In countries facing economic hardship, governments have more limited possibilities at their disposal to support families, even if they are convinced that such policies are needed. Some governmental attitudes toward family policy might be associated with public opinions on family-related issues and policies. These associations are analysed here using the family policy regimes and the PPAS data on people's opinions of relevant issues.

To that end, several items from different questions have been selected. They concern: respondents' attitudes towards marriage and children (statements 1–6 in Table 1.6), opinions on family policy measures (statements 7–9), and opinions about possible impacts of institutional childcare on children's development (statements 10–11). Only positive choices have been taken into account to calculate the relevant percentages presented in Table 1.6.

Some of the respondents' attitudes and values vary according to the family policy implemented by the national government. For example, respondents from countries belonging to the "Day care" regime were much less frequently in favour of the statement: "The best child care is by the child's own parents" than respondents living under the other regimes (64% vs. 83–91%), who were more markedly in favour of the public day care system. In addition, they did not believe that children under institutional care would experience problems in the later life.

Differences across the family policy regimes, as demonstrated by Table 1.6, allow one to distinguish "profiles" of public opinions on family-related values and relevant policy measures, including impacts of institutional care on children's development.

In the "Day care" regime countries, respondents are in favour of institutional day care (statements 11 and 12). They also defend free choice for starting a family – there was little support for the statement "People who want children ought to get married" (statement 2). Correspondingly, bringing up children in lone-parent families was allotted the same value as in two-parent families (statement 3). Also the statements related to the financial support provided by the government were less widely accepted (statements 7–9). This indicates the nature of the societies in which the regime is practiced: Provision of several welfare benefits is widely accepted,

Table 1.6 Responses to the question 'Do you tend to agree with the following statements?' by family policy regimes (as a percentage of positive responses)

Statements	Family policy regimes				
	Day care	Income transfer	Labour market	Imposed home care	Total
1. Married people are generally happier than unmarried people	37	26	24	52	34
2. People who want children ought to get married	34	42	36	59	47
3. One parent can bring up a child as well as two parents together	52	42	39	39	41
4. I like having children because they really need you	46	67	41	82	69
5. I believe it's your duty towards society to have children	24	45	7	54	43
6. I do not believe you can be really happy if you do not have children	31	36	6	52	39
7. An allowance at the birth of each child	68	70	42	92	79
8. A substantial decrease in the cost of education	58	74	68	90	81
9. Better housing for families with children	67	78	40	92	81
10. It is good for a child's development if he/she is already partly taken care of by other members of the family/friends at an early age	78	62	32	56	56
11. Children who are in a day care centre most of the week will be more likely to experience problems in later life	12	29	42	44	37
12. The best child care is by the child's own parents	64	83	85	91	87

Notes: The table includes different items of the relevant questions from the standardized questionnaire (only positive choices included)

Statements 1–3: question CL 4, statements 5–7

Statements 4–6: question CL 5, statements 4–6

Statements 7–9: question CF4, statements 6, 12, 13

Statements 10–12: G2 all statements

All differences between the family policy regimes are statistically significant (at the 0.000 level)

family forms alternative to married couples are approved of within society, and people seem to be satisfied with that.

The "opinions profile" in the "Income transfer" regime resembles that of "Day care", but the deviations of relevant percentages from the averages given under "Total" are smaller.

For respondents who live under the "Labour market" regime, almost all figures were well below average. In particular, low percentages for statements 5–6 about the values of children indicate that respondents did not accept the arguments such as "It's your duty towards society to have children" or "You can't be happy without children". They accepted an option to live without children, but if they had children, they preferred to take care of the children by themselves. Since figures related to statements 5 and 6 were also exceptionally low as compared with the corresponding figures in other regimes, it would indicate strong individualism and independence.

Respondents' profiles in the "Imposed home care" regime were clearly exceptional as compared with the other regimes: Their attitudes towards marriage (Statement 1) and having a child showed that marriage was still an important arrangement for being happy and having children, and that children made parents happier than childless persons. Also the statements about family benefits provided by governments received very strong support (statements 7–9). Altogether, marriage, children and home care of children were much more valued than in other family policy regimes. However, governments were unable to meet these expectations, except child-care provision, which was exceptionally low in these countries.

1.8 Conclusions

The DIALOG countries, as other European countries, will face the same fate of a falling population size at the latest around 2050. To ensure generation replacement and compensate for childless (10/15%) and one-child (15/20%) families, there would have to be 45/15% of two-child families and 30/50% of three-child families (Avramov and Cliquet 2003a). This illustration of necessary shifts in family composition by number of children to compensate for the considerable share of the population remaining childless or having only one child clearly documents how challenging it is to bring the total fertility rate closer to the replacement level, and for current family policies and generous social polices to focus more on promoting an increase in fertility and more favourable family settings.

Low fertility has spread to most of the DIALOG countries. The CEE countries, along with Italy, Greece and Spain, belong to the lowest-low fertility countries (TFR below 1.3). Serious implications of that situation are illustrated by the fact that the population will be halved in 65 years if the TFR stabilises at a level of 1.5. The halving process will already be faced in 32 years if it stabilises at a level of 1.1 (Billari et al. 2004). The seriousness of the current fertility trends is demonstrated in the Czech Republic, Italy, Lithuania, Poland, Romania and Slovenia, where the TFR has already dropped close to 1.2. Due to these very low fertility levels, these countries will encounter massive economic and social problems.

Grant et al. (2004) have listed the unfavourable economic consequences of this demographic transition. The detrimental consequences for European economies include the following:

- as the working-age population decreases in size, countries will experience declines in human capital, which potentially reduces productivity;
- pension and social insurance systems can become heavily burdened;
- the ability to care for the expanding elderly population will decline;
- the elderly will face sharply increasing health care needs and costs.

This chapter focuses on interrelationships between the existing population and family policies in the DIALOG countries and on the socio-economic conditions. Additionally, associations between the family policy types and public opinions have been studied.

The DIALOG countries were grouped into four family policy regimes, based mainly on the generousness of public support to families. These regimes can be ordered as follows in terms of their level of generosity in family support: "Day care service" model, "Income transfer" model, "Labour market" model, and "Imposed home care" model. These groups were found to overlap closely with the clusters that were formulated by use of socio-economic, demographic and gender equity contextual variables.

This overlap implies that governments created their family policies to a considerable extent according to the available financial resources. Some countries limited their public support to means-tested benefits, mostly targeting low-income families. They also paid less attention to gender equity issues. Besides economic resources, ideological issues also affected the government's approach to family policies. The choices made (or measures implemented) were associated with demographic changes in these countries.

Family policy regimes have been found to be associated with public opinion on family-related issues and family policies. Respondents in "Imposed home care" regimes attached much greater value to marriage, children and home care of children than respondents of the other policy regimes. They also strongly supported family benefits provided by governments. Paradoxically, governments were unable to meet these expectations of their citizens. That gap between citizens' expectations and limitations in government support for families contributes to low fertility in these countries.

Respondents' expectations and actual public policy are better matched in the "Day care service" and "Labour market" regimes. Respondents of the former regime relied on and valued day care more than the others. Respondents of the latter regime disregarded childbearing as a societal duty, and valued the individual freedom to have children. They like, however, to take care of children by themselves. It is difficult to judge whether public opinion had an impact on public policies, or vice versa. Be that as it may, the fertility rates were higher in these countries than in two other groups. This finding could entail some political implications for population policies.

When it comes to population-related trends, the article concentrated on the rates of natural increase and net migration. "Labour market" countries (the Netherlands, Switzerland and Cyprus), Belgium (Flanders) ("Income transfer" country) and Finland ("Day care service" country) had the highest rate of natural increase from the viewpoint of family policy regimes. "Income transfer" countries (Germany, Austria and Italy) and Slovenia ("Day care service" country) were able to maintain high rates of net migration. "Imposed home care" countries had low and usually negative rates of natural increase, as well as of net migration. Family policy types as such were closely associated with population growth in DIALOG countries.

A well-functioning labour market with low unemployment and an advanced social security system seem to have been appealing for immigrants in the DIALOG countries. These properties, together with high part-time female employment rates, have been associated with higher fertility rates in the very same countries. However, female-friendly family policy ("Day care service" model, and a high percentage of expenditure on families and children in terms of GDP) have not been associated with higher population growth and fertility.

In addition, young motherhood has not counteracted declines in fertility and natural increase in the "Imposed home care" countries. Unfavourable economic and social conditions seem to play a dominant role. All these findings show how difficult it is to isolate some single macrodeterminants that could be argued to promote higher fertility or population growth in those countries.

According to the country reports, none of the DIALOG countries had specific programs for addressing population policy, such as low fertility. In contrast, in most of the CEE countries current governmental population policy attitudes seemed to be very passive and mostly more restrictive. In some of these countries, pro-natal policies had been pursued prior to transition, and the contrast between the past and the present was clear. Individual freedom and choice appear to be highly valued in all countries. Many scholars and policy-makers indeed doubt whether it is possible to influence people's reproductive behaviour in a positive sense. (Avramov and Cliquet 2003a).

It was stated in many national reports that reducing the benefits, weakening child care facilities and generally insufficient attention to family policy have influenced the declining fertility levels, family welfare and the postponement of child bearing. Hungary is a good example to illustrate the family policy effects on fertility. Unlike many other transition countries, it managed to preserve its rich family policy to some degree in the early 1990s after the fall of communism. As a result, fertility declined modestly as compared to the other CEE countries. However, the "Bokros package", which reduced many family benefits around 1995, clearly exacerbated the decline in fertility.

All in all, many authors of the country reports (Söderling and Laitalainen 2005) argued that the interplay between the demographic changes and family policy could not be presented by some direct causal relationships, since values, the economy, population and policies are in a complex interrelationship. Some authors from the CEE countries held the opinion that there is a need to secure economic growth and create a stable population policy oriented towards families and children, and to improve labour market conditions and gender equality before fertility levels can rise.

Appendix

Contextual indicators for the DIALOG countries

Demography	BE2	CZ	DE	EE	IT	CY	LT	HU	NL	AT	PL	RO	CH	SL	FI
1. Life expectancy at birth, females	81.1	78.7	81.3	77.1	82.9	81	77.5	76.7	80.7	81.7	78.7	74.8	83	80.5	81.5
2. Mean age of women at first marriage	26.7	26.5	28.8	25.5	27.9	26.5	24.0	24.6	28.2	27.2	23.4	23.9	28.2	26.7	29.1
3. Mean age of women at birth of first child	27.5	25.3	28.4	24.6	28.1	26.3	24.2	25.1	28.7	26.5	24.8	22.8	28.9	26.5	27.7
4. Live extramarital births	17.3	23.5	23.6	56.3	9.7	24.9	25.4	29	29.1	33.1	13.1	26.7	11.7	37.1	39.5
5. International migration stock/% of total pop.	8.6	2.3	8.9	26.7	2.8	6.3	9.7	3.0	9.9	9.3	5.4	0.4	25.1	2.6	2.6
Economy and social policy															
6. Per capita GDP (in PPS) EU–25 = 100	116	67.2	109.9	46.3	108.3	82.9	42.1	58.2	126.7	121.3	45.3	28.5	(120)	74.8	113.5
7. Human development index	.9	.87	.93	.85	.92	.88	.84	.85	.94	.93	.85	.78	.90	.94	.94
8. Social expenditure, percent of GDP	27.7	21.9	32.2	10.1	25.6	(15)	16.6	12.9	27.6	28.5	18.5	11.9	20.8	26.6	25.8
9. Expenditure on families and children, percent of GDP	2.5	1.8	3.3	(1.5)	1.0	(1.0)	1.3	0.3	1.2	3.0	0.9	0.3	1.1	2.4	3.0
10. Poverty rate after social transfers	1.3	8	13	18	19	15 2003	17	11	12	12	16	17	9	11	11
Employment															
11. Economically-active people. aged 30–34	74	74	77	72	64	86	88	64	78	80	79	74	78	93	80

(continued)

Demography	BE2	CZ	DE	EE	IT	CY	LT	HU	NL	AT	PL	RO	CH	SL	FI
12. Female full-time employment rate (20–39)	24.3	55.6	41.6	53.7	26.9	64.4	44.4	51.4 (45)	14.2	39.3	45.8	46.2	16.3	70.4	51.6
13. Female part-time employment rate (20–39)	31.1	7.7	29	8.5	16.9 all M+F	6.6	11.5 all M+F	(6.4)	62.8	30.1	10.0	10.9 all	55.3 all	6.0	18.8
14. Unemployment rate, females (20–64)	8.7	9.4	8	9.9	12.4	3.6	14.7	4.7	3.6	3	19.6	7.7	2.6	7.2	8
15. Unemployment rate, aged under 25	18.5	16.9	14.2	19.3	23.1	9.7	23.8	12.0	5.0	6.7	41.8	21.0	7.7	15.3	21.0
16. Ratio of female-to-male earned income	50	56	52	63	45	47	67	59	53	36	62	58	50	62	70
Education and public opinion															
17. Females in tertiary education	63	35	48	74	53	25	72	50	57	61	69	30	37	70	94
18. Early school-leavers, 18–24	9.9	5.7	12.6	9.8	20.7	10.2	13.4	11.8	14.3	10.2	5.6	22.1	(10)	3.3	7.3

Sources: Variables 1–4, 8–9, 13–14: http://www.vaestoliitto.fi/in_english/population_research/research_projects/dialog/ (Dialog WP4, country reports)
Variable 5: United Nations: International Migration Report 2002 (Dept. of Economic and Social Affairs, Population Division, NY. 2002
Variable 6–7, 16–17: UNDP: Human Development Report 2004. Cultural Liberty in today's Diverse World, NY 2002
Variable 10, 15, 18: http://epp.eurostat.cec.eu.int/portal
Variable 11–12: http://laborsta.ilo.org/cgi-bin

Chapter 2
Demographic Knowledge and Evaluation of Demographic Trends

Jürgen Dorbritz

Abstract The following article seeks to describe and explain the state of knowledge among the population concerning the scale of demographic trends and the prevalent attitudes towards demographic change. The level of knowledge concerning the number of inhabitants of the country in question, as well as of future trends, can considered to be relatively good. Greater deviations between the actual population size and the number estimated can be found in those countries which have a relatively large population (Germany, Italy and Poland). The fact that a large section of the responses can be found within the 5% confidence interval also speaks in favour of the quality of the estimations. Furthermore, respondents' anticipation of future demographic trends is relatively accurate. It is noticeable with regard to the formerly Socialist countries that a large section of the population expects further negative trends to result from the massive fall in the birth rate in the nineties. At the same time, there is support for a future increase in the number of inhabitants. In none of the countries was a fall regarded as a preferred trend. The relatively precise estimations of the population size are set against the considerable deviations observed between the actual proportion of elderly people and the figures estimated. The proportion of 65-year-olds and older is considerably overestimated in all countries. It is presumed that the connection between ageing and the danger posed to the social security systems is known, and that it is this situation, which is perceived as a threat, which is the source of the overestimation. In general terms, the ageing of the population is regarded as a negative trend. The respondents are largely in agreement on this in all the PPAS countries. A differentiated view is developed of the trends which are relevant in terms of family demographics. Across-the-board criticism is observed of change in the family. Such criticism is however less widespread with regard to the declining significance of marriage as the basis for partnership-based cohabitation. By contrast, there is firm rejection of trends which point towards the dissolution of the family (divorce, childlessness and one-parent families).

Keywords: Population · Ageing · Birth · Marriage · Divorce

J. Dorbritz
Federal Institute for Population Research, Wiesbaden, Germany
e-mail: juergen.dorbritz@destatis.de

C. Höhn et al. (eds.), *People, Population Change and Policies: Vol. 2: Demographic Knowledge – Gender – Ageing,* © Springer Science+Business Media B.V. 2008

2.1 Introduction

The intention is to analyse below the extent of knowledge among the populations with regard to some aspects of the demographic situation in their countries, how aware they are of demographic change, as well as which changes find acceptance, and which are rejected. The scale of the differences which arise between the participating countries is demonstrated, as is whether different ways of thinking occur in individual social groups. Finally, factors influencing demographic knowledge are calculated using logistic regression.

All countries participating in the Population Policy Acceptance Study take a more or less unambiguous stance towards the problems of demographic change. All the countries must tackle the consequences of demographic ageing; they have birthrates which do not guarantee the replacement of the parents' generations, are faced by a higher divorce rate, high proportions of extramarital live births, a falling marriage rate, rising childlessness or increasing proportions of one-person households.

The demographic situations in the PPAS countries are by no means identical, and the course taken by demographic change is not uniform. One should merely consider that the PPAS included both western countries which have had low birthrates for a long time, and formerly Socialist countries for which today's lowest-low fertility situation is still a relatively new phenomenon. It is therefore presumed that the course taken by demographic trends in the past influences both knowledge concerning magnitudes, and their evaluation. Section 2.2 of this article will therefore firstly provide an overview of the demographic situations and current trends.

The topic of demographic change is attracting increasing public attention in Europe, and naturally also in the countries of the PPAS. In particular the ageing of the population and its consequences for the social security systems have created new social challenges. These are the subject of discussion not only in the individual countries, but also at European level. For instance, these topics are discussed in the Green Paper entitled "Confronting demographic change: a new solidarity between the generations" which appeared in 2005 (page 1 et seqq.), the success of which the Commissioner of the European Union, Vladimir Spidla, specifically referred to in the closing presentation of the international PPAS results in November 2005 in Stuttgart. "Europe is facing today unprecedented demographic change. (...)European and national level public policies must take these demographic changes into account. This is the goal of the preparatory action adopted by the European Parliament in 2004 which seeks to better take into account the impact of demographic changes in all the relevant policies." The European Population Conference organised in the spring of 2005 by the Council of Europe's Population Committee, which featured a broad dialogue between politicians and researchers, is also an indication of increased awareness of the topic. In a publication in preparation for the conference, Charlotte Höhn (Höhn 2005, 116) raises the following questions and brings them to the attention of those in the political arena: "The political assessment of unavoidable consequences for pensions, health expenditures and long-term care will raise difficult questions. Which social security system is demographically sustainable? Which reforms can be done? Will the population in working age be ready to pay higher contributions?. . . How successful will be the concept of active ageing?"

In this context of growing public awareness of demographic change, the PPAS was to provide information on the state of knowledge regarding demographic trends and on attitudes towards the current changes. The respondents were called upon to estimate the size of the population, the number of immigrants and the proportion of the foreign population, the proportions of the elderly and of the younger population, as well as the average life expectancy achieved. At the same time, they were asked to make a statement on the significance of the institution of marriage, on the increasing incidence of non-marital cohabitation, growing childlessness, the increasing divorce rate or the fall in the birth rate.

2.2 The Demographic Situations

The space provided in this publication does not permit the provision of a detailed description of the demographic trends in the PPAS countries. For this reason, it is only possible to outline the general trends and major differences between countries.

The ageing population is the all-dominating demographic process of our time. This situation looms more or less large in all participating countries. Three different demographic situations can be identified here.

Firstly, the western and southern European countries with a birthrate which has been low for many years already and a high, and rising, life expectancy. These include Austria, Germany and Italy. The birthrate had already fallen markedly in Germany and Austria between 1965 and 1975, in the period of Europe's Second Demographic Transition. The fall in the birthrate did not take place in Italy until the eighties. The Total Fertility Rate currently reaches a level of 1.4 in Austria, and 1.3 and 1.2, respectively, in Germany and Italy (Fig. 2.1, Table 2.1). Life expectancy in these countries reaches comparably very high levels, and has risen notably since 1980. The life expectancy of men is between 75.5–77.0 years, and that of women between 81.3–82.9 years.

Secondly, the western European countries, where the fall in the birthrate is less pronounced, but which also record a considerable increase in life expectancy, similar to the countries of the first group. This group of countries is formed by Belgium, Finland and the Netherlands. The progression of the second fall in the birth rates in Europe did not lead to such a steep fall in the Total Fertility Rate in these countries as it did for instance in Germany or Italy. The birthrate in the Netherlands is currently 1.73 children per woman. It is 1.72 in Finland and 1.62 in Belgium (Fig. 2.1, Table 2.1). Life expectancy at birth reaches values that are similar to those in group 1 (men: 75.1–76.2 years, women: 81.6–82.9 years). Because of the birthrate, still very high as a result of the very late start of the fall in the birth rates (TFR 2003: 1.98), and of the high life expectancy, Cyprus also belongs to this group of countries.

Thirdly, the central and eastern European reforming states   Czech Republic, Estonia, Hungary, Lithuania, Poland, Romania and Slovenia. With the exception

(a)

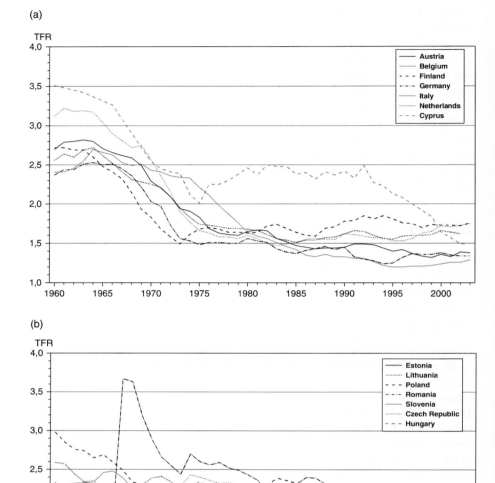

Fig. 2.1 Total Fertility Rates in western and southern European PPAS countries, 1960 to 2003 (b)
Total Fertility Rates in central and eastern European PPAS countries, 1960–2003
Source: Council of Europe, Recent demographic developments in Europe 2004

2.3.2 *The Expected and Preferred Size of the Population*

Table 2.4, column 2 shows the results of the medium variant of the UN demographic projection to 2020. Moderate falls in the population size were predicted for the majority of countries (Belgium, Czech Republic, Estonia, Finland, Hungary, Italy, Poland, Romania and Slovenia). Only for Lithuania, the Netherlands and Cyprus are slight increases in the population size forecast.

The expectations of the population regarding future trends only partly concur with the UN projections. 65.2% of respondents in the Netherlands expect the population size to be bigger in 2020 than today. This concurs with the trend of the UN projection. Only 6.0% expect a fall in the population size. The Netherlands are among the countries which have shown a constant demographic growth rate for many years as a result of both migration and fertility. It can be presumed that this has contributed to widespread expectations of demographic growth. In the case of Lithuania, the second country for which the UN forecast demographic growth, there is a wide gap between the prognosis and the expectation among the population. In Lithuania, 79.4% expect the population size to fall in future, and only 6.6% expect it to increase. However, it can be observed that Lithuania recorded considerable falls in its population size in the nineties. These were the result of both a mortality surplus and of a negative migration balance. Here too, the population's expectation concurs with the actual trend prior to the time of the questionnaire. The Netherlands,

Table 2.4 Number of population in 2020 and expected and preferred size of population *(in millions, %)*

Countries	Number of population 2020* (in millions)	Expected size of population in 2020, all respondents (in %)			Preferred size of population in 2020, all respondents (in %)		
		Larger	The same	Smaller	Increase	The same	Decrease
Belgium	10, 244	46.1	22.9	31.0	35.2	48.5	16.3
Czech Republic	9, 895	19.3	27.8	52.9	54.9	40.4	4.7
Estonia	1, 127	–	–	–	77.1	21.8	1.1
Finland	5, 165	–	–	–	40.1	57.9	2.0
Hungary	9, 021	12.4	14.5	73.1	76.8	21.0	2.2
Italy	53, 861	–	–	–	42.0	50.9	7.1
Lithuania	3, 483	6.6	14.0	79.4	72.8	25.3	1.9
The Netherlands	16, 507	65.2	28.8	6.0	8.7	61.2	30.1
Poland	37, 741	9.0	23.4	67.5	38.9	50.9	10.3
Romania	21, 026	19.5	18.7	61.8	73.6	21.5	4.9
Slovenia	1, 890	17.0	26.4	56.6	61.5	35.2	3.4
Cyprus	0, 832	30.5	38.8	30.7	74.3	23.2	2.5

Source: Population Policy Acceptance Study; United Nations, World Population Prospects, 2000 Revision
*UN projection, medium variant

and to a certain extent also Cyprus, are exceptional in the expectations of the trends
in the population size. A slightly upward trend is forecast for Cyprus. By contrast,
the population most frequently expects that the number of inhabitants will remain
constant (38.8%), 30.7% presume that it will fall, and 30.5% that it will rise.

The UN forecast falls in the population size for the other countries. A large
section of the population in Belgium expects different trends. 46.1% presume that
the population size will be larger in 2020 than today. In the Czech Republic, Hungary, Poland, Romania and Slovenia, the respondents' expectations of a fall in the
population size concur with the result of the projection. In Lithuania and Hungary,
for instance, the vast majority, at 79.4% and 73.1% respectively, expects negative
demographic trends.

The expectations of the population agree with the result of the prognosis in 6 out
of 8 countries. However, it cannot be presumed that the demographic knowledge
of the population also includes the UN demographic prognoses. The populations in
the PPAS countries nevertheless also have a good level of knowledge regarding this
matter. It is presumed that, since current trends in particular are expanded in the
medium variant in the prognoses, the respondents have orientated their expectations
in line with the current situation. This has already been described above for the
Netherlands. The other countries in which expectations and prognoses point in the
same direction are exclusively the formerly Socialist countries. It can be presumed
that the populations have derived their expectations from the current demographic
crisis. All the formerly Socialist countries are likely to be affected by the massive
fall in the birth rate in the nineties and the consequent fall in the population size,
even if it is no longer the case that all countries, such as the Czech Republic and
Slovenia, continue to record a fall in the population size today (Table 2.2).

The expected trends and the trends preferred by the respondents do not agree
in any instance. The majority of the formerly Socialist countries form a cluster (Table 2.4). Large sections of the population in the Czech Republic, Hungary,
Lithuania, Romania and Slovenia expect a fall in the number of inhabitants. Equally,
large sections prefer demographic growth. On the one hand, Belgium and the
Netherlands deviate from this evaluation pattern. The largest section of respondents
expects demographic growth to continue, but would prefer the situation to remain
as it is. On the other hand, a majority of Cypriots thinks that the population size
will remain unchanged, but would prefer future growth. In none of the countries did
a majority prefer a future fall in the population size. This possibility was preferred
most frequently in the Netherlands, at 30.1%.

2.3.3 The Proportions of the Elderly Among the Population

In contrast to knowledge regarding the population size and its future trends, there
are considerable differences between the actual proportions among the population
of people who are 65 and older and the estimations (Table 2.5). It can be observed
as a general trend that the proportions of the elderly are significantly overestimated.
This is most notable in Estonia, where 21.7% points lie between the actual value and

the estimation. The smallest differences can be found in Germany and the Czech Republic, each with 13.9% points.

In none of the countries in which this question was asked does the proportion of the elderly exceed 20%. It is the highest in Germany, at 16.2%, and the lowest in Cyprus, at 11.7%. By contrast, the estimations are around 30%. The highest proportion of the elderly, at 36.9%, is presumed by Estonians in their country. The lowest value, at 27.8%, is to be found in the Czech Republic. Yet another general trend in evaluation is noticeable: In each of the PPAS countries, women estimate the proportion of 65-year-olds and older to be higher than men. Particularly notable differences can be found here in the Netherlands.

A hypothesis to explain the situation found here can be formulated as follows: In contradistinction to trends in the population size, demographic ageing cannot be perceived as a largely neutral process. The populations are aware of the link between demographic ageing and the risk to the social security systems. This is perceived as a matter for future concern. Based on the perception of a threat, the respondents believe that the proportion of the elderly is much higher than it really is. Women are more likely to be concerned by this situation, which could lead to a greater overestimation in comparison to men.

2.3.4 Opinions on the Ageing of the Population

The ageing of the population is expressed both in the increase of the proportion of 65-year-olds and older, and in the fall in the proportion of younger people. Both aspects were to be evaluated in the PPAS (Table 2.6).

Table 2.5 Real proportion and estimation of the proportion of people aged 65 and over in PPAS countries by men and women (in % points)

Countries	Proportion of people aged 65 and over (in %)	Estimated pro-portion of people aged 65 (in %)			Difference between real proportion and estimation (in % points)			Min. esti-mation	Max. esti-mation
		Total	Men	Women	Total	Men	Women		
Czech Republic	13.9	27.8	27.0	28.5	13.9	13.1	14.6	4	80
Estonia	15.2	36.9	36.0	37.4	21.7	20.8	22.2	5	80
Germany	16.2	30.1	28.5	31.8	13.9	12.3	15.6	3	95
Hungary	14.7	33.5	31.9	35.2	18.8	17.2	20.5	1	84
Lithuania	13.6	33.3	32.2	34.2	19.7	18.6	20.6	1	85
The Netherlands	13.6	32.0	29.7	34.2	18.4	16.1	20.6	1	100
Poland	12.3	28.4	27.9	28.8	16.1	15.6	16.5	1	85
Romania	13.5	29.2	29.0	29.3	15.7	15.5	15.8	1	89
Slovenia	14.1	29.4	28.4	30.3	15.3	14.3	16.2	2	78
Cyprus	11.7	29.4	28.1	30.6	17.7	16.4	18.9	3	77

Source: IPPAS; Council of Europe, Recent demographic developments in Europe 2001

The assessment of both processes was approximately similar in all participating countries. The ageing of the population is judged to be a largely negative demographic trend. Those answering "bad" or "very bad" make up the largest group within the population in all countries. This answer is in fact given by the absolute majority in the majority of countries. This supports the hypothesis developed in the above section, according to which the negative consequences of demographic ageing are known, and hence the process is evaluated as an unfavourable trend.

It is only the differences between countries which are to be discussed. When it comes to an evaluation of the increasing proportions of the elderly, it is only respondents in Belgium who do not conform to the general pattern of responses. In Belgium too, the largest group answered "bad" or "very bad", at 43.2%, but

Table 2.6 Opinion on rising number of 65-year-olds and over and declining proportion of young people in PPAS countries (in %, means)

Countries	Opinion on rising number of people aged 65 and over				
	Excellent/ good	Neither good, nor bad	Bad/very bad	Means, men	Means, women
Belgium	21.7	35.0	43.2	3.27	3.23
Czech Republic	4.8	23.6	71.6	3.93	3.91
Estonia	5.5	26.6	68.0	3.83	3.79
Finland	–	–	–	–	–
Germany	6.5	22.0	71.5	3.98	3.88
Hungary	–	–	–	–	–
Italy	22.8	18.8	58.4	3.36	3.35
Lithuania	4.3	23.9	71.8	4.00	3.86
The Netherlands	–	–	–	–	–
Poland	6.3	28.5	65.2	3.75	3.72
Romania	5.3	23.1	71.6	4.03	3.96
Slovenia	17.0	26.5	56.5	3.52	3.55
Cyprus	–	–	–	–	–
Countries	Opinion on declining proportion of young people in 50 years				
	Excellent/ good	Neither good, nor bad	Bad/very bad	Means, men	Means, women
Belgium	10.4	35.0	54.6	3.50	3.52
Czech Republic	4.2	19.9	75.9	3.96	3.99
Estonia	–	–	–	–	–
Finland	3.9	19.7	76.5	3.91	3.93
Germany	2.1	14.1	83.8	4.23	4.20
Hungary	1.1	7.9	91.1	4.38	4.37
Italy	2.3	9.2	88.5	3.86	3.86
Lithuania	1.4	9.2	89.4	4.23	4.28
The Netherlands	8.0	39.1	52.9	3.50	3.49
Poland	6.9	28.1	65.0	3.72	3.70
Romania	–	–	–	–	–
Slovenia	2.4	9.6	88.0	4.21	4.22
Cyprus	4.0	8.7	87.3	4.31	4.30

the proportions in the other countries are much higher, being in a range of 56.5% (Slovenia) to 71.8% (Lithuania). Even more negative are the attitudes to the falling proportions of the younger population. These trends are regarded as negative by a majority of respondents in all countries. Narrow majorities can be found in the Netherlands (52.9%), and also in Belgium, at 54.6%. The most unfavourable views are to be found in Hungary, where 91.1% responded "bad/very bad", followed by Lithuania (89.4%) and Italy (88.5%). It should be stressed here that it is the process of demographic ageing which is being judged negatively. This however by no means indicates negative or inimical attitudes towards the role of the elderly in society.

No direct link can be found between the demographic situation and the evaluation of the shifts in proportions between the main age groups. The level of life expectancy and the actual proportion of the population among 65-year-olds+ does not correlate with the negative view of the increasing proportions of the elderly or the declining proportions of younger people. Instead, it is possible to determine that the evaluation of the two demographic aspects of ageing tends to be more negative in the formerly Socialist countries. The ageing of the population is a relatively new manifestation in these countries, and negative consequences are perceived more acutely in crisis situations, as caused by the system transformations. Both are likely to lead to highly negative views.

2.3.5 The Evaluation of Family-demographic Trends

The evaluation of family-demographic trends which express different aspects of the changes in the family has been strongly differentiated. At the same time, the valuations differ considerably from one country to another. Table 2.7 shows the median values calculated using a five-tier scale between the scale points "very positive" and "very negative".

It can be ascertained in very general terms that there is a tendency for the medians to be larger than three. This means that there are more negative than positive evaluations. The respondents in the PPAS countries are hence more critical in their attitudes to change in the family.

The negative views are least prominent if demographic change expresses a decline in the significance of the family. This concerns both the aspect of co-habitation in an unmarried partnership, as well as unmarried co-habitation with children. There is a tendency across the countries for the items "Increasing number of couples who live together unmarried", "Increasing number of births among unmarried couples" and "Declining number of marriages" to record the fewest negative views.

The responses are considerably more negative if the demographic trends express the collapse of the family, family being understood as co-habitation in a spirit of partnership by parent(s) with children, not necessarily based on marriage. Once more, this tendency was observed across all the countries for the items "Increasing number of divorces", "Increasing number of children being an only child" and "Declining number of births".

Table 2.7 Opinion on family-related demographic trends in the PPAS countries, all respondents (means)

Countries	Increasing number of couples who live together unmarried	Increasing number of couples who decide to remain childless	Declining number of marriages	Declining number of births	Increasing number of children in a one-parent family
Austria	2.89	3.70	3.27	3.95	3.52
Belgium	2.63	3.24	3.10	3.58	3.73
Czech Republic	2.95	3.76	3.40	4.12	4.09
Estonia	2.31	2.97	2.58	2.63	2.83
Finland	3.10	3.80	3.59	4.03	4.21
Germany	2.97	3.80	3.36	4.16	3.88
Hungary	3.28	4.38	3.89	4.58	4.69
Italy	3.04	3.34	3.23	3.71	3.79
Lithuania	3.30	4.02	3.75	4.21	4.17
The Netherlands	2.64	3.05	2.99	3.02	3.84
Poland	3.30	3.72	3.55	3.81	3.95
Slovenia	3.02	4.00	3.46	4.21	4.13
Cyprus	3.14	4.18	-	4.29	4.15

Countries	Increasing number of children being an only child	Increasing number of persons who live alone	Increasing number of births among unmarried couples	Increasing number of divorces
Austria	3.50	3.49	3.19	4.00
Belgium	–	3.27	3.09	4.13
Czech Republic	3.71	3.72	3.38	4.26
Estonia	2.63	2.91	2.38	2.81
Finland	3.94	3.93	3.31	4.33
Germany	3.68	3.60	3.07	3.96
Hungary	4.25	4.63	4.16	4.57
Italy	3.47	3.61	3.22	3.68
Lithuania	3.64	3.99	3.38	4.19
The Netherlands	3.57	3.11	2.86	4.09
Poland	3.53	3.75	3.72	4.14
Slovenia	3.85	3.96	3.38	4.15
Cyprus	3.77	3.66	4.27	4.44

Source: IPPAS

If one analyses the data by countries, some stable response patterns are shown between the countries. Estonia, Belgium and the Netherlands are countries which tend towards low median values, in other words towards greater acceptance of the trends. A distant stance towards the classical model of partnership and family is to be found more frequently in the western and northern countries of Europe. It has been found in Chapter 4 of Volume 2, using the comparison of PPAS1 with PPAS2, that an increase in the significance of family-orientated values has taken place in the Netherlands. This so-called re-traditionalisation has not led, however, to a situation in which the Netherlands have become a country where intolerance towards change in the family has become predominant. There is less tolerance of demographic trends which place the family in question in the formerly Socialist countries Hungary, Slovenia and also Lithuania, as well as in Cyprus. In particular for Hungary, it is noticeable that the valuation of the traditional family typical of the formerly Socialist countries remains unchanged.

2.4 Multinomial Logistic Regressions to Calculate the Influencing Factors on the Evaluation of Family-Demographic Trends

On the formation of the models: In order to be able to describe the impact of various influencing factors on the family-demographic trends, four different models were calculated using multinomial logistic regression. These models differ, firstly, as to the dependent variables that were used. Two statements have been selected from those in Table 2.7. Firstly, a variable has been selected which depicts the distant stance towards the institution of marriage, and which has been evaluated relatively positively (the increasing number of unmarried couples living together). Secondly, the statement "Increasing number of children spending a part of their childhood with only one parent" was valued highly negatively as an independent variable, indicating as it does the collapse of the traditional family. Secondly, two groups of independent variables were formed. On the one hand, the indicators size of munici- pality (rural area or small village, smaller or medium-sized town, city), educational groups (lower: primary or lower secondary education, medium: higher secondary education, higher: post-secondary education) and age groups (20–39 years, 40–59 years) were included. Secondly, since these are family-demographic trends, two indicators of the family situation were included in the model (children: yes, no; partner: yes, no), which were broken down further into two age groups. Four re- gression models emerge in the combination, the results of which are contained in Tables 2.8–2.11. The forecast percentages are shown, which express the probabil- ity of how many persons in the individual groups regard the increasing number of unmarried couples living together as more positive or the increasing number of one-parent families as more negative. Only the main effects have been incorporated in the models.

Model 1: Growing number of unmarried couples living together by size of mu- nicipality, education and age (Table 2.8)

Age, region and education all have a major influence on the evaluation of the trend towards the increasing number of unmarried couples living together. The in- fluence of age is highly significant in all countries included in Table 2.8. Equally significant influences emerge in the majority of countries by the municipality size. Only in the Czech Republic and Lithuania is there no significant influence. The influence of the level of education on the evaluation of this family-demographic trend appears to be rather slight. Significant influences were found in the Czech

Table 2.8 Results of the Multinomial Logistic Regression Analysis, evaluation of the trend "growing number of unmarried couples living together" by region, age and education, highly positive and somewhat positive (probabilities)

Area	Educational level	Age group	Countries				
			Belgium	Czech Rep.	Finland	Germany	Hungary
Rural area or village	Lower	20–39	50.3	45.2	28.3	38.1	19.5
		40–59	42.1	33.3	19.3	28.0	15.4
	medium	20–39	44.4	33.9	25.0	30.4	22.1
		40–59	36.9	24.3	16.7	22.2	17.6
	higher	20–39	27.6	21.8	18.7	26.8	16.6
		40–59	21.9	15.5	12.1	19.4	12.9
Smaller medium-sized town	lower	20–39	48.8	51.8	30.9	38.0	24.3
		40–59	40.4	40.7	21.4	28.3	19.9
	medium	20–39	43.0	39.6	27.4	30.2	27.4
		40–59	35.4	30.2	18.7	22.3	22.6
	higher	20–39	26.5	25.9	20.7	26.5	21.0
		40–59	20.8	19.3	13.7	19.4	16.9
City	lower	20–39	51.2	47.6	32.9	43.7	25.2
		40–59	43.2	35.9	23.3	34.1	20.9
	medium	20–39	45.1	36.0	29.3	35.0	28.3
		40–59	37.8	26.4	20.4	26.9	23.7
	higher	20–39	28.8	23.3	22.2	30.9	21.8
		40–59	22.6	16.8	15.0	23.5	17.9

Table 2.11 Results of the Multinomial Logistic Regression Analysis, evaluation of the trend "increasing number of children spending a part of their childhood with only one parent" by age, child and family situation, highly positive and somewhat positive (probabilities)

Own child(ren)	Partner situation	Age group	Countries										
			Austria	Belgium	Czech Rep.	Finland	Germany	Hungary	Italy	Lithuania	Netherlands	Poland	Slovenia
No	Yes	20–39	50.4	67.3	82.1	88.8	69.6	96.4	82.9	88.1	70.5	77.2	87.5
		40–59	53.5	60.4	85.1	88.6	74.5	95.0	76.2	89.9	70.5	78.2	84.7
	No	20–39	39.7	60.6	71.4	81.4	54.2	92.9	86.1	81.3	56.4	70.4	82.6
		40–59	42.6	52.5	75.1	81.1	60.4	89.8	80.0	84.0	56.3	71.6	78.7
Yes	Yes	20–39	55.3	69.4	76.6	88.4	70.1	95.6	70.8	88.2	74.1	78.9	89.7
		40–59	58.2	62.2	81.8	88.3	75.1	94.3	61.9	90.2	74.0	79.8	87.2
	No	20–39	44.0	61.9	64.3	80.9	54.3	91.8	76.0	81.7	60.9	72.4	85.0
		40–59	46.9	52.9	70.9	80.7	60.7	89.0	67.6	84.6	60.8	73.5	81.1

Source: IPPAS

Republic, Finland, Germany and Cyprus. The connections are not significant in the former Socialist countries of Hungary, Lithuania, Poland and Slovenia. It is presumed that differences in education played a less prominent role in the former Socialist countries, and that the social change which took place after 1990, with the re-evaluation of education and qualification levels and redefinition the social elites, has restricted the differentiating significance of this characteristic. If there are significant differences in evaluation, the directions taken by the connections in the countries are identical, and can be formulated as follows:

Age: The probability that unmarried cohabitation is evaluated more positively is higher in the age group 20–39 than in the age group 40–59.

Region: The more urban the region is, the greater is the chance that the increase in instances of unmarried cohabitation is valued positively.

Education: A more surprising connection is shown for education. The lower the educational level, the higher is the probability of a positive evaluation of unmarried cohabitation. It can be stated as a hypothesis for further investigations of these facts that tolerance towards new living arrangements has now become common at the lower educational levels, whilst it is possible that re-traditionalisation has taken place in the higher educational groups.

The evaluations become stronger in the interrelation between age, education and region, and lead in some cases to considerable differences between the social groups. This is exemplified by Belgium and Germany. Age and educational group show a highly significant influence in Belgium. The probability to evaluate unmarried cohabitation positively is 50.3% in the group "lower level of education/age 20–39", but only 21.9% in the group "higher level of education/age 40–59". The influence of all three characteristics is significant in Germany. The chance of a positive view being taken is 43.7% in the group "city/lower level of education/20–39". It is only 19.4% in the contrasting group "rural area or small village/higher education/40–59".

Model 2: Growing number of unmarried couples living together by number of children, partner situation and age (Table 2.9)

The model shows once more the highly-significant context of age in the evaluation of the growing number of unmarried couples living together. An exception is the Netherlands, which however was not included in Model 1 because of the data available. The family situation, i.e. whether or not one has children of one's own, or whether one lives together with a partner, unexpectedly exerts an influence on the evaluation of the demographic trend. Significant differences in evaluation can be found across the board in Austria, Germany and Italy. Highly significant differences can however be found only in Germany. The direction of the age-related influence was already described in Model 1. This is as follows for the partner and the child situation: Those who live with neither partner nor children are more likely to accept the increased significance of unmarried cohabitation than those with a partner and a child/children. The differences in evaluation are however not as pronounced as those linked to age, education and region. The example of Austria shows that the probability of regarding this trend in a positive light is 41.5% among those in the age group 20–39 who have neither a partner nor children. It is 33.7% in the same age group among respondents with a partner and a child/children. The influence of the partner situation is not significant in the Czech Republic, Finland, Hungary, Lithuania or the Netherlands. This applies to Belgium, Hungary, Poland and Slovenia in terms of whether respondents have children.

Model 3: Growing number of one-parent families by size of municipality, education and age (Table 2.10)

Model 4: Growing number of one-parent families by number of children, partner situation and age (Table 2.11)

The dependent variable has been changed in Models 3 and 4. Now, the growing number of children is to be evaluated who spend at least a part of their childhood with only one parent. This is an item which generally came across a high level of rejection. Significant differences in evaluation are more seldom found, and are weaker in comparison to Models 1 and 2. It is presumed that the respondents generally reject this demographic trend so strongly that differences in evaluation between social groups are less pronounced. Model 3 in particular, when compared with Model 1, with the characteristics region, education and age, has taken on reduced significance when it comes to explaining differences in evaluation. In Models 3 and 4 in particular, age serves less frequently to explain the differences.

There are significant age-related differences in the evaluation of the increasing number of one-parent families in Model 3 in three countries (Belgium, Germany, and Cyprus), whilst education-related differences are found in five countries (Belgium, the Czech Republic, Germany, Poland and Slovenia), and regional differences occur in four countries (Germany, Slovenia, Poland and Cyprus). Highly significant differences are rare. Differences in significance with regard to all three characteristics are found only in Germany. The directions of the evaluations can be described as follows: The probability of a negative evaluation of this trend is higher in the age group 40–59 than in the younger age group. This direction is typical of Germany and Cyprus. In Belgium, the rate of rejection is higher in the younger age groups. In terms of education, the probability of a negative evaluation increased with increasing educational qualification. Here, therefore, one finds, as in the model, the more traditional evaluations among individuals with higher educational qualifications. As to regional differences, the rejection falls as municipality size increases. As in the other models, there are considerable differences in the combination of the characteristics. Germany is selected as an example since only there have highly significant differences been found in all three characteristics. The lowest probability of rejection, at 51.6%, can be found among low-education younger people in cities, and the highest among persons who are older, live in rural areas and have a higher level of education (74.3%).

It is shown in Model 4 that it is above all the partner situation which leads to significant differences in the evaluation. This was found for eight countries (Austria, Belgium, the Czech Republic, Finland, Germany, Hungary, the Netherlands and Poland). It is surprising that the child situation exerts virtually no influence. A significant connection exists only in Italy. As to the partner situation, anyone living with a partner has a much higher probability of rejecting the trend. The connection is highly significant in the Netherlands, for instance. The probability of rejection in age group 20–39 years, no children, but with a partner, is 70.5%. In the same group, but without a partner, it is only 56.4%. If at all, the influence of the children situation (own children, yes or no) can be labelled with a greater probability of rejection among those who live without children. It can be presumed that those who have no partner can more easily imagine being a lone parent than those with a partner.

2.5 Discussion of the Results

Demographic change and its multifarious consequences are no longer being discussed only among population researchers, but have reached a broad public. This is shown by the fact that at least in some cases the population has relatively precise knowledge of the magnitude of demographic processes (population size), and makes a differentiated evaluation. A broadly-negative view of demographic trends is developed in the population if demographic change is regarded as a threat. This particularly applies to demographic ageing. The connection between demographic ageing and a danger to the social security systems is known to the majority of the population, and is to be regarded as the cause of the strongly negative evaluations. At the same time, the magnitude of the trends which are regarded as threatening (demographic ageing) is significantly overestimated. This overestimation is likely to be emphasized by the frequency with which these topics are covered by the media.

From a family-policy point of view of the results, a distant stance or indifference towards the institution of marriage should be pointed to. The consequences drawn: "if partnership, then marriage" and "if children, then marriage" appear to be dissolving, while by contrast the consequence "if children, then partnership" continues. The distant stance towards marriage cannot however be regarded as constituting such a stance towards the family. In the opinion of the respondents, marriage is no longer regarded as being necessary for family formation, but family, for which marriage is not absolutely necessary, is still categorised as a children-friendly institution.

Differences in evaluation can still be found between the western and the former Socialist countries. A distant stance towards the classical family model can be found more often in the western and northern countries of Europe. It can be presumed that those orientations which date back to the Socialist era have been conserved and are changing only gradually. Until the end of the eighties, a change in values such as had taken place in the western countries was impossible in these countries for a variety of reasons. Hence, the totalitarian regimes had prevented the spread of individualistic orientations, and an extremely pronatalist family policy helped conserve the esteem attached to the concept of the family. The results of this situation appear to echo to the present day.

Welfare state regimes can differ by how far they extend in one or another direction. More conservative regimes emphasise liberty; socio-democratic states shore up welfare state institutions and activities more in order to help the socially disadvantaged.

All welfare states aim to improve the everyday life of their citizens and to equalise social disparities. Welfare states guarantee social rights for every citizen. Their activities usually pertain to four spheres (Skuban 2004):

- Social security: coverage of life risks (disease, unemployment, need for care, etc.);
- Families: indirect or direct transfers;
- Guarantee of equal opportunities for all citizens by providing an educational system; and
- Regulation of the labour market.

Above all, the advantages of welfare state activities depend on economic prosperity, since the resources expended for benefits first have to be accumulated. In contrast, the welfare state contributes to the economic system by increasing productivity and stabilising economic demand. In political terms, welfare states help to balance the power distribution between employers and employees and reduce social disparities. In social terms, they stabilise private life arrangements and human capital. In cultural terms, welfare states are an outcome of the Western model, placing strong emphasis on the coverage of those who find themselves at a disadvantage within society.

If one tries to distinguish and categorise welfare states, Esping-Andersen's (1990) typology of welfare state regimes has to be taken into account sooner or later. Andersen categorized three broad regimes:

1. The liberal welfare states have rather moderate social security systems and a low level of benefits. There is a relatively pronounced orientation towards the market system and demand for intra-family solidarity. It is financed by taxes and can be found mainly in Anglo-Saxon countries, and partly in Switzerland.
2. The conservative welfare states are strongly influenced by Catholic social doctrine. The principle of subsidiary stipulates that that the State should not intervene before family resources have been expended. This system is financed mainly by social security contributions ("pay-as-you-go system") and is found largely in Austria, Italy, France and Germany.
3. The mainly tax-funded Social Democratic system aims to achieve equality at the highest level possible by installing a system where all citizens are included. The individual's independence is promoted by focusing on the principle of solidarity. A high level of social services is developed. Representatives of this type are the Scandinavian countries.

However, this typology is not carved in stone. Facing the abovementioned economic and demographic challenges, several variants of Esping-Andersen's classification have been devised, resulting in less sharp demarcations between the different types distinguished. Scholarly criticism has concentrated for instance on a lack of historical perspective or of family/gender aspects (Fux 2008). New advances have further fleshed out the theory and increased the number of types, countries and dimensions.

Fux (in this volume) also elaborated a typology of welfare systems, partly based on the analysis of the PPAS countries. Starting from the assumption of different "trajectories of modernization", Fux distinguishes between four main groups of countries and welfare regimes by their cultural and socio-structural characteristics:

1. The etatistic (Protestant) Scandinavian cluster;
2. A group of Eastern European countries with a still traditional background despite the secularization going on alongside the transformation;
3. A cluster of Catholic countries, subdivided into those with strong secularization and welfare systems (a) and those with underdeveloped welfare systems (greater emphasis on the family) and non-secularized structures (b);
4. A cluster of Eastern European countries in which the Catholic ones tend towards a familialistic trajectory (a) and the Protestant ones tend rather towards an etatistic trajectory (b).

According to Fux' typology, the countries of our analysis can be classified as follows: Finland in Cluster 1; Romania in Cluster 2; Germany in Cluster 3a; and Lithuania, Poland and Slovenia in Cluster 4a.

As mentioned above, an important aspect of looking at welfare state regimes is the dynamic perspective: Especially in recent times they are transforming and reforming rapidly, and some scholars speak of a crisis (Evers 1993). One main type of reform is to expand the pay-as-you-go system to include a funded system in order to diminish financial burdens and safeguard benefits. Leisering and Berner (2001) regard this as a major shift from a welfare state providing transfers and benefits towards a regulating one where the steering and coordination of welfare state activities assume a more prominent place.

The change in the structure of the welfare systems leads to a broader mix of social benefits with more private services, instead of being purely focused on the State. Evers (1993) refers to this trend as a "welfare mix" or "welfare pluralism" with four levels where benefits are offered:

- The free market;
- The state;
- The intermediate sector (voluntary organisations, etc.); and
- The informal (private) sector.

Evers and Svetlik (1993) therefore claim a more sector-oriented view of the welfare state since each of the areas has certain (dis)advantages, premises and benefits. Leisering and Berner (2001) expanded the welfare mix concept by introducing the idea of a "welfare linkage", which places greater emphasis on the interlinkages between welfare activities at different levels.

When it comes to the health/long-term care and care institutions, the changes in welfare state systems lead to an increasing need for alternative institutions and care options due to the demographic and economic pressure placed on the state system. The pluralism of welfare systems results in an increasing importance of alternative benefit-providers. Having said that, the roles and responsibilities of the care-providers also change as the welfare systems alter. There is a general need to ensure that the process of privatisation does not necessarily lead to increasing disadvantages, inequalities and risks.

3.1.4 Care for the Elderly: Institutional Structures and International Differences

The demographic impacts on the general level of welfare states described above can also be observed for the area of (long-term) care for the elderly. The demographic pressure will increase substantially. As a consequence, the future group of potential care-receivers among the elderly will dramatically grow, since age-related disabilities and the need for long-term care are closely linked to ageing. In addition, today's care structures will undergo a major change, as families become smaller, birth rates remain low, the number of single persons increases and female employment rates rise (since women are the main care-givers), in short: The potential for informal and familial care-givers will diminish through several processes (Hörl and Schimany 2004). This raises the question of adequate alternatives.

According to Eisen (1999), there are two main ways to tackle the risk of needing long-term care: the "individual principle" and the "social principle". The individual principle means that the citizen tries to cover the risk by taking out private insurance or savings plans. The social principle comprises all laws that try to regulate benefits (in)directly, but also the implementation of the social security system. There are several other characterisations which differentiate the two systems.

If we look at the countries in our analysis, one has to be careful in comparing the systems, since cultural values influence which model a society chooses and by the time develops. A well-known approach towards a consistent typology of care systems is the following (Eisen 1999):

- The "Bismarck" model (social security and welfare state);
- The "Beveridge" model (emphasis on national welfare services); and
- The "Jefferson" model (stronger emphasis on the individual).

However, it should be stressed that a country cannot be assigned to one single group only. Germany is an example where the newly-introduced long-term care insurance (1995) is one pillar of the social security system, but where various institutions also operate in the informal sector. Moreover, the former socialistic Eastern European countries have experienced a dramatic socio-economic transformation with different paths and success stories which also affected the welfare systems.

Characterising health and care policies in the PPAS countries raises further problems (Lamura 2003). One example is the heterogeneous terminology used in care for elderly and its institutions. Another problem is the differences between the national care systems, which hamper cross-country comparisons. Finally, statistical information and data are sometimes not available or are not gathered according to the same standards.

Lamura (2003) distinguishes between the following institutions of care systems:

- One common denominator of all countries is some form of national **health care**. This comprises hospital care, hospices, interim health care and community care.
- **Social care** comprises home care, day care services and residential care – on a state or private level.
- **Informal care** includes several forms of care-giving by the family, but also by volunteers, help from the neighbourhood or friends.

It seems that the level and extent of services for elderly people differ widely between European countries, as do the principles and policies which are implemented to tackle the duty of health (long-term) care. Governmental awareness of the increasing need for care and its implementation in health and social policies was rather poor in all parts of Europe – with the exception of the Scandinavian countries, where policies were adapted to societal changes at an early stage and the level of institutionalisation (of long-term care) is comparably high. One reason for the lagging behind of the adaptation may be the belief (at least among politicians in some countries) that the elderly should receive long-term care primarily from their families. Substantial differences therefore exist between European countries.

For example, Finland is a country with high standards of services for the elderly and a high degree of institutionalisation (the proportion of the elderly in long-term care, e.g. nursing or residential homes). However, especially due to the high cost of institutional care, policies have been implemented to use community-based or informal alternatives instead (Noro 1998). Policies therefore focus more and more on these sectors – despite the fact that the informal/familial sector has a limited potential due to its demographic shrinking. According to Noro (1998), there was also a shift in Finland towards home-based care during the 1970s due to economic constraints. Since then, policies have aimed to keep as many elderly people as possible in private housing – not necessarily cared for by family members or friends. The objective was to "promote independent living and reduce institutional care" (Noro 1998, 6). However, Evers and Leichsenring (1994) accentuated the regional differences among the municipalities which are responsible for care services.

Other countries did not react very actively to (demographic) change and the changing needs. Traditionalistic countries such as Poland continued to emphasise informal care by family members. In contrast, the former care system was socialistically centralised and hierarchical, which is why Hrynkiewicz (1993) rated it as ineffective and ripe for removal. Despite this, most elderly care was provided by family members without much help from the State. The transition towards a modern welfare mix was difficult, and this was to be expected: "The passivity of the people and mistrust of the State, being so widespread among volunteers, were the most serious obstacles slowing down the shifts in the welfare mix" (Hrynkiewicz et al. 1993, 218). Moreover, "(. . .) the health service reforms [in Poland, *the authors*] introduced in 1999 did not specifically address the situation of older people" (Lamura 2003, 9). On the other hand, Poland is a country still in transition and undergoing dramatic economic and social changes, and problems in implementing adequate policies do not therefore come as a surprise.

The interrelationship of attitudes towards care and different "cultures" as determinants of welfare regimes was mentioned above. A specification of this idea was elaborated by Klie and Blinkert (2002), who analysed "cultures" of attitudes towards care among a group of Germans aged 40–60 in a dynamic perspective (between two surveys). As Klie and Blinkert state, insights into such attitudes can help to answer several questions: Which people have the highest willingness for private/family care; in which way did this willingness change; and what implications can be derived for local and regional policies? The results suggest that acceptance of institutional care is especially high among the liberal middle class, but rather low in the traditionalistic, conservative groups of the population. Moreover, it is alarming that especially the proportions of people with higher acceptance of family care decreased the most pronouncedly between the two surveys. The authors concluded that care systems have to concentrate more closely on institutional care and cannot rely on the willingness to provide private care.

3.2 Methodology

As mentioned in the introduction to this chapter, we aim to find an empirical answer to the question as to whether the attribution of governments' responsibilities is an explanatory variable for the preference of "who should care" for the elderly. Therefore our empirical analysis is based on two indices. Firstly, we aim to obtain information about attitudes towards the responsibility of governments. This is the dimension where we measure expectations of public welfare policy. We created one variable which can express the general viewpoint as to whether high or low demand is placed on the State. Secondly, we would like to know which setting of care for the elderly is preferred by respondents. Equally, we would like to work with just one variable which expresses attitudes as to whether care for elderly people is a private or an institutional matter. The construction and use of those two indices will be described in the following two sub-chapters.

3.2.1 The Governments' Responsibility Attribution Index (GRAI)

The first index for our analysis is the Governments' Responsibility Attribution Index (GRAI), which is constructed from the IPPAS item battery headlined attribution of the responsibility of each government concerning different areas. The index was constructed on the basis of seven items of one set from the IPPAS database, which included the following questions regarding the government's responsibility:

- Looking after the elderly (CI1a);
- Availability of adequate housing for everyone (CI1b);
- Facilitating female labour force participation (CI1c);

- Facilitating opportunities for women to combine a job with raising children (CI1d);
- Facilitating opportunities for men to combine a job with raising children (CI1e);
- Taking care for young job-seekers (CI1f); and
- Providing adequate health care for all (CI1g).

These are of course different topics, but the idea for constructing this index is based on the assumption that the overall ascription of governments' responsibility can be more or less seen as being independent of the concrete content. Our aim is to identify a stance of what people think about the state's responsibility in general and not on a particular subject or domain. All in all, they measure the same dimension. To prove this statement, we carried out a reliability analysis for the item set. The result of 0.84 for Cronbach's Alpha is relatively high and supports our suggestion. We therefore believe that this index is useful for our analysis because it gives an estimation of the overall attribution of governments' responsibility under the restriction of the items available in the IPPAS database. In this matter we can use it as a dependent variable if we use the country as an independent variable to reveal the differences in expectations towards the welfare states under study. In addition, we will use a single variable from this battery to reveal country differences regarding care for the elderly: The item which measures exactly the attribution of responsibility towards this issue.

The most important point is that we have the possibility to work with this index as the **independent variable** to prove our initial assumptions as to whether expectations of the welfare state serve to explain preferences regarding responsibility in care for elderly people.

For the construction of this index, we simply made a single variable from these seven items by calculating a mean value from all the answers. This mean value was calculated such that all answers (they are numeric codes; for example: 1 = "Completely responsible" to 4 = "Not responsible at all")[1] have been summed up and finally divided by the number of items, in this case seven. The advantage of using a mean value instead of an additive one is that we have the same level of values as in the original, single variables. The next step was to calculate these values into three categories for the attribution of governments' responsibilities in all evaluated areas. The index values have been distributed into three equal parts: One for the "High and medium responsibility" category (value 1 up to approx. 1.67), two for the "Low responsibility" category (above approx. 1.67 to approx. 2.33) and three for the "No responsibility" category (above approx. 2.33 to approx. 3).

In the following chapters we will use the abbreviation GRAI for this composite variable as the instrument for measuring expectations of the welfare state on the level of attributing its duties.

---

[1] Originally there is a five-tier scale per item, except in the survey in Germany, which has four categories. It was therefore necessary to reduce the scale to a three-tier level. The categories "Completely", "Quite" and simply responsible have been combined to category 1 "high or medium responsibility attribution"; the two other categories are "low" and "not", which are the same in the original variable.

3.2.2 The "Care for the Elderly Index" (CFEI)

The second index is constructed from 17 items obtained from the IPPAS database. The use of this index aims to find three different preferences of respondents regarding care for the elderly. The first preference is the "institutional category", which relates to an overall attitude that care for elderly people is a matter for professional, public facilities, voluntary, charitable and church organisations and for-money private services, or whether it is a state-related, fundamentally institutionalised affair. However, it is the opposing category to the second one which we called the "familial category". The preference represented here is related to the sum of the attitudes that care is a private concern: Relatives, children, family members, friends, etc., should care for elderly people. The third category aims to represent respondents who are indifferent persons whose preference in this matter is neither institutional nor familial.

These categories are related to the content of the items from two batteries in the IPPAS database. In both item sets, the original variables are based on a five-point scale with 1 standing for "Could not agree more" to 5 for "Disagree completely". In the first battery, the questions are related to the measurement of opinion towards care for the elderly in general, who is or should be responsible. The respondents were confronted with statements[2] with which they can concur or disagree within the scale. These statements have been interpreted as familial if they represent a preference that care for the elderly is a private concern, and as institutional if they state that it is not. In the second battery, they were questioned as to which persons or institutions should be responsible for caring for elderly people if they need help in daily life.[3]" In this battery, the question of "who should care" is clearly measured in such a way that respondents simply chose the strength of agreement or disagreement on the responsibility of a certain person, group or institution to care for elderly people.

We decided to construct this index on the basis of a score ranging from 0 to 4 for every answer to each item from each respondent. The index consists of a scale of 5 scores:

1. 0 = neither institutional nor familial;
2. 1 = fully institutional;
3. 2 = rather institutional;
4. 3 = rather familial;
5. 4 = fully familial.

---

[2] The CFEI is based on the variables a3a to a3i and a4a to a4h from the IPPAS database. Please see for further details the codebook or the questionnaire in the annex to this volume.

[3] This battery (A4) consists of the following persons, groups or institutions: "Spouse", "Children", "Other family members", "Friends or neighbours", "A public facility", "Voluntary and charitable organisations", "Church organisations" and "Persons or private services for a fee (expenses deductible from tax)".

Respondents concurring with items representing an institutional preference obtained a score of 1 for "Could not agree more" and a score of 2 for "Agree somewhat". Concurrence with items representing a familial preference obtained a score of 4 for "Agree somewhat" and a score of 5 ("Could not agree more"). Disagreement was calculated inversely: If a respondent disagrees with an item representing an institutional preference, a score for familial attitudes was obtained, and vice versa if a person disagrees with an item representing familial preferences. For example: A person who disagrees on an item which represents familial preferences would get a score of 1 or 2.

In order to obtain one composite variable from all the scores for each item, we decided to have a mean value for the "Care for the Elderly Index". We summed up all scores and divided this sum by the number of items (17). Similar to the construction of GRAI, we reduced these resulting values into three categories: "neither institutional nor familial", "institutional" and "familial".

In addition, we have to mention that reliability is slightly lower, with a 0.725 for Cronbach's Alpha, but this is however satisfactory from our point of view. We will use the abbreviation CFEI for this index below.

3.3 Results

3.3.1 Attribution of Governments' Responsibility

As described in the methodological section, we used an index (GRAI) to measure the overall attributions for governments' responsibility from the respondents of the selected DIALOG countries. Figure 3.2 shows the comparison of the results for the seven countries.

All in all, the attribution of governments' responsibility is mostly distributed at medium or high levels. The derogation in Slovenia and Poland is interesting, as these countries have a significantly different distribution of the strength of attribution. Whereas nearly all respondents in Lithuania attributed the government with medium or high responsibility and only 4% see a low or no responsibility, in comparison, 30% of respondents in Poland see no prominent responsibility of the government for their lives.

As described in the theoretical part, Poland and Slovenia belong to the Eastern European Catholic cluster of welfare states tending towards a familialistic trajectory. In these two cases, the classification into the welfare state typology corresponds with the results of our analysis. The responsibility attribution is high but significantly lower than in other countries. We carefully assume that the familialistic trajectory has an influence on the degree of the expectation on the welfare state such that people more often regard certain areas as a private (or familial) concern. Another problem is that the pattern does not fit with Lithuania, which also belongs to this cluster (according to Fux), but where we calculated a very high GRAI value.

5%, and for Eastern Germany, at 2% for the "institutional" category and 3% for the "familial" category. We have negative and lower values for the deviation in Finland, Western Germany, Lithuania and Romania. That means that the expectations towards welfare states are lower if respondents prefer "institutional" care, and that it is higher if they prefer familial care.

Similar results are to be found for the relationship between expectations of the welfare state concerning care for the elderly and attitudes as to "who should care". Table 3.2 shows the results obtained if we associate this single item with the CFEI.

The table above illustrates major differences between the countries concerning attitudes towards the responsibility attribution in the area of care and help for elderly people. Corresponding to the previous results of the overall GRAI, Finland is also a special case in the analysis of the single item. We can again observe more than 10% of Finnish respondents who prefer neither institutional nor familial care, and approximately 80% who prefer institutional care, once more irrespectively of the expectations placed on the welfare state.

As already mentioned, the differences between the degree of attribution and the CFEI are not very significant – they are below 10% (Fig. 3.6). The pattern is interesting nonetheless: The deviations point in the same direction in all the countries, regardless of whether we are regarding the "familial" or institutional category. A tendency towards pattern formation is revealed. Lithuania and Romania are special cases: Those respondents who have high expectations of the government prefer less institutional care. On the other hand, people who prefer familial care can be found more commonly in the "high/medium" category for responsibility attribution concerning care for the elderly than in the "low/no" category. We suppose that the level of confidence in institutional care is lower here than in other countries, although expectations made of the government in this area are high. All in all, these results

Table 3.2 CFEI by attribution of governments' responsibility to care for the elderly in %

Governments' responsibility: Taking care for the elderly		CFEI		
		Institutional	Familial	Neither
FI	High/medium	80.0	7.7	12.3
	Low/no	78.3	8.5	13.2
DE-E	High/medium	69.2	28.3	2.6
	Low/no	64.6	33.3	2.0
DE-W	High/medium	71.0	26.8	2.2
	Low/no	63.7	30.3	6.0
LT	High/medium	62.5	36.3	1.2
	Low/no	64.8	28.6	6.7
PL	High/medium	55.8	42.0	2.2
	Low/no	49.1	49.1	1.8
RO	High/medium	49.7	49.1	1.2
	Low/no	54.3	45.0	0.7
SL	High/medium	60.5	37.7	1.9
	Low/no	52.2	44.7	3.1

Source: IPPAS

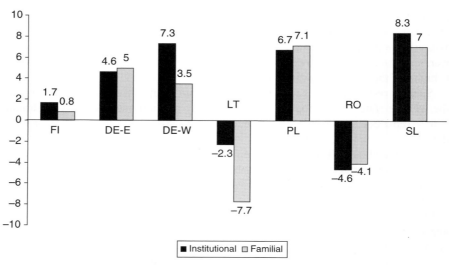

Fig. 3.6 Deviation of percentage between high/med, and low/no RA ("to take care for the elderly") by CFEI
Source: IPPAS

are also not strong enough to provide an answer to our initial question as to whether expectations made of the welfare state might impact preferences as to who should care for elderly people.

3.5 Conclusion

On the basis of the IPPAS data, we have to abandon the hypothesis that expectations of the welfare state have an effect on the preference of whether institutions or family members should care for the elderly. It is evident that citizens from the countries under study see an overall high level of responsibility for governments in different areas which affect private life and especially care for old people. However, even that does not mean that they prefer care to be organised by institutions – the preference as to "who should care" does not appear to cohere with the responsibility attribution.

The association between the degree of responsibility attribution and the preference of who should care for old people is very slight and insignificant in all countries. Having said that, the direction of the low association is interesting: We found concordance in five out of seven countries. Those respondents with high expectations of the welfare state prefer institutional care, and those with low expectations prefer familial care. In Lithuania and Romania, however, the results show discordance. The percentage of respondents who have low expectations towards the state and prefer institutional care is higher than those who have high expectations, and vice versa.

In general, institutional care is preferred to familial care. One exception is constituted by Romania, where we found that approximately half of respondents prefer institutional care and the other half prefer familial care. An interesting case is Finland, where we found the highest level of preference towards institutional care, while care by family members is far less frequently favoured when compared to the other countries in the study. Among Finnish respondents, one also finds the highest percentage of respondents who are indifferent.

As regards our research question, we have to conclude that the attribution of governments' responsibility or expectations of the welfare state cannot be used as an explanatory variable for the question of "who should care". We assume different drives which lead to the decision or preference as to whether care for the elderly is a private or institutional matter. We believe that a further analysis focused on the individual level and on different attitudes could reveal clearer correlations and explanations of the preferences. However, our results show that the overall high demand on the welfare state which we found for the countries under study does not lead to higher demand on the state for care for elderly people.

Chapter 4
Changing Attitudes on Population Trends and Policies?

A comparison between the first and second rounds of the PPAS

Jürgen Dorbritz

Abstract The article seeks to compare the results of the current DIALOG project (PPAS2) with the previous questionnaire which was carried out in the first half of the nineties (PPAS1). Even if it is not always possible to make a comparison because of the restricted number of countries, as well as of changed indicators and problems, some notable changes are nevertheless shown in attitudes towards demographic trends and demographically-relevant policies. The ageing of the population is judged to be negative, in particular the fall in the proportion of young people among the population. Negative evaluations were found more frequently in PPAS2. Among the family-demographic trends, criticism is most frequently leveled at those which signify changes in the traditional family. The comparison revealed changes in the significance of marriage as a basis for partnership and for cohabitation with children. The associated change in attitudes which can be observed is not the same across Europe. In the Netherlands, for instance, unmarried cohabitation, a fall in the birthrate or childlessness were regarded as less negative at the start of the nineties than is the case today. The change of attitude took an opposite course in Italy, with tolerance tending to increase. Attitude patterns can still be found in the Czech Republic and Hungary, even after 2000, which are derived from the former Socialist era, with the family being held in very high esteem. Whilst a change of attitude can be observed in the Czech Republic, virtually no differences as against the PPAS1 can be found in Hungary. The author would like to stress the changes in desired fertility which have taken place in the past ten years. Desired fertility is very low in the German-speaking area in particular. The frequent wish to remain childless is noticeable in this context. A major conclusion drawn by the PPAS is that there are high proportions of women who would like to reconcile family and work, and that the trend has risen even further in comparison to the nineties. Many are in favour of

J. Dorbritz
Federal Institute for Population Research, Wiesbaden, Germany
e-mail: juergen.dorbritz@destatis.de

part-time work, flexible working hours and improvements in the childcare situation. This indicates an increased desire to reconcile family and work, also shown in the ideals of reconciliation of family and work, where having children and working part-time are favoured.

Keywords: Ageing · Marriage · Birth · Children · Family · Family policy

4.1 Introduction

The DIALOG – PPAS study evaluated in this book (referred to hereinafter, and only in the present article, as PPAS2) is based on the so-called PPA (hereinafter referred to PPAS1), a survey also providing comparisons at European level on the acceptance of demographically-relevant policies, carried out at the beginning of the nineties. The full title at that time was: "European Comparative Survey on Population Policy Acceptance (PPA)". PPAS1 was carried out in different manifestations in the individual countries from September 1990 to December 1992. The period of the PPAS2 questionnaire was 1999–2004.

The main results of the first PPAS have been published in two volumes, edited by Hein Moors and Rossella Palomba (1995); Rossella Palomba and Hein Moors (1998) entitled "Population, Family and Welfare", the first volume containing national results and the second devoted to comparisons between the countries.

This article aims to compare the results of the two rounds of the PPAS. The comparison takes place in various demographic areas, the focus being clearly on the change in attitudes towards marriage, family and children. The detailed evaluations cover the topics of evaluation of demographic ageing, attitudes towards marriage, family and children, desired fertility, evaluation of family policy measures, preferred forms of reconciliation of family and work, and general value systems. Such comparisons appear to be valuable in that not only a demographic change has taken place in Europe in comparison with the beginning of the nineties, but also the relevant conditions for the evaluation of demographic trends and policies have changed. These also include a heightened public perception of demographic ageing and the increasingly critical discussion of the consequences for the social security systems. Demographic change hence directly impacts the respondents and leads to a new quality in the evaluation. Also worthy of mention are the changes in the former Socialist countries of central and Eastern Europe, which were not yet so clearly reflected in demographically-relevant attitudes at the beginning of the nineties as was the case in the second round of the PPAS. Results are available for three countries (regions), namely Hungary, Eastern Germany and the Czech Republic.

Before the results of the two surveys are compared, a few restrictions need to be pointed out:

- Not all countries which participated in the first round also took part in PPAS2. Spain and Switzerland did not take part in the second round. Several new countries have been added in the shape of Poland, Romania, Slovenia, Estonia,

Lithuania, Finland and Cyprus for which no data are available from the first round. If one looks separately at Western and Eastern Germany, recommended because of continuing differences in attitude, along with Austria, Belgium, the Czech Republic, Hungary, Italy and the Netherlands, eight comparative regions are available.

- The questionnaires used in the first and second rounds are no longer identical. The wording of the questions and scales have been changed to some extent because of experience from the first round; new questions have been added or old ones omitted.
- Different age restrictions in the various samples are also a cause for concern. In order not to distort matters here, only the data for 20- to 40-year-olds have been evaluated.

All this makes it more difficult, but not impossible, to compare the two surveys, whilst explaining why in some cases there are only four or five countries for which it was possible to carry out the comparative analyses.

4.2 The Change in the Age Structure of the Population

The fall in the proportion of young people and the increase in the proportion of the elderly among the population were to be evaluated. Table 4.1 presents the proportions of those respondents who evaluated the trends as bad.[1]

Demographic ageing is judged in negative terms by the population. It can however be observed that the fall in the proportion of younger people among the population is evaluated more negatively than the increase in the proportion of the elderly. This is a result which had already been found in the first round of the PPAS, and was confirmed in the second round. It is likely to be an expression on the one hand of reservations with regard to the low birthrate, and on the other hand of the

Table 4.1 Opinion on the rising number of older people and the declining proportion of young people in countries of PPAS1 and 2, all respondents, age group 20 up to 39 (very bad, in %)

Countries	PPAS	Decrease of young people			Increase of older people		
		Total	Men	Women	Total	Men	Women
Belgium	PPAS1	63.2	64.2	62.6	40.1	44.6	37.6
	PPAS2	59.2	57.4	60.9	53.1	53.7	52.4
Czech	PPAS1	61.5	61.4	61.5	–	–	–
	PPAS2	73.5	68.0	78.0	72.8	74.1	71.8
Italy	PPAS1	73.7	71.3	76.1	50.1	52.0	48.5
	PPAS2	88.9	89.2	88.7	59.5	60.2	58.7
The Netherlands	PPAS1	51.3	50.0	52.6	39.2	40.0	38.3
	PPAS2	52.2	49.9	54.4	–	–	–

[1] The five-tier scale in the PPAS2 has been converted to a three-tier scale, combining the points good and very good, as well as bad and very bad.

two-sided view taken of elderly people. There is naturally a negative evaluation of demographic ageing, along with its social consequences. At the same time, the respondents have parents and grandparents whose high life expectancy is definitely not regarded as negative. What is more, a positive view is taken of the role of the elderly in society as a result of their experience and knowledge. This is presumed to be the reason why two aspects of the uniform process of demographic ageing are given different evaluations. The proportion of those who regard the fall in the number of young people as an unfavourable trend ranges from 51.3% (Netherlands, PPAS1) to 88.9% (Italy, PPAS2). A range from 39.2% (Netherlands, PPAS1) to 72.8% (Czech Republic, PPAS2) was found for the evaluation of the increase of the proportion of the elderly.[2]

Because of the data available, a comparison of the evaluation of the increase in the proportions of the elderly between PPAS1 and 2 is only possible for two countries: Belgium and Italy. A notable increase can be discerned in both countries as to the proportion of those regarding this as an unfavourable trend. The proportion increased in Belgium from 40.1% to 53.1%. An increase from 50.1% to 59.1% can be ascertained in Italy. A possible explanation can be expressed as follows: The level of knowledge among the population as to demographic ageing and its consequences has increased in comparison with the beginning of the nineties. Ageing is more often perceived as a threat to the social security systems, and hence judged in a more negative light.

There are different trends in the view of the fall in the proportion of young people among the population (the evaluations in four countries are comparable here). It is evident in Italy and the Czech Republic in PPAS2 that more respondents consider this trend to be bad. The proportion in the Czech Republic increased from 61.5% to 73.5%, and in Italy from 71.3% to 88.9%. The evaluations in the Netherlands have remained virtually unchanged, a slight increase from 51.3 to 52.2% being recorded. Belgium even experienced a slight fall, from 63.2 to 59.2%.

It can be discerned in general terms that the changes in proportion in the age structure of the population, tipping the scales towards the elderly, were regarded as less critically at the beginning of the nineties than is the case today.

4.3 The Evaluation of Family-demographic Trends

A whole series of family-demographic trends were to be evaluated, covering a range from the fall in the birthrate, via childlessness and unmarried cohabitation with children, through to divorces. Data are available for six countries.

It can be observed in general terms that approval of the current change in the family-demographic trends is rare. The greatest acceptance is found for the increasing number of couples in unmarried cohabitation, the birth of children to unmarried

---

[2] The relatively considerable differences between the PPAS countries are discussed in the article entitled "Demographic Knowledge and Evaluation of demographic trends" in this volume.

parents and the fall in the marriage rate. The increasing numbers of divorces, the growing number of children in one-parent families, the fall in the birthrates and the increasing proportion of persons opting to live alone tend to be viewed highly critically. Seen in detail, there are very major differences between the countries, as well as in the trends from PPAS1 to PPAS2 (Table 4.2).

Table 4.2 Evaluation of family-demographic trends in countries of PPAS1 and 2, all respondents, age group 20–39 (very positive in %, means)

Countries	PPA	Increasing number of unmarried couples		Increasing number of couples opting to remain childless		Drop in the number of marriages		Fall in the birthrates	
		Very pos.	mean	Very pos.	mean	Very pos.	mean	Very Pos.	mean
Austria	PPA1	33.1	2.92	10.4	3.72	8.2	3.64	6.8	3.93
	PPA2	39.5	2.69	10.5	3.58	13.5	3.13	5.5	3.86
Belgium	PPA1	–	–	–	–	–	–	20.6	3.25
	PPA2	46.2	2.49	16.0	3.16	14.4	3.01	7.7	3.60
Czech R.	PPA1	12.6	3.40	3.9	3.98	4.4	3.80	3.1	4.06
	PPA2	35.8	2.78	6.5	3.67	13.8	3.21	2.3	4.11
Hungary	PPA1	19.1	3.02	–	–	2.3	3.60	.7	4.11
(only women)	PPA2	27.2	2.97	2.2	4.37	5.4	3.65	1.0	4.57
Italy	PPA1	28.1	2.90	18.5	3.22	15.1	3.21	11.8	3.61
	PPA2	25.5	2.99	26.4	3.28	31.3	3.18	10.8	3.72
The Netherlands	PPA1	68.3	2.17	35.0	2.70	33.3	2.76	57.0	2.42
	PPA2	45.1	2.53	20.5	2.93	23.0	2.85	20.9	2.92

Countries	PPA	Increasing number of children in a one-parent family		Increasing number of persons who live alone		Increasing number of births unmarried couples		Increasing number of divorces	
		Very pos.	mean	Very pos.	mean	Very pos.	mean	Very pos.	mean
Austria	PPA1	8.2	3.88	6.2	3.86	8.8	3.46	3.0	4.24
	PPA2	10.6	3.46	12.5	3.40	18.8	3.04	3.7	4.02
Belgium	PPA1	–	–	–	–		–	–	–
	PPA2	4.2	3.71	12.2	3.14	26.5	2.85	1.4	4.15
Czech R.	PPA1	.5	4.53	1.7	4.20	2.9	3.88	–	4.72
	PPA2	3.3	3.96	3.8	3.75	12.1	3.23	1.2	4.22
Hungary	PPA1	.6	4.43	.2	4.30	.9	4.02	.2	4.50
(only women)	PPA2	.2	4.71	.3	4.68	3.3	3.97	1.2	4.53
Italy	PPA1	1.0	4.37	11.8	3.45	7.4	3.63	3.1	3.95
	PPA2	10.6	3.75	15.7	3.61	32.1	3.14	12.1	3.70
The Netherlands	PPA1	8.0	3.56	28.6	2.96	37.8	2.86	.7	4.15
	PPA2	6.6	3.66	16.1	3.01	38.4	2.69	4.4	4.01

The increasing number of unmarried couples

This is the demographic trend towards which respondents took the least critical stance. This trend was most broadly accepted in PPAS1 in the Netherlands, with a mean of 2.17 (calculated on the basis of a five-tier scale ranging from very good [1] to very bad [5]). And a low mean value in Belgium in PPAS2 also shows a positive view of unmarried cohabitation. The trend is viewed in highly negative terms in the first round of the PPAS in the Czech Republic and Hungary, still reflecting the traditional attitudes dominant in the former Socialist countries. A change of attitude can be discovered in all participating countries, but progressing in a variety of directions. The proportion of positive evaluations has increased in Austria, the Czech Republic and Hungary, whilst acceptance has fallen in Italy, and in the Netherlands in particular.

The increasing number of childless couples

Childlessness has few proponents. Rejection is most common in the Czech Republic and in Hungary, whilst a comparably positive evaluation can be found in the Netherlands in PPAS1 and in Italy in PPAS2. The critical view of childlessness has remained virtually unchanged since the beginning of the nineties. Only in Italy has agreement with this development increased. In turn, an increase in the proportion of critical evaluations can be found in the Netherlands.

The decline in the number of marriages and the fall in the birthrate

Neither demographic trend is regarded as a favourable development. Once more, rejection is particularly pronounced in the two former Socialist countries Hungary and the Czech Republic. Marked changes as against PPAS1 are only discernible in a small number of cases. The positive view taken in Italy and the Czech Republic has increased when it comes to a fall in the number of marriages. The decline in the birthrate is seen much more critically in the Netherlands and in Belgium than at the beginning of the nineties. In the Netherlands, for instance, the proportion of those who answered very positive fell from 57.0 to 20.9%. It is presumed that the fall in the birthrate is much more commonly connected to demographic ageing, and hence receives a more critical evaluation.

Growing number of children in one-parent families and increase
in the number of divorces

These are the two trends which tend to be agreed with least. High means indicate that very many respondents judged these to be bad or very bad. There are virtually no differences in evaluation between the two questionnaire periods. Only Italy constitutes an exception, where the increase in acceptance is still low.

The increase in the number of those living alone

The increase in the number of single persons is almost never regarded in a positive light. The trend finds most agreement in the Netherlands and in Italy. As with the
evaluation of the other family-demographic trends, a decline in the number of positive evaluations here can be observed in the Netherlands, coupled with an increase
in Italy. Equally, the extremely negative view of living alone taken in Hungary and
the Czech Republic fits the picture which has already been drawn.

Increasing number of extramarital births

The evaluation of the increase in the rate of extramarital births is highly differentiated in the countries of the PPAS. A relatively large proportion in PPAS2 in the
Netherlands, Belgium and Italy consider it to be positive that marriage and the birth
of children are decoupled. This situation already existed in the Netherlands in the
first round of the PPAS. A clear increase in acceptance has been recorded in Italy
and also in Austria. Very low agreement values are found once more in Hungary
and the Czech Republic, while the Czech Republic also records an increase in the
proportion of respondents who answered very good.

To close this section, three results are to be emphasised from the evaluation of
family-demographic trends:

Firstly, a largely critical view is taken of the dissolution of the traditional patterns
of family formation. This however applies less to marriage as a basis for cohabitation in a spirit of partnership, and also not to extramarital births and unmarried
cohabitation with children. By contrast, respondents are primarily concerned about
the trends reflecting a threat to cohabitation with children, irrespective of the kind of
partnership-based living arrangement. The distant stance towards marriage emerging in Europe is also shown in the next section, which is devoted to the significance
of this institution.

Secondly, as above in the judgment of family-demographic trends, major sdiffer-
ences in Europe can be found which have not fundamentally changed from PPAS1
to PPAS2. It should also be stressed that the change in attitudes is not progressing
in the same direction. The greatest tolerance towards the changed picture of the
family can be found in the Netherlands. It is remarkable however that this tolerance
was more pronounced at the beginning of the nineties, in other words that a re-
traditionalisation has taken place in the ten years which have ensued. In this context,
the thesis is being developed that the heightened public perception of the ageing of
the population has led to a more negative view being taken of those changes in
the traditional family structures which lead to the fall in the birthrate. By contrast,
the situation in Italy, a country which is frequently regarded as familialist, is very
different. In the first round of the PPAS, change in the family-demographic trends
was held in a highly negative light. In the second wave of questionnaires, a clearly
higher level of agreement with the changes could be found in almost all areas in
most cases.

Thirdly, the situation in the former Socialist countries should be pointed out. A tendency can be found towards marked differences as against the attitudes in the western countries. Highly positive evaluations of the traditional picture of the family were found in PPAS1 in both Hungary and the Czech Republic. These differences have essentially been retained. This applies very much to Hungary, whilst in the Czech Republic a change of attitude, tending towards the western patterns, could be observed in some areas.

4.4 The View of the Institution "Marriage and Family"

This view appears to be particularly significant, especially from the point of view of changes in partnership-based living arrangements, in which the institution of "marriage and family" takes on a major conduct-norming function. Two indicators have been selected in order to portray a change in the attitudes towards the institution of "marriage and family". Firstly, the institution of marriage was to be evaluated using the statement "Marriage is an outdated institution". The aspect of cohabitation with children is portrayed with the statement "If a single woman would like to have a child but not a long-term partnership, this should be accepted" (Table 4.3).

In general terms, the institution of marriage still finds a high level of acceptance in the majority of European populations. The highest agreement with the statement that marriage is an outdated institution is to be found among men in Germany in PPAS2. 33.1% of 20- to 39-year-old men in Western Germany and 39.6% in Eastern Germany agreed. An even greater proportion of women accept the institution. 25.4% of women in Western Germany, and 31.3% of women in Eastern Germany, agreed with this statement in PPAS2. Such differences are typical of all the countries which were included in the analysis.

A relatively distant stance towards marriage is also found in the other western countries (Belgium, Austria and the Netherlands). Agreement with the statement that marriage is an outdated institution is less common in the Czech Republic and Italy, by contrast.

If one compares the trends between PPAS1 and PPAS2, a clear development can be identified. Rejection of the institution of marriage has clearly increased in Europe in comparison with the beginning of the nineties. Agreement with the statement to be evaluated has clearly increased both among women and men in all countries observed. The proportion of agreement increased from 15.3 to 29.5% among for instance Austrian men, from 14.1 to 26.4% among men in the Netherlands, and from 20.0 to 31.3% among women in Eastern Germany.

Trends in the Czech Republic also appear to be worthy of note. The institution still found unrestricted agreement shortly after the end of Socialism. Only 3.1% of women and 8.5% of men agreed with the rejection. This shows the continuation of attitudes that were typical in the Socialist era, with high acceptance of and esteem for marriage and the family, which also expressed itself in a relatively high birthrate, a small number of unmarried people and low childlessness. The increases in PPAS2,

Table 4.3 Evaluation of the institution "marriage and family" by men and women in PPAS countries, age group 20–39 (in %)

| Countries | PPAS | Marriage is an outdated institution* | | | |
| | | Men | | Women | |
		Agree	Disagree	Agree	Disagree
Austria	PPAS1	15.3	80.7	13.3	81.3
	PPAS2	29.5	70.5	25.5	74:5
Belgium	PPAS1	–	–	–	–
	PPAS2	30.3	45.6	20.7	58.9
Czech	PPAS1	8.5	84.3	3.1	93.7
	PPAS2	21.3	78.7	12.2	87.8
Germany W	PPAS1	26.3	60.3	23.4	65.8
	PPAS2	33.1	66.9	25.4	74.6
Germany E	PPAS1	25.5	61.4	20.0	67.8
	PPAS2	39.6	60.4	31.3	68.7
Italy	PPAS1	12.0	84.6	11.3	86.1
	PPAS2	19.7	74.5	16.1	78.1
The Netherlands	PPAS1	14.1	80.5	13.8	79.1
	PPAS2	26.4	73.6	18.1	81.9

| Countries | PPAS | If a single woman would like to have child but not a long-term partnership, this should be accepted* | | | |
| | | Men | | Women | |
		Agree	Disagree	Agree	Disagree
Austria	PPAS1	82.8	13.7	88.4	9.2
	PPAS2	85.0	15.0	90.7	9.3
Belgium	PPAS1	59.1	21.8	56.2	23.9
	PPAS2	49.9	25.5	63.1	16.5
Czech	PPAS1	42.5	45.5	48.9	40.2
	PPAS2	78.8	21.2	80.5	19.5
Germany W	PPAS1	78.2	12.5	81.1	10.9
	PPAS2	84.5	15.5	88.4	11.6
Germany E	PPAS1	88.4	6.4	91.5	4.7
	PPAS2	93.4	6.6	96.1	3.9
Italy	PPAS1	17.4	75.5	16.5	77.2
	PPAS2	21.7	67.7	19.5	71.4
The Netherlands	PPAS1	28.4	59.3	40.1	45.5
	PPAS2	59.0	41.0	63.2	36.8

*The difference to 100% is accounted for by the item "neither agree nor disagree"

to 12.2% among women and to 21.3% among men, indicate a change of attitude which continues to the present day. This result is also significant in the framework of the discussion of the degree to which change in the patterns of family formation in the post-socialist reform states is only a symptom of the crisis, or of whether new patterns are becoming established. Taking the Czech Republic as an example certainly indicates that the influence of institutional change on family formation has increased. This favours a hypothesis that a return to the old patterns of family formation is less likely than progressing towards western-orientated patterns.

The change of attitude among men in particular should also be pointed out in this context. Rejection of the institution of marriage has advanced faster among men than among women. This is noticeable in all countries. The Netherlands can be taken as an example of the situation. Rejection of the institution has increased from 14.1 to 26.4% among male and from 13.8 to 18.1% among female respondents between PPAS1 and PPAS2. Similarly distanced stances towards the family are shown in desired fertility, here in particular the trend towards desired childlessness, and also among attitudes towards children (cf. Sections 4.5 and 4.6). It appears to be an almost pan-European situation that men increasingly take up a distanced stance towards the family.

The child-orientated second aspect of the question of whether it is acceptable if women fulfil their desired fertility without resorting to the institution of marriage or living in a long-term partnership is widely accepted, with the exception of Italy (Table 4.3). The greatest degree of agreement with the statement, at 93.4% among men and 96.1% among women, is found in Eastern Germany in PPAS2. The increases over PPAS 1 are slight since agreement with the statement was also very high in the first round. The same applies to Western Germany and Austria.

The decoupling of marriage/partnership and having children found virtually no agreement in PPAS1 in Italy (men: 17.4%, women: 16.5%), the Netherlands (men: 28.4%; women: 40.1%) and also in the Czech Republic (men: 42.5%, women: 48.9%). Whilst in Italy this more traditional attitude is also shown unchanged in PPAS2, marked increases are recorded in the Czech Republic and the Netherlands.

The results of the Population Policy Acceptance Study show, if one disregards Italy, that a further deinstitutionalation has taken place in people's attitudes towards the institution of "marriage and family". This is shown in the increasing proportions of respondents who consider the institution to be obsolete and in the high and increased proportions who accept the decoupling of marriage and partnership and cohabitation with children (a central aspect of the institution).

4.5 Desired Fertility

Attention has already been drawn for quite some time to changes in desired fertility in some European countries. One should mention here first and foremost the evaluations of the Eurobarometer by Fahey and Spéder (2004), which have already indicated the low desired fertility in the German-speaking area. The PPAS now offers the possibility to demonstrate trends in comparison with the first half of the nineties. Both the number of average desired children, and the structure of desired fertility, should be discussed.

Table 4.4 Desired number of children by women and men in PPAS countries, age group 20–39

Countries	Desired number of children (average)			
	Women		Men	
	PPAS1	PPAS2	PPAS1	PPAS2
Austria	2.11	1.84	1.98	1.78
Belgium	2.15	1.86	2.12	1.81
Czech Rep.	2.16	1.97	2.18	2.02
Western Germany	1.70	1.72	1.68	1.56
Eastern Germany	1.79	1.78	1.65	1.46
Hungary	2.21	1.90	–	1.90
Italy	–	1.92	–	1.86
The Netherlands	2.01	1.98	1.78	1.98

To start with, it can be established that despite all the discussions on change in desired fertility it is still the case that more than half of the women and men questioned in the PPAS countries would like to have more than two children (Table 4.4). If one takes a look at the average values, however, it is then only men in the Czech Republic who want more than two children, with an average of 2.02.[3] Comparably high values in desired fertility are also achieved among women and men in the Netherlands and in Hungary. The lower measured values for Germany are noticeable. Women in Western and Eastern Germany would still like to have an average of 1.73 and 1.78 children respectively. Hence, replacement of the parents' generation is not even achieved in terms of desired fertility. Again, German men clearly want to have fewer children, accounting for 1.59 children in the West and 1.53 children in the East.

The desire for precisely two children is dominant in the parity-specific structure of desired fertility. This is the largest group in the second round among both women and men in all PPAS countries, but no longer necessarily forms a majority. 58.3% of women in the Czech Republic would like to have two children. In Austria, by contrast, it is only 35.1% (Table 4.5). The countries then differ as to the second-largest group. Among women and men in Austria and Eastern Germany, among women in Belgium, and among men in Hungary, it is this group which only wants to have one child. Women and men wanting three or more children form the second-largest group in all other countries. One should not overlook the fact that a relatively large number of respondents now do not want to have any children at all. This group is relatively large among women only in Western Germany, at 16.6%. One also finds high proportions among men in the Netherlands and Belgium, in addition to Germany, with no desired fertility. The highest value was observed in Western Germany, at 27.2%.

Compared with the desired fertility observed at the beginning of the nineties, the average amount and also the structure of desired fertility have changed in the majority of countries.

---

[3] It should be pointed out here that desired fertility is also higher than two in other PPAS countries (e.g. Finland). These countries have not been included here since no comparative data are available from the first round.

76   J. Dorbritz

Table 4.5 Desired number of children by women, men and parities in PPAS countries, age group 20–39 (in %)

Countries	Desired number of children by parity (%)							
	Women PPAS1				PPAS2			
	0	1	2	3+	0	1	2	3+
Austria	7.6	12.9	51.6	27.9	8.2	32.7	35.1	24.0
Belgium	5.8	16.2	46.9	31.1	10.4	22.7	45.3	21.5
Czech Rep.	1.4	9.8	64.3	24.5	6.9	15.0	58.3	19.8
Western Germany	15.0	23.2	44.0	17.7	16.6	14.5	53.7	15.3
Eastern Germany	5.6	29.6	49.1	15.7	5.8	28.7	50.6	14.9
Hungary	0.3	11.9	61.8	26.1	3.2	15.6	53.7	27.4
Italy	–	–	–	–	7.1	18.9	53.4	20.6
The Netherlands	15.1	5.5	50.8	28.6	12.9	7.3	49.2	30.7

Countries	Desired number of children by parity (%)							
	Men PPAS1				PPAS2			
	0	1	2	3+	0	1	2	3+
Austria	9.4	14.4	51.9	24.2	11.1	33.5	34.4	21.1
Belgium	7.1	14.9	46.1	31.9	15.3	19.6	43.3	21.8
Czech Rep.	3.0	7.0	63.8	26.2	6.4	19.6	50.4	23.6
Western Germany	16.0	21.4	46.9	15.7	27.2	13.0	40.0	19.8
Eastern Germany	9.3	31.8	47.2	11.7	21.1	24.2	45.0	9.6
Hungary	–	–	–	–	7.7	20.6	53.7	18.0
Italy	–	–	–	–	9.1	16.9	56.9	17.1
The Netherlands	18.0	9.2	55.6	17.3	17.5	5.3	52.7	24.4

On the average number of children: The exceptions to this trend are to be found in the Netherlands and in Germany. Average desired fertility among women has remained constantly high in the Netherlands, being now 1.98 (PPAS1: 2.01). It has in fact risen once more among men from, 1.78 to 1.98. This trend concurs with the findings already made in which a return to family-orientated attitudes has been ascertained in the Netherlands. The situation in Germany for the desired fertility of women can be described at a very low but constant level. A noticeably lower desired fertility of 1.70 was already ascertained in Western Germany in the first round (PPAS2: 1.73). The values for Eastern Germany are 1.79 (PPAS1) and 1.78 (PPAS2). Among men, by contrast, a further reduction has taken place – in Western Germany from 1.68 to 1.59, and in Eastern Germany from 1.65 to 1.53.

Negative trends can be stated for all other countries. There have been notable reductions in Austria, Belgium and Hungary. The desired fertility of women in Austria fell from 2.11 to 1.84, and in Belgium from 2.15 to 1.86. The consequence of this is that there is now little difference in desired fertility between Austria, Belgium and Germany, at least among women. The number of children wanted by men in

Germany is noticeably lower than in the other countries. A considerable decline can also be discerned for Hungary. Since the initial level was a very high 2.21, however, Hungary is also still among the countries with higher desired fertility in the second round, at 1.90. The fall in the Czech Republic was moderate both among women and men.

On the parity-specific structure of desired fertility: Although an orientation to the two-child family was found in both rounds of the PPAS, it became less significant between the two rounds in relative terms. The desired family size has tended to become smaller. The desire for the parities zero and one has tended to increase. Seen in detail, however, highly differentiated trends have taken place which because of the large amount of data are to be portrayed separately by parity and for each country:

Austria: There are virtually no increases in desired childlessness. However, a considerable re-distribution has taken place among women and men of the parities two and three-plus to one. For instance, this can be described for Austrian women. In PPAS1, 51.6% desired two children (PPAS2: 35.1). By contrast, the desire for one child has increased from 12.9% to 32.7%.

Belgium: Desired childlessness has roughly doubled, having increased among women from 5.8% to 10.4%. There is hardly any change in the desire for one and two children. However, the desire for three and more children has declined.

The Czech Republic: The desire to remain childless was virtually negligible in the first round of the PPAS. It increased to a low level in PPAS2 (women: 6.9%). The desire for only one child has also increased slightly. By contrast, the desire for two children and for three and more has dropped slightly. All in all, the structural changes in desired fertility are slight.

Germany: Not only were there different fertility regimes in the two regions of Germany, but also specific desired fertility structures. The desire to remain childless is common in Western Germany. The high values of the desire to have no children in the first round, at 15.0% (women) and 16.0% (men), have remained constant among women, whilst among men it has risen to 27.2%. Among Eastern German women, these values have remained unchanged at 5.6% (PPAS1) and 5.8% (PPAS2). Among men the desire for no children has increased tangibly to 21.1%. Accordingly, the shifts in the parity structures have remained slight among women. Among men the increase in significance of the parity zero has taken place by virtue of declines in all other parities.

Hungary: Data are only available for women. The parity structure has only changed minimally in comparison to other countries.

Netherlands: The changes in the Netherlands run counter to the general trend. The desire for no children has fallen slightly among women, from 15.1% to 12.9%, whilst it has remained unchanged among men. In comparison with the Czech Republic or Hungary, the desire for childlessness is still at a high level. The desire for one child is low, by contrast to which very many respondents would like to have two or more children. This situation has not changed in the comparison of the two rounds of questionnaires.

4.6 The Significance of Family Policy Measures

One of the central elements of the PPAS is to ascertain the family policy expectations within the populations. To this end, a number of possible future measures have been stated for evaluation. The five measures which have had the greatest agreement are listed in Table 4.6.

It applies equally to PPAS1 and PPAS2 that the expectations of family policy measures in the population are high. Approval of the most important measures by in some cases more than 90% of respondents is an indication of this. Only a small number of countries fall outside the evaluation pattern, first and foremost Belgium and the Netherlands, above all in PPAS1. The generally very high importance of possible measures is even stronger in the former Socialist countries. Here are two examples of this: In the first PPAS, round 98.8% of respondents in Hungary and 95.4% of Eastern Germans had come out in favour of improving housing for families. In the Czech Republic, 93.5% voted for improved parental leave arrangements. The greater expectations in the Eastern European countries can be explained from their Socialist past. The governments of these countries had already started to introduce in some cases strongly pronatalist-orientated demographic policy measures in the seventies. However one may judge the impact of such measures, their effect was obviously that they aroused great expectations of state family policy among the population. This effect can still be seen relatively clearly in the second round in Hungary and Eastern Germany.

Changes can however also be observed in what the populations in the PPAS countries consider desirable in terms of family policy. In the trend, this change can be described in terms of upgrading the measures making it easier to reconcile family and work. This is a finding which concurs with the change in the ideals of reconciliation of family and work. The measures which were relevant to reconcilability were also already highly significant in the first round of PPAS. The five most important measures in each of the countries are two to three measures aimed to improve the reconcilability conditions. The important measures were "More and better part-time work opportunities", "Flexible working hours for working parents" and "Better day-care facilities for children younger than three years". At the same time, one can see for PPAS1 that an improvement in housing for families was classed as the most important measure in three countries/regions (Western and Eastern Germany, Hungary). What is more, it reached second place in Austria.

Reconcilability-orientated measures have been placed in the first position in PPAS 2 in 6 out of 8 countries/regions. Only in Hungary has better housing, and in the Czech Republic lower wage and income tax, been voted the most important measure of future family policy. At the beginning of the 21st Century, therefore, the dominant measures of family policy expectations are those which are to make it easier to reconcile family and work. Financial support-orientated measures have hence by no means become insignificant, particular importance attaching to "Lower wage and income tax" and to a "Substantial rise in child allowance". This applies in particular to the former Socialist countries, where with the removal of women from the labour market and the financial uncertainty in the social transitional phase

Table 4.6 Preferences for family policy measures in PPAS countries, all respondents, age group 20 up to 39 ("very in favour" and "somewhat in favour", in %)

Countries	PPAS1 Family policy measures	%	PPAS2 Family policy measures	%
Austria	1. More and better part-time work opportunities	91.2	1. More and better part-time work opportunities	90.8
	2. Better housing for families with children	91.1	2. Lower wage and income tax	89.0
	3. Lower wage and income tax	90.4	3. Flexible working hours for working parents	89.0
	4. Better day-care facilities for children >3 years	90.2	4. Improved parental leave arrangements	88.8
	5. Flexible working hours for working parents	90.2	5. Better day-care facilities for children <3 years	82.6
Belgium	1. Allowance for non working parents	69.8	1. More and better part-time work opportunities	85.1
	2. Rise in child allowances	66.6	2. Flexible working hours for working parents	81.9
	3. More and better part-time work opportunities	65.9	3. Lower wage and income tax	81.4
	4. Child-care facilities for school going children	64.1	4. Better day-care facilities for children <3 years	73.2
	5. Improved parental leave arrangements	51.7	5. Substantial decrease in the costs of education	71.8
Czech Rep.	1. Improved parental leave arrangements	93.5	1. Lower wage and income tax	89.2
	2. Flexible working hours for working parents	92.1	2. Allowance for non working parents care	87.6
	3. Allowances for families with children	91.4	3. Improved parental leave arrangements	87.1
	4. Allowance at birth of each child	90.9	4. Substantial rise in child allowance	86.3
	5. Lower wage and income tax	90.8	5. More and better part-time work opportunities	85.1
Western Germany	1. Better housing for families with children	92.7	1. Flexible working hours for working parents	89.8
	2. More and better part-time work opportunities	91.2	2. More and better part-time work opportunities	89.2
	3. Flexible working hours for working parents	90.4	3. Better day-care facilities for children <3 years	88.9
	4. Lower wage and income tax	90.3	4. Lower wage and income tax	87.6
	5. Improved parental leave arrangements	89.9	5. Improved parental leave arrangements	84.4
Eastern Germany	1. Better housing for families with children	95.4	1. Better day-care facilities for children >3 years	92.5
	2. More and better part-time work opportunities	94.5	2. Flexible working hours for working parents	90.8
	3. Better day-care facilities for children >3 years	94.5	3. More and better part-time work opportunities	90.8
	4. Flexible working hours for working parents	93.7	4. Child-care facilities for school going children	89.1
	5. Allowances for families with children	93.5	5. Better day-care facilities for children <3 years	88.8

Table 4.6 (continued)

Countries	PPAS1 Family policy measures	%	PPAS2 Family policy measures	%
Hungary	1. Better housing for families with children	98.8	1. Better housing for families with children	95.8
	2. Lower wage and income tax	96.7	2. Substantial decrease in the costs of education	93.1
	3. More and better part-time work opportunities	96.4	3. Substantial rise in child allowance	92.4
	4. Flexible working hours for working parents	95.5	4. Lower wage and income tax	91.6
	5. Allowance for non working parents	78.9	5. Income-dependent allowance for families	90.9
Italy	1. Better day-care facilities for children <3 years	94.4	1. More and better part-time work opportunities	88.7
	2. Lower wage and income tax	89.3	2. Lower wage and income tax	88.2
	3. Improved parental leave arrangements	88.5	3. A substantial rise in child allowance	88.1
	4. Flexible working hours for working parents	88.4	4. Better day-care facilities for children <3 years	87.7
	5. Allowances for families with children	85.9	5. Better housing for families with children	80.9
The Netherlands	1. More and better part-time work opportunities	76.0	1. More and better part-time work opportunities	80.2
	2. Cheaper schools for children	71.7	2. Flexible working hours for working parents	75.6
	3. Improved parental leave arrangements	69.6	3. Improved parental leave arrangements	75.5
	4. Better day-care facilities for children <3 years	66.6	4. Better day-care facilities for children <3 years	68.6
	5. Better day-care facilities for children >3 years	66.6	5. Lower wage and income tax	67.9

after the end of Socialism, the financial security of the family has gained greater attention.

The following conclusion can be drawn from this section for future European family policies: A combination of financial support and family-friendly working hours arrangements is what young European women and men expect for the future. In this respect, the western countries have been calling louder for working hours arrangements and the former Socialist countries for reductions in financial burdens.

4.7 Reconciliation of Family and Work

Women aged from 20–39 were asked for their view on the ideal method of reconciling family and work. A distinction was made here according to full-time and part-time work or leaving work altogether and the number of children.

The majority of women in the PPAS countries would like to have children and work. This statement applies just as much today as at the beginning of the nineties. Childlessness coupled with full- or part-time employment is unpopular.

Also, completely or temporarily leaving work, if one has children, plays only a subordinate role (Table 4.7).

If one summarises the different numbers of children desired and working hours models, many more than half wish to combine having children and working. The highest values can be found here in Belgium. In the first round of questionnaires, 75.4% had selected a reconciliation model. The figure in the second round was 80.2%. Similarly strong reconciliation aspirations can be found in Italy. In PPAS1, it was 81.1% who considered it to be ideal to combine family and work. The value has fallen slightly in PPAS2, to 75.5%. Considerable significance is also attached to the ideal of reconciliation in the East of Germany. 73.1% in PPAS1 and 70.5% in PPAS2 consider one of the reconciliation models to be ideal.

Aspirations towards reconciliation have considerably increased in Western Germany and the Netherlands in a comparison of the two PPAS questionnaires. An increase from 38.5% to 53.8% can be recorded in Western Germany, and from 51.1 to 60.4% in the Netherlands.

If a detailed distinction is made by individual models, it is shown that the respondents would like to have two children and to work part-time. With the exception of Western Germany, this is the model named most frequently in the first round. The countries vary when it comes to the second most frequently-named models. Leaving work as long as the children are small has a relatively high value in Western Germany, the Netherlands and Italy. Full-time work with one or two children is more frequently considered to be ideal in Eastern Germany and Belgium.

The most important result of the comparison made here is the increased desire in Europe to reconcile family and work in parallel. This can be seen on the basis of the change in attitudes in Western Germany and the Netherlands. A pronounced orientation can be seen here towards part-time work. However, the breadwinner-homemaker model has also retained its significance in those countries in which it was frequently regarded as ideal at the beginning of the nineties.

Over and above this, a whole series of changes has taken place in individual countries. One can observe for Belgium that the very high significance of reconciling full-time work in the first round has given way to part-time work. With regard to Germany, three particularities are to be noted. *Firstly*: Western Germany is the region in which childlessness in conjunction with full-time work was more frequently named as an ideal reconciliation model. This also corresponds to the actual situation, with high proportions of women who are childless. The unfavourable framework for reconciliation is considered to be the cause of this, leading to a need to decide between family and job/career. *Secondly*: The classical breadwinner-homemaker model, in other words leaving work altogether when children come along, has become much less significant and shows the fact that a paradigm shift is taking place in Western Germany in attitudes towards a reconciliation orientation. *Thirdly*: Considerable differences when it comes to reconciliation-related ideals can be identified between Western and Eastern Germany. Whilst Western Germans' preferences pursue the current model of family policy with a high proportion of women who leave work when children come along, the model of GDR family policy can still be found in Eastern Germany. This is reflected in the high proportions of those who want

Table 4.7 Ideal choice for reconciliation of paid work and family, female respondents, age group 20–39 in PPAS countries (in %)

Countries	PPA	Full-time No children	Full-time One child	Full-time Two children	Full-time More than two	Part-time No children	Part-time One child	Part-time Two children	Part-time More than two	No work as long as the children are small	No work at all if there are children
Belgium	PPAS1	3.5		34.0		1.2		41.4		8.4	7.4
	PPAS2	5.3		13.5		1.2		66.7		10.2	3.0
Western Germany	PPAS1	14.5	6.8	3.6		2.8	12.8	15.3		22.7	20.1
	PPAS2	9.8	4.7	5.4	1.4	1.6	13.6	26.5	6.1	23.7	4.2
Eastern Germany	PPAS1	9.9	22.0	14.5		1.0	12.0	24.6		9.4	4.9
	PPAS2	6.5	19.9	19.1	3.7	.6	9.6	21.9	7.0	8.7	2.0
Italy	PPAS1	4.3	12.5	11.3		1.9	15.3	42.0		12.7	
	PPAS2	1.4	4.3	6.6		.8	14.0	50.6		22.1	
The Netherlands	PPAS1	2.3	2.3	3.5		4.2	3.5	41,8		24.2	
	PPAS2	7.6	5.9	5.2	54.5					19.9	6.9

to have children and work full-time. It can be stated for Italy that a polarisation of attitudes has taken place. On the one hand, the significance of reconciliation on the basis of part-time work has increased, whilst on the other hand the proportion of those who consider the traditional model to be ideal has also risen.

4.8 Value Orientations

In order to be able to depict the diversity of orientations to be evaluated more compactly, scaled down, the results of the questionnaires have initially been processed with a factor analysis. In a second step, those value orientations which identify individualistic attitudes are observed specifically according to the number of children.

The comparison is made much more difficult above all by the small number of comparative countries, and by the fact that the prescribed values of the two rounds are not completely identical as to the number and the formulations of the questions. Nevertheless, some interesting results do emerge.

4.8.1 The Dimensions of the Values

To start off, a brief overview of the most important values is to be given in the first and second rounds of the PPAS. In both PPAS rounds, those values were allotted the greatest significance which express cohabitation as partners with children. In the first round of the PPAS, these were mainly child-orientated values such as "Being able to give enough care and attention to your children" and "Being able to give your children a proper education". These values are among the three most frequently named in all the participating countries. A general difference in the evaluation was found between the western and the former Socialist countries. In the western countries, the structure of the values is also typified by the considerable significance of individualistically-orientated values. These include "Striving for self-fulfilment" and "Having enough time for yourself and for your own interests". The aspect "Having enough income/money" plays a more prominent role in the former Socialist countries, something which can be explained by the material uncertainty of the population in the phases of social transition at the beginning of the nineties (Philipov and Dorbritz 2003).

Child-orientated values were not explicitly surveyed in the second round of the PPAS. The continuing dominance of family-orientated values is reflected in the importance attached to living with one's partner in harmony and the orientation to providing security to those close to one. The harmonious partnership was categorised as the most important area of life in almost all countries. In Hungary and the Czech Republic, for instance, more than 95% of respondents answered "very important" or "important". Equally, (as a rule place 2) "Providing security for people close to you" has been categorised as extremely important. The tendential differences in the significance of materialist and idealistic orientations between western and former

Socialist countries have remained. Thus, the value "Having enough income/money" has been placed at first place in Hungary, with a mean of 1.19 (calculated with a five-tier scale). The value takes second place in the Czech Republic and Poland, with a mean value of 1.43.

Only the data from the Czech Republic and Germany are available for a concrete comparison of the two rounds of the PPAS. Table 4.8 shows the results of the factor analysis, in particular the allocation of the items to the factors. In the PPAS1, there is a clear result with three largely identical factors. Both in Western and Eastern Germany, and in the Czech Republic, the factors "self-fulfilment", "family and children" and "gender equality" have been found with largely concurring items. The factor "family and children" is constituted by three items in Germany and in the Czech Republic: Firstly "Give care and attention to children", secondly "Give children a proper education", and thirdly "Complete and happy family life". Similarly strong concurrence is found for the two other factors. In the Czech Republic and Eastern Germany, the factor "self-fulfilment" contains the factors "Striving for self-fulfilment", "Having a professional career" and "Respected outside the family". Instead of "Respected outside the family" in Western Germany "Enough time for yourself and interests" forms an element in this factor. The third factor thus contains two items which in the first portray the striving towards gender equality ("Time for household and job", "Equal division of household tasks"). The third item belonging here is "Living according the rules of faith".

Completely different developments can subsequently be observed for Germany and the Czech Republic in PPAS2. A relatively strong constancy is to be observed for Germany, whilst a notable change in the basic structure of the values has taken place in the Czech Republic. The two factors "Self-fulfilment" and "Family" were taken up again in Germany. The factor "Self-fulfilment" has remained unchanged in Western Germany as against the beginning of the nineties. "Striving for self-fulfilment" and "Respected outside the family" have been retained in Eastern Germany, whilst the work orientation has been exchanged for a leisure orientation. The factor "family" is still there, by contrast, but because of the value scale which has been re-defined in some cases, with new or re-worded statements, new items have been combined with this factor. It is now formed by "Living with partner in harmony" and "Providing security for people close to you". The third factor has taken on a completely new face. The orientation towards gender equality has given way to a prosperity orientation. "Living in a nice, spacious house" and "Having enough money" are part of this factor in both regions of Germany. In Western Germany they are supplemented by "Having holidays at least once a year", and in Eastern Germany by job satisfaction.

In the Czech Republic, the factors have taken on a largely new character in contradistinction to Germany. Prosperity-related orientations (house, holiday) have been added in the factor "Self-fulfilment". The items orientated towards money and income, as well as career, are contained in the factor partnership. The third factor "Gender equality" has been replaced by the factor "Outside family" with the orientations towards own interests, to respect outside the family and to time for friends. A result is confirmed here which was already found with the evaluation of the

Table 4.8 Results of the factor analysis, classification of the items to factors in PPAS countries, all respondents, age group 20 up to 39

Countries	PPAS	Factors/Items		
		Factor 1	Factor 2	Factor 3
Western Germany	PPAS1	*Self-fulfilment*	*Family/Children*	*Gender equality/Religion*
		Having a professional career	Give care and attention to children	Living according the rules of faith
		Striving for self-fulfilment	Give children a proper education	Time for household and job
		Enough time for yourself and interests	Complete and happy family life	Equal division of household tasks
	PPAS2	*Self-fulfilment*	*Family*	–
		Having enough time for friends	Living with partner in harmony	Living in a nice, spacious house
		Striving for self-fulfilment	Providing security for people close to you	Having holidays at least once a year
		Enough time for yourself and interests		Having enough money
Eastern Germany	PPAS1	*Family/Children*	*Self-fulfilment*	*Gender equality/Religion*
		Give care and attention to children	Having a professional career	Living according the rules of faith
		Give children a proper education	Striving for self-fulfilment	Equal division of household tasks
		Complete and happy family life	Respected outside the family	Time for household and job
	PPAS2	*Self-fulfilment*	*Family*	*Wealth*
		Having enough time for friends	Living with partner in harmony	Having enough money
		Respected outside the family	Providing security for people close to you	Being satisfied in job
		Striving for self-fulfilment		Living in a nice, spacious house
Czech	PPAS1	*Family/Children*	*Self-fulfilment*	*Gender equality/Religion*
		Complete and happy family life	Striving for self-fulfilment	Living according the rules of faith
		Give care and attention to children	Respected outside the family	Time for household and job
		Give children a proper education	Having a professional career	Equal division of household tasks
	PPAS2	*Self-fulfilment wealth*	*Partner/Job/Income*	*Outside family*
		Living in a nice, spacious house	Living with partner in harmony	Enough time for yourself and interests
		Striving for self-fulfilment	Having enough money	Respected outside the family
		Having holidays at least once a year	Being satisfied in job	Having enough time for friends

Table 4.8 (continued)

Countries	PPAS	Factors/Items		
		Factor 1	Factor 2	Factor 3
Italy	PPAS1	*Self-fulfilment*	*Profession/Income*	*Household/Children*
		Striving for self-fulfilment	Having a professional career	Equal division of household tasks
		Satisfied and happy with your life	Having enough money	Time for household and job
		Respected outside the family	Living in a nice, spacious house	Give care and attention to children

demographic trends and the institution of marriage and family. In contradistinction to Hungary, the evaluation patterns in the Czech Republic have become more western. This is likely to be also based on the trend towards prosperity and leisure orientations in the general values.

Italy is included in Table 4.7 although the data are only available for the first round. Italy is the country, determined in the sections on marriage and family, in which a marked turning away from marriage and family was identified in the period between the two PPAS rounds. Hence, it is to be studied using the values whether an indication of the change in attitude can already be found at the beginning of the nineties. This is clearly the case. Italy is the only country in PPAS1 which does not have a children/family factor, in contradistinction to Germany or the Czech Republic. Similar to these two countries, a "Self-fulfilment" factor could be found. The two other factors are formed by items orientated towards work, income and gender equality. Only in the third factor is a child-orientated item represented, with "Give care and attention to children". It must therefore be presumed that the lack of a child-orientated factor in the structure of the values with the Italian respondents in PPAS1 favoured the establishment of distant stances towards marriage and family noted in PPAS2.

4.8.1.1 Number of Children-specific View

In this step, attention is turned to the change in significance in those values which portray individualist orientations. These values are analysed specifically for numbers of children. It was asked with how many children one can still achieve the stated values (Table 4.9). The concentration on the individualist values is owed to the special significance of the concept of individualism in the explanation of the low birthrate. Two new comparison countries have been added in the shape of Hungary and Italy.

In general terms, as with all items to be evaluated, including for the individualistic ones, the majority of respondents here consider these values also to be feasible with two and more children, or that the number of children is irrelevant. If one focuses the analysis on the number of children-specific answers, it is possible to ascertain special results in three ways.

Table 4.9 Individualistically-oriented value orientation, realization by number of children in PPAS Countries, all respondents, age group 20–39 (in %)*

Countries	PPA	Having enough time for yourself			Having enough income			Striving for self-fulfilment		
		0	1	2+	0	1	2+	0	1	2+
Czech	PPA1	14.3	23.5	41.2	8.7	17.2	33.7	13.3	18.2	24.5
	PPA2	9.4	25.6	39.9	13.7	19.3	32.7	15.1	14.5	28.6
Western	PPA1	21.8	31.1	35.6	23.0	21.9	31.9	24.7	18.4	22.0
Germany	PPA2	25.5	33.5	28.1	31.8	32.5	23.9	38.5	19.4	16.3
Eastern	PPA1	14.1	36.8	42.7	21.4	29.7	29.9	13.6	27.1	28.5
Germany	PPA2	19.8	41.3	26.1	32.5	35.6	18.8	30.1	26.7	15.7
Hungary	PPA1	9.7	25.2	48.9	13.5	27.1	39.7	–	–	–
	PPA2	11.8	20.0	33.8	14.1	15.3	35.1	11.1	15.5	31.6
Italy	PPA1	12.0	25.7	40.5	9.8	16.1	30.7	9.1	17.3	30.0
	PPA2	9.8	18.5	40.4	14.6	23.9	34.2	11.1	19.0	36.8

*Difference to 100%: answer "Does not matter"

Firstly: The proportion of those who think that these values can be realised with two or more children has fallen in comparison between the two rounds. This applies in particular to Germany and Hungary. In the PPAS1, for instance, 48.9% of respondents in Hungary answered that "Having enough time for yourself" is also feasible with two or more children. In the second round of the PPAS, it was only 33.8%. A similar change in the evaluation took place in Germany, in particular in Eastern Germany. There, the proportion fell from 42.7% to 26.1%, whilst in the Czech Republic and Italy there were virtually no changes in the evaluation. Similar trends are shown with the evaluation specific to the number of children of the areas "Having enough income" and "Striving for self-fulfilment". In comparison to this, opposing trends can be observed in the Czech Republic and Italy. The proportion of those who consider it possible to strive for self-fulfilment with two or more children has increased.

Secondly: The changes described at *Firstly* have not led to a situation in the Czech Republic, Hungary and Italy in which the realisation of the values is considered to be possible only with one or no child. Such a situation has come about in PPAS2 only in both regions of Germany. This relates to the values "Having enough income" and "Having enough time for yourself". The implementation of these values is now only considered possible with one child. An example clarifies the change: At the beginning of the nineties, 42.7% of Eastern Germans still felt that it was possible to realise the value "Having enough time for yourself" with two or more children. In 2003, this proportion fell to 26.1%. By contrast, 41.3% now take the view that this is only possible with one child.

Thirdly: One should point to the special situation in Germany in the context of this analysis. With the three values put up for evaluation, it is the Germans who are most frequently of the opinion that this can be best realised without children. The proportions of these answers have indeed increased in comparison between the two rounds of questionnaires. This applies particularly to Eastern Germans, but also to Western Germans. It is already evident in Western Germany in PPAS1 that a relatively large number answered with "no children". This response pattern was not yet so common in Eastern Germany, but it has now also become established there, as shown by the results of PPAS2. In 1992, 24.7% of Western Germans believed that "Striving for self-fulfilment" could only be achieved without children (Eastern Germany: 13.6%). Until 2003, these values had increased to 38.5% (Western Germany) and 30.1% (Eastern Germany). Comparable changes can also be observed in making sufficient income. The results portrayed here for Germany can be inserted seamlessly into other demographic findings. Actual childlessness in Germany is extraordinarily high in a European comparison (Dorbritz 2006). This also applies to the desire to remain childless (cf. on this Section 4.5: Desired fertility). As a result, there is now talk in Germany of a culture of desired childlessness. From a demographic research point of view, a close link can be observed between individualist values and desired childlessness which is to be seen as one of the bases of the spread of childlessness.

4.9 Discussion of the Results

The change in demographically-relevant attitudes and values in comparison to the situation found at the beginning of the nineties encompasses several general trends, as well as country-specific developments which ran in completely different directions. It even appears that different trends in the individual countries of the PPAS are more noticeable than joint development directions. The results of the PPAS agree with the heterogeneity in the European family formation patterns ascertained by Harry Kuijsten (1996, 141). "In the area of the second demographic transition the European family map has grown more diversified rather than more uniform, and ultimate fears for a sort of 'MacDonaldization' of European family structures, with people snacking in the take-away relationship store, seem completely unwarranted."

Probably the most important change of attitude ascertained in the European PPAS countries is the trend towards reconciling family and work. It was already very common in the former Socialist countries, but it has also become more so in the Western European countries. There are two indications of this trend. Firstly, the proportion of women has increased who consider it ideal to reconcile family and work. Secondly, those measures have become more significant with possible, future measures of family policy which make it easier to reconcile family and work.

The second general change of attitude observed relates to the judgment of marriage as a basis for cohabitation in a spirit of partnership. One can see a widening distance towards marriage. It should be particularly stressed in this context that it is not a turning away from the family, but only a distancing from the traditional form of family based on marriage. This result of the PPAS is of considerable importance for family policy. Wherever married people are the primary addressees of family policy measures, the impact of family policy will be restricted.

Also noteworthy are the country-specific situations ascertained in the PPAS. The different attitudes on marriage and family between the Western and former Socialist

countries have not disappeared. Even in the reunified Germany, different evaluation patterns have been retained. The trend is for more traditional stances towards
marriage and family to be found in Eastern Europe than in Western Europe. The
Eastern European countries appear to form a less homogeneous group today than
was the case at the beginning of the nineties. The examples of Hungary and the
Czech Republic are indicative of the process of drifting apart. Whilst a relatively
high level of constancy in attitudes was found for Hungary, a change of attitude is
afoot in the Czech Republic. Contradictory trends in evaluation can also be found
in the "Western" countries. One may almost speak of re-traditionalisation in the
Netherlands. The very high tolerance towards the decline in the significance of
marriage and change in the family measured at the beginning of the nineties has
considerably weakened. The contrary trend was observed for Italy. The highly familialist attitudes in the first round of the PPAS have given way to broad tolerance
towards unmarried developments.

Finally, mention should be made of the specifically individualistic situation in
Germany. Germany is the only one of the countries under comparison in which not
only a more distant stance towards marriage, but also an increasing aversion towards
having children was ascertained. It was in Germany that the most frequent responses
were obtained that marriage is an out-of-date institution, where the desire to remain
childless is most common, and where the realisation of individualistic values is most
frequently considered possible only if one remains childless. This is an expression
of a polarisation of attitudes. In Germany, as in no other country, an albeit still
relatively small group in the population has come about which quite deliberately
opts against family formation.

Part II
Comparative Delphi-study

Chapter 5
2030: Another Europe?

Results from the Policy Dephi Study

Rossella Palomba and Piero Dell'Anno

Abstract This chapter presents the results of a Europe-wide research project based on a policy Delphi, the aim of which was to design population and society scenarios up to 2030. The policy Delphi is a research method particularly suitable to allow experts, working independently, to act as a whole while dealing with complex problems. We used the Delphi technique as a method of social construction of scenarios in the field of population and welfare polices. Three main issues were dealt with in terms of policy developments: population ageing, family and fertility, and gender roles. Scenarios were designed following the inputs, comments and suggestions provided by the 15–20 "experts" selected in each country (totalling 250 experts) who collectively contributed towards the creation of the scenarios through an iterative, innovative multi-method approach which integrates Delphi, Appreciative Inquiry and SWOT analysis. The experts – who are strictly anonymous – were all influential persons who may well help re-shape the future.

Keywords: Future scenarios · Europe · Policy delphi · Gender roles · Family and fertility · Elderly population

5.1 Pioneering the Future, Studying European Policy Scenarios

The future – especially the long-term future – is a time that needs to be better explored from the point of view of the desires, dreams and plans of both individuals and social groups. While the future is an under-investigated time, the techniques to study the future are less well developed than others. Notwithstanding this fact, policy-makers, decision-makers, pressure groups and citizens often ask questions about the future: What will our future look like? Can we design policies which result

R. Palomba
Istituto di ricerche sulla Popolazione e le Politiche Sociali, Consiglio Nazionale delle Ricerche, Rome, Italy
e-mail: r.palomba@irpps.cnr.it

in real improvements in citizens' quality of life? Will current political controversies be solved, and if so how? How will current demographic issues such as population ageing or fertility decline develop in the future? The answers to such complex questions cannot come from disciplinary, sectoral or market studies because these analyses offer only limited visions of what might take place. Moreover, these studies are not at all sufficient to individuate policies aimed at a real social improvement and to suggest appropriate and integrated policy actions to achieve these policy goals.

Governments, businesses, organizations and citizens seek to understand the future better, since we will all be living and working in a future world that promises to be different than today. When people think of changes that might take place in future, they highlight better opportunities for their lives for better ways to positively influence the future that should not just come of itself, but must be created. Almost anything can be created *if* we have a vision of what we want to create and are also committed personally to that vision.

It is also important to remember that while the past, present and future are all somehow interconnected, the only moment from which to change the future is in the present, because the present is the only time from which our thoughts or actions can actually be changed. Most people, as well as most businessmen and politicians, only look ahead as far as four to five years ahead in their planning (in politics until the next election). However, it is important to look further ahead and take a long-range perspective into the future up to twenty to fifty years from now to be sufficiently courageous in the effort to take off from the present. This is the reason why in our study we extended our perspective up to 2030.

Since, by its nature, the future has not yet happened, those who intend to study the future have had to develop a number of methodologies and techniques. Traditional forecasting techniques extrapolate the future from the present and the past, and are based on data which already exist or can be generated. This future may be defined as the probable future on the basis of current knowledge of the situation. For example, in demographic projections, experts set a number of hypotheses, mainly based on extending past developments of current quantitative trends into the future. These hypotheses are often too limited or fail to describe the complex reality under consideration because potential synergies with other sectors of society cannot be fully considered, or because rapid and unexpected changes of the observed phenomena occur. Thus, the probable future often becomes an academic exercise, relevant to understand what will probably happen, if all the conditions we set are confirmed.[1]

It is important to remember that many alternative futures may exist, including probable, possible and preferable futures. Designing preferable alternative futures, and showing how we can plan to get from the present to this more desirable future, calls for different intellectual approaches and methodologies, which range from quantitative to creative methods, and various combinations in between. Methods

---

[1] As demographers, we of course know that population ageing is unavoidable. What we do not know is how we will live in a greying society, and more importantly, how we would like to live in a greying society.

for studying the preferable future do not generally pretend to be able to predict the future, although assessing the feasibility of alternative futures is an important aspect of these studies. Rather, these methods are designed to help policy-makers, decision-makers and citizens to gain a better understanding of desirable future alternatives in order to make better decisions today.

As described by Schwartz (1996), scenarios of the future are visions of what may become reality. Building scenarios of the future is therefore "a method for articulating the different pathways that might exist tomorrow, and finding appropriate movements down each of those possible paths". In brief, scenario planning is the process by which experts create several alternative images of the future, aiming to make strategic decisions: It is about making choices today with an understanding of how they might turn out.

The DIALOG project has included in its work-plan a study aiming to design population and society-policy scenarios. Scenarios were designed following the inputs, comments and suggestions provided by the 15–20 "experts" selected in each participating country (making up a total of 250 experts) who collectively contribute to create the scenarios through an iterative, innovative multi-method approach which integrates the Delphi technique, Appreciative Inquiry and SWOT Analysis. The experts – who are strictly anonymous – were all influential persons who may well help re-shape the future.

Three main issues were dealt with in terms of policy developments: population ageing, family and fertility and gender roles. The three issues are socio-demographic developments which are extremely relevant for Europe in 2030: They influence the economic decisions taken at national and European level; they shape the welfare systems and impact on labour market policies and trends. In addition, they modify European citizens' everyday lives through changes in the family organisation, working life and use of services.

Fifteen European countries (Austria, Belgium (Flanders), Cyprus, the Czech Republic, Estonia, Germany, Finland, Hungary, Italy, Lithuania, the Netherlands, Poland, Romania, Slovenia and Switzerland) participated in the study from spring 2003 to autumn 2004. An additional study was conducted at the level of European international organisations.

The panels – which were set up in each of the fifteen countries – comprised a highly diverse set of experts, namely: policy-makers, industrial organisations, entrepreneurial associations, lobbies and pressure groups, trade unions, journalists, church representatives and religious associations, gender equity institutions, academics, representatives of the cultural world (writers, art directors, poets, musicologists, etc.), local administrators and representatives of best practices in the field of population policies.

5.2 Methodological Approach

The methodological mechanism sprang from a collective idea of the DIALOG research group (composed of researchers and experts coming from different disciplines),with the aim in mind of designing future population scenarios and of applying methodologies which were intended to integrate complexity theory and the thoughtful exercise of dialogue. (Palomba et al. 2005). Scenarios were made up of policy objectives and practical methods of achieving them. One natural consequence of this idea has been the construction of a multi-method process that comprises the following methods:

- Policy Delphi, a method conceived in order to integrate into a consensus the voice of experts who possess a varied series of backgrounds both in expertise and in experience (Linstone and Turoff 1975).
- Appreciative Inquiry, a process using dialogue in order to identify the positive elements that characterise our present and bringing them into the definition of an idealised future (Cooperrider and Srivastva 1987).
- SWOT[2] Analysis, to evaluate the strong points and the weaknesses in both the scenarios and the present situation, and to identify the opportunities and threats that could stand in the way of bringing the scenarios to fruition in 2030.

The first point in the definition of future scenarios was the definition of the questionnaire (every country constructed its own questionnaire independently under the supervision of the IRPPS – Institute of Population and Social Policies), designed – with respect to every voice in the survey – to integrate polarised points of view (varied sources were used, such as the European Union's strategic guidelines, manifestos of political parties, scientific material from specialised journals, etc.). The questionnaire was structured in three sections dedicated respectively to population trends, political objectives integrated with critical factors for success (or measurements of achievement) and controversial policy issues.

The policy Delphi is composed of four rounds of interviews during which a questionnaire is submitted to the experts/panellists. The policy Delphi investigated three topics, namely: gender roles, family and fertility and growth of the elderly population.

In each of the four rounds, in order to corroborate the views and information pertaining to the three topics and to allow respondents to react to and assess differing viewpoints of the other panellists, the questionnaire was designed as follows:

- *Population trends*: The panellists were asked to design desired future population trends on the basis of historical trends, their knowledge, perception and intuitions. Trends were submitted to the panellists in graphic format (i.e. historical curves of various demographic trends from 1980 up to the present day).
- *Policy objectives*: The panellists were asked to select a variable number of policy objectives – depending on the interview round – in the field of population, given a thirty year time-frame up to 2030 and to list of up to three key success factors for each selected policy objective.
- *Controversial policy issues*: The panellists were asked to express their views,

---

[2] SWOT stands for Strengths, Weaknesses, Opportunities and Threats. See also Part III.

and to highlight the effects deriving from the adoption, rejection or the lack of controversial policy issues proposed in the list.[3]

For each of the three areas surveyed (family and fertility, gender roles and growth of the elderly population), the objectives were defined (15 for each theme on average, with a total of 45), as well as the political measures intended to bring about each objective (again, about 15 per objective, with a total of about 670 suggestions for each questionnaire per country).

Once the construction and revision of the questionnaire was complete, the process of surveying began with the first cycle of interviews. The survey process included the following four interview cycles in the course of one year:

Phase 1, Discovery: Two weeks before the experts were interviewed, each of them received two brief reports on demographic trends and political measures regarding the three research issues (ageing, family and fertility, gender). The two documents were written without making value judgements and comments in order to avoid influencing the members of the panel. In the course of the first survey cycle, the panellists described – always in terms of the three themes – the present, the evolution in the future, and how they would like to see society evolve from today to 2030 (their "*dreams*"). The information relative to the dreams were synthesised in a list of ideal wishes that helped to construct the scenarios presented to the panel in the course of the fourth and last phase. Attached to this first, descriptive section (typical of the first phase), was a compilation that had as its goal the collecting of experts' responses to the questions in the questionnaire in all three above-mentioned sections.

The information gathered in the first phase was used and developed in order to construct the second questionnaire, which formed part of the second phase.

Phase 2, Dreaming: In the second phase, the panellists were asked to express their own opinions on the combined answers obtained from the whole panel during the first phase. The new questionnaire omitted positions that were not extreme and not sufficiently representative of the will of the experts. In the course of this second phase, the experts were asked to:

- observe the range of population trends suggested in the first phase and to re-evaluate the trends on the basis of their desiderata. Each graph takes on the shape of a pair of scissors, having as the points of the scissors the lower and the higher levels indicated by the panellists in the previous round,
- attribute to all the policy objectives over a determined threshold a valuation, in terms of desirability, based on a four-tier scale. The experts were to associate three critical factors to each of the policy objectives considered Desirable or Very Desirable, and indicate the relative level of importance based on a scale of importance, and

---

[3] Controversial Policy Issues will not be considered in this chapter. They were very country-specific, making a comparative perspective impossible.

- outline the positive and negative effects which could result from the application of controversial policies.

Phase 3, Design: The interviews conducted over the course of the third phase have substantially the same structure as those of the second phase. The experts are once again asked to:

- observe the graphed population trends – in their scissor form cleared of extreme positions – and to outline the trend based on their desiderata,
- indicate three political objectives for each of the three themes which are the objects of the survey and qualify their desirability based on a three-level scale, and to qualify them according to their feasibility on the same scale, and
- consider the positive and negative effects that result from the application of controversial policies and have been collected in the preceding phase, and to evaluate these policies based on a scale of desirability and feasibility.

Phase 4, Destiny: Between the third and fourth phases, the data were analysed and developed in order to construct four scenarios set into a feasibility and desirability matrix according to political goals, critical success factors, controversial policies and the list of dreams built on the basis of information gathered in the first round. Population trends were not integrated into the scenarios, but continue to stand on their own. The four scenarios were thereby presented to the experts who were then invited to select the scenario which they wish to see achieved by 2030. Each expert is then asked to evaluate the scenario he/she has selected using the SWOT analysis technique. Population trends were once again treated according to the method used in the course of the preceding phases.

5.3 Co-creating the Future 2030 in Europe: Synthesis of National Scenarios

The dream for Europe up to 2030 coincides with better quality of life for its citizens, a simple concept which carries a positive and concrete vision of the future. While it is obvious that political interventions should move towards an improvement of collective well-being, in reality this is rarely achieved in an integrated way. Deci-sion – makers and policy-makers very often intervene in a specific sector of society which they consider to be a priority, and do not consider existing synergies with other sectors of society. The development and social progress of individuals and societies are inextricably intertwined. The "segmented" approach to policy-making organised differently by institution and by policy areas may thus improve one aspect of society and appear to somehow damage other.

Well-being and welfare need to be better defined through the specific target groups of the population benefiting from them. The working-age population, and working women in particular, have emerged from our study as a privileged target group. The basic idea which emanates from each national study is the need to re-shape the labour market in terms of working schedule, workers' rights and concern for the needs of both social partners.

Current economic rules are pushing the labour market towards increasing flexibility. Our panellists would like to see a labour market for 2030 that, whilst respecting and being attentive to the points of view of businesses, as well as to the unavoidable constraints imposed by international competitiveness, helps build a cohesive, new society that is collectively committed to the future, in which marginalization, discrimination and gender imbalances will be a nightmare of the past. How to realize this better future society depends on the national context and on the starting point of each European country.

According to all the countries participating in the policy Delphi study, the common objective for 2030 is the identification of policies tailored to achieve a better balance between citizens' various parts of life, namely work, family and free time.

It is hardly surprising that countries[4] where part-time work is less wide-spread (the Czech Republic, Italy, Poland, Slovenia and Hungary) ask for policy actions that aim to promote and sustain easier access to part-time work. Austria, Estonia, Finland, Germany and Switzerland wish for effective flexibility in working time. In particular, Finland, the Netherlands and Switzerland would like to see actions aimed at encouraging employers to take into account the family responsibilities and needs of male and female workers.

As long as there is a widespread conviction within the workplace that there must be a hierarchy in the values and behaviour of the employees based on the view that work is more important than any other aspect of people's lives, the career and employment opportunities of those who make different choices or who are forced to find a compromise between work commitments and personal life will be necessarily limited. The idea of having to reconcile work and family or to find a work-life balance still implies a dichotomy between two parts of life which fail to communicate properly, and require people to somehow divide their time between the two. This divide between the private and public spheres in the life of European citizens – due to market demands and work environment needs – is a major obstacle in the achievement and even the design of policies which are based on individual needs, and above all on women who most often continue to bear the principal burden of family responsibilities.

The new vision implies a considerable change in attitudes, labour market structures and working patterns in the public and private sectors. Poland and the Netherlands suggest changes in the attitudes of employers towards their employees who have children, in particular women, thus reconsidering the possibility of also introducing family-friendly labour market laws from the perspective of attitude changes. Other countries, namely Slovenia and the Czech Republic, would like to achieve better reconciliation of work and family by means of an increase in the social value of the family. Media campaigns may help to realise this objective, as suggested by

---

[4] Below we speak of and name countries although of course only the condensed view of panellists from these countries is expressed.

the Slovenian panellists. It should be noted that the Czech panellists would like to shift away from a performance-oriented society in 2030, and thus overcome the dichotomy between the two spheres of life, namely work and family.

Poland, Cyprus and the Netherlands also highlight the relevance of changing gender roles, promoting an equal share of family tasks between men and women as a starting point to change the organisation of work.

All the countries consider a priority for the future well-being of Europe to eliminate discrimination and stereotypes concerning gender roles. Austria, Cyprus, the Czech Republic, Hungary, Italy, Lithuania, Poland and Switzerland suggest actions aimed at having women acquire better and more visible positions in the labour market and in social, economic and political life, simplify the tasks and commitments of mothers and reduce the pay gap between men and women. Germany and Belgium (Flanders) identify policy actions above all aimed at fostering a higher participation of men in domestic chores and in child care.

As emerged from our study, one of the European priorities should be to step up investments in the realisation of a society that is well aware of its ageing process. All the panellists in dreaming the future in quantitative terms have identified a very considerable share of the elderly out of the total population in 2030. For example, the panellists envisioned a future where life expectancy at birth is on average ninety years for both sexes, and in Poland even 120 years for men and women. What is considered even more important is that those years should be spent in good health and without marginalization problems.

The vast majority of the measures suggested by the panellists can be broken down into three main categories: increasing protection of the elderly by securing their economic, physical and emotional security with regard to the risk of poverty, vulnerability and isolation (Estonia, Finland, Hungary, Lithuania, Netherlands, the Czech Republic, Slovakia and Slovenia); increasing participation of elderly people that refers to the need to establish a greater and more active social role for the elderly (Austria, Belgium (Flanders), Cyprus, Estonia, Finland, Germany, Italy, the Netherlands, Poland, Romania, the Czech Republic and Switzerland); improving the image of the elderly that refers to the need to define a more positive, less degrading and less discriminatory idea of elderly persons and their capacities (Italy, Lithuania, Romania and Slovenia). The achievements of these objectives pursuing a wide-spread improvement in the quality of life of European citizens would indeed generate greater social cohesion playing the key role of strength in sustaining the future. Its limits lie not in society, but in the decision-making process adopted to shape the future. "I dream of a society where old age will no longer be considered a phase of mere survival but a stage of life where we can pay attention to social activity, travel and culture", says one of our respondents, highlighting the importance that a longer and healthy life span is a reasonable wish of all of us, and that it should become the target of adequate policy actions.

5.4 Increasing Feasibilty, Highlighting Potential Threats

SWOT analysis is a method that allows us to use existing and acquired knowledge to comment on the characteristics of scenarios and to complete an analysis, drawing up a framework on the basis of which strategies can be designed. In particular, the SWOT analysis allows the panellists (and us) to audit their selected scenarios, stressing the positive and negative effects related to implementation in an imagined future.

With SWOT analysis, respondents are asked to analyse problems from four different and opposing points of view. It is a logical procedure developed inside managerial and business organisations, which evaluates internal and external risks and opportunities related to a project's feasibility, and defines strategic actions for the success of the project itself.

The internal factors are the so-called strengths and weaknesses of the project, while the external factors are the so-called opportunities and threats. The internal factors are an integral part of the system under evaluation and in which it is possible to intervene to achieve the desired goals; the external factors cannot be directly addressed, and may positively or negatively influence goal achievement.

We asked the panellists to indicate the strengths, weaknesses, opportunities and threats related to the feasibility of the scenario they have selected for 2030. The feasibility of the scenario is thus strengthened because in implementing policy actions related to the future scenario it will be necessary to rely upon strengths, alleviate weaknesses, maximise opportunities coming from outside and reduce risks deriving from changes in the national and international context. The main results are shown in the scheme below and commented in the following paragraphs.

Table 5.1 Results of the SWOT analysis

Strengths	Opportunities
Spread of solidarity	Increasing social cooperation
Gender equity	Economic growth
Raising fertility	Improvement of attitudes towards the elderly
Changing values and attitudes	A child-oriented society
Quality of life (improvement)	A broader role for NGOs
Weaknesses	Threats
Too much idealism – Utopia	Materialism, individualism, egoism
Conflicts and incompatibilities	System inertia
Financial problems	Lack of funding
Role of the State and of the private sector	Economic crisis, instability
	Political instability
	Political distrust
	Difficulties in changing values and attitudes
	EU role

5.4.1 Strong Points

In the list of the resources and strong points that are seen inside the scenarios indicated by the panellists in every country, we found quite a large convergence on different issues related to the general environment that should support the realisation of the scenario. In first place, we found two very "idealistic" issues expressing a need and a hope for justice and social cooperation, such as solidarity and gender equity (Table 5.1). A different modulation of these factors is found among countries regarding solidarity: Intergenerational aspects are stressed in the Czech Republic, Estonia, Hungary and Slovenia, while the inclusion of all groups of society is highlighted by Italy, Lithuania and the Netherlands. This element is expected in Germany as a general societal orientation.

The second effect of implementation of the "dreamed" scenarios in seven countries is the achievement of gender equity. This is considered in Italy, Slovenia, Germany and Switzerland mostly from the point of view of the family: parents sharing the task of childrearing and housework, achieving a balance between maternal and parental leave, fathers facing up to their responsibilities. The promotion of women's role in society, equal opportunity on the labour market and a fair salary system, are additional ways to indicate the positive effects of achieving gender equity in the wished-for society of the future. Raising fertility is also indicated as a positive goal (Cyprus, Austria, Estonia, Hungary and Poland).

Strictly linked to gender issues is the theme of flexibility considered in many countries (Finland, Italy, the Netherlands, Poland and Slovenia) as the best way to combine work and family life, while in Switzerland the focus is on a flexible retirement scheme.

In many countries the strong idealistic approach of the panellists includes the theme of freedom, meant both as choice for people to have the kind of family they desire (the Czech Republic and Poland) and, in a broader sense, as the possibility of having greater freedom and autonomy for all citizens (Germany and the Netherlands).

In a coherent view with previous points and policy priorities, some countries (namely the Czech Republic, Italy and Poland) forecast a growing social appreciation of family values, while others (Cyprus, Lithuania and Switzerland) wish and expect a more general and deeper process of changing values and attitudes regarding cultural and social mentality, particularly focussing on gender roles.

Finally, an overall improvement of the quality of life is a strength envisaged by a number of countries (Lithuania, Italy and Poland), only Italy stressing the role of the widespread use of new technologies.

It is to be noted that two countries (Cyprus and Germany) highlighted the importance of designing long-term policies, abandoning the narrow view of implanting short-term actions aimed at solving problems instead of changing the future.

5.4.2 Points of Opportunity

Among the possible points for sustaining the scenarios from outside, six countries (Austria, Germany, Italy, Lithuania, Romania and Switzerland) stressed that the scenarios will enforce social cohesion and integration between the various social groups. As a result of this future society being more integrated and less hindered by social conflicts, it will naturally support the implementation of the desired policy actions. As a further opportunity reinforcing social cohesion, Cyprus, Estonia, Finland and the Netherlands favour an improvement of attitudes towards the elderly that will act as a cultural catalyst of the concrete realisation of the scenarios. A well-integrated, cohesive society will constitute the best possible environment for couples who wish to have children. This is the reason why Cyprus, the Czech Republic, Estonia, Finland, Hungary and Switzerland perceive in the realisation of a child-oriented society as foreseen for the scenarios an additional opportunity for making the desired society sustainable.

It goes without saying that economic growth is a necessary factor for achieving the political goals by 2030. Last but not least, three countries (Cyprus, the Czech Republic and Romania) consider a deep-rooted role of NGOs to be a supporting and accompanying factor in implementing the scenarios.

5.4.3 Weak Points

The third component of the SWOT analysis looks at the weaknesses existing in the future scenarios. The comparative reading of the various SWOT analyses produced at national level highlight the fact that the policy objectives and their related key success factors present some common, weak points that can be grouped under four major headings, namely:

The implementation of the scenario is difficult, given that

- its scenario content is utopistic;
- its policy objectives are incompatible;
- its existing financial problems might hinder its achievement; and
- it calls for an excessive role to be played by the state.

The weaknesses vary depending on the countries though representing common ground for a large majority of them. A comparative reading of the first of the four weaknesses shows that seven countries (Estonia, Germany, Poland, Romania, Slovenia, Switzerland and the Czech Republic) believe their scenarios to be idealistic. The reason for calling a scenario idealistic varies from country to country. In Slovenia, for example, a risk of superficiality of some of the measures is mentioned, the Swiss panellists believe that some of the measures are not sufficiently concrete, the Czechs stress that the scenarios lack the practical tools to achieve the policy objectives.

The second weakness evokes the conflicts and incompatibilities within the scenarios. Five countries believe this to be a relevant characteristic of the scenarios, namely: Hungary, Italy, Poland, the Czech Republic and Germany. In Germany we have found a general feeling of mistrust towards the future and a lack of belief that the required political consensus might be obtained to achieve the policy objectives and to implement the related measures. The conflicts and incompatibilities in Hungary, Poland and Italy are suspected to lie in the divergent evolvement of gender roles and the family requirements.

The third weakness has a financial dimension. Austria, Estonia, Lithuania, Poland, Romania and Belgium (Flanders) believe that the achievement of the objectives will be slowed down by the financial constraints and the lack of financial resources existing in their societies. In Belgium (Flanders), there is additionally a common feeling that the issue of pensions will contribute towards creating financial constraints.

Last but not least, scenarios will be constrained by the excessive role that the state and the private sector play in the development of our societies. This is the belief in Switzerland, Poland, the Netherlands and Cyprus.

5.4.4 Points of Threat

As expected, the policy-makers themselves are considered to be one of the major threats to the realization of the scenarios because of their scarce interest in policies which go beyond their mandate (Table 5.1). Very often, in fact, when the government changes the political goals change accordingly. This is the reason why Belgium (Flanders), Germany, Lithuania and the Netherlands indicate political instability as a possible threat to scenario implementation, and Romania, Slovenia and Switzerland identified political mistrust as a risk to the realisation of the imagined future society.

Additional risk factors lie on the economic side: lack of funding and international economic instability may make the scenario unsustainable.

Social systems are characterised by a deep-seated inertia which makes it difficult to achieve changes and slows their implementation. This is a warning very clearly expressed by Belgium (Flanders), the Czech Republic, Hungary, Germany, Italy and Slovenia. More specifically, difficulties in changing values and attitudes of common people have been highlighted in the Czech Republic, Germany, Lithuania and Slovenia, while the diffusion of materialistic, individualistic and egoistic values and behaviour are considered a threat in Belgium (Flanders), Germany, Italy, Lithuania, Netherlands, Poland and Slovenia.

EU enlargement is surprisingly perceived as a threat in Lithuania and Romania, where people are worried by the fact that further enlargement will result in a "double standard for newcomers and old members". The same concern is perceived in the Netherlands, while Italy stressed the danger of a passive role of the EU and the risk of a double standard between Northern and Southern countries.

5.5 Desired Future Population Trends

This section of the study aimed at highlighting future desired population trends up to 2030. Each country decided independently which population trends amongst the themes investigated by the scenario planning to submit to the panel of experts. Trends also varied in number country by country (from five to 18). While diversity was a distinctive point in the research, in order to highlight national priorities and characteristics, eight trends turned out to be the same in the fifteen countries. These eight where the object of a comparative horizontal analysis, and are: number of inhabitants, fertility, elderly population, marriage rate, marital instability, extramarital births, age at first motherhood and female labour force participation.

As stated above in this article, the research was conducted over four rounds of interviews, meaning that the panels of experts were called four times to express their opinions, wishes and points of view. The same happened for the section aiming at expressing desired future population trends whose final aim was to understand if, when, and in which direction the panels where reaching consensus on future trends. A consensus on some of the topics under investigation was already reached in the first round of interviews, showing convergence on an ideal future at the very early stages; others had to go through the entire process, or most of it, whilst for some others convergence was never reached.

The trends do not correspond to a demographic forecasting logic, but – in line with the overall methodology applied – are the result of wishful thinking based on current opinions of the status quo. The comparative analysis can be summarised as follows:

Number of inhabitants: This trend shows two major positions, namely those countries which wish to see a population increase in the years to come, and those which hope to see the number of inhabitants maintained at current levels. Those countries (Germany, Lithuania, Poland and Slovenia) which are aiming at an increase are proposing a slight growth of the curve, while higher growth is suggested in Italy. Five countries wish for "zero population growth". Overall, the demographic future is not expected to be much different today in order to maintain the current social organisation and avoid the risks that are associated with a growing population. Remarkably, nobody wishes the population to decline, nor do they believe that it will do so.

Fertility: All in all, 2030 is a time of desired fertility increase, albeit with different levels being recorded in the various countries. In fact, while in Austria, Germany and Italy the fertility increase is close to replacement level, in Belgium (Flanders), Estonia, Poland and Switzerland the future 25 years are desired to be characterised by more than two children per woman. Between these two expectations are positioned those of Lithuania, the Netherlands, Romania and Slovenia, showing a desire for growth in line with the current situation. Last but not least, the panellists in Hungary dreamed of an increase in the birth rate, which they however regarded as *"questionable"*. With this, the Hungarian panellists are the most realistic dreamers.

The elderly: Dreaming has proven to be a difficult exercise when designing the future presence of the elderly in our societies. The panels were of course well informed on the topic; the dream is therefore an informed one and extremely concrete. As a result, the great majority of countries has envisaged an increase in the size of the elderly population. Only in the Czech Republic, Cyprus, Estonia and Italy was an expectation shown of a decline or of stabilisation in the presence of the elderly.

Marriage rate: 2030 is deemed a time of narrow growth of the marriage rate. A tendency towards an increase in the trend is expected in six countries out of eleven. In fact, the panels in Germany, Hungary, Lithuania, Poland and Slovenia have forecast a small percentage growth, while in the Czech Republic this growth is expected to be more rapid. The preferred marriage rate varies in Switzerland, Romania, Estonia, Italy and Austria from a small increase to a decrease. Marriage does not of course coincide with cohabitation, and its significance might still have a religious dimension for many.

Marital instability: is certainly not an expectation for the future. The tendency is expected to move towards stabilization and a decrease in separation and in the divorce rate (half of the countries) with some tendencies even expecting no divorce at all. The wish to witness a decline in divorces is strongly driven by the desire to ensure children their right and to meet their need to live with both parents. Here we have an example of truly pious wishful thinking.

Extra-marital births: Children born to unmarried couples are an unclear issue in the countries were this trend has been submitted. In fact, out of nine countries where the issue was approached, three showed the desire towards an increase, three wished to see stabilization at the current level, while three others ended up the cycle of interviews without proving a clear tendency in the future. This issue is less and less important in modern societies, as a stigma is no longer associated with having children within or outside marriage.

Age at first motherhood: The common tendency in Europe is to postpone the founding of a family, and the age of women at first birth is continuously rising as a consequence. The anticipated trend shows a progression toward the higher part of the scale in all the countries investigated. It remains a mystery how the fertility increase which panellists dream of would materialise.

Female labour force participation: Many policy papers and economic studies are quite determined in affirming that future economic growth in Europe hinges on a higher female employment rate. Somewhat sustained growth in female participation in the labour market has been observed in most countries in the recent past, with the exception of some of Eastern European ones. The recent increase has narrowed country differences, bringing about homogeneity amongst European regions and shaping a less heterogeneous labour market, at least from a gender perspective. The trends coming out of the policy Delphi highlight European-wide agreement amongst the panels to sustain higher female participation and to increase wealth production via their higher participation in the labour market. The only exception in this commonly-shared trend is Hungary, where a moderate decrease in the trend has been mentioned. In some countries (Austria, Germany, Italy and Lithuania), 2030 is a year of goal attainment in women's equal involvement in the labour market, whilst in others the growth is expected to be less impressive.

5.6 Conclusions

Overall, Europe in 2030 is a socio-political and economic arena within which stake-holders dream of better quality of life on behalf of citizens. If we consider the arena as a complex system, we can assume on the basis of the results provided within the scenarios that the system will outperform itself if all stakeholders remain actively involved: not only in laying the basement "bricks", but also in designing its archi-tecture. There are no sectorial priorities: Overall system performance is the priority. This is due to the strong interconnections existing between economic growth and social development.

An approach which is process- or content-based, even though it might generate interesting vertical results, will not guarantee the overall balanced growth that is expected to sustain the well-being of our societies and therefore our population (no matter their gender, age, territorial location, employment situation and oth-ers). Europe's development should be promoted considering national specificity, even though the path should unavoidably take into consideration work, family and free-time.

If we consider the future as a space and time where our visions might become reality, then today is the time when those visions should be transformed into political objectives and actions to make these visions become true.

European stakeholders have recommended that well-being and welfare should become a high priority. This important target should concentrate on reshaping the labour market. Reshaping means integrating workers' rights and work-schedules in a balanced dialogue of all parties concerned. Flexibility and competitiveness are certainly important to exist in the global arena, but shortcuts are not the path to take. Flexibility is key if it sustains social cohesiveness and equal rights, but certainly not if it exacerbates the existing social disequilibrium.

In 2030 there is a fundamental assumption that needs to be challenged: work over everything else in people's lives. This of course challenges the way in which we design and build our working environment and the rules that regulate it. The ageing process and the increasing participation of women in the labour market are key success factors of our growth, and not barriers. We simply need to remove the secular stereotypes on the basis of which we have built our societies so far.

Another Europe will be here in 2030 only if we choose to believe that we can do it. This implies challenging the assumptions generating status as "elderly" and their alleged inabilities, and therefore reconsidering their contribution to socio-economic development, challenging the idea that competitiveness matters more than work-life balance and the existing labour market structure and working patterns in the public and private sectors.

2030 is closer than we think. 2030 starts today. Therefore, we have to begin to think differently and to act consistently, think collectively and in a dialogue-based manner. This is the very fundamental change we require, a challenging one that can generate the change to establish another Europe, the Europe that its citizens want.

In closing this study, a few words should be said concerning the experience of conducting a qualitative study on what participants would like the future to be. There is an ontological transformation awaiting anyone who decides to conduct future research. It quickly becomes obvious quite that neither the past nor the future actually exists, but only memories, projections and perceptions. However, both the past and the future guide current actions. When blended with the topics of social change and improving quality of life, the value of research into a desirable future emerges as an absolute imperative. Without the ability to plan, project and envision what we want to create, the ability to prepare for the future is hopeless. However, without hope, without dreams, there is no future.

Chapter 6
Action Programs of Socio-political Actors

A Cross-national Comparison, Taking Account of Contextual Factors and the Opinion of the Populace

Alfred Bertschinger

Abstract Interaction between political actors and their environment is the subject of this study. Firstly, future action programs of experts in social policy covering the areas ageing and family are outlined and compared. Secondly, the focus given by those experts is placed in the context and the populace's opinion. A cross-national, quantitative approach is followed whereby 14 DIALOG countries are studied. There is evidence to suggest that the panellists react to contextual factors: On the one hand, they react to demographic changes, which create needs, whilst on the other they try to intervene actively in a social situation. Furthermore, the study shows that the people react differently. Experts and the populace do not base their appreciation on the same assumptions. Divergence between the two groups is discernible.

Keywords: Social policy · Action programs · Advocates · Cross-national comparison · Comparative method

6.1 Introduction

The formulation of political issues is the beginning of the policy process. Social problems do not exist "per se". They are taken up by social actors and brought into politics, where they are framed and measured and, if a consensus is reached, implemented. The Delphi study aimed to shape the future by defining relevant policy objectives (for more details see Chapter 5 by Rossella Palomba and Piero Dell'Anno in this volume). Political actors in every country (a highly diverse set of experts) were chosen to define them. Round one functioned as a selection of a possible future reality. In round two, this reality was rated. What does this future reality look like? Are there differences or similarities between the countries studied? These are the

A. Bertschinger
Sociological Institute of the University of Zurich, Zurich, Switzerland
e-mail: a.bertschinger@freesurf.ch

C. Höhn et al. (eds.), *People, Population Change and Policies: Vol. 2: Demographic Knowledge – Gender – Ageing*, © Springer Science+Business Media B.V. 2008

first questions asked in this article: a cross-national comparison that tries to figure out the shape of the future. A second question is, if those advocates react to the changing environment, is there interplay between societal change and policies, and are political actors aware of opinions within the populace?

6.2 The Theoretical Framework

Policy analysis understands public policy as a set of interconnected policy decisions and actions in the sense of an action program (Binder, Kübler 2003, 6). This program is goal-oriented, which entails an intention to change social facts (Durkheim) that are perceived as problems. Policy programs contain normative directions, as well as concrete strategies to achieve the desired situation. The individual is seen as a rational actor whose actions are motivated through (a) a system of beliefs and (b) an assessment of the situation. In contradistinction to classical political action models, which reduce the action of actors to goal, situation and measure, our action concept is more complex. It is reconstructed as an actor who acts on the basis of (a) a specific intention and (b) a specific assumption about the effect of his behaviour, and who intervenes with (c) certain measures in (d) a defined situation (Kaufmann 2005, 109). Underlining this concept is a definition of social policy as an intensifying process of state intervention in societal circumstances (Kaufmann 2005, 27). It stabilises society and transforms production and reproduction circumstances (2005, 74).

6.2.1 The Advocacy Coalition Framework Theory (ACF)

A theory which aims to explain the policy process and policy change over time is the Advocacy Coalition Framework (ACF) theory, formulated around 1990 by Sabatier and Jenkins-Smith (Sabatier and Jenkins-Smith 1993, 1999). The theory incorporates and broadens the broadly-accepted stage model of the policy process: "We argue that conceptions of policy subsystems should be broadened from traditional notions of 'iron triangles' [state/market/society] – (...) – to include actors at various levels of government active in policy formulation and implementation as well as journalists, researchers, and policy analysts who play important roles in the generation, dissemination, and evaluation of policy ideas" (1993, 17). They point to the role of changing social and economic conditions and "the interaction of specialists within a specific policy area as they gradually learned more about various aspects of the problem over time" (1993, 15).

According to their system-theoretic perspective, a basic distinction between system and environment is introduced. The environment is conceptualised as (a) contextual factors: socio-economic conditions and social structure and (b) fundamental cultural values, which build up a system of beliefs. The policy subsystem is constituted by political actors who can be aggregated into advocacy coalitions composed of various people from governmental and private organisations "who share a set of normative and causal beliefs" (1993, 18), who have certain resources, and who act collectively. It is usual for two coalitions (A and B) to face each other with different opinions and conflicting strategies regarding a certain issue. Those conflicting strategies are normally mediated by "policy brokers", "whose principal concern is to find some reasonable compromise that will reduce intense conflict" (1993, 18). The result of the negotiation is a governmental program which produces policy outputs.

6.2.2 Design of the Study

The ACF approach is adapted and slightly modified for the purpose of this study. The policy subsystem is given concrete form, and named a social policy subsystem. External factors are referred to as context. A box named populace is included in addition to contextual factors. A "nested" structure is assumed which leads to a multi-level approach. Two levels of analysis are identified: The units of analysis at the first level are nation-states, and at the second level they are policy makers. The actors are seen as rational players whose actions are motivated through a system of beliefs.[1] Figure 6.1 illustrates the design of the study:

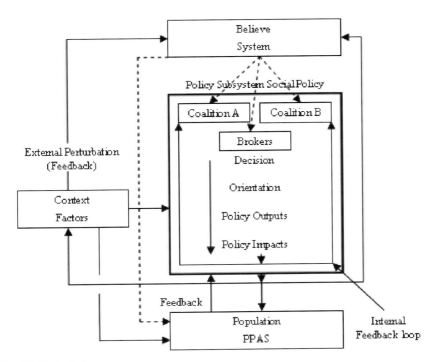

Fig. 6.1 Study design

---

[1] For nation-states, an aggregation of advocates' systems of belief is assumed according to the forces of coalitions.

In the centre is the social policy subsystem. Political actors form coalitions; on the basis of their decisions, policy implementation starts (policy process) and action programs are constituted. Three interaction levels are identified:

- **Within system interaction**: The subsystem constitutes an evaluation process (internal feedback loop); the result of the feedback is policy-oriented learning.
- **Interaction between contextual factors and policy subsystem**: Contextual factors produce external perturbations, which produce resonance within the subsystem. Knowledge of contextual factors influences the decision-making process.
- **Interaction between the populace and the policy subsystem**: As soon as policies are implemented, the reaction of the populace takes place. Their feedback is transformed and integrated into the internal feedback loop.

The focus of this study lies at the latter two interaction levels. The influence of contextual factors on policy-makers' decisions is supported by other researchers: Gauthier argues that, concerning family policies, "demographic changes have acted over time as major catalysts" (Gauthier 1996, 199). They created new needs and prompted governments to intervene. In her conceptual framework, she introduced three interaction channels: Firstly, demographic changes attract researchers to study the social phenomena under observation. Secondly, there is a response from the public and other social actors (advocates). Finally, the response of the government takes place.

6.2.3 Hypothesis

The research question for the following sections is how conditions external to the subsystem explain the variation between countries. Based on the theoretical assumption above, we formulate the following hypothesis:

Hypothesis: Emphasis on a specific dimension depends on factors outside the subsystem. It is anticipated that the panellists will react to demographic and structural changes, and that they will be aware of the opinions of the populace.

6.3 The Comparative Method

According to Ragin (1987), two distinctive approaches for comparative social sciences can be identified. On the one hand, the case-oriented or qualitative method with its focus on cases as wholes sees cases as a combination of conditions and tries to identify conditions which explain the variation between countries. This method is limited to a small number of theoretically-defined cases, and is sensitive to historical trajectories.

On the other hand, the variable-oriented or quantitative approach, which is theory centred, is concerned less with understanding specific outcomes, and more with assessing the correspondence between relationships. This method investigates the relationship between general features of social structure conceived as variables by verifying for intervening factors. The quantitative approach, focussing as it does on statistical calculation, encounters severe statistical problems. The analysis is limited because of the usual small number of countries under observation, the so-called small N problem (Gelissen 2002, 19ff; Callens 2004, 7). Furthermore, the variables show causal complexity (multiple causation), which makes it difficult to use multiple dependent variable approaches (Ragin 1987, 19–34). The so-called Galton problem has to be considered, which poses the general question of whether nations could be treated as independent. Processes within and between societies could be an explanation of the observed correlation (Callens 2004, 7). Last but not least, there is the so-called black-box problem, which addresses the question of causal interference and the unknown processes behind it (2004, 7). This ties up the problem of multiple causation and the questionable assumption of the causal relationship itself. Given an awareness of these restrictions, this study follows a quantitative approach.

6.4 Analytical Framework

The first level of analysis concerns nation-states. The policy objectives have to be classified to compare them. To develop a classification system is one of the major tasks for comparativists. "Frameworks provide a foundation for inquiry by specifying classes of variables and general relationships among them" (Schlager 1999, 234). It is important to define the level on which a certain variable appears (over- and sub-ordination of variables), as well as their interaction.

The process of classification was two-sided: On the one hand, results from current research (especially results of the Delphi study itself) were taken into account; on the other hand, the empirical data were observed. A qualitative approach is taken: Firstly, the data are analysed in a qualitative manner, and then categories derived from research literature are confronted with the results. 336 Policy Objectives (POs) had to be classified; only six were excluded. The classification system is displayed in the subsequent sections.

6.5 Scope and Limitations of the Study

This synchronic analysis displays the situation around 2003 in the DIALOG countries under observation. The picture outlined is an outcome of different historical trajectories, which are not discussed here; the focus is on desired social policies of the future, as outlined by experts. The three themes under consideration are Ageing, Family & Fertility and Gender. The geographical region is Europe, with its division into Eastern and Western countries. 14 DIALOG countries are analysed (Austria,

Belgium (Flanders), Switzerland, Cyprus, the Czech Republic, Germany,[2] Estonia, Finland, Italy, Lithuania, the Netherlands, Poland, Romania and Slovenia).

The analysis contains a linguistic blurredness: The POs, which were classified, are formulated in a general way. To avoid mistakes, the classification was sent to the partners for approval. Furthermore, consideration needs to be given to the researchers' impact: The lists of desired future policies presented to the experts were designed by researchers. They were advised by the co-ordinators of the Delphi study to integrate a wide range of issues, but a selection still had to be made. This selection is to a certain degree arbitrary. Even though the panellists had the opportunity to address and add missing issues, the first selection is directive. Finally, the reliability of the results depends on the validity of the panels. The purpose was to compose a highly-diverse panel, including various political actors. It is presumed that the partners selected the participants carefully and followed the guidelines issued by the co-ordinators. The selectivity of the panels is a problem giving rise to major concern. There is no representativeness, and the results are questionable. Another problem "that plagues comparative research is the difficulty in finding valid and reliable empirical indicators of the independent variables" (Korpi 1989, 315). The selection is to a certain degree arbitrary and has to be underpinned by theory.[3]

6.6 Ageing

Demographic ageing and the fertility decline, which are observed among European societies, give rise to adaptation processes. The call for security and protection, and the integration of the elderly into society, are matters of political discourse. The course for the future has to be set. The problem of sustaining pension systems, and the fear of social isolation of a whole group of people, circles around the heads of political actors. How are they reacting to this challenge?

6.6.1 Classification Framework

To classify the POs within the theme of ageing, results from the comparative Delphi report were integrated (Palomba et al. 2005). According to Palomba et al., the panellists are seeking to achieve a better "quality of life" for European citizens. This is also the case for the elderly. Quality of life in its broadest meaning is a "multi-dimensional welfare term that means good 'objective' living conditions and a high degree of 'subjective' well-being, and it also includes collective welfare in addition to the individual satisfaction of needs" (2005, 67. cf. Glatzer

---

[2] Existing differences between Eastern and Western Germany are ignored.

[3] Additionally, it is advisable to select variables carefully because the small number of cases restricts the amount of variables chosen.

and Mohr 1987). Furthermore, the Delphi study showed that the concept "quality of life" can be broken down into three main categories: Protection, Participation and Image.

"Protection refers to securing the economic, physical and emotional safety of elderly people with regard to their risk of poverty, vulnerability and isolation" (Palomba et al. 2005, 69). The concept of protection is again multi-dimensional. Three sub-dimensions are identified: economic, physical and emotional protection.

"Participation refers to the need to establish a greater and more active role of the elderly in society" (2005, 69). In this sense, participation comes close to the concept of "active ageing" that was introduced by the World Health Organisation in the late 90ies. It was defined as "the process of optimising opportunities for health, participation and security in order to enhance quality of life as people age" (Avramov and Maskova 2003b, 26). According to this definition, the concept stays in direct interaction with the above-mentioned achievable goal to enhance quality of life. Two different approaches towards "active ageing" can be distinguished. Firstly, an approach which focuses "on the active way of spending the increased free time after retirement" (2003b, 24). Secondly, an approach which focuses on economic activity as labour force participation. These two sub-dimensions appear also in the data.

Finally, the sub-dimension Image refers "to the need to define a more positive, less degrading and discriminatory idea of who elderly persons are and what they are capable of doing" (Palomba et al. 2005, 69).

To subsume the theoretical concept, the Table 6.1 shows the classified dimension in hierarchical order:

The categories were weighted in relation to the total amount of POs within a country. The weighting is seen as the strength of a certain dimension, the level of priority is given by the panellists.[4]

The following analysis has to prove how the different variables interact with each other. The interaction is expected on the horizontal level, and the focus of the analysis lies on the three intermediate dimensions: Participation, Protection and Image.

Table 6.1 Classification framework ageing

Participation	Quality of life Protection	Image
Labour Force	Economic	
Social Inclusion	Physical	
	Emotional	

---

[4] The weighting is problematic: Firstly, different appreciation of the issues within the panels is ignored, secondly, the weighting is more robust as several POs are subsumed under one dimension. A small number of POs within a dimension leads the classified dimension to be over-weighted.

6.6.2 Priorities Set by the Panellists

The highest dimension Quality of Life was present in six countries (Austria, Cyprus, the Czech Republic, Estonia, Finland and the Netherlands). The other DIALOG countries did not address this issue directly.

Protection (which was present in all countries) was given priority; the average of all countries is 62%. A level below 50% is only reached by the Netherlands (29%) and Estonia (40%). Participation was present in 13 DIALOG countries, with only Cyprus not addressing this issue. The overall mean is 28%. Participation is particularly focussed on by the Netherlands (57%), the Czech Republic (42%), Estonia (40%) and Slovenia (38%). Finally, the category Image was addressed by nine DIALOG countries. The average is below 10%. Five did not address this issue directly (Austria, Switzerland, Lithuania, Poland and Romania). The Czech Republic addressed this issue with only one PO. The weight in relation to the total amount of POs is almost zero. The variable was additionally given binary coding (present/absent), the Czech Republic being coded as 0.

6.6.3 The Inner Consistency of the Data

The test for inner consistency revealed that the dimensions Participation and Protection are very closely correlated ($r = -0.829$). Figure 6.2 shows the distribution of the countries:

DIALOG countries with a high level of Protection show a tendency to have a low level of Participation, and vice versa. The Netherlands focus most on Participation, and one finds the Czech Republic, Estonia and Slovenia in a medium position. The rest of the DIALOG countries place their focus more on Protection.

Image is weakly correlated with the two other dimensions. As the DIALOG countries which did not address this dimension, were removed, the correlation augmented. As a result, there is a tendency for countries with a high level of Participation to show a lower level of Image, and vice versa ($r = -0.5$). The correlation between Protection and Image is positive, but is too low to make any substantial statement.

6.6.4 Operationalization and Method

As *dependent variables*, we use the intermediate dimensions found in the data: **Participation**, **Protection** and **Image**.

The *explanatory variables* at country level were operationalized as follows: firstly, a general spatial **East/West** indicator is introduced to test for geographical differences. Secondly, a cultural variable (inspired by Stein Rokkan (Flora 2000)) is introduced regarding the dominant **religion** (0: Catholic and Orthodox, 1: Protestant

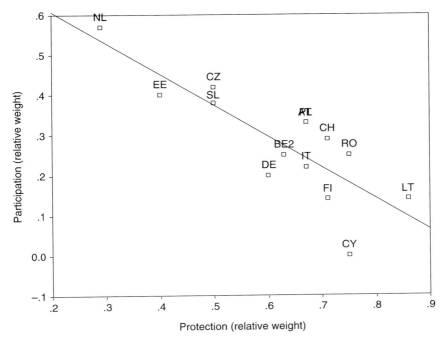

Fig. 6.2 Relation between participation and protection

and mixed). As contextual variables we use socio-demographic results taken out of Workpackage 4 (Kontula and Miettinen 2005):

- **Proportion of persons aged 65+ in percent, 2002**. This indicator is seen as a measure of the progressing demographic ageing of European societies.
- **Employment rate among men aged 60–64, around 2000**: an indicator of economic activity among elderly people. The male rate was considered because it displayed higher coefficients. There are no data for Switzerland.

As a general indicator of economic performance regarding the "pluralist industrial hypothesis" (Korpi 1989, 315), we use a variable from Eurostat, 2002: **Per capita GDP in relation to the European average**, set at 100. Data are missing for Switzerland.

The explanatory variables at population level were taken from the IPPAS database.[5] First, the indicator **preference of strong government responsibility in elderly care in percent** was selected.[6] This variable is associated with the dimension of Protection. It is available for ten DIALOG countries (data are missing for

---

[5] Weighted data were used.

[6] Using only cases which rated the government's responsibility as complete or held the government to share a large part of the responsibility.

Austria, Switzerland, Estonia and Italy). Furthermore, the variable **first preference to enable elderly people to work after retirement in percent** was selected. This variable is associated with the dimension of Participation. It is (only) available for eight DIALOG countries. There are no data for Austria, Switzerland, Cyprus, Finland, Italy and the Netherlands. The aggregation of individual data ignores different response patterns of the respondents caused by effects such as age and sex.

Finally, the variable **minimum pension** in Euros of every country around 2000 was selected (There are no data for Germany, the Netherlands and Romania).

As clarified above, it is impossible to calculate complex statistical models with only 14 cases. The analysis is restricted to interrelations, and is therefore more descriptive in nature. The first step is to identify predictors, which may explain the different priorities allotted by the panellists. The explanatory variables are expected to show multiple causation, and therefore interfering variables are identified and their influence is eliminated. In a second step, the dependent variables are related to the populace's preferences; interactions and probable differences are displayed.

6.6.5 Results

The correlation of the explanatory variables revealed that our expectation of multiple causation came true.[7]

The next step of the analysis is the correlation of the explanatory variables with the dependent variable to test relationships. At first sight, correlation displayed the worst case scenario, in that no substantial interrelation was found. By exploring the relationships graphically and removing outliers, the overall view gained greater clarity.[8]

6.6.5.1 Interplay Between Panellists and Contextual Factors

The results of the correlation (Fig. 6.3) show that the country panellists react to contextual variables. Countries with a low employment rate among the elderly show a strong focus on **Participation**, and vice versa ($r = -0.81$). The countries seem to group together; countries with a low employment rate and a high focus on Participation are Austria, Belgium (Flanders), the Czech Republic, Poland and Slovenia. Countries positioned in the middle are Germany, Finland, Italy, Lithuania and Romania. Cyprus is a special case (Participation $= 0$). The outliers Estonia and the Netherlands were excluded.

Two intervening variables were identified – lower but substantial coefficients were found. Countries with a small amount of minimum pension in Euro show a higher

---

[7] It is not intended here to outline the several interrelations, but we have to keep in mind that they exist.

[8] To keep as many countries as possible in the analysis, outliers were defined separately for every relation. Results are displayed after verifying for outliers.

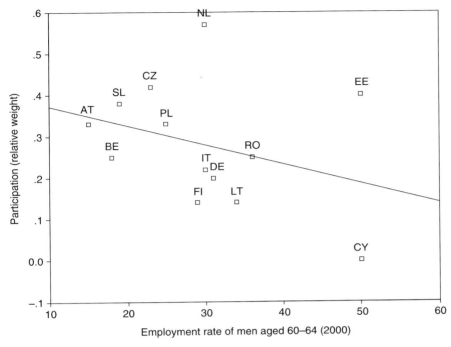

Fig. 6.3 Relation between participation and employment rate

focus on Participation, and vice versa (r = −0.625), whereby Lithuania and Cyprus were excluded. Countries with a small proportion of people aged 65+ show a higher focus on Participation, and vice versa (r = −0.412); Cyprus was excluded. When the intervening variables were verified, the correlation coefficient (r) rose to –0.93.

Correlation with **Protection** and with **Image** shows no clear results.

6.6.5.2 Interplay Between Panellists and Populace

The next step in the analysis relates the focus given by the panellists on people's opinions. Firstly, predictors of the PPAS variables are worked out. It is shown that there is an interplay between people's preferences and contextual data; therefore, people are aware of the situation in which they live.

The strongest predictor for the preference concerning governmental responsibility to enable elderly people to work after retirement is the employment rate among men aged 60–64. The strong relationship is, in contrast to the panellists, positive (r = 0.919): the higher the employment rate among men, the higher the preference for policies to encourage work after retirement. When the influence of intervening variables was verified, the correlation coefficient (r) rose to a level of 0.98.

The strongest predictor for opinion concerning governmental responsibility in elderly care is the minimum amount of pension in Euros. The strong relationship is positive (r = 0.881). An intervening variable was found: the percentage of persons aged 65+ (r = 0.7). When the intervening variable was verified, the correlation coefficient (r) fell to a level of 0.8.

Participation correlated with the preference for the elderly to continue working brought about a relatively substantial correlation of r = −0.583, Estonia being excluded. When the intervening variable was verified, the relationship became obscure (r = −0.16).

Protection correlated with the preference concerning governmental responsibility for care brought a negative correlation of r = −0.467 (the Netherlands and Slovenia being excluded). When the minimum pension in Euros was verified, the correlation rose to –0.6.

These results display a discrepancy between the populace and the panellists. The tendency is for stronger focus on the part of the panel to be accompanied by lower preference within the populace, and vice versa. Table 6.2 shows the differences between the two groups, whereby negative differences imply a stronger preference on the part of the populace, and positive ones a higher focus on the part of the panellists (there are no data for Austria, Switzerland or Italy):

Table 6.2 shows that the populations of Estonia, Lithuania and Romania focus more strongly on **Participation** compared to the panel of those countries. The Czech Republic, Poland and Slovenia display an inverse pattern. There, the focus of the panel is stronger. The groups in Germany and Belgium (Flanders) are the most like-minded.

The picture changes when it comes to the issue of **Protection**. Belgium (Flanders), the Czech Republic, Germany, Finland and the Netherlands show a discrepancy in that the populace focuses more on Protection than the panellists do. The panellists' focus is stronger in Cyprus, Lithuania, Poland and Slovenia. The two groups correspond well, with small differences in Finland, Romania and Slovenia.

There is a strong contrast between eastern and western countries when it comes to the issue of Protection. People in the West want a greater emphasis to be placed

Table 6.2 Interplay between the panellists and the populace

Country	Focus on participa-tion	Preference for work	Difference	Focus on protection	Preference for care	Difference
BE 2	25%	19%	6%	63%	88%	−25%
CY	0			75%	65%	10%
CZ	42%	17%	25%	50%	70%	−20%
DE	20%	19%	1%	60%	88%	−28%
EE	40%	57%	−17%	40%		
FI	14%			71%	79%	−8%
LT	14%	27%	−13%	86%	55%	31%
NL	57%			29%	65%	−36%
PL	33%	16%	17%	67%	54%	13%
RO	25%	38%	−13%	75%	76%	−1%
SL	38%	0	38%	50%	43%	7%
Average	28%	24%	4%	62%	68%	−6%

on Protection than the panellists do. In contrast, the discrepancy in eastern countries goes in the opposite direction, in that the panel would like to see a stronger focus (exception: the Czech Republic).

6.6.6 Conclusion

There is evidence that the panellists react to contextual variables. The awareness of a low employment rate among the elderly leads the panellists to place the focus of future policies on Participation. Furthermore, the analysis showed that the populace reacts differently to contextual variables; the awareness of a high employment rate among elderly people leads to a preference for policies which encourage work after retirement. The demand for governmental responsibility in elderly care is seen in the context of the minimum pension amount; a bad economic situation of the elderly creates a demand for governmental activities.

The results furthermore display a discrepancy between the populace and the panellists. The attitudes of experts and the populace do not match. Only a small number of countries reach convergence between the two groups.

6.7 Family, Fertility and Gender

"Since the turn of the century, the family in industrialised countries has undergone major transformation" (Gauthier 1996, 1). Fertility decline led to smaller family sizes, marriage became less popular and divorces became more common. Women no longer aspire to the traditional role as a housewife; they are well educated and push into the labour market. Politics have reacted to these transformations. How do political actors design future policies? What are the priorities which they set, and do political actors react to contextual factors and preferences of the populace?

6.7.1 Classification Framework

As several correspondences between the themes Family & Fertility and Gender appeared in the data, the two subjects are treated together. As a theoretical background, the typology of motives for family policy from Kaufmann was integrated (Kaufmann 2002). It was placed in the context of the results of the Delphi study (Palomba et al., 2005). Kaufmann's typology acts as a basis for the assumption that public debates on family issues have a certain rhetoric. The term "family rhetoric" means the expression and the diagnosis of a problem and the proposals to solve it. It contains "implicit normative assumptions, which may be shaped by tradition or by the dynamics of social movement" (Kaufmann 2002, 426). Kaufmann distinguishes between eight different arguments which may serve to motivate political intervention affecting the family. Four of them appear in the data.[9]

Identified by Palomba et al. are four themes/problems which appear in the final scenarios of the Delphi study (cf. Palomba 2005, 9): (1) the increase in the number of births, (2) child-friendly policies, (3) improvement in men's and women's work-life balance, (4) changes in male and female roles. Those themes have to be included in the categorical framework.

The theme *increase in the number of births* corresponds with what Kaufmann labels *pro-natal orientation*. Within this motive, the focus lies on the importance of demographic reproduction. The insufficiency of the birth rates is recognised, and an attempt is made to implement policies to increase fertility.

The next motive, which is translated into a category, is the *child orientation*, which focuses principally on children's well-being. The government has to provide the necessary framework for public provision of children's needs. Derived from this motive is the demand for *child-friendly policies*.

Another category derives from Kaufmann's *family orientation* which "focuses on need and equality and underscores the economic disadvantages related to taking on family responsibilities" (Kaufmann 2002, 427). One argument is child and family poverty. This issue does not appear in the identification of relevant themes by Palomba; nevertheless, it appears within the data. The family orientation demands *family-friendly policies*.

The last two themes of Palomba's priority list, the improvement in the *work-life balance of men and women* and *changes in male and female roles*, were subsumed under Kaufmann's *gender orientation*: "on the one hand, this points out that the economic and social disadvantages of living in a family are solely faced by women ... on the other hand, it argues for the equality of men and women with regard to participation in the labour market as well as to assuming familial responsibilities" (2002, 428). According to that definition, two sub-dimensions were worked out: on the one hand, the aspect of equality, and on the other, disadvantages faced by women. The equality dimension is seen as a superior category. Besides disadvantages faced by women, three other sub-dimensions of equality were distinguished: the work-life balance, which includes as sub-categories the issues of female labour force participation, intrafamilial equality and the change of gender roles.

To subsume the theoretical concept, Table 6.3 shows the classified dimension in hierarchical order:

After the classification, the dimensions were weighted as clarified above (see Section 6.6.1). The following analysis has to prove how the different variables interact with each other. Interaction is expected to take place on the horizontal level, the focus of the analysis lies on motives. The vertical level implies a causal order, which begins with normative assumption and ends with concrete strategies to reach the goal.

---

[9] The labels of the motives were changed by the author for clarification.

Table 6.3 Classification: family, fertility and gender

Action program			
Child orientation	Family orientation	Gender orientation	Pro-natal orientation
Child-friendly policies	Family-friendly policies	Equality	Active policies to increase fertility
		Work-life balance	
		Changing gender roles	
		Intrafamilial equality	
		Disadvantages	

6.7.2 Priorities Set by the Panellists

Gender orientation was given priority (mean: 61%). It is present in all countries within a range of 53%–73%; the highest levels are reached by Austria, the Netherlands, Belgium (Flanders) and Poland (over 68%). *Family orientation* followed, which generated an overall priority of 22%. It was addressed by all DIALOG countries with a range between 9% (Estonia) and 42% (Switzerland). The *pro-natal orientation* was addressed within a range of 0% and 27% (Estonia); only Switzerland did not address this issue. In seven DIALOG countries, this motive was mentioned by one PO.[10] The last dimension, *child orientation,* was addressed by eight DIALOG countries. Six DIALOG countries did not address this issue directly (Austria, Belgium (Flanders), Switzerland, Cyprus, Germany and Romania). The overall priority given is 6%. The variable was additionally given binary coding (present/absent).

6.7.3 The Inner Consistency of the Data

The test for inner consistency did not provide any substantial results. The four dimensions are weakly correlated, but tendencies became apparent. The relationship between *child* and *family orientation* is negative: countries with a higher focus on child-friendly policies display a lower focus on family-friendly policies, and vice versa. There is a close to zero relationship between *child orientation*, the *pro-natal* and the *gender orientation*. The relationship between *family* and *gender orientation* is negative (if one excludes Switzerland and Estonia) (r = −0.515). The same negative relationship appears with the *pro-natal orientation* (r = −0.447). Hence, countries with a higher focus on family-friendly policies display a lower focus on *gender* and on *pro-natal orientation*. Finally, the most substantial relationship is observed between *gender* and *pro-natal orientation* (r = −0.658, if one excludes

---

[10] The differences in weight are caused by the different amount of total POs of the countries. The variation between those countries may be doubted.

Switzerland and Estonia). Countries with a high focus on gender display a low focus on active policies to increase fertility, and vice versa.

We have to keep in mind when it comes to the following analysis that Switzerland and Estonia follow a different pattern: Switzerland with its strong focus on family-friendly policies and the absence of active policies to increase fertility, and Estonia with its strong focus on the latter issue.

6.7.4 Operationalization and Method

We use as *dependent variables* the four motives for family policies mentioned above: **child orientation, family orientation, pro-natal orientation** and **gender orientation**.

The *explanatory variables* at the country level were operationalized as follows: As in the previous section, three general indicators are used: **East/West, religion** and **per capita GDP in relation to the European average**. These variables are taken into account in every motive.

Contextual data out of Workpackage 4 and IPPAS data are associated with the dependent variables. The aggregation of PPAS data to the country level ignores different response patterns of the respondents caused by effects such as age and sex.

Two indicators are associated with *child orientation*: the **total fertility rate** (TFR 2002) and the **proportion of families with three and more children in percent** (2002). There are no data for Cyprus or Romania. These two indicators reflect different reproductive and family behaviour patterns.

Associated with *family orientation* is the **proportion of families with three and more children in percent** (2002) and an indicator from the PPAS: **more emphasis should be placed on family life in the future**, agreement in percent per country. This variable is available for ten DIALOG countries (There are no data for Belgium (Flanders), Switzerland, Cyprus or Romania).

Associated with *pro-natal orientation* are the **TFR** (2002), the **average population growth rate**[11] (1996–2002) and the PPAS indicator: **disapproval of the declining number of births in percent**. Only people who rated this issue as "very bad" were considered. This indicator is available for eleven DIALOG countries (There are no data for Switzerland, Estonia, Italy or Romania).

Associated with *gender orientation* are two indicators which are seen as central determinants for gender equality: the **labour force participation of women aged 20–29** in percent (2002, There are no data for Belgium (Flanders)) and **part-time employed of women in percent** (2002). As an indicator from the PPAS, the opinion is selected concerning **governmental responsibility in facilitating female labour force participation**.[12] Data are available for nine DIALOG countries (countries not available: Austria, Belgium (Flanders), Switzerland, Estonia and Italy). Indicators

---

[11] This indicator reflects the trends concerning population development.

[12] People responding with complete and quite responsible. Weighted data were used.

of female economic activity are not sufficient; other indicators on resources and power should be integrated (Pinnelli 2001, 47), therefore a variable from the Human Development Index database is introduced: **Gender Empowerment Index**[13] (GEM 2004).

The analysis follows the same methodological approach as clarified above (see Section 6.6.4).

6.7.5 Results

The correlation of the explanatory variables revealed the truth of our expectation of multiple causation.[14]

The next step of the analysis is the association of the explanatory variables with the dependent variable to test for relationships. At first sight, the interrelation did not display a substantial correlation (with the exception of *gender orientation*). Exploring the relationships graphically and removing outliers gave the overall view greater clarity.[15]

6.7.5.1 Interplay Between Panellists and Contextual Factors

The results of the correlation show that the panellists of the countries react to contextual variables. The strongest predictor for **gender orientation** is the labour force participation of females aged 20–29 (r = 0.675). By excluding the countries with the highest focus on this issue (Austria, the Netherlands and Poland) the correlation coefficient was increased to 0.896. By verifying the intervening variable (GEM), the relationship became weaker, but remained stably positive. Figure 6.4 displays the distribution of the countries:

The panellists from Austria and the Netherlands placed the highest emphasis on the *gender orientation*; they displayed high female labour force participation. An exception is Poland: a high focus by the panellists and medium female labour force participation. The other countries form two groups: Italy, Romania, the Czech Republic and Estonia display a lower focus by the panellists and low female labour force participation. Switzerland, Cyprus, Finland, Germany, Lithuania and Slovenia take a medium position.

The focus on **child orientation** given by the panellists is generally low; it is absent in six countries. The correlation with the dependent variables brought not only few tendencies to the surface. The motive is negatively correlated with the

---

[13] The GEM subsumes four aspects of gender equality: seats in parliament held by women in percent, female legislators, senior officials and managers, female professional and technical workers and the ratio of estimated female to male earned income.

[14] It is not intended here to outline the several interrelations, but we have to keep in mind that they exist.

[15] To keep as many countries as possible in the analysis, outliers were defined separately for every relation. Results are displayed after verifying for outliers.

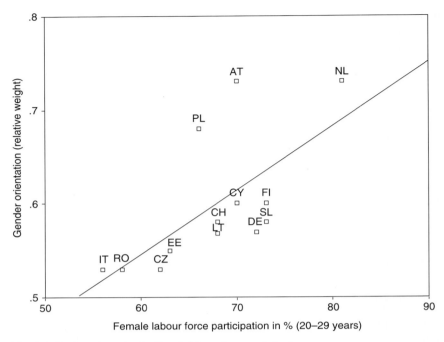

Fig. 6.4 Gender orientation by female labour force participation

TFR, per capita GDP and the proportion of families with three or more children. The strongest predictor is the TFR. The tendency is for a lower fertility rate to lead to a stronger focus on child-friendly policies, and vice versa. When the intervening variables were verified, the relationship remained stable but negative. Furthermore, there is a tendency for countries in the East to focus more on children-related issues.

The most substantial predictor for **family orientation** is per capita GDP. Exclusion of Estonia and Poland caused the correlation coefficient (r) to increase to –0.667. When the intervening variables were verified, the relationship became weaker, remaining stable but negative. Hence, countries with a high economic performance show a lower level of *family orientation,* and vice versa.[16] Furthermore, a connection was revealed between religion and the focus on family issues: Catholic countries focus more closely on family-friendly policies (Switzerland excluded).

The focus on **pro-natal orientation** given by the panellists is low. Estonia, Germany and Romania are exceptions, with a value in excess of 20%. The correlation of the dependent variable with the explanatory variables on the interval level brought no clear results. A substantial correlation coefficient (eta = 0.76) was reached by introducing the indicator religion (by excluding Switzerland and the

---

[16] It should be kept in mind that western countries displayed a high economic performance.

Netherlands). There is a tendency for panellists of Catholic and Orthodox countries to focus less closely on the pro-natal dimension.

6.7.5.2 The Interplay Between the Panellists and the Populace

The next step of the analysis relates the focus given by the panellists with peoples' opinions. It was possible to compare three out of the four dimensions with variables from the IPPAS.[17] First, predictors of peoples' preferences are worked out. It is shown that there is an interplay between people's preferences and contextual data; people are aware of the situation they live in. Subsequently, the variables are placed in the context of the dependent variables.

The strongest predictor of agreement of the government's responsibility in facilitating female labour force participation is female labour force participation itself. The strong relationship (excluding Germany) is negative, in contradistinction to that of the panellists ($r = -0.855$). Hence, the higher the female labour force participation, the lower is peoples' agreement to governmental responsibility. The strongest predictor of emphasis on family life in the future is per capita GDP. The strong relationship is negative ($r = -0.806$, excluding Poland). Higher economic performance leads to a lower emphasis on family life, and vice versa.[18] The strongest predictor for disapproval of the decline in fertility by the people is the TFR. The relationship is negative, but the coefficient is not robust ($r = -0.495$). Hence, there is a tendency for a higher TFR to lead to lower disapproval by the people, and vice versa.

Gender orientation and the preference for female labour force participation are negatively correlated. When the intervening variable female labour force participation was verified, the relationship became weaker but remained negative. The relationship between *family orientation* and the emphasis on family life by the people is highly positive ($r = 0.8$, Estonia being excluded). When per capita GDP was verified, the positive relationship remained strong. The relationship between the *pro-natal orientation* and the disapproval of the decline in fertility by the people is not robust, but is positive ($r = 0.495$). Hence, there is a tendency for disapproval of the decline in fertility to correspond with the panellists' *pro-natal orientation*.

The results display in one case clear convergence between the populace and the panellists: The panellists' focus on family issues corresponds with the preferences of the populace ($r = 0.8$). The outlier is Estonia with a low focus by the panellists and a high focus by the populace. The levels differ widely: The agreement of emphasis on family life is very strong (range: 87%–99%), the range of the panellists' focus is rather small (9%–29%). Figure 6.5 displays the distribution of the countries and the predicted relationship (Estonia being excluded):

Lithuania matches best: a high focus on family-friendly policies by the panellists and a strong emphasis on family life by the populace (99%). An intermediate group

---

[17] Weighted data were used.

[18] Weighted data were used.

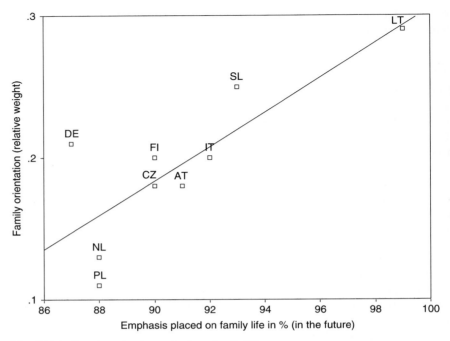

Fig. 6.5 Family orientation by emphasis on family life

also matches well. This group is formed by Austria, the Czech Republic, Finland and Italy, with a medium focus on family-friendly policies and a high emphasis on family life. The highest deviation from the predicted value is shown by Germany; here, the panellists show a high focus on family-friendly policies, the populace's emphasis being low in comparison with to the other countries. Slovenia displays the same picture with a smaller deviation. The panellists of the Netherlands and Poland display a lower focus on family issues than expected, of which Poland shows the higher discrepancy in comparison to the predicted value.

No clear tendency is detectable within the other two dimensions. Table 6.4 shows the differences between the two groups, whereby negative differences imply a stronger preference of the populace and positive differences a higher focus by the panellists. (There are no data for Switzerland, Romania and Slovenia):

The *gender orientation* of the panels is strong (>53%). The people display a different pattern: The highest value is found in Germany, where about 80% consider the government to be responsible; high values are allotted in Cyprus, the Czech Republic, Poland, Romania and Lithuania. The lowest levels are found in Finland and the Netherlands. In seven out of nine DIALOG countries the panellists' focus on *gender orientation* is stronger compared to that of the people. Exceptions are Germany and Romania, which show a converse pattern. The Netherlands displays the highest difference, and approximate convergence between the two groups is reached in Cyprus and the Czech Republic.

Table 6.4 Interplay between the panellists and the populace

Country	Gender orientation	Responsi-bility for female lfp	Difference	Pronatal orienta-tion	Disapproval of fertility decline	Difference
AT	73%			9%	20%	−11%
BE	69%			8%	10%	−2%
CY	60%	54%	6%	10%	42%	−32%
CZ	53%	45%	8%	18%	31%	−13%
DE	57%	79%	−22%	21%	36%	−15%
FI	60%	32%	28%	13%	24%	−11%
LT	57%	37%	20%	7%	30%	−23%
NL	73%	22%	51%	7%	2%	5%
PL	68%	47%	21%	5%	19%	−14%
RO	53%	63%	−10%	20%		
SL	58%	35%	23%	8%	30%	−22%
Mean	62%	46%	16%	11%	24%	−13%

The issue of correspondence between *pro-natal orientation* and disapproval of the fertility decline is different. Within eight countries, the peoples' focus is stronger compared to the focus given by the panellists. Cyprus displays the greatest difference, a converse pattern is found in Estonia. Convergence between the two groups is reached in Belgium (Flanders) and in the Netherlands.

6.7.6 Conclusion

There is evidence that the focus on a certain motive for family policy is influenced by contextual factors. The panellists react to high female labour force participation with a strong focus on gender issues. The structural change created new needs, and experts respond to the new situation. The people show an inverse pattern: A low female employment rate creates a strong demand for governmental activities. The comparison of the two groups revealed that the panellists' focus on gender issues is stronger, the differences vary and convergence is approximately reached only in Cyprus and the Czech Republic. Germany and Romania display an inverse pattern: There, the people are strongly in favour of the government shouldering responsibility for female labour force participation.

Concerning *family orientation*, the two groups correspond well: Strong economic performance in a country (western countries) leads to a lower focus on families. The outlier Switzerland, with its strong focus, may be explained by its minor development of family policy (Fux et al. 1997, 27ff).

Concerning *pro-natal orientation*, the people's disapproval of the decline in fertility is stronger compared to the panellists. The outlier Estonia shows an inverse pattern. Convergence is reached only in Belgium (Flanders) and in the Netherlands, where the level of disapproval is rather low.

6.8 Final Comments and Discussion

This study aimed to find out whether, and if so how, political actors react to contextual factors within the social policy subsystem, and whether they are aware of the opinions circulating among the populace. The thematic focus lay on future ageing and family policies, and the classification system outlined the fact that the panellists focused on only a few dimensions. Even though the study stands on "sandy" ground concerning the selectivity of the panels, the small number of countries considered and the selection of the explanatory variables, there is evidence that political actors react to contextual factors. On the one hand, the experts try to intervene actively in a social situation, whilst on the other hand they react to demographic changes which created needs. Both a reactive-compensatory and a constitutive-shaping (Huf 1998) intervention policy appears in the data. Moreover, it was shown that the populace reacts differently, and that their appreciation of a particular issue is based on different assumptions. There is a divergence between these two groups; one can of a culture of experts, which does not often match the people's opinion. There is a need for further population policy acceptance studies to better understand the people's expectations and attitudes and to transmit the results into the political system.

Case-oriented work is needed to better understand the decision-making of the panellists and the coalitions which they form. Conflicts which appear within a country have to be looked at carefully, and the situation of every country has to be taken into account. Intra-system interaction – which was not part of the remit of this study – also has to be examined on a country level in order to find out about policy-oriented learning.

This study did not provide robust results, but constituted an attempt to explore the interaction between experts and the environment. Further studies are needed to confirm the evidence.

Chapter 7
Making Dialog Possible

The View of Delphi Panellists and Citizens on Female Employment

Adele Menniti and Maura Misiti

Abstract The chapter analyses comparatively the results of a policy Delphi study on gender roles, family and fertility, as well as ageing, conducted in 15 European countries and the results of the Population Policy Acceptance Study (PPAS) examining preferences and attitudes of European citizens on the same topics. The comparative analysis focuses on female employment; the sources utilised are the national Delphi reports and some synthesis reports drafted within the DIALOG project. The analysis underlines interesting insights showing both convergence and differences among citizens and opinion leaders. In fact, while in some cases policy actions proposed by the Delphi panellists are in line with citizens' values and preferences, in others their policy priorities indicated a certain distance with the lifestyles preferred by the population.

Keywords: Gender roles · Work-life balance · Policy delphi · Female labour force participation

7.1 Introduction

This chapter analyses comparatively the results of a policy Delphi study on gender, family and fertility, as well as ageing, conducted in 15 European countries and the results of the Population Policy Acceptance Surveys studying the opinions and preferences of European citizens on the same topics.[1] The analysis focuses on a specific theme, namely female employment.

A. Menniti
Istituto di ricerche sulla Popolazione e le Politiche Sociali, Consiglio Nazionale delle Ricerche, Rome, Italy
e-mail: a.menniti@irpps.cnr.it

[1] It should be noted that Switzerland did not carry out the PPAS and that some specific topics considered in this chapter are not included in a number of national PPAS questionnaires. Nevertheless, in order to make the greatest use of the information gathered in the project, all DIALOG countries have been considered in our analysis.

C. Höhn et al. (eds.), *People, Population Change and Policies: Vol. 2: Demographic Knowledge – Gender – Ageing*, © Springer Science+Business Media B.V. 2008

The sources used for this comparative analysis are the national Delphi reports[2] and some synthesis reports drafted for the DIALOG project. For the purpose of this article we have mainly taken into account the synthesis reports on Gender Issues (Philipov 2006), Work and Parenthood (Kotowska et al. 2006) – as part of the PPAS surveys – and the comparative Delphi Study (Dell'Anno et al. 2005), while the report on Child Friendly Policy (Esveldt and Fokkema 2006) has been considered by analysing the relationship between female work and fertility.

The chapter is divided into two sections: The first aims to describe the views of citizens and opinion leaders on the roles of women and men in paid and unpaid work. The second section focuses on the desires of European citizens with regard to part-time female employment and the position of opinion leaders on this female employment pattern. Each section starts with a brief introduction of the current debate on the topic. The chapter ends with some conclusive comments.

More specifically, the scope of this chapter is to try to identify similarities and dissimilarities between the preferences and the attitudes of Europeans and the policy actions proposed by the European panellists who participated in the Delphi. This attempt to compare stakeholders' and citizens' views on population issues can be considered as a further input to the debate on citizens' participation and involvement in the decision-making process, namely in the field of social policies. In fact, the relationship between a government and its citizens is a priority for democracies. Nevertheless, governments everywhere have been criticised for being remote from the people, not being attentive enough to public opinion, and not seeking participation. One example of this disaffection is the erosion of voter turnout in elections, falling membership of political parties and declining confidence in key public institutions. Calls for greater government transparency and accountability have grown louder as public and media analysis of government action increases in intensity (OECD 2001). At the same time, new forms of representation and participation in the public sphere are emerging in all democratic countries. These efforts are however too often focused on specific issues where public interest is already high, such as the environment or consumer protection, and have not found sufficient imitation throughout government as an integral part of the whole democratic and law-making process.

Population issues such as ageing, gender roles, as well as fertility and family, have grown to be very hot topics on all European governments' agendas and cover both private and public life. Increasing attention is therefore devoted to ascertaining how to deal with these matters, also involving a general re-think on welfare policy approaches. The participation and the engagement of people in policy-making appears to be crucial in this context to assure a broad consensus and, at the same time, the effective implementation of new policies.

---

[2] The national Delphi reports were prepared by Abuladze (2004), Demographic Research Centre (2004), Department of Sociology-School of Social Studies (2004), Esveldt (2004), Fux and Bertschinger (2004), Hautaniemi (2004), HCSO Demographic Research Institute (2004), Intercollege (2004), Kotowska et al. (2004), Manea (2004), Stropnik (2004), van Peer and Desmet (2004), Vienna Institute for Demography (2004).

The challenge is how to spread this type of consultation and participation to all areas of government. To reach this goal, governments should develop and use appropriate tools, ranging from traditional opinion polls of the population at large to consensus conferences with small groups of stakeholders. At the same time, it is crucial to broaden and improve the communication process, especially when this is intended to stimulate public discussion, to raise awareness and to understand community needs. In other words, it is necessary to introduce a new quality of governance that enables public institutions to catalyse and manage different contributions with the goal of helping to draft and build new policies. It is thus clear that public institutions are requested to have a strong willingness to enter into a dialog with citizens and different communities to enable stakeholders in participating and defining programs and strategies. We believe that the DIALOG project experience is an important step in this direction.

7.1.1 PPAS and Delphi: Two Methodological Approaches

The comparative analyses do not fully match, due to various reasons that we will be listing below.

Firstly, the PPAS used a structured questionnaire, with pre-defined questions and answers. This format lacks flexibility and denies the respondent the possibility of commenting further or adding details and/or inputs clarifying his/her point of view. Respondents answered by choosing the pre-coded answers closest to their opinion. Of course, the focus of the PPAS is to identify differences in attitudes within the population and across countries.

The policy Delphi study followed a different approach.[3] In this methodology, panellists are in fact encouraged not only to express their views within a series of predefined, open questions, but are also recommended to further enrich the questions by suggesting additional topics. Last but not least, policy Delphi aims to reach a "collective consensus", and so it does not tend to highlight nuances in the positions of the national panellists. This means that individual points of view are considered important only if they match or meet the general consensus within the panel.

Secondly, while the PPAS used the same questions in each participating country, the Delphi study is built on questions that, whilst they are based on a common structure of interview guidelines, are individually formulated for each of the countries involved. It fact, the goal of the Delphi study is to highlight, within the three broad issues, national specificities that need to be addressed and resolved in the view of the national panels.

Thirdly, a time issue has to be considered. In fact, while the PPAS gathered the opinions that citizens had at the time of the interview, policy Delphi drafts scenarios for the year 2030. In this respect, the latter identify those policy actions to be

---

[3] Detailed information on the methodology used in the Delphi study can be found in Palomba and Dell'Anno in Chapter 5.

implemented in the following thirty years, while the PPAS highlights the current preferences of the population that may not necessarily match the preferences of the same population in 2030. Time, of course, not only determines potential change in the attitudes and preferences of a given population, but also in the composition of the population itself. In fact, the adults in 2030 are not the adults interviewed in our PPAS surveys.

Finally, while policy Delphi aims to describe policy actions relevant to a given country and its overall population, the PPAS illustrates those attitudes and preferences that are relevant for the individuals.

These differences create some difficulty in comparing PPAS and Delphi findings. At the same time, this exercise is highly challenging and, as can be seen later on, it provides interesting insights into convergence and differences among citizens and Delphi panellists. In fact, while in some cases policy actions proposed by the panellists are in line with citizens' values and preferences, in other cases they differ from the population's preferred lifestyles.

7.2 Should Women Work or Not?

The need for increased participation by women in the labour market is of paramount importance for several reasons. The growth in the number of working women is considered crucial to sustain and improve the economic performance of European families, to achieve women's independence, to guarantee the sustainability of the welfare system and pension schemes, and to respond to the decline in and the ageing of European populations, as well as of the working-age populations. This issue is particularly relevant taking into account both the economic impact that female employment has in European countries, and the existing relationship between female labour force participation and fertility behaviour. Some remarks will be made on the latter issue in the conclusions, considering the major findings of the DIALOG report on child-friendly policy (Esveldt and Fokkema 2006).

The under-representation of women in the labour market is characterised by both the unbalanced participation of the two genders, and by women's lower economic status. The existing gender imbalance compromises European competitiveness and is a waste of valuable human resources, considering the high level of female education and talent. Therefore, women's participation in the labour market requires specific attention and means that the issue is highly relevant in a social, cultural, political and economic perspective.

7.2.1 The View of Citizens

PPAS deals with the issue of female employment from two main viewpoints, namely attitudes on gender roles toward work and family, and preferences towards the so-called partnership-employment model.[4] This model considers three typologies: The first concerns the couple or family where the male partner works full-time and the female stays at home ("male breadwinner model"), the second refers to a couple or family where the male works full-time and the female works on a part-time basis ("modernised male breadwinner model"), and the third relates to a couple or family where both partners work, either full- or part-time ("dual-earner model"). In the comparative analysis we start by merging the two latter models and labelling it the "dual-income model". Later we of course distinguish between the modernised male breadwinner model and the dual-earner model.

7.2.1.1 Attitudes Towards Female Paid Work

The PPAS findings highlight a high level of consensus on the two following statements:[5] "*Most women have to work today to support their families*" and "*Both men and women should contribute towards the household income*". A large majority of respondents (around 80%) find themselves in strong agreement or in agreement with these two statements. On the other hand, female paid work as a way to gain independence is not considered at the same level of agreement; in fact the consensus on the statement "*Work for a woman offers the best opportunity to be independent*" ranges between 40 and 80%. Moreover, the fulfilment attained through paid work versus unpaid work, as well as the preference towards a division of labour opposite to the asymmetric male breadwinner model, encountered a medium level of agreement: In fact, only a minority of respondents agree that "*Being a housewife is just as fulfilling as working*" and that "*It is not good if the man stays at home and cares for the children and the woman goes out to work*" (Table 7.1).

The social and cultural value of female work is particularly important for some sub-groups of the population and countries, while it is considered to be of lesser importance when compared with the economic value. Therefore citizens attach a high value to female work, especially when considering its financial aspect.

The high level of agreement on "economic" statements ("*Most women have to work today to support their families*" and "*Both men and women should contribute towards the household income*") strongly indicates the existence of favourable grounds for an increase in demand for women's employment in Europe.

The importance attached to female work obviously shows some differences between and within individual DIALOG countries. In general terms, agreement with balanced gender roles is more explicit in Western Europe than in Central and Eastern Europe, as well as amongst highly-educated respondents and younger generations (Philipov 2006, 46–47). It is worth noting that in the Netherlands there is a diffuse awareness that women do not consider family and the children a priority, and that

---

[4] For a detailed analysis of the PPAS findings on gender roles and on work and parenthood, see Philipov 2006 and Kotowska et al. 2006.

[5] The questions on gender roles were put in Austria, Estonia, Germany, Hungary, Italy, Lithuania, the Netherlands, Poland, Romania and Slovenia.

Table 7.1 Concurrence (*) with the statements on gender roles

	Low	Medium	High
Economic aspects		NL	AT, EE, DE,
Most women have to work today			HU, LT, IT,
to support their families.			PL, RO
Both men and women should			AT, EE, DE,
contribute towards the household			HU, LT, PL,
income.			RO
Child-related aspects			
A pre-school child will probably		AT, EE, DE,	
suffer if his/her mother works.	NL	HU, LT, PL, RO	IT
The relationship between a			
working mother and her children			
can be just as close as that of a		EE, HU, LT, PL,	
non-working mother.		RO	AT, DE, NL
All in all family life suffers if the		EE, DE, HU, LT,	
woman works a full-time.		NT, RO	
Patriarchal aspects	AT, EE, DE, HU,		
For a man work should be more	LT, NL, PL, RO,		
important than the family.	SI	IT	
Work is good, but what most			
women really want is a home and			
children.	AT, DE, NT	EE, LT, PL, RO	HU
Being a housewife is just as		AT, EE, DE,	
fulfilling as working.	LT, RO	HU, IT, NL, PL	
Most women are not as	AT, EE, DE, HU,		
ambitious in their work as men.	LT, IT, NL, PL, RO		
A man has to earn money; a			
woman should look after the		AT, HU, LT, PL,	
home and the family.	EE, DE,	RO	
It is not good if the man stays at			
home and cares for the children		EE, HU, IT, LT,	
and the woman goes out to work.	AT, DE, NL	PL	RO
Emancipatory aspects			
Work offers the best opportunity		EE, DE, HU, LT,	
for a woman to be independent.		IT, NL, PL	AT, RO
Women who work are highly		EE, DE, HU, LT,	
respected.		NL, PL, RO, SI	
Family life often suffers because			
men concentrate too much on		AT, DE, LT, NL,	
their work.		PO, RO	EE, HU, IT

*Agreement less than 30% = low; 31–70% = medium; >70% = high
Source: Philipov 2006

the economic value of female work is lower than in other countries while, in the meantime, a high level of acceptance of a reversal of family and gender roles can be seen. On the other hand, Lithuanians and Hungarians show a high level of agreement with regard to the need for female work for economic reasons, together with a high level of attachment to traditional family roles.

Women and younger people appreciate paid female work more than men and the older generation (Philipov 2006). Therefore, it seems that young women are highly determined to play an active role in the labour market, being convinced that paid work can ensure their well-being as well as that of their families. This trend is probably bound to increase in the next few years, as new generations enter the labour market.

The increase in female employment can certainly provide many advantages, but at the same time it may also create frictions and conflicts at individual, familial and social level. In particular, it poses for society the challenge of improving the work-life family balance. In the private sphere, women wishing to enter gainful employment might push for a review of the couple relationship in order to reach a new stability. In Europe, the work-life family balance is a widely-debated topic that needs fast and satisfactory responses and solutions in order to guarantee an improvement in quality of life for all citizens, especially in the perspective of a possible and desired increase in the number of working women and mothers.

European citizens also foresee unfavourable consequences in the growth of female paid work not only for women, who have to develop adequate strategies to combine the dual role of workers and wives/mothers, but also for their families. This is a matter of concern especially for families with small children and the question of whether they might suffer as a result of the limited amount of time their mothers can spend at home and dedicate to them.

7.2.1.2 Are Citizens Calling for an Increase in Female Employment?

Data on the preferred partnership-employment model show that the two-income model is highly popular[6] (Table 7.2). In the DIALOG countries considered, a minority of respondents selects the male breadwinner model, which is chosen to be ideal by less than 30% of respondents, with the sole exception of Lithuania (45.9%). In fact, the percentage of respondents that prefers this model is the highest there among the countries surveyed. This result confirms the high value attached to the family by Lithuanians. The Netherlands, Poland, Cyprus and Estonia are positioned in the middle of the range: Around 23–28% of respondents in these countries prefer for their partnership/family the model where only men work.

Looking at the differences between the achieved and the preferred male breadwinner model (Kotowska et al. 2006), it emerges that there is an unmet demand for female work in the majority of countries. In fact this model is more commonly practised than preferred in every country except Lithuania and the Netherlands, where a wider diffusion of the male breadwinner model is requested. It is worth noting that, while the difference in the Netherlands is small (around 5%), the gap in Lithuania is higher (around 15%).

---

[6] The question as to the preferred partnership-employment model was submitted in ten countries, namely Belgium (Flanders), the Czech Republic, Estonia, Finland, Germany, Italy, Lithuania, the Netherlands, Poland and Slovenia.

Table 7.2 Preferences concerning the male breadwinner model and the two-income model by country (% ranked), men and women living in a couple with the woman aged 20–49

	Male breadwinner model	Two-income model
Romania	6.2	93.8
Belgium – Flanders	12.0	88.0
Slovenia	17.6	82.4
Italy	19.4	80.6
Estonia	22.6	77.4
Cyprus	23.1	76.9
Poland	23.1	76.8
Netherlands	27.8	72.2
Lithuania	45.9	54.1

Source: Kotowska et al. 2006

7.2.2 The View of the Delphi Panellists

European agendas should include affirmative action on female employment among its policy priorities. This is an explicit call by the "opinion leaders" interviewed in our Delphi surveys. The panellists clearly stated their views on this topic in different sections of the study: Population Trends, Controversial Policy Issues, Policy Objectives and Key Success Factors. In fact, many scenarios resulting from our Delphi studies deal with a variety of elements related to female employment.

Some aspects more closely related to the choice of working or not working (the trend on female employment and the promotion of housework activities), as well as some features related to the conditions of female participation in the labour market (their under-representation in high-level positions) will be analysed below.

7.2.2.1 Will Women Participate in the Labour Market? The Trends

The vast majority of countries which participated in the Delphi study asked their Delphi panellists to propose desired future trends of female labour market participation (14 out of 15). Finland dealt with the issue by analysing a specific feature of the involvement of the female gender in the labour market, including the trend on "the proportion of women in the highest executive positions in big business". An analysis of the countries' findings on the position of Delphi panellists on female labour market participation showed a tendency toward an increase in the number of working women in all the countries, the only exception being Hungary.

Therefore, even if we can say for certain that the dream of the Delphi panellists is to see growth in female labour market participation, it is the speed of this development that is being questioned. In some countries, such as Austria, Belgium (Flanders), Italy, Lithuania, the Netherlands and Switzerland, there is a high percentage of working women (more than 70%). In the other countries, namely Cyprus, Estonia, Germany, Poland and Slovenia, the percentages are lower, but even there the Delphi panellists clearly uphold the idea that future European societies will witness a growing number of working women.

7.2.2.2 The Recognition of Household Work

The desirable increase in female employment expressed by the European Delphi panellists is further strengthened if one considers their positions regarding unpaid work and the promotion of female work at more senior levels. In this section, we will deal with those Policy Objectives related to the domestic role of women and to the desire of considering or not considering the recognition of unpaid work as a priority by 2030.

Among the countries that included this issue in their Delphi study, only four reached a consensus on the higher level of esteem attached to household work. In these countries, recognition of unpaid work has been invoked via different tools such as the extension of pension benefits to housewives (the Czech Republic, Germany and Hungary) and tax relief for family members who take care of children and households (the Czech Republic).

The number of countries where Delphi panellists rejected policy actions rewarding household activities is higher than the number of those invoking them. Delphi panellists in Germany, Italy and Poland did not agree on the "need to support women who want to be housewives and mothers"; Delphi panellists in Lithuania and Italy dropped the Policy Objective related to the "maintenance of conservative gender roles"; Delphi panellists in Belgium (Flanders), the Netherlands and Poland did not consider the "promotion of the 'male breadwinner' model". Finally, Delphi panellists in Cyprus, the Netherlands and Romania did not accept the idea of financial recognition of family work, while Delphi panellists in Switzerland rejected the idea that to be a "housewife and mother is the backbone of the family".

On the other hand, Delphi panellists in Switzerland reached a consensus on the changed role of men within society ("the promotion of the father's responsibilities") via the financial acknowledgement of family work. It is to be noted that, notwithstanding the Dutch PPAS respondents favouring the male breadwinner model to some extent, Dutch Delphi panellists did not accept the two measures aiming to promote it, namely "the promotion of the male breadwinner model" and "the recognition and payment of housewives". This position may be explained with the strong support panellists gave to the economic independence of women (Esveldt 2004).

As a general comment, we may say that in a considerable number of countries Delphi panellists did not accept the idea of reinforcing the traditional role of women, and thus did not agree to make housework an activity to be promoted in the future. This does not mean that European panellists do not appreciate domestic work, but that policies should rather be directed towards the integration of women in the labour market and the reconciliation between paid and unpaid work. In fact, policy Delphi results show strong support for child-rearing activities through the improvement of childcare facilities and a more family-friendly work environment with the promotion of part-time, flexi-time and ad-hoc leave.

In brief, according to the national panels, policy makers should develop a framework for the reconciliation of work and family, for equal opportunities and for the attenuation of gender roles.

7.2.2.3 Women and Work: The View of the Delphi Panellists on the Position of Women

The policy Delphi findings attribute a key role to work issues and to female partic-ipation in the labour market in building the future Europe. In general terms, Delphi panellists envision a labour market capable of playing a pivotal role in improving our societies. The labour market is expected to be – in the minds of panellists – more respectful of personal and family life and gender equality (Dell'Anno et al. 2005).

As is already known, gender affects not only the quantitative aspect of participa-tion in the labour market, but also the conditions for participation. Amongst them, the quality of female work and working conditions are receiving heightened atten-tion at institutional level (European Commission 2002; European Parliament 2002). In this respect, Delphi panellists have expressed a specific need for increased attention.

As has been shown, although female paid work is largely recognised to be a fundamental instrument to ensure financial sustainability for families in Europe, there is still a certain degree of resistance to its growth due to individual atti-tudes (Philipov 2006) and to unfair practices still characterising work environments. These attitudes and practices impair the working conditions and the position reached by working women. In that respect, one widely-recognised solution is the improve-ment of family and work reconciliation. This issue has been widely discussed else-where (see also Palomba and Dell'Anno in Chapter 5) and – as we will see in Sec-tion 7.3.2 of the present chapter – a convergence has emerged amongst citizens and Delphi panellists indicating part-time work as a viable solution for improving the work-life balance.

The Delphi findings have provided valuable information on "women and work", allowing for a more accurate study of the relationship. In fact, Delphi panellists put forward a series of "corrections" needed to overcome some of the negative aspects of the condition of working women, aware that they are still in a "weak" position in the labour market.

Next, we will consider those Policy Objectives (POs) contained in the countries' Delphi scenarios in which paid female work was explicitly mentioned. Therefore, those POs that reached a consensus among the Delphi panellists, those that have been retained during the Delphi selection procedure, will be examined. In order to precisely address the issue of paid female work, we excluded some POs that, though related to the position of women in society, do not tackle the position of women in the workplace.[7]

The selected POs highlight a number of common issues that have recently entered the debate on the relationship between women and work and that have been included

---

[7] Here are some examples of the excluded POs: "support the right to self-fulfilment for men and women"; "policies that would overstep the marginal position of the woman in society", "increase female participation in social and political life"; "balance out the social weight of women and men"; "grant more opportunities to women"; "adopt specific legislation for the enhancement of women's participation in the social/political arena".

in the agenda of European institutions (European Foundation for the Improvement of Living and Working Conditions 2002). As a whole, a specific area of attention has emerged for the issue of gender equality.

POs such as "the promotion of women in leading positions" and "the establishment of equal opportunities in workplaces" highlight the need to implement specific actions to combat discrimination against women, both from an economic point of view and in terms of their difficulty in entering and remaining in the labour market.

As highlighted in Table 7.3, these Policy Objectives were common to many countries, while some national specificities emerged in others. It is the case of measures that make it possible to get back into the labour market after childbearing (Cyprus, Italy, Lithuania and Romania) or increased earnings in female-specific jobs (Austria). A special case appears to be Finland, where there are many POs aiming to improve the position of Finnish women in the labour market. In Finland, equal participation by men and women in the labour market – both in terms of the labour force participation rate and of the unemployment rate – and a low impact by parenthood on female working life have been achieved. Therefore, Finnish Delphi panellists have stressed specific topics (vertical segregation, temporary work contracts of young women, valorisation of female abilities, requirement of wage transparency, promotion of equal wages) that need to be dealt with and resolved (Hautaniemi 2004).

In conclusion, Delphi panellists called for a labour market in which women can occupy high-level managerial positions and are enabled to fulfil their potential in the same way as their male counterparts.

7.2.2.4 The Unresolved Issue of Gender Quotas

We have seen how the role and the status of women in future societies are considered key elements by the Delphi panellists.

In "real" and "dreamed" societies, the gender equity debate, both in the family, in the workplace and in politics, is a subject that raises strong interest but which

Table 7.3 Policy Objectives related to the position of women in the labour market

–	Increasing the earnings in female-specific jobs, (Austria).
–	Promoting women in leading/decision-making positions (Austria, Cyprus, the Czech Republic, Germany, Finland, Italy, the Netherlands and Romania).
–	Increasing the number of mothers who return to the labour market after giving birth (Cyprus, Italy, Lithuania and Romania).
–	Advancing equality in working life/Creating equal opportunities for men and women in the labour market/ Preventing gender discrimination in employment and at the workplace/Eliminating wage inequality between the genders (Austria, Germany, Estonia, Finland, Lithuania, Poland, Slovenia and Switzerland).
–	Encouraging women to take on a different kind of responsibility (Finland).
–	No longer making a distinction between female and male jobs (Finland).
–	Guaranteeing the permanency of the work contracts of young educated women (Finland).

Source: National Delphi Reports

is also controversial. The issue of the under-representation of women in top-level positions, as well as that of the policies needed to correct this imbalance – such as the introduction of gender quotas – should therefore not be absent from this analysis.

In fact, recent years have seen a surge of interest worldwide for provisions to increase the representation of women in top-level positions in the various sectors of society, including politics.

Although highly controversial, gender quotas are being introduced in an increasing number of countries around the world. In more than 50 countries, quotas for election to public office are now stipulated in the statutes of major political parties, demanding that a fixed minimum, often 30%, of the parties' candidates for election to national parliament must be women.

Underscoring the high level of controversy surrounding this issue is the fact that only Finland[8] has included the issue of a female quota in the labour market among the Policy Objectives for their 2030 scenarios. In all other countries, the problem has been addressed in the Controversial Policy Issues (CPI) section. While the issue has remained controversial in Cyprus, the unanimous opinion of the Delphi panellists from the other countries was to reject the adoption of quotas (Table 7.4).

This only confirms the ambiguity and difficulty which policy-makers must confront in dealing with an issue which seems to spark strong disagreement for measures "imposing" an increase in the numbers of women in top-level positions. However, the panellists' recognition of the need for action to counterbalance the weak position of women in the labour market is highly unambiguous. On the other hand, it is quite difficult to identify from PPA surveys a clear indication of citizens' attitudes towards the same issue since it has not been specifically addressed.

The high value that is attributed to the family and to children (NIDI 2005) would not seem to favour a broad consensus for more widespread involvement of women and mothers in the labour market, often a necessary pre-requisite for those who wish to occupy top-level positions. While a positive attitude is indeed emerging towards

Table 7.4 Controversial Policy Issues related to quotas in the countries where it was considered

–	Women's quotas should not be prescribed for the public service, Parliament and the provincial governments. (Austria)
–	Specific mandatory quotas for female employees in public institutions, in Parliament and the local governments should not exist. (Hungary)
–	Quotas should not be reserved for women in public sector offices, in Parliament, and in the regional authorities. (Germany)
–	Women's quotas should not be implemented in leadership positions. (Lithuania)
–	The percentage of women in Parliament should not be regulated by law. (Poland)
–	Legislation that will safeguard a quota of posts for women in the civil service, in Parliament and district authorities. (Cyprus, CPI on which a consensus has *not* been reached)

Source: National Delphi Reports

---

[8] The PO is: The equal participation of women and men at different levels of society, the related Key Success Factors: Gender quotas for companies' executive boards, boards of directors and the representative bodies of labour market organisations.

the recognition of gender equality (see Table 7.1), this could create some conflicts as these new rights for women are no longer just "theory" but must actually be implemented in daily life. A difference in the results between PPAS and Delphi seems to emerge, although it is important to note that the "time" factor may significantly influence this issue.

7.3 How Much Should Women Work?

The increasing diversification of working time schedules is one of the most recent and important changes in the employment structure in European countries. One of the most evident indicators of this is the rise in the rate of part-time work. The strengthening of international competition, new production methods and forms of organisation, increased unemployment, and rising female participation rates, contribute to this increase (Fagan 2003).

Part-time employment has been widely recognised as a tool for promoting market flexibility, for improving family policy and for redistributing existing employment (thereby reducing unemployment). From the employers' side, a spread of part-time work may provide greater flexibility in responding to market requirements. Working part-time may offer parents the possibility to better reconcile working life and care responsibilities. For policy-makers, the increase in part-time work may reduce the number of job-seekers (ILO 1997). EU employment policy papers explicitly encourage the social partners and public authorities to modernise the organisation of work by developing part-time work, as well as through other flexible working arrangements.

Information on reasons for choosing to work part-time clearly show that in a number of countries (such as Germany, Austria, the United Kingdom and Switzerland) a large percentage of adult women work part-time because of care responsibilities (towards children and the elderly). Part-time employment has been central to growth in employment today, especially for women (Jaumotte 2003). However, the trend shows differences across countries. The average proportion of part-time work declined significantly in the Nordic countries (due to women's transition to full-time jobs) and increased in some other European countries, excluding Central and Eastern Europe. Countries where this share is high comprise the Netherlands, Austria, Belgium and Germany. By contrast, the Central and Eastern European countries, as well as Finland, have a lower share of part-timers.

The PPAS and Delphi findings provide interesting insights into the preference of this type of employment.

7.3.1 The View of the Citizens: A Call for Part-time Working Arrangements

The preferred partnership-employment model in the majority of the PPAS countries is the dual-income couple/family. Major differences emerge within the two-income model when it comes to the preferences expressed concerning female working time arrangements: part-time (the modernised male breadwinner model) and full-time (the dual-earner model) (Table 7.5).

In Belgium (Flanders) and Italy, the majority of respondents prefer to combine women's part-time employment and men's full-time economic activity. The Central and Eastern European countries have a lower preference towards the modernised male breadwinner model than the Western countries. Romanians show the lowest level of preference with regard to the modernised male breadwinner model.

When examining differences between preferences and practices (Kotowska et al. 2006), greater demand was observed for better reconciliation of paid work and the family. This reconciliation was called for via an increase in the modernised male breadwinner model, even though that model is more commonly desired than practised in all countries but the Netherlands. The differences are visibly stronger in Italy, Belgium (Flanders) and Lithuania despite the fact that this model is more frequently adopted in Italy and Belgium (Flanders) than in post-socialist countries.

The PPAS results highlight the fact that in the DIALOG countries the incidence of part-time work amongst respondents varies considerably from on country to another country. The discrepancy between preferences and practices is much higher in the case of the modernised breadwinner model compared with the other two. Last but not least, the results showed unmet demand for part-time work for women and mothers, apart from in the Netherlands.

It should be noted that in the DIALOG project the subject of part-time work has not only been called for to address the work-life balance issue, but also as a measure to improve European family policies. As a matter of fact, this measure is one of those which attracts the highest level of support: 86% of European citizens interviewed are in favour of improving opportunities to work part-time (Esveldt and Fokkema 2006). This result confirmed the high level of interest that the population

Table 7.5 Preferences concerning partnership-employment models, countries ranked by modernised male breadwinner model (%), men and women living in a couple with the woman aged 20–49

Country	Male breadwinner model	Modernised male breadwinner model	Dual-earner model
Belgium (Flanders)	12.0	53.7	34.3
Italy	19.4	51.7	28.9
Netherlands	27.8	30.9	41.3
Cyprus	23.1	30.6	46.3
Lithuania	45.9	28.8	25.3
Slovenia	17.6	26.1	56.3
Poland	23.1	22.5	54.4
Estonia	22.6	22.0	55.4
Romania	6.2	14.6	79.2

Source: Kotowska et al. 2006

attached to this type of job. It is nevertheless important to be aware of the possible drawbacks which part-time work may entail regarding job stability, wage level, and career opportunities (Kotowska et al. 2006).

7.3.2 Part-time Working: Findings from the Delphi Study

Considering the importance attached to part-time working by both citizens and European institutions, it does not come as a surprise that this issue frequently appears as a policy action to be sustained in the future Europe. Out of the 14 participating countries, Delphi panellists from Austria, Belgium (Flanders), the Czech Republic, Germany, Hungary, Italy, Lithuania, the Netherlands, Poland, Slovenia and Switzerland collectively called for an increase in the number of part-time jobs. By contrast, panellists in Cyprus, Estonia and Finland wished to observe growth in flexi-time opportunities; only in Romania did neither part-time nor flexi-time arrangements appear as suggested measures.

The increase in part-time employment was pointed out as a tool to correct a variety of problems, ranging from restructuring the labour market, through the work-life balance to an increase in the fertility rate. In five countries, the enhancement of part-time working is a key element for a better work-life balance, and in two countries it is explicitly aimed to increase the number of births (Germany and Poland).

If we look at the importance of part-time working, besides the problems related to child rearing and work-family reconciliation, we find that this working arrangement plays an important role in the attainment of other relevant Policy Objectives. In fact, part-time working is considered a useful measure to promote work opportunities amongst the elderly (Austria); to obtain a flexible transition from working life to retirement (Switzerland and the Czech Republic), and to fight family poverty (Switzerland). According to these approaches, part-time working is seen in a broader perspective that goes beyond the association with women's work-family reconciliation. It can be used to counteract early retirement, to guarantee a smooth transition from working life to retirement, and to sustain the pension system.

How to promote part-time working? According to the Delphi findings, different actions might be put forward. Lithuanian Delphi panellists favoured fiscal measures (to grant tax relief to employers who create flexible part-time posts) as well as awareness campaigns (a change in employers' attitudes, creating an awareness that part-time working is important for society). Polish panellists aimed at changing the economic value of part-time working (the productivity of part-timers is higher than that of full-time workers), while Slovenian Delphi panellists opted for legislative support (facilitate a shift from full-time employment to part-time employment). Slovenian Delphi panellists additionally took into account an aspect frequently mentioned and related to the economic consequences of opting to work part-time: The panel concurred with the statement to "consider part-time working (six hours per day) as full-time employment in terms of pension insurance entitlements" in order to counteract the low level of pension benefit which part-timers might accrue.

A further suggestion related to the promotion of part-time working among fathers. The latter represents an interesting finding. From one side, it underscored the desire to see fathers increasingly involved in child-rearing activities and contributing to work-family reconciliation, whilst from the other it suggested the possibility to de-genderise part-time work. In fact, as is well known, this type of work is not widespread among the male population, the only exception being the Netherlands. Delphi panellists in Germany, Italy, Hungary, Poland, the Netherlands, Slovenia and Switzerland have explicitly indicated male part-time work as one of the policy actions to be implemented in the future. It is worth noting the position of the Dutch panellists, who do not link part-time work to caring activities but see it as a tool for achieving other policy objectives. In the Netherlands there seems to be a convergence with the PPAS respondents, who did not call for even more part-time working in order to combine work and parenthood.[9]

In conclusion, we observe that the majority of European Delphi panellists imagine that increasing the level of female part-time working is an adequate policy measure to sustain the reconciliation between work and caring/family responsibilities. In this respect, a convergence emerged with the ideals of citizens and the measures which they call for. Some differences did nevertheless emerge: Delphi panellists, in fact, calling for an increase in the number of part-time male workers, showed a more open attitude towards a change in gender roles. By contrast, PPAS respondents, having a tendency to consider part-time working as a working model suitable for women, appear to remain attached to traditional gender roles.

7.3.2.1 The Involvement of Fathers in Family Activities

Men's roles in domestic work in Europe have been extensively addressed in the countries participating in the Delphi study. In fact, the unequal distribution of domestic work affects the availability of men and women in the labour market. Some issues especially related to the role of fathers (and of men in general) in family life have therefore been included in many countries' Delphi studies.

The promotion of fathers in childcare activities reached a consensus in eleven out of 15 countries. Many policy actions intended to increase male participation within the family have been proposed. Some of these are the introduction/extension of parental leave to fathers (Austria, the Czech Republic and Finland), the elimination of stereotypes such as on the inability of fathers to effectively take care of children (Italy), tax relief for employers in order to encourage them to employ

---

[9] In fact, the Dutch Delphi panellists would like to see an increase in the number of part-timers among fathers in order to promote a "more equal division of work and care between women and men". The latter seems to be in line with the attitudes of Dutch respondents who have the least traditional opinion of the reversal of gender roles. Finally, Dutch Delphi panellists would like "To increase the number of working hours of women to a minimum of 28 hours per week", with the aim in mind of increasing women's economic independence. This priority might be due to the high level of women part-timers, which prevents them attaining an adequate standard of living (Esveldt 2004).

Part III
Gender Roles

Chapter 8
Family-related Gender Attitudes

The Three Dimensions: "Gender-role Ideology", "Consequences for the Family", and "Economic Consequences"

Dimiter Philipov

Abstract This article discusses gender attitudes of adults aged below 40 towards the division of labour in the family. It presents a comparative analysis of ten European countries. Three dimensions of gender attitudes are considered: gender-role ideology, family consequences and economic consequences of women's participation in work. The results indicate that modern gender roles, as described by the "gender ideology" dimension, are less prevalent in the former socialist CEE countries, as compared to Western European countries. Modern gender roles are least prevalent in familistic Italy, where the family consequences dimension is considered. Factors that have an effect on attitude formation do not reveal an explicit international pattern. Decreasing religiosity, higher education and women in work correlate positively with increasing preference in modern gender roles, but the results are not equal for the three dimensions. Intentions to become a parent seem to be correlated with the "gender ideology" and to a lesser extent with the "family consequences" dimension. In general, the gender-ideology dimension seems to best represent gender attitudes.

Keywords: Gender attitudes · Gender and family · Gender roles · Gender-role ideology · Gender and fertility intentions

8.1 Introduction

It has become customary in contemporary European societies for women to participate in the paid labour market, and frequently to do most of the household work as well. Women thus shoulder the dual burden of labour participation and work in the home, while this is rarely true for men. Gender inequality persists in family roles

D. Philipov
Österreichische Akademie der Wissenschaften – Institut für Demographie, Vienna, Austria
e-mail: dimiter.philipov@oeaw.ac.at

C. Höhn et al. (eds.), *People, Population Change and Policies: Vol. 2: Demographic Knowledge – Gender – Ageing*, © Springer Science+Business Media B.V. 2008

and chores. Women's dual burden is an obstacle to childbearing and childrearing. They may prefer to postpone or indeed may reject childbearing until they become well established in their jobs. As a result, births decrease, or come when the mother is older.

It is from this perspective that the population policy acceptance study (PPAS) integrated the gender dimension of the family. In principle, the PPAS covers different aspects of gender roles, but only some partner countries chose to include all of the gender role questions. The survey focuses on attitudes towards gender roles in the family, and to a lesser extent on attitudes towards governmental policies and gender practices in the family. This chapter deals with the first of these issues for persons aged between 20 and 40. The choice of this age group stems from the fact that it comprises people who are of peak child-bearing age, and hence gender differences can have a significant influence on family life. The gender items included in the PPAS form three main dimensions of gender attitudes: gender-role ideology, family consequences of women in paid work, and economic consequences of women in paid work. The main research aim in this chapter is to study in an international comparative perspective the three dimensions in the families of young European adults.

The three gender dimensions are first studied descriptively and then in a multivariate framework. They are subsequently tested for significance with regard to intentions to become a parent.

The study is based on a comparative analysis of the countries in which the gender module of the PPAS was implemented, namely: Austria, Estonia, Germany (broken down into its Western and Eastern regions), Hungary, Lithuania, the Netherlands, Poland and Romania. Limited information for Italy and Cyprus was also used in the descriptive analysis.

8.2 Theoretical Background and Research Questions

The division of labour in the family was polarized until several decades ago: The man was usually the single breadwinner, and the woman took care of the household tasks. Today this model of family care has lost its prevalence. It has become common for women to work for pay, and their contribution to the family income has become a must in an overwhelming number of European families. At the same time, women keep on doing most of the chores, and childcare in particular. A well-known dilemma has arisen: work or family? The incompatibility of career and motherhood is a particularly pronounced component of this dilemma. One solution of the latter could be achieved most conveniently by having fewer children, or indeed none at all. Another possible solution is the sharing of all household activities between the man and the woman. This is the gender attribute of the topic.

The compatibility of gainful employment and family labour is a multi-dimensional problem (Esping-Andersen 2002). In this paper we consider three dimensions of the gender roles in the family: ideological views, family consequences of women and men in work, and economic consequences of women and men in work. The gender emphasis in the three dimensions is placed on women.

Ideational changes that have taken place in contemporary societies during the last couple of decades refer to an overall shift from traditional to modern and post-modern values (Inglehart 1997). Where population issues are considered, this shift results in the second demographic transition, characterized by falling marriage and birth rates, rising divorce rates and non-marital cohabitation and a rise in extra-marital fertility (Lesthaeghe 1995). Changes in the value systems towards a rise in post-modern values are described by Lesthaeghe and Surkyn (2002) as: (i) accen-tuation of individual autonomy; (ii) rejection of all forms of institutional control and authority; and (iii) rise in expressive values connected to self-realisation, self-fulfilment and the quest for recognition.

Individual autonomy implies that people take independent decisions regarding their personal lifestyles and biographies and remain independent from other indi-viduals and institutions. Economic autonomy is essential for this purpose, particu-larly for women. Rejection of institutional control is an important means to achieve individual autonomy. Thus, a decision to have a child or a decision to work rather than stay at home as a home-carer becomes less influenced by social norms, the Church and other institutions. The rise in the desire for self-fulfilment and recog-nition is also a significant motive for women's labour force participation. Hence, each of the three components of ideational change supports women's decisions to participate in gainful employment. The conflict can be partially resolved by equal sharing of household work between men and women (see also Oppenheim-Mason and Jensen (1995).

When women spend time with their children, they contribute to higher child quality through better health, development of higher abilities and skills, and mainte-nance of selected social contacts. This work is known in New Home Economics as home production (Becker 1981). Hence, the family consequences, particularly for the children, of the mother being in work may be reflected in lower child quality. Joshi (2002) gives a recent detailed analysis for British women (see also Gornick and Meyers 2003).

The economic consequences of women in work include an increase in the house-hold income, and achievement of economic autonomy for women. The latter is nec-essary not only to accomplish individual autonomy: In times when unions are less stable, economic independence is crucial for women who may become single once more, even if only temporarily. A woman's earnings will obviously no longer con-tribute towards the household income if she stays at home to look after the children. The higher the earnings, the higher the opportunity costs of childrearing (Becker 1981).

The above description indicates the importance of two major theoretical ap-proaches: that of ideational shifts, and an economic one. We view the dilemma of work and family from these two theoretical points of view.

In this paper, we discuss attitudes towards gender roles in the family that consider primarily the compatibility of careers and family. We will analyse gender-related attitudes by asking the following questions:

Do contemporary gender-role attitudes include an ideational component? How do people perceive the consequences of the contemporary egalitarian gender roles for the family? What are their attitudes to the economic consequences?

The research is based on international comparative analysis. The former socialist countries of Central and Eastern Europe form a special group in this analysis. They had a centralised market structure and state-promoted gender equality in labour participation. Hence, gender attitudes might be expected to bear certain special features in this part of Europe (Jahnert et al. 2001). The following research question suggests itself:

How do countries in Europe differ with regard to gender role attitudes? In particular, do people in the former socialist Central and Eastern European countries have any specific gender-related attitudes compared to other European countries?

To provide a better outline of the former socialist countries, we divide Germany into two parts: Western and Eastern, as is often done in demographic analyses (Braun et al. 1994; Rosenfeld et al. 2004).

The PPAS survey was not conceptualized as a tool for testing specific demographic theories. Therefore, some other relevant theories cannot be addressed with the available data. By way of example, Hakim (1999) argues that women have different preferences for work and family, and she distinguishes between three models of the family on that basis. McDonald (2000a) raises the hypothesis that fertility is lower in societies where institutional gender equality is achieved but gender practices remain traditional, and that it is higher where both institutional gender equality is high and gender practices are uniform.

Numerous authors identify the connectivity between welfare state regimes and aspects of gender equality (e.g. Esping-Andersen 1999; Korpi 2000; Sainsbury 1996; Geist 2005; Gauthier 2002). However, due to the limited number of DIALOG countries for which data on gender are available, the data are not a sufficiently solid base for a comparison of gender attitudes by welfare state regimes.

8.3 Measurement of Gender Issues in the PPAS: Methodological Considerations

The PPAS studies attitudes towards gender roles in the family by using a specified gender module that contains 14 items. Three of them remained unused.[1] Each item is a question regarding the attitude towards a specific gender role, and the answer is categorised with a Likert scale (completely agree, agree, neither agree nor disagree, disagree, completely disagree). The eleven items are presented in Table 8.1.

---

[1] One was not used because the respondents showed virtually unanimous disagreement (item G2e in the PPAS questionnaire). The other two were not used because they do not match, at least statistically, any of the three dimensions used in the study (items G1h and G2f).

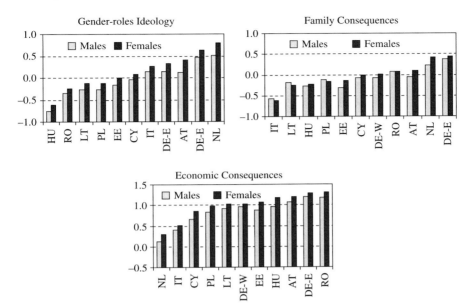

Fig. 8.1 Means of composite variables representing three gender dimensions, males and females aged below 40, countries ordered by magnitudes for females

value of a mean is +2 and the minimum is –2. Means below 0 indicate that traditional gender role values are dominant in comparison to contemporary ones.

The panel in Fig. 8.1 that charts the gender ideology dimension shows a significant difference between the ten countries. Lower means are observed in the former socialist countries, and particularly in Hungary, which implies that acceptance of women's traditional gender roles is more prevalent in these countries than in the Western countries. The mean is considerably higher in the latter, and in the Netherlands in particular. Eastern Germany is an exception to the group of former socialist countries with its position next to the Netherlands. The figure also shows that men hold more traditional attitudes towards gender ideology than women, and this holds true for all countries. It is also observed that the means are lower than zero in the countries of Central and Eastern Europe, which indicates a prevalence of traditional attitudes over modern ones. The means are close to zero in the two Southern European countries, while in the Western countries they are significantly higher than zero. In the latter countries there is therefore a prevalence of contemporary attitudes towards gender roles relative to traditional ones.

The means corresponding to the family consequences dimension reveal a slightly different picture. Italy is the country in which the respondents have the most negative perception of the consequences of women's work for the family. The group of the former socialist countries follows, with respondents from Cyprus and Western Germany being slightly more negative than Romanians. Negative family consequences are expressed least frequently in the Netherlands and Eastern Germany. Differences between men and women are not as explicit in this dimension as in the previous case, and in some countries there are no such differences. The means are lower than or close to zero in all countries except the Netherlands and Eastern Germany. Hence, in only one country and one part of Germany do we observe the predominance of perceptions that women's work does not bring about negative consequences for the family.

The strong prevalence of traditional family values in Italy is well known (Dalla Zuanna and Micheli 2005). We find that they have a significant affect on the family consequences dimension of gender roles.

The economic consequences dimension reveals a different country pattern. The Netherlands is the country in which the economic consequences of women's work are assessed as being the least significant. Gender attitudes in this country are less bound to the economic consequences as compared to other countries. This is likely to be the result of the combined action of social and gender-related policies which do not require women to work in order to achieve autonomy, or to support their families. We also note low values of the means in Italy and Cyprus. It is most likely that the familistic culture that is dominant in Southern Europe is disassociated from the perception of a necessity for women to work. Unlike in the previous two dimensions, the Netherlands and Eastern Germany are divided towards the polar positions in the range of countries. The differences in the attitudes of men and women are visible in this dimension, although they are not as large as in the gender ideology dimension. The means are all higher than zero, thus indicating a full prevalence in Europe of the positive assessment of the economic consequences of women's work.

Next we present comparisons of the three dimensions. We concentrate on women only because the inferences for men are similar.

Figure 8.2 exhibits the three graphs for the dimensions from Fig. 8.1 related to females. A salient finding is that the economic dimension is considerably higher than the other two, except for the Netherlands. The difference is greatest in the CEE countries, as well as in Italy, Austria and Western Germany, where the family consequences dimension is considered. Another observation is that the differences between the gender role ideology dimension and the family consequences dimension are not very great, except for Italy, and the latter is placed slightly below the former.

8.5 Multivariate Analyses of the Three Dimensions

In the present section we use three regression equations, where the dependent variables represent the gender dimensions, differently constructed as compared to the composite variables described above. The difference is that instead of adding the items, principal factor analysis was used. We retain one factor for each dimension separately, and this factor is the desired dependent variable. Similar to the compos-

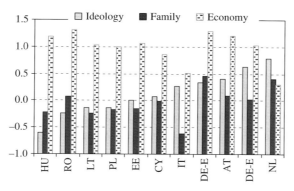

Fig. 8.2 Three gender dimensions: Gender role ideology, family consequences and economic consequences, for females aged below 40

ite variables discussed in the previous section, an increase in the value of a factor denotes an increase in acceptance of modern gender roles.[4]

Since the three dimensions are interrelated from a theoretical point of view, as mentioned above, it can be expected that the error terms in the regression equations will be correlated. Hence it is convenient to apply seemingly unrelated regression (SURE).

The explanatory variables are the same within each country for the three regression equations. Hence, SURE gives the same asymptotically-unbiased coefficients as the ordinary regression (Greene 2000). By applying SURE we obtain more information on the correlation of the errors in the three equations. This is a preferred approach to study the correlation between the three dependent variables because the inclusion of one or two of them as explanatory variables in the equation of the third one would make them endogenous. The correlation of the errors can provide information on the effect that a sudden change, such as a shock, in the circumstances defining one variable will have on the other variables.

The list of explanatory variables is short because of significant incompatibility of other variables among the countries. We retained the following ones:

- *Age*. It increases from 18 to 39.
- *Marital status*. Three marital states are considered: married, cohabiting, and single. The first of these is taken as a base.
- *Number of children*. All the respondent's children are considered, regardless of whether they are biological, step-children or adopted.
- *Religiosity*. It is measured with the question: "What role does religion play in your life: (i) very important role, (ii) important role, (iii) not an important role, (iv) no role at all." The variable is taken as continuous, and it measures decreasing religiosity. Thus measured, religiosity is subjectively self-assessed.

---

[4] The results of the factor analyses were sometimes unsatisfactory in that the uniqueness of some items was undesirably high. The last item in the gender ideology dimension, which refers to men, was not used because it was insignificant (uniqueness usually above 0.90 and factor loading much smaller than that of the other items).

- *Working status.* This variable is constructed on the basis of the information available in the questionnaires. Two states are considered: working (base category), and not working. Information on employment is insufficient and cannot be used in this analysis.
- *Education.* It is measured in three levels: below secondary, secondary completed, and higher than secondary. Compatibility of education among different countries is a standard problem in international comparative analyses. The PPAS database includes recoded variables that overcome problems of incompatibility as far as possible. We use the recoded variable for education.
- *Equivalised household income.* We use a variable available in the dataset. It is measured in the local country's currency (the surveys were carried out before the introduction of the Euro). As a result, the estimated coefficient in the equations is very small because it reflects the effect of an increase in income by one unit (for example one Shilling in Austria). We present it multiplied by 1,000.

The set of explanatory variables differs among the countries because some of them were not measured. (Income was not measured in Estonia, Lithuania and Romania; number of children and religiosity were not measured in Romania, and cohabitation was not measured in Poland.). They are the same for the three equations within a country. Hence, the estimated coefficients are the same as when applying ordinary linear regression. Through the seemingly unrelated regression we achieve more information on the correlation of the errors.

Tables 8.3 and 8.4 display the coefficients for the three equations for eight countries where gender attitudes were measured. The results in the tables indicate a number of inferences that are worthy of note, although they are difficult to systematise. We discuss the coefficients of the explanatory variables in sequence. In this discussion we disregard the magnitude of the coefficients and consider only their signs: A positive sign means that an increase in the corresponding variable is associated with an increase in acceptance of modern gender roles, and a negative sign indicates an association with increased acceptance of the traditional gender roles.

Age is statistically significant in few countries as regards men. An increase in age in Austria and Western Germany is positively related to an increase in acceptance of more egalitarian gender roles (the first dimension). The Netherlands can be added to the list with its positive coefficient, although it is not statistically significant. This completes the list of Western European countries. Estonia and Hungary join this list, while men in the remaining Central and Eastern European countries reveal decreasing acceptance of egalitarian roles with advancing age, although this inference only takes on statistical significance in Romania. Approximately the same association is also observed in the other two dimensions, although statistical significance is rarely achieved and, if it is, for other countries than those cited above.

Age is more frequently statistically significant for women. The negative sign in the gender roles ideology dimension shows that older women are less inclined to accept egalitarian gender roles in Austria, Lithuania and Poland, but that they are more egalitarian in Eastern Germany and Hungary. Converse signs for age are

Table 8.3 Seemingly unrelated regressions for three gender dimensions, males aged below 40

	AT	EE	DE-E	DE-W	HU	LT	NL	PL	RO
Dimension 1: Gender ideology									
Age × 100 (increasing)	1.82[b]	0.16	−0.53	2.20[b]	0.95	−0.01	0.44	−0.46	−1.18[b]
Marital status:									
− married (base)	0	0	0	0	0	0	0	0	0
− cohabiting	0.28[a]	−0.11	0.15	−0.19	0.00	0.16	0.06	(dr.)	0.07
− single	0.12	−0.02	0.28[c]	−0.18	0.17	−0.01	−0.09	0.08	−0.07
Number of children	−0.01	0.01	0.11[c]	−0.06	−0.04	−0.12[b]	0.03	0.01	–
Religiosity (decreasing)	0.01	0.08[c]	0.10	0.10[c]	0.06	0.27[a]	0.09[b]	0.04	–
Working status:									
− works (base)	0	0	0	0	0	0	0	0	0
− does not work	0.39[a]	0.07	−0.19[c]	0.20	0.09	−0.15[c]	0.45[a]	−0.06	0.09
Education:									
− lower than secondary	0.16	0.02	−0.16	−0.08	−0.34[a]	−0.09	−0.14	−0.09[c]	−0.26[a]
− secondary (base)	0	0	0	0	0	0	0	0	0
− higher than secondary	0.01	0.13[c]	0.26[b]	0.17[c]	0.14	0.02	0.23[a]	0.24[a]	0.04
Income (× 1000)	0.19[a]	–	0.10	−0.06	0.93	–	0.01	–	−0.17
Dimension 2: Family consequences									
Age × 100 (increasing)	−0.29	0.02	−0.97	1.49	−0.94	−1.77[c]	1.20	−0.34	−2.31[a]
Marital status:									
− married (base)	0	0	0	0	0	0	0	0	0
− cohabiting	0.14	−0.04	−0.18	0.00	0.18	0.34[c]	−0.10	(dr.)	0.28
− single	0.00	0.06	−0.13	−0.05	−0.05	0.06	−0.10	0.07	−0.16

Table 8.3 (continued)

	AT	EE	DE-E	DE-W	HU	LT	NL	PL	RO
Number of children	-0.03	-0.06	0.10	-0.05	-0.14[b]	-0.13[b]	-0.06	-0.02	—
Religiosity (decreasing)	0.00	0.13[b]	0.15[c]	0.18[a]	0.15[a]	0.12[b]	0.11[b]	-0.02	—
Working status:									
− works (base)	0	0	0	0	0	0	0	0	0
− does not work	0.04	-0.09	0.03	0.05	-0.09	-0.15	0.34[b]	0.10[b]	-0.24[c]
Education:									
− lower than secondary	0.28[c]	-0.34[b]	-0.23	-0.15	-0.10	0.33[b]	-0.28[b]	-0.05	0.04
− secondary (base)	0	0	0	0	0	0	0	0	0
− higher than secondary	0.08	-0.09	0.09	0.10	0.05	0.14	0.16	0.11	0.22
Income (× 1000)	0.08	—	0.18	-0.01	-0.34	—	0.02	—	0.29
Dimension 3: Economic consequences									
Age × 100 (increasing)	1.45	1.65[b]	-0.94	0.98	1.07	0.45	0.27	-0.10	-0.70
Marital status:									
− married (base)	0	0	0	0	0	0	0	0	0
− cohabiting	0.10	0.22[b]	0.22[c]	0.07	-0.01	0.05	0.02	(dr.)	0
− single	-0.14	0.07	0.00	0.11	0.19[b]	-0.10	-0.02	-0.04	-0.44[b]
Number of children	-0.15[a]	-0.10[b]	0.10	0.03	-0.01	0.08	-0.07	0.04	-0.15
Religiosity (decreasing)	-0.07[c]	0.01	0.09	0.14[a]	0.08[b]	-0.03	0.05	0.02	—
Working status:									
− works	0	0	0	0	0	0	0	0	0
− does not work	0.11	-0.07	-0.28[b]	0.06	-0.02	0.00	-0.10	0.14[a]	0.23
Education:									
− lower than secondary	-0.12	0.13	0.24	-0.11	-0.02	0.27[b]	0.02	-0.02	-0.13
− secondary (base)	0	0	0	0	0	0	0	0	0
− higher than secondary	-0.25	-0.03	-0.11	-0.25[a]	-0.17	-0.14[c]	-0.02	0.04	0.14
Income (× 1000)	0.16[c]	—	0.00	-0.06	0.25	—	0.01	—	-0.30
N	263	263	189	224	290	273	251	994	214

Note: Emboldened text indicates statistical significance: [a] p > 0.015; [b] p > 0.055; [c] p > 0.105

Table 8.4 Seemingly unrelated regressions for three gender dimensions, females aged below 40

	AT	EE	DE-E	DE-W	HU	LT	NL	PL	RO
Dimension 1: Gender ideology									
Age × 100 (increasing)	-1.26[c]	-0.86	1.48[c]	0.19	1.82[b]	-2.31[b]	-0.51	-0.82[b]	-0.31
Marital status:									
– married (base)	0	0	0	0	0	0	0	0	0
– cohabiting	0.05	-0.03	0.33[a]	-0.08	0.00	-0.32[b]	-0.23[a]	(dr.)	-0.23
– single	0.10	0.08	0.13	0.15	0.12	-0.12	-0.20[b]	0.11[b]	0.13
Number of children	0.09[b]	-0.14[a]	-0.03	-0.01	-0.12[b]	-0.17[a]	-0.08[c]	-0.03	–
Religiosity (decreasing)	0.01	0.05	0.08	0.17[a]	0.06	0.06	0.14[a]	0.06[b]	–
Working status:									
– works (base)	0	0	0	0	0	0	0	0	0
– does not work	-0.11	-0.15[b]	-0.10	-0.17	0.05	-0.13	-0.15[b]	-0.12[a]	0.03
Education:									
– lower than secondary	-0.28[a]	-0.10	-0.02	-0.20	-0.19[b]	-0.02	0.04	-0.16[a]	-0.23[a]
– secondary (base)	0	0	0	0	0	0	0	0	0
– higher than secondary	0.48[a]	0.06	0.52[a]	0.47[a]	0.15	0.30[a]	0.27[a]	0.20[a]	0.10
Income (× 1000)	0.08	–	0.03	-0.01	1.46[a]	–	0.00	–	1.35[a]
Dimension 2: Family consequences									
Age × 100 (increasing)	0.12	1.91[c]	-0.67	0.99	1.37	-1.95[c]	-0.98	-0.73[c]	-0.46
Marital status:									
– married (base)	0	0	0	0	0	0	0	0	0
– cohabiting	0.05	0.17	0.12	0.04	0.09	-0.01	-0.15	(dr.)	0.08
– single	-0.03	0.17	0.09	0.40[a]	-0.02	0.01	0.01	0.04	-0.08

Table 8.4 (continued)

	AT	EE	DE-E	DE-W	HU	LT	NL	PL	RO
Number of children	0.01	−0.19[a]	−0.11[c]	−0.02	−0.04	−0.02	−0.02	−0.03	—
Religiosity (decreasing)	0.00	0.14[a]	0.14[b]	0.15[a]	0.08[c]	0.05	0.19[a]	−0.01	—
Working status:									
− works (base)	0	0	0	0	0	0	0	0	0
− does not work	−0.19	−0.04	−0.13	−0.19	0.13	−0.12	−0.47	−0.10	−0.07
Education:									
− lower than secondary	−0.26a	−0.20	−0.04	−0.12	−0.22	0.48 b	−0.10	−0.02	−0.11
− secondary (base)	0	0	0	0	0	0	0	0	0
− higher than secondary	0.23 a	0.12	0.31 a	0.18 b	0.02	0.18 c	0.21 b	0.20 a	0.04
Income (× 1000)	0.08	—	−0.05	0.05	0.06	—	0.05a	—	0.57
Dimension 3: Economic consequences									
Age × 100 (increasing)	−0.11	0.06	−0.70	1.00	0.27	0.22	−1.19[b]	0.80[b]	−0.53
Marital status:									
− married (base)	0	0	0	0	0	0	0	0	0
− cohabiting	0.21[a]	0.06	0.12	0.10	0.00	−0.06	0.18[b]	(dr.)	−0.09
− single	0.11	0.04	0.07	0.23[b]	0.03	−0.01	0.18[b]	−0.03	−0.05
Number of children	−0.07[c]	0.00	0.01	−0.06	−0.04	0.00	0.03	−0.04[c]	—
Religiosity (decreasing)	0.03	0.05	0.09[c]	0.06	0.04	0.00	0.09[a]	−0.01	—
Working status:									
− works	0	0	0	0	0	0	0	0	0
− does not work	−0.08	−0.19[a]	−0.15[c]	−0.07	0.01	0.02	−0.34[a]	−0.03	−0.07
Education:									
− lower than secondary	−0.01	−0.02	−0.27[b]	0.05	0.04	−0.07	0.13[c]	−0.02	0.19[b]
− secondary (base)	0	0	0	0	0	0	0	0	0
− higher than secondary	−0.02	−0.05	−0.22[a]	−0.12	−0.04	−0.01	−0.03	−0.08	−0.11
Income (× 1000)	−0.08	—	0.00	−0.11	−0.10	—	−0.01	—	0.43
N	412	414	275	276	361	323	324	1099	246

Note: Bold indicates statistical significance: [a]p > 0.015; [b]p > 0.055; [c]p > 0.105

observed in the other two dimensions as well, although the variable is statistically significant in a smaller number of countries.

The marital status of men is rarely a significant determinant of gender attitudes. The statistically-significant coefficients are positive with one exception (Romania), which indicates that cohabiting or single men are more amenable to modern gender roles as compared to married men. The marital status of women is also infrequently statistically significant. It is worth noting that non-married women in the Netherlands are likely to have more traditional attitudes towards gender ideology as compared to married women, but that the inverse correlation is observed where the economic consequences are considered. This and several other country-specific observations require more extensive study.

The number of children takes on an explanatory value in two countries for each dimension where males are considered. However, it is frequently significant among women in the explanation of gender ideology. With the exception of Austria, in all the other countries the coefficient of this variable has a negative sign for this dimension: A larger number of children is associated with more traditional perceptions regarding gender roles as far as the ultimate role of women in the family is considered.

Religiosity goes a long way in most of the countries towards explaining the phenomenon which has been observed. For both men and women, a fall in religiosity relates to an increase in acceptance of modern gender roles, and to a reduced degree of concern when it comes to family and economic consequences of modern gender roles. The association is most frequent for the "family consequences" dimension. Although statistical significance is not observed in any of the three dimensions for Austrian and Lithuanian women, the positive values of the coefficients indicate that the same association is likely to hold.

The effect of men's employment status is rarely significant, and the direction of the association with a gender dimension sometimes differs from one country to another. The effect of women's employment status takes on a more detailed structure. The coefficient is negative in all cases, which indicates that non-working women are more inclined than working women to hold to traditional gender roles in all three gender dimensions.

Education is another variable with a well-structured effect. In the "gender ideology" dimension, men and women with education higher than secondary are more likely to accept modern gender roles than those with secondary education, and the latter are more likely to do so when compared with persons having education lower than secondary. In brief, the higher the level of education, the more likely it is that a person will accept the contemporary gender roles. The only exceptions are observed among men in Austria and Lithuania, and among women in Estonia. The same inference is restricted to a smaller number of countries where the family consequences are considered. Interestingly, statistical significance for men with higher education is not observed in any country. The positive signs of the coefficients do however support the inference made for the first dimension. Statistical significance is not as widespread in the third dimension as in the other two. However, as the signs of the coefficients indicate, persons with higher education are more likely to accept negative economic consequences of women working than those with secondary education.

Equivalised household income is rarely significant, even for the economic consequences dimension. Its effect can be generally disregarded, with the exception of women's attitudes towards gender ideology in Hungary and Romania.

We discuss here one additional result not conveyed in Tables 8.3 and 8.4. We run the same regressions for respondents in both sexes with the inclusion of a variable on the sex of the respondent. We found that women in virtually all countries are more willing than men to accept the modern directions taken by gender roles in the three dimensions. The exceptions were found in Hungary, the Netherlands Poland and Romania for the "family consequences" dimension, and in Romania for the "economic consequences" dimension.

We used the same set of variables to study the three gender role dimensions. This provides us with an idea of how a change in one explanatory variable will effect each one of the three dimensions. Consider for example women in Western Germany (Table 8.3): An increase in education will be correlated with an increase in the acceptance of the egalitarian gender roles as reflected by the first dimension; it will have a minor impact in the same direction on attitudes related to family consequences, and a negative effect on attitudes related to the economic consequences of modern gender roles. The error terms of the three regression equations can have a similar effect. For example, an increase in the error term will increase attitudes towards egalitarian gender roles, and will at the same time have an effect (positive or negative) on the attitudes considered in the other two equations. It is therefore appealing to learn more about the correlation between the error terms. To this end, we applied the Breusch-Pagan test for independence of the residuals using Stata (StataCorp 2003).

We found in 17 out of 18 regressions (for nine countries and separately for males and females) statistical significance for $p = 0.001$, and statistical significance was achieved for Romanian males at $p = 0.03$. Thus, the overall correlation of the residuals supports the theoretical presumption as to the interrelated nature of the three dimensions.

Next we report the statistical significance for the three pairs of dimensions, estimated for each separate regression. Statistical significance is considered for $p = 0.05$. The ideology and the family consequences dimensions were found to be significantly correlated in all cases except for Austrian men (the p-value is 0.09). The correlation coefficients are higher for women as compared to men. The gender ideology and the economic consequences dimensions are not correlated, except for men in Western Germany and women in Estonia, the Netherlands and Romania. The family consequences and the economic consequences dimensions are correlated in about half of the regressions: for men in Austria, Estonia, Lithuania, the Netherlands and Poland, and for women in Austria, Eastern Germany, Hungary (p-value = 0.056), the Netherlands and Lithuania (p-value = 0.09). The correlations for Lithuanian men and Hungarian women have a negative sign.

How can we interpret these statistical findings? The error terms are frequently considered in statistics as describing a certain unanticipated change in the system of study. As an example, we may think of the adoption and introduction into practice of a new legal act. Supposing that such an act causes a rise in positive attitudes towards egalitarian gender roles, the statistical findings discussed in the previous paragraph tell us that there will be an increase in positive attitudes towards there being fewer family consequences when women work, and no change in attitudes towards economic consequences of women's work. Supposing that the legal act causes an increase in the positive attitudes towards there being fewer economic consequences, this change will not have an effect on attitudes towards gender ideology, and will only have a positive impact on attitudes towards family consequences in some countries. Finally, supposing that the legal act has a positive effect on attitudes towards family consequences, it will also have a positive impact on the gender ideology dimension, and in some countries on the economic consequences dimension. It emerges that an unexpected "shock" on the family consequences will have a greater impact on the other two dimensions in comparison with the impact of an unexpected shock on gender ideology or on the economic consequences dimensions.

8.6 Gender Attitudes and Desired Fertility

In a study of the gender dimensions of the family, it is important to learn about the association between gender attitudes and intentions to have children. To this end, we ran a logit model where the dependent variable referred to intentions to have or not to have a(nother) child, and the independent variables included those discussed in the previous section, as well as the three factor variables representing the three gender dimensions.[5] Respondents who were not certain of their answer to the question as to intentions to have a child were grouped together with those who answered with certainty that they did not want to have a(nother) child. Table 8.4 displays the results.

The preliminary runs of the model indicated that there was no statistically-significant effect of the three gender factors for intentions to have or not to have a second- or higher-order child. We therefore focus here only on intentions to have a first child, i.e. on the intention to become a parent in the first place. The application of the model requires several aspects to be explained. The number of respondents who are not determined to become parents at some point is relatively small from the point of view of a statistical model. The lowest number of such respondents was observed among Hungarian women (17 cases) and Estonian women (31 cases). Hence the results of the logit model are not as stable as we would have liked. We display in Table 8.5 the values of the coefficients for each of the gender factors and the corresponding p-values. All other variables are treated here as control variables. They include age, union status, religiousness, education, working status

---

[5] In a logit model the dependent variable can take on one of two values, in our case a positive or a negative intention to have a(nother) child. In the ordinary regressions the dependent variable is continuous.

and household equivalised income. Religiosity is considerably correlated with the gender factors, as it was found in the previous section; however, its removal from the set of explanatory variables does not have a significant effect on the results. The same inference applies to education. Here we only discuss the impact of the gender variables on the intentions to have a first child. Age is not a factor of primary significance for the intentions considered here. Were respondents aged below 35 instead of 40 considered here, the results of the model would not have changed considerably. A final comment refers to the interrelatedness of the gender factors that might influence the results of the model. Running the logit without any of the factors would have had a considerable impact on the results.

Apriori we would expect that an increase in the factor for gender ideology, i.e. an increase in the acceptance of modern gender roles, would correlate with lower intentions to ever become a parent, as far as the ideational theoretical approach indicates. We would therefore anticipate the coefficients of this factor to be lower than one. The second and third gender factors, corresponding to the "consequences for the family" and the "economic consequences" dimensions, can *apriori* be expected to be positively correlated to the intentions because an increasing value of the factor corresponds to the acceptance of a decrease in the consequences of the woman being in work. Hence we would expect the values of the coefficients to be greater than one.

The results shown in Table 8.5 indicate that the factor representing gender ideology is statistically significant in four countries: for Austrian men, Estonian women, both men and women in Western Germany, and men in Romania. However, the values of the coefficients for men in Austria and Western Germany are higher than one, thus indicating that men who are more inclined to accept modern gender roles are more willing to become parents. This result runs counter to a conventional understanding of the ideational theoretical approach. In the other three cases in which gender ideology was found to be significant in shaping intentions to become a parent, the coefficient is lower than unity, and thus concurs with the *apriori* expectations.

The second gender dimension, "family consequences", is significant for both men and women when it comes to the formation of intentions to become a parent in Hungary. The values of the coefficients are inverse for both sexes, again an observation for which there is no immediate explanation. Accepting a statistical significance indicated by a *p*-value of 0.12 would add women in Estonia here. The third dimension, "economic consequences", was not found to be significant in any country.

The overall results give some evidence that the gender ideology dimension is the most influential in the formation of intentions to become a parent. The economic consequences dimension is likely not to have any impact on the formation of these intentions, and the family consequences dimension were only found to be significant in Hungary. It is difficult to discern any pattern of country differences, except for the commonality of the impact of the ideological factor on men in Austria and Western Germany.

Table 8.5 Intentions to ever become a parent: odds ratios for three gender dimensions, men and women aged below 40 (by age, marital status, religiosity, working status, education, household equivalised income)

	Men		Women	
	coef.	P-value	coef.	P-value
Austria	$N = 146$		$N = 168$	
Ideology	2.17	0.02	1.54	0.28
Family consequences	1.04	0.95	1.07	0.88
Economic consequences	0.51	0.16	1.43	0.43
Estonia	$N = 176$		$N = 245$	
Ideology	1.37	0.52	0.20	0.01
Family consequences	0.83	0.53	1.61	0.12
Economic consequences	0.71	0.45	0.53	0.30
Germany, Eastern	$N = 91$		$N = 70$	
Ideology	1.14	0.79	1.78	0.29
Family consequences	1.32	0.54	1.09	0.83
Economic consequences	1.79	0.24	1.34	0.65
Germany, Western	$N = 70$		$N = 107$	
Ideology	1.75	0.08	0.41	0.07
Family consequences	0.64	0.23	1.12	0.79
Economic consequences	1.08	0.83	0.46	0.17
Hungary	$N = 119$		$N = 115$	
Ideology	0.53	0.15	0.58	0.36
Family consequences	3.19	0.01	0.24	0.03
Economic consequences	1.66	0.50	1.25	0.15
Lithuania	$N = 100$		$N = 72$	
Ideology	0.84	0.69	0.99	0.97
Family consequences	1.02	0.96	1.43	0.45
Economic consequences	1.11	0.84	1.44	0.52
The Netherlands	$N = 141$		$N = 153$	
Ideology	0.99	0.99	0.62	0.28
Family consequences	1.59	0.20	0.99	0.97
Economic consequences	1.40	0.47	1.32	0.50
Poland	$N = 546$		$N = 437$	
Ideology	0.95	0.79	1.17	0.38
Family consequences	0.90	0.54	0.10	0.82
Economic consequences	1.28	0.16	0.96	0.82
Romania	$N = 110$		$N = 94$	
Ideology	0.41	0.08	2.56	0.15
Family consequences	1.15	0.74	1.07	0.93
Economic consequences	1.06	0.87	0.14	0.33

8.7 Summary Conclusions

The results of our analysis suggest that the "gender ideology" dimension is the one that provides the most information as regards the attitudes of men and women towards gender roles, as against the "family consequences" and "economic consequences" dimensions.

A descriptive analysis of the data indicates that modern gender roles, as described in the "gender ideology" dimension, are considerably less prevalent in the CEE countries than in Western European countries. Moreover, mean values of the composite variables indicate that gender role ideology in the CEE countries is more traditional than modern on average, while in the Western countries it is more modern than traditional. Women are more orientated towards modern gender roles than men. The same inferences are less explicitly observed for the "family consequences" dimension, and even less so for the "economic consequences" dimension. However, the "family consequences" dimension indicates the predominance of traditional attitudes in a familistic country such as Italy. The "economic consequences" dimension is the one where respondents from all countries cluster towards agreement that economic consequences of work for women are rather positive than negative.

Next we carried out regression analyses that aim to explain the descriptive comparative observations. The results are not as satisfactory because no particular cross-country pattern could be traced. The regressions did not depict an unambiguous distinction among the three dimensions in the gender attitudes. It is worth noting that regressions do a better job of explaining phenomena among women than among men.

In general we find that age and marital status are not as depictive as it could be expected. In particular, we do not find convincing evidence that cohabiting persons have more modern attitudes than married or single persons. The findings indicate that the number of children correlates negatively with an increase in modern gender attitudes, and that this relationship is more pronounced in the gender ideology dimension. Decreasing religiosity relates positively with the increase in the modern orientation of gender attitudes, and this is mostly observed in the case of the family consequences dimension, but also in the ideology dimension. The same holds for the increase in education. Women not in work are more traditional than those who do work, whether full-time or part-time.

Gender ideology is more frequently significant in the shaping of intentions to become a parent than the family consequences dimension, while the economic consequences dimension was not found to be significant in any of the countries considered in the analyses. The gender ideology has an inverse effect on men's and women's intentions to become parents. While its effect on women is as expected, i.e. modern attitudes correlate with lower intentions to become parents, the inverse correlation is observed for men.

The study bears several caveats. The gender module has not been applied uniformly in all participating countries. The multivariate analyses include a restricted number of variables because of the cross-country incompatibility of the relevant data. Finally, extreme response and agreement bias may have a pronounced effect on the inferences.

It can be summarised that the gender ideology dimension of gender attitudes is of primary significance to gaining an understanding of gender issues related to work in the family and to gainful employment.

Chapter 9
Gender and Fertility

Attitudes Towards Gender Roles and Fertility Behaviour

Kerstin Ruckdeschel

Abstract Two hypotheses are tested in this contribution: (1) The existence of preference types related to the value-of-children and the emancipation dimension, showing a similar profile in a cross-national comparison. It was possible to confirm this
hypothesis. We found a home-centred preference type with high fertility intentions
and a work-centred type with lower intentions. (2) The relation between structural
opportunities provided by family and gender policy, and the gap between intended
and achieved fertility. It was also possible to prove this hypothesis at least partly.
Finally a positive impact of child oriented preferences on closing the gap between
intended and achieved fertility dominating structural opportunities was found.

Keywords: Gender · Preference type · Fertility · Fertility intentions · European
comparison

9.1 Introduction

Europe looks back at the end of the 20th century on a constant decline in fertility
rates taking place over a period of more than 50 years. At the same time, a fundamental change of values has taken place. The two developments come together
in the so-called theory of the second demographic transition. The perception of
the role of women in family and society has changed profoundly in the course of
this transition. The second wave[1] of women's emancipation in the 1960s led to a
growing participation of women in education and on the labour market, at the same

---

K. Ruckdeschel
Federal Institute for Population Research, Wiesbaden, Germany
e-mail: kerstin.ruckdeschel@destatis.de

[1] The equal rights movement at the end of the 19th and the start of the 20th century is generally
referred to as the first wave of modern feminism; younger feminists are calling themselves the third
wave.

C. Höhn et al. (eds.), *People, Population Change and Policies: Vol. 2: Demographic
Knowledge – Gender – Ageing*, © Springer Science+Business Media B.V. 2008

time caused by and further enforcing the change of values. Nevertheless, not all societal institutions changed, or if they did they did so only slowly, thus increasing the gap between individual, especially female expectations and structural opportunities. Women were confronted with competing demands from the family and from the labour market, and seem to have responded to this dilemma by reducing their fertility.

In this contribution, we would like to examine the connection between female orientations regarding gender roles and structural opportunities provided by family and gender policies, and their consequences for fertility. After a short introduction to the theoretical background, we present a typology of work-parenthood preferences, and compare the fertility of the different preference types. Finally, these results are examined in relation to country-specific structural opportunities in view of exploring the effects of family- and gender-related policies.

9.2 Theoretical Background and Hypotheses

9.2.1 Modern Gender Roles

Individual and societal modernity are not always developed to the same degree in modern societies. As Safilios-Rothschild (1970, 18) stated "even when a society is modern, it does not follow that all individuals in it are equally modern. On the contrary, individuals may be quite modern despite the fact that the overall society is still traditional", and vice versa. This applies especially to the perception of women's roles in society. For a long time, motherhood was at the core of women's self-perception, with a growing importance since the middle of the 19th century (Schütze 1991, 19ff.; Shorter 1975, 263 et seqq.). From then on, approximately until the middle of the 20th century, a lot of tasks formerly performed by women, e.g. in the context of household production or education, were assigned to other institutions, leaving only child and family care to the female realm. Accordingly, women's interest concentrated on children, the latter becoming the very meaning of female existence (Herwartz-Emden 1995; Schenk 1988). An idealised model of motherhood emerged where the "responsibility for mothering rests almost exclusively on one woman (the biological mother), for whom it constitutes the primary if not sole mission during the child's formative years." (Glenn 1994, 3). This changed with the feminist movement in the 1960s, when women, after having gained legal equality, also claimed full social and economic equality. In this process, it was becoming more important for a woman to be independent, i.e. to have a job and to have her own income. In the course of this "equal opportunities revolution" (Hakim 2002, 434), women increasingly obtained opportunities to choose what to do with their lives. Although there may still be obstacles, increasing numbers of women are accepting this idea and trying to live up to it. In the course of this change, motherhood became just one lifestyle option among others, even though still a very important one.

The changes mentioned above are related to two different value systems at the individual level: on the one hand women's increasing independence and ability to achieve self-realisation by leading their own lives, made possible by labour market participation, on the other hand the personal value of children. These two independent dimensions may be combined in several ways by the individual. Catherine Hakim (1999) developed a typology of individual lifestyle preferences of women which may be helpful in this respect. Based on the notion of women's free choice of lifestyle in modern industrialised societies, she presents a classification of three types of women's work-family preferences. The *home-centred woman* prefers home and family to work. The *work-centred woman* is characterised as career-oriented, or in a broader sense is defined as preferring something other than motherhood. Finally, the *adaptive woman* would like to combine motherhood and employment. Empirical data show that the adaptive type is the most common in modern societies, such as Great Britain, ranging from 40% to 60% of all women, whereas the other two types constitute significant minorities (Hakim 1999, 2001, 2002). The different value systems underpinning those types also become visible in their fertility. The work-centred type consists mainly of childless women, whereas we find mostly mothers among the home-centred type (Hakim 2002).

However, fertility is not only an outcome of individual preferences, but also of structural opportunities. Peter McDonald (2000a,b) documented the effect of differences in gender equity in social institutions on fertility. He concluded that fertility is low in countries where gender equality has developed to different degrees in different institutions, i.e. where it is low in family-oriented institutions and high in individual-oriented ones, e.g. the labour market. This happens because women have to meet different demands in those different spheres. Being regarded solely as an individual on the labour market means requests in terms of availability and mobility which are not compatible with the demands of a family.

Both family and gender policy determine the general framework for female labour market participation by regulating access to the labour market in legal as well as in normative terms. "Normative" in this context means the influence of social norms with regard to mothers' employment. Thus, women of the home-centred type may find that a more conservative family policy suits their ideals, while it may hinder the work-centred type in choosing how they would like to live. On the other hand, the work-centred type may feel happy with a family policy which enables women to participate constantly in the labour market whilst also having a family, something which may not fit the ideals of the home-centred type as well. This brings us back to the difference between societal and individual modernity, mentioned above. Depending on the match or mismatch of individual preferences and structural opportunities, women may adapt their actual fertility behaviour. In our case, depending on the match or mismatch of the work-family preference type and structural opportunities provided by family policy, women may be able to achieve their intended fertility (match), or may be forced to reduce their actual fertility compared with intended fertility (mismatch).

9.2.2 Fertility Intentions

In this contribution we would like to study the link between fertility and individual preferences. We cannot use fertility already achieved as a measure, since this may only give a partial picture of the total fertility to be expected. Furthermore, actual fertility is the outcome of previous attitudes, which may have changed in the meantime, and may no longer have any causal relation to other actual preferences. For that reason, we use the concept of *fertility intentions*. Fertility intentions are a measure of an individual's present attitudes, and can thus be linked to other attitudes held at the present time. However, fertility intentions, in contrast to actual fertility, are a weaker measure insofar as they indicate an intention with no guarantee of its realisation. If we suppose that in individual intentions the probability of their realisation is already considered by taking into account the individual's resources and structural opportunities, this peculiarity enables us to measure via intended fertility the individual evaluation of these external factors.

9.2.3 Hypotheses

The question to be addressed in the present contribution is whether differences in the match of individual preferences and structural opportunities lead to differences in achieved fertility compared to fertility intentions. We will develop a family-work preference typology slightly differing from Hakim's in order to show that the different preference types also differ in their fertility intentions. Our hypothesis is that the preference types do have different fertility intentions which are type-inherent. We therefore expect to find the same pattern of differences in all countries under study. However, the realisation of the intentions should strongly depend on the structural opportunities available in the respective countries, and should therefore differ from one country to another. To test these hypotheses, the aforesaid preference typology will be developed. Next, fertility intentions will be described, comparing actual with intended fertility. Finally, the findings will be related to structural opportunities in the respective countries.

9.3 Methods

A modified family-work preference classification will be developed on the basis of the information available in the IPPAS database. Since the main focus of the present analysis is on the perception of women's roles in family and society, and this perception varies widely between men and women, the analysis will be restricted to women only, leaving a comparison with men for another contribution. The second focus of interest concerns fertility intentions and their realisation, leading us to concentrate on women in their fecund age range. Accordingly, the analysis will be further restricted to women between the ages of 20 and 39. The upper boundary of

39 has been chosen because our interest lies in additional fertility intentions, which should have a chance of still being realised. The lower boundary is a question of data availability and comparability. Fertility intentions are computed as the sum of children already born, current pregnancy (+1) and additionally intended children. In our case, fertility intentions are measured via a clear affirmation, i.e. "don't know" answers are counted as "no additional children". This leads to rather conservative results, i.e. intended fertility will tend to be under – rather than overestimated.

The empirical part consists of a number of descriptive analyses the statistical significance of which is tested by means of ANOVA procedures if necessary. General linear modelling has been chosen for multivariate analyses (for further details see Schoenmaeckers, Callens, Vanderleyden in this volume).

9.4 Modelling of Family-work Preference Types

With regard to the two issues on which we would like to focus, i.e. the value of children and the importance attached to female self-realisation aside from the traditional role of women, we try to develop a typology which is as close to Hakim's as possible. Following her classification, women who assign higher subjective priority to their own children than to female self-realisation may be called "home-centred". Women who fully support the idea of the importance of female self-fulfilment and independence, mainly through labour force participation, may be called "work-centred". Women who consider both priorities as very important for their individual lives may be called "double performers". The latter represent only part of Hakim's so-called "adaptive" group, which is highly heterogeneous and includes all women not belonging to one of her other two categories. In contrast, we restrict the group to women who attach a high value to both children and emancipation and, therefore, this group takes on a different designation. In our own typology, we distinguish a fourth group, including all women who think neither of children nor of employment as their very first priority. Part of this category is found in Hakim's *adaptive type*, and part of it in her *work-centred type*, where she also places women with high aspirations in arts, sports, politics or similar fields (Hakim 2002, 435).

9.4.1 Measurement of the Two Preference Dimensions in the IPPAS

The items which we would like to use for constructing the family-work preference typology are not available for all countries. Therefore, only eight different countries can be included in the analysis. We nevertheless ultimately obtain nine cases because Eastern and Western Germany differ widely with regard to the dimensions under consideration, and are therefore analysed separately.

The classical value-of-children scale was applied in the IPPAS. Reliability analyses confirmed that the inclusion of all items of this scale was the best way to proceed in the further analysis and, moreover, guaranteed comparability. Nevertheless, in

some countries not all items were asked in the questionnaire and, therefore, the
scale had to be reduced to fewer items in those cases. Table 9.1 presents all items,
their availability in the respective countries, and Cronbach's alpha value for each
country.

Each item could be answered on a scale ranging from 1 "fully agree" to 5 "do not
agree at all". An index has been constructed using these items, once again ranging
from 1 to 5. This has been reduced to a bipolar variable, where women with values
in the upper third of the scale, i.e. between 1 and 2.5, were categorised as having
a high value-of-children, and all other women as having a low value on that scale.
The results for this dimension are shown in Fig. 9.1. As can be seen, the percentage
of women with a high score on the value-of-children index ranges from 80% in
Hungary to 10% in the Netherlands (Fig. 9.2). It seems to be especially high in ex-
communist countries and particularly low in the Netherlands. This result confirms
the findings of Dorbritz and Fux (1997) on the first PPA. Exceptional positions in
this range of countries are taken by Cyprus on the one hand, with a relatively high
score for a Western country, and by Estonia on the other hand, with a relatively low
score for an ex-communist country.

For the second dimension under consideration, the IPPAS includes a scale on
attitudes towards traditional gender roles.[2] This allows us to measure a modern

Table 9.1 Items of value-of-children dimension

	AT	EE	DE-E	DE-W	HU	LT	NL	PL	CY
The only place where you can feel completely happy and at ease is at home with your children	x	x	x	x	x	x	x	x	x
I always enjoy having children near me	x	x	x	x	x	x	x	x	x
You can be perfectly satisfied with life if you have been a good parent	—	x	x	x	x	x	x	x	x
I like having children because they really need you	x	x	x	x	x	x	x	x	x
It is your duty towards society to have children	x	x	x	x	x	x	x	x	x
You can not be really happy without having children	—	x	x	x	x	x	x	x	x
The closest relationship you can have with anyone is with your own child	x	x	x	x	x	x	x	x	x
Cronbach's Alpha	.774	.733	.804	.858	.696	.776	.762	.787	.776

Source: IPPAS; x available; - not available
AT Austria; EE Estonia; DE-E Eastern Germany; DE-W Western Germany; HU Hungary;
LT Lithuania; NL The Netherlands; PL Poland; CY Cyprus

[2] The IPPAS also includes a gender scale containing two items relating to the importance of female employment. An analysis of reliability however produced unfavourable results for this scale.

		Value of children	
		+	−
Emancipation	+	double performer	work-centred
	−	home-centred	others

Fig. 9.1 Family-work preference typology

concept of female self-realisation via the rejection of traditional role models. This dimension has been confirmed by separate factor analyses. Four items have been tested for their reliability, and as a result three items have been chosen to set up that scale. In order to ensure a certain degree of international comparability, countries with smaller Alpha have also been included in the analysis. The Netherlands and Cyprus only asked two out of the three items, and for Hungary factor analysis and reliability results led us to omit the third item also. The wording of the items, their availability and reliability are shown in Table 9.2.

An emancipation index has been built out of these three items in which women who strongly reject the idea of a life as a mother and homemaker are classified as high-scoring, i.e. they have a score of 3.5 to 5 on the index scale. The country results for the emancipation index produce a nearly perfect mirror image of the results for the value-of-children index. Hungary, Poland and Lithuania show the lowest proportion of women with a high score on that dimension, whereas the Netherlands and Western Germany are at the other end of the scale. This time there seems to be an even more perfect distinction between the Western countries and the Eastern, former socialist countries, with only one exception. Eastern Germany shows the

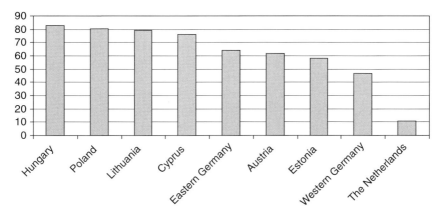

Fig. 9.2 Percentage of women aged 20–39 with a high score on the value-of-children index
Source: IPPAS

Table 9.2 Items of the emancipation dimension

	AT	EE	DE-E	DE-W	HU	LT	NL	PL	CY
What most women really want is a home and children	x	x	x	x	x	x	x	x	X
Being a housewife is just as fulfilling as working for pay	x	x	x	x	x	x	x	x	X
A man has to earn money; a woman looks after the home and family	–	x	x	x	–	x	–	x	–
Cronbach's Alpha	.708	.487	.722	.729	.593	.617	.408	.524	.624

Source: IPPAS

highest score on this scale. This can be explained in historical terms, given that during the socialist regime East Germany had one of the highest female labour participation rates among the socialist countries and even world-wide (Schneider 1994, 79), and social norms dating back to that period still appear to dominate individual orientations.

9.4.2 Constructing the Typology

Out of the two indices "value-of-children" and "emancipation", a family-work preference typology has been constructed according to which each woman was classified. The types should be seen as ideal types. Following Hakim's method, the typology consists of the types presented in Fig. 9.1:

a) *home-centred*, i.e. women with a high score on the value-of-children index and a low score on the emancipation index

b) *work-centred*, i.e. women with a high score on the emancipation index and a low score on the value-of-children index

c) *double performer*, i.e. women with a high score on both indices, the value-of-children index and the emancipation index

d) *other*, i.e. women with a low score on both indices, the value-of-children index and the emancipation index

The distribution of the four types in the respective countries is shown in Fig. 9.3. Once again, a clear distinction can be made out between so-called Eastern and Western countries. In Eastern countries, we find a clear dominance of *home-centred* women, with Hungary at the top. The three other types never account for more than approximately 10% of the respective population, and can be neglected in these countries except for Estonia. In Estonia the "others" category is rather strong in numbers. The proportion of home-centred women is much lower in the Western countries, and gives way to the other types with no clear dominance of either one. Home-centred women are a strong majority in Cyprus and Austria compared to the other

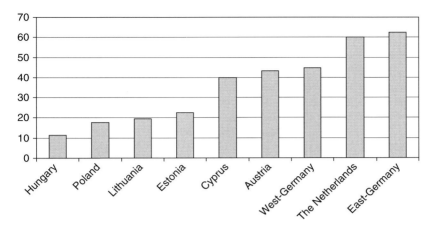

Fig. 9.3 Percentage of women aged 20–39 with a high score on the emancipation index
Source: IPPAS

Western countries. However, the next most important type in Cyprus is constituted by double performer women, whereas in Austria it is work-centred women. Eastern Germany is the only country where the double performer type is the most important, and home- and work-centred women take up nearly equal proportions. Finally, the Netherlands deviate from all the other countries. Here, the work-centred type is the most important one, whereas the numbers of double performer and home-centred women are negligible. In particular in the Netherlands, but also in Western Germany and Estonia, the "others" category is rather strongly represented. This category consists of women who rated high neither on the value-of-children scale, nor on the emancipation scale. This constitutes a sort of remainder category which is not relevant for the testing of our hypotheses. We will not therefore be exploring the preferences of this last type in this contribution.

9.4.3 Socio-demographic Characteristics of Preference Types

The three preference types under consideration can be expected to differentiate according to age and fertility, two major aspects of our analysis. Furthermore it is to be expected that the preference types also differ according to marital status insofar as marriage and children are still strongly interlinked in some of the countries. Finally, education has to be checked for, as it could be related to orientations towards a professional career.

Table 9.3 presents mean age and mean number of children, indicating significant differences between the preference types in the respective countries.[3] Regarding

---

[3] ANOVA procedure.

Table 9.3 Mean age, mean number of children, proportion married and proportion with higher education of preference types; women aged 20–39

	AT	EE	DE-E	DE-W	HU	LT	NL	PL	CY
Mean age									
Double performer	32.58	31.50	35.12	34.31	33.75	33.32	(35.20)	32.06	32.02
Home-centred	34.34	33.66	34.40	33.94	32.20	34.32	(36.47)	33.52	33.39
Work-centred	31.96	30.98	32.25	33.59	32.62	(31.19)	33.40	28.44	28.09
Diff.[a]	**	*	**					***	***
Mean number of children									
Double performer	1.37	1.21	1.38	1.29	1.28	1.43	(1.78)	1.48	1.50
Home-centred	1.76	1.65	1.34	1.40	1.64	1.69	(1.92)	1.92	1.83
Work-centred	1.00	0.89	0.77	0.73	1.00	(0.73)	0.89	0.89	0.71
Diff.[a]	***	***	***	***	**	***	***	***	***
% married									
Double performer	59	(43)	39	52	54	75	(78)	80	68
Home-centred	71	44	46	59	62	71	(75)	81	71
Work-centred	37	(23)	22	27	(41)	(46)	51	53	51
Diff.[b]	***	*	***	***	*	*	*	***	**
% with high (post secondary) education									
Double performer	33	(65)	38	41	(29)	82	(11)	24	57
Home-centred	12	43	20	22	10	65	(4)	15	32
Work-centred	60	59	46	49	(19)	(81)	49	(26)	75
Diff.[b]	***	*	***	***	***	*	***	**	***

Source: IPPAS

Note: () small numbers: n < 30; significance level: *< .05; **< .01; ***< .001; [a]ANOVA; [b]Chi^2

marital status and education, the proportion of women currently married and the proportion of women with post-secondary education is shown for the respective types.

We find significant differences in five out of the nine countries when it comes to mean age. However, in all countries, except in Hungary, it is always the work-centred type which is the youngest. The differences between the work-centred and the home-centred types are very small in Hungary, and are not significant. It is the home-centred type which is the oldest in six out of nine countries; this difference is statistically significant in three cases. The double performer type is oldest in the other three countries.

We find significant differences in all countries with regard to the mean number of children. Work-centred women have the lowest number of children everywhere. There is however some variation between the countries. The average number is as small as 0.71 for Cyprus, and reaches 1.00 for Austria and Hungary. The mean number of children for the other two preference types is higher. As could have been expected, it is always the home-centred type, defined as valuing children more highly than the other types, that has the largest number of children. Eastern Germany is an exception. Here, the double performer type has a slightly higher number of children. These results can mainly be explained by the differences in the mean ages of the respective preference types, as shown by an analysis of variance. However, the preference type also has a significant but small impact of its own (Appendix Table 9.8).

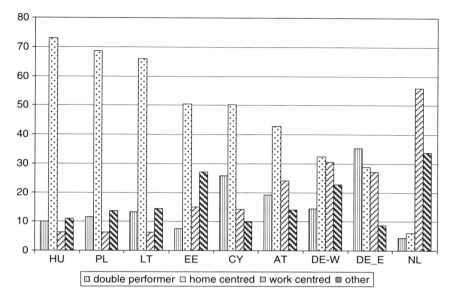

Fig. 9.4 Distribution of women according to the preference typology, ranked by proportion of "home-centred" women
Source: IPPAS

As far as marital status is concerned, a clear pattern can be distinguished here as well, i.e. the proportion of married people is much higher among home-centred than among work-centred women, whereas double performers often take an intermediate position. To check whether these results are type-inherent attributes or whether it is a simple age effect, a logistic regression model has been applied modelling the effect of age and work-preference type on the probability of being married. The results confirm a significant positive impact of age in all countries[4] and an additional significant negative impact of the work-centred type in six out of the nine countries (A, EE, D-E, D-W, LT, PL).[5]

Finally, higher education is also found more frequently among work-centred and least frequently among home-centred women, while double performers are again somewhat in between. Once again, logistic regression has been applied to test for age effects. This time, a significant effect for age could be observed in four of the countries (D-E, LT, NL, CY). In seven of the countries, the home-centred type had a significantly lower probability of having attained higher education (A, D-E, D-W, HU, LT, PL, CY) and in two countries the work-centred type had a significantly higher probability of having attained higher education (A, NL). This confirms our hypothesis that there is an interrelation between education and career aspirations.

---

[4] The higher the age the higher the chance of being married.

[5] Tables not shown.

These results give us a first idea of how to characterise the different preference types. While the home-centred type mainly includes married women with children, having attained a lower or secondary educational qualification, the work-centred type constitutes the opposite. The latter more often comprises women with higher educational attainment, has a smaller number of children, is less often married, and is on average younger than the other two types. The double performer type, finally, lies somewhere in between. Although there are age effects, the differences can also be traced back to type-inherent characteristics. While the pattern is similar for all countries, except for some outliers, the degree of difference can vary between countries.

9.5 Fertility Intentions of Preference Types and Their Realisation

9.5.1 Fertility Intentions of the Preference Types

The differences in the average number of children between the preference types are, as we have shown, partly caused by the differences in mean age. For our purposes, however, it is more interesting to know whether and if so by how much they differ in their fertility *intentions*. According to our hypothesis, intentions should be largely independent of country-specific structures and more inherent to the respective preference types themselves. Table 9.4 shows that fertility intentions follow the same pattern as already achieved fertility, i.e. work-centred women not only have fewer children than home-centred women, but also want fewer children in total. The differences are significant, except for Lithuania. However, although the pattern is the same for all countries, there are major differences in the level of intended fertility. In five of the countries under study, home-centred and double performer women would like to have more than two children on average. In Hungary, only the intended fertility of home-centred women is above two children. In the two regions of Germany, as well as in Lithuania, home-centred women would like to have fewer than two children on average. The threshold of two children is mentioned here because Bongaarts (2001, 277) calls it a crucial divide for the further development of fertility in Europe. In

Table 9.4 Intended fertility of preference types and realisation; women aged 20–39

	AT	EE	DE-E	DE-W	HU	LT	NL	PL	CY
Intended fertility (mean number of children)									
Double performer	2.01	2.30	1.81	1.92	1.98	1.80	(2.16)	2.00	2.58
Home-centred	2.30	2.34	1.78	1.98	2.30	1.97	(2.49)	2.31	2.66
Work-centred	1.64	1.88	1.34	1.25	1.75	(1.65)	1.84	1.53	2.27
Diff.	***	*	***	***	**		*	***	*
Difference between fertility intentions and realisation									
Double performer	0.25	1.09	0.44	0.64	0.68	0.38	(0.38)	0.53	0.98
Home-centred	0.36	0.68	0.43	0.57	0.63	0.27	(0.57)	0.38	0.68
Work-centred	0.10	0.99	0.56	0.50	0.72	(0.92)	0.86	0.64	1.45
Diff.	**	*				***		**	***

Source: IPPAS

Note: () small numbers: n <30; significance level: *<.05; **<.01; ***<.001

his opinion it will become harder to get back to replacement fertility when fertility intentions fall below that threshold. In all countries except Cyprus, work-centred women intend to have fewer than two children. This can be explained by Cyprus being a typical Southern European country, where a high value attaches to children.

Unlike the mean number of children, intended fertility is not mainly caused by an age-related effect. The results of a variance analysis show that it can be attributed to the preference types in five out of the nine countries under consideration, and in two other countries it has an additional effect together with age (Appendix Table 9.9).

9.5.2 Fertility Intentions and Structural Opportunities

According to our hypotheses, the differences between achieved and intended fertility should not be related to properties of the different preference types, but to societal background factors. Table 9.4 shows that there are significant differences between achieved and desired fertility in five out of nine countries. In Poland and Cyprus, it is work-centred women who are far from having reached their desired fertility; this holds also for Eastern Germany, Hungary and the Netherlands, although the results for these countries are not significant. The double performer category shows the biggest difference in Estonia and Western Germany, and in Austria it is the home-centred type. Although it is often the work-centred type in which the differences are greatest, this result is not due to the type itself but to an age effect (Appendix Table 9.9). This confirms our first hypothesis, i.e. while differences in achieved fertility are caused by an age-related effect, the differences in fertility intentions are type-inherent.

With our second hypothesis, we suggest a relation between structural effects and individual fertility behaviour. Hence we have to consider family and gender policies in the countries included in our analysis. We focus on means of reconciliation of family and employment which by and by became an issue in gender policy, where a shift "from equal opportunities measures to reconciliation of employment with family life" (Hantrais 2000, 18 et seq.) could be observed. The main reason behind this process was the insight that equal opportunities could only be ensured by an equal access to gainful employment and an equal share of unpaid work between men and women. Lohkamp-Himmighofen and Dienel (2000) classified 17 European states according to their reconciliation policies, taking into account parental leave and the provision of child care. They found six models of reconciliation policy models: the egalitarian model, the labour market demographic model, the liberal labour market orientation model, the three-phase model, the Mediterranean family-based model and the socialist Eastern European model (Lohkamp-Himmighofen and Dienel 2000, 60 et seq.)

With respect to the countries in our analysis we get three groups:

1. Three-phase model: Austria, Germany and the Netherlands

In these countries (except Eastern Germany) for a long time the male-breadwinner model has been favoured. Motherhood is generally considered to be incompatible with economic activity outside the household. If paid employment of mothers couldn't be prevented, part-time work was preferred. The notion of the "three phases" refers to the temporary withdrawal of mothers with small children from the labour market. The model of the male breadwinner is still widely practised in these countries, although a change towards a more egalitarian model can be observed (Lohkamp-Himmighofen and Dienel 2000, 64).

2. Mediterranean family-based model: Cyprus

The group includes only Mediterranean countries where the care for children is considered to be a private matter of families with no support from the state, including a persisting traditional notion of gender roles. Regulations for parental leave in these countries are poorly developed and implemented and "European directives did not appear to have brought about any significant improvements in arrangements for combining paid work and unpaid work" (Lohkamp-Himmighofen and Dienel 2000, 65).

3. Socialist Eastern European model: Lithuania, Hungary, Poland, Estonia

In the former socialist countries women's participation in the labour market was supported by a relatively high provision of child care facilities. In the 1990s the closing down of a lot of these facilities led to serious problems in reconciling paid work and family life for women. At the same time parental leave was extended and thus led to new forms of reconciliation (Lohkamp-Himmighofen and Dienel 2000, 65).

The typology of Lohkamp-Himmighofen and Dienel is supported by the results of Beat Fux (Vol. I in this contribution) who developed a more general welfare state typology but without special considerations concerning gender topics. Nevertheless the three-phase model and the Mediterranean family-based model are comprised in Fux' forth cluster and the Eastern European countries in his third. In a finer classification the Netherlands could be distinguished from Germany and Austria as being more individualistic and Estonia as being more etatistic than the other Eastern European countries. However, for the validity of the analysis a broader classification is preferable.

The comparison of the different policy regimes with the gaps between intended and achieved fertility has to be carried out by multivariate analysis in order to check for age effects. A general linear model (GLM) has therefore been applied. This model has estimated the impact of the different preference types, the policy models and age on the difference between intended and achieved fertility. To measure the effect of the aggregated variables at national level, i.e. the policy models, we had to work with a pooled database containing all countries. The results are shown in Table 9.5.

The GLM produces significant results, albeit the effects are not very strong. We find the expected effect of age on the difference between intended and achieved fertility: the older the respondent, the narrower the gap between intended and achieved fertility. Contrary to our hypothesis, one of the preference types shows a significant impact. The home-centred type has a significantly smaller gap between intended and achieved fertility even when controlled for age and policy model in comparison to

Table 9.5 Results of GLM analysis for effects of preference types, family and gender policy on difference between intended and achieved fertility

Covariate effects/Intercept		B coeff.	Sign. level	
	Intercept	2.869	.000	***
Preference types	double performer	−0.053	.156	
	Home-centred	−0.120	.000	***
	work-centred	Ref.		
Policy model	Three-phase model	0.034	.207	
	Mediterranean model	0.327	.000	***
	Eastern European model	Ref.		
Age	(cov.)	−0.069	.000	***

Source: IPPAS

Note: significance level: * <.05; ** <.01; *** <.001; R^2 .314

the work-centred type. So preferences seem to be stronger than possible restrictions by external political conditions. Nevertheless, policy models also seem to have a significant effect on reaching one's fertility intentions. At least the Mediterranean model contributes to a widening of the gap between intended and achieved fertility. However, as this group consists of only one country this could also be due to data restrictions and should not be explored further.

In conclusion, the analysis indicates a positive impact of preferences towards children which seem to be independent of structural opportunities. The impact of policy models on the other hand could only be proved for the Mediterranean model. There low state intervention and a high dependence on family networks widen the gap between intended and achieved fertility in comparison with the Eastern European model. Nevertheless, we have to be cautious not to over-interpret this result as a large number of unmeasured influences can be involved.

9.6 Conclusion

It was possible to group women in the nine countries analysed according to their preference towards the individual importance of children and employment. The most prevalent type is constituted by home-centred women. They are very important in all of the post-socialist countries, but also in Austria and Cyprus. A clear polarisation between the home-centred and work-centred types can be found in the Western region of Germany, whereas the Eastern part is the only region where the double performer ideal predominates. The Netherlands finally are the only country where the work-centred type clearly predominates. The international comparison confirmed the similarity of the types in all countries. We found home-centred women to be married more often, less well educated on average and older than other women. They have high fertility intentions, and also high achieved fertility in comparison to the other types. The opposite is the work-centred type, which is younger, less frequently married and better educated, concentrating on achieving self-realisation and independence by means of their own careers. These women want fewer children and show a wider gap between desired and achieved fertility than home-centred women.

As far as fertility intentions are concerned, we found a strong correlation between preference type and these intentions. Home-centred women have the highest expectations, averaging more than two children, with Cyprus at the top. In the post-socialist countries, the intended number of children of the home-centred type exceeds two children as well. Exceptions are formed by the two regions of Germany and Lithuania, where even the home-centred type, i.e. the type with the highest intentions, would like to have fewer than two children.[6] The work-centred type, on the other hand, never reaches two children with its intended fertility, the only exception being Cyprus. Thus we find the same pattern in all countries, but on very different levels as a result of cultural and structural differences. Nevertheless, in seven out of nine countries, the home-centred type is the one with the highest fertility intentions and the highest achieved fertility. A substantial shift in preferences in those countries could lead to lower intended fertility, and indeed to lower achieved fertility in the future.

Our second hypothesis related the difference between the desired and achieved fertility of the preference types to living conditions shaped by family and gender policy regimes. We succeeded in showing that the Mediterranean policy model, where the emphasis lies on the private networks and traditional gender roles, does have a negative impact on the gap between intended and achieved fertility. More important, we succeeded in showing an independent positive impact of child oriented preferences on the closing of this gap which could be interpreted as the prevalence of individual orientations over structural opportunities.

Appendix

Table 9.6 Distribution according to preference typology in %; women aged 20–39

	AT	EE	DE-E	DE-W	HU	LT	NL	PL	CY
				%					
Double performer	19	7	35	14	10	13	(4)	11	26
Home-centred	43	50	29	32	73	66	(6)	69	50
Work-centred	24	15	27	30	6	(6)	56	6	14
Other	14	27	9	23	11	14	34	14	10
N	623	401	569	646	695	421	405	1418	562

Source: IPPAS

Note: () small numbers: n < 30

---

[6] It should not however be forgotten that we are working with a very conservative measure of fertility intentions here.

Table 9.7 Results of analysis of variance: effects of age and preference type on achieved fertility, women aged 20–39

	AT			EE			DE-E		
Source of variance	df	F	p	df	F	p	df	F	p
Age	1	175.47***	.000	1	218.72***	.000	1	184.68***	.000
Preference type	2	17.57***	.000	2	5.80**	.003	2	12.01***	.000
Int. error	563			268			511		
	DE-W			**HU**			**LT**		
Source of variance	df	F	p	df	F	p	df	F	p
Age	1	197.37***	.000	1	273.37***	.000	1	51.51***	.000
Preference type	2	24.76***	.000	2	12.78***	.000	2	9.15***	.000
Int. error	490			631			356		
	NL			**PL**			**CY**		
Source of variance	df	F	p	df	F	p	df	F	p
Age	1	65.14***	.000	1	599.74***	.000	1	285.71***	.000
Preference type	2	14.15***	.000	2	11.46***	.000	2	8.95***	.000
Int. error	266			1285			428		

Source: IPPAS
Note: significance level: *<.05; **<.01; ***<.001

Table 9.8 Results of analysis of variance: effects of age and preference type on fertility intentions, women aged 20–39

	AT			EE			DE-E		
Source of variance	df	F	p	df	F	p	df	F	p
Age	1	0.23	.632	1	5.24*	.023	1	0.52	.471
Preference type	2	15.61***	.000	2	2.54	.081	2	11.50***	.000
Int. error	451			268			499		
	DE-W			**HU**			**LT**		
Source of variance	df	F	p	df	F	p	df	F	p
Age	1	1.99	.159	1	1.55	.214	1	0.08	.774
Preference type	2	26.31***	.000	2	8.99***	.000	2	1.67	.189
Int. error	474			621			355		
	NL			**PL**			**CY**		
Source of variance	df	F	p	df	F	p	df	F	p
Age	1	12.75***	.000	1	118.54***	.000	1	3.10	.079
Preference type	2	6.82**	.001	2	9.14***	.000	2	2.19	.113
Int. error	266			1271			428		

Source: IPPAS
Note: significance level: *<.05; **<.01; ***<.001

Table 9.9 Results of analysis of variance: effects of age and preference type on difference fertility intentions – achieved fertility, women aged 20–39

	AT			EE			DE-E		
Source of variance	df	F	p	df	F	P	df	F	p
Age	1	86.28***	.000	1	156.6***	.000	1	267.7***	.000
Preference type	2	6.60**	.001	2	0.85	.430	2	0.27	.763
Int. error	451			268			499		
	DE-W			HU			LT		
Source of variance	df	F	p	df	F	p	df	F	p
Age	1	218.4***	.000	1	491.08***	.000	1	108.3***	.000
Preference type	2	1.89	.153	2	1.76	.174	2	6.31**	.002
Int. error	474			621			355		
	NL			PL			CY		
Source of variance	df	F	p	df	F	p	df	F	p
Age	1	142.35***	.000	1	360.73***	.000	1	259.06***	.000
Preference type	2	0.37	.692	2	0.65	.521	2	4.43*	.013
Int. error	266			1271			428		

Source: IPPAS

Note: significance level: *<.05; **<.01; ***<.001

(C)   "Subsequent generations could profit from the presence, knowledge and experience of the aged";
(D)   "The elderly are no longer productive and take away resources from society";
(E)   "The elderly are an obstacle to change";
(F)   "The elderly are a burden for society";
(G)   "The elderly are an important resource for emotional support".

By and large the seven statements cover two domains. Statements (A), (B), (C) and (G) would be associated with the social or emotional sphere, while statements (D), (E) and (F) would be associated rather with the economic sphere.

From the inception of the analysis it was decided to transform these seven "attitude" variables into one single index variable. The main argument was that within each domain there must be a considerable overlap between each of the statements. The attitude of each respondent would not be measured on the basis of one single statement, but would reflect an overall attitude based on several statements. Also, there would be the extra attraction that attitude would be measured over a wider range (the range directly depends on the number of statements included in the index and the number of categories for each statement).[2]

It was decided not to include statement (D) because of its ambiguity; citizens may feel that the elderly are no longer productive without however "taking resources from society".[3]

Eventually, the OAP index is constructed in such a way that it receives a value of "6" when the respondent has answered "strongly agree" to all six statements and a value of 30 when he/she has answered "strongly disagree" to all statements.

Figure 10.3 (Appendix, p. 211) presents the frequency distribution (in %) of the OAP index. Figure 10.3 shows a bimodal distribution with a skewed pattern to the left, implying that there are a greater number of citizens having a positive than citizens with a negative attitude toward the elderly.[4] The two peaks are at a value of "6" (a modest 6.5% for a clearly positive attitude) and at a value of "12" (16.9%), which is about half-way between an extremely positive and a neutral attitude (i.e. values 17 and 18, each with 3%).

In other words, the negative opinion which citizens show with respect to the rising number of older people cannot be interpreted as a negative attitude toward

---

[2] All statements include five categories that follow an identical pattern, ranging from "strongly agree" via "agree", "neither agree, nor disagree", "disagree" to "strongly disagree". For obvious reasons, because of the particular phrasing, the order of categories of statements (D), (E), and (F) needs to be reversed to make them comparable with the categories of statements (A), (B), (C), and (G).

[3] In fact this is likely to be the reason for a (slightly) higher non-response for statement (D) as compared to the other statements. Another "technical" consideration for not including statement (D) in the index variable is that the information is missing for Austria. Not excluding it would have implied an analysis including data from only seven countries instead of eight.

[4] From a more technical point of view, the smaller peak value (of 6.5%) may also be interpreted as an indication of truncation, i.e. a curtailing for the presence of respondents with a "very positive attitude" (assuming that the distribution of the index is normal).

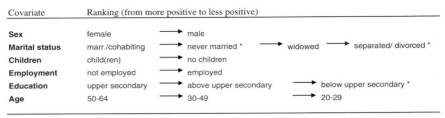

Covariate	Ranking (from more positive to less positive)

Covariate				
Sex	female ⟶ male			
Marital status	marr./cohabiting ⟶ never married * ⟶ widowed ⟶ separated/ divorced *			
Children	child(ren) ⟶ no children			
Employment	not employed ⟶ employed			
Education	upper secondary ⟶ above upper secondary ⟶ below upper secondary *			
Age	50-64 ⟶ 30-49 ⟶ 20-29			

* = effect insignificant

Fig. 10.1 Ranking of covariates

the elderly. The fact that citizens generally continue to take a favourable view of the role which older people may play in society, in spite of their concerns related to "population ageing", was also the conclusion reached after looking at the results of all seven statements separately: "[...] the overall picture is one of a positive opinion about older people, a large majority of citizens (roughly 80%) believing that older persons have a social role to fulfil in society and only a minority (30%–40%) seem to regard older people as an obstacle to change or as a burden" (Schoenmaeckers et al. 2006, p. 21).

Finally, it should be noted that the results are based on data for a total of eight countries/regions: Austria, the Czech Republic, Eastern Germany, Western Germany, Estonia, Lithuania, Poland and Slovenia. The DIALOG countries that are missing do not have information on one or more of the seven statements that constitute the basis for the OAP index (or do not have the required information for one or more of the covariates used in the GLM analyses).

10.1.2 Choice of a Multivariate Technique (GLM)

The statistical procedure used in the present analysis is General Linear Modelling (GLM), a simple procedure for regression modelling (SPSS 2003). GLM does not require any specific characteristic from the variables. The procedure allows the use of a continuous variable as the dependent variable (here the OAP index) and covariates that are categorical (see further).

The results provide an estimate for an "intercept" (which can be interpreted as a base-line value: see immediately below) and for the effects for each but one of all covariate categories, one category being taken as a reference category; the intercept corresponds to the estimated value of the dependent variable for those observations for which covariates take the characteristics of the reference category.

A logical choice for the analysis would have been multi-level analysis (Callens 2005; Snijders and Bosker 1999) since one of the overall objectives of the DIALOG programme is to identify country differences, if there are any. This option did not seem to be expedient, and had to be rejected in view of the small number of countries (8) that could be included in the analysis.

10.1.3 Choice of Covariates

The following variables have been included as covariates in the multivariate procedure: age, sex, marital status, educational level and employment; "country" has also been introduced as a covariate in one "preliminary" analysis.

- **Age:** In spite of the fact that "age" does not seem to exert a major influence on the opinion which citizens have with respect to the rise in the number of older people, it is the first variable that comes to mind as a required covariate. According to Matilda Riley (1987), a sociologist who has done pioneering work on the subject of age stratification in society, an individual confronts his or her own life-course experiences with environmental events and societal changes. Their behaviour, attitudes and opinions are an outflow of this confrontation. Psychologists formulate the issue somewhat differently as follows: "[...] the basic question for ontogenetic psychology[5] [is] how behaviour becomes organised and differentiated over a lifespan" (Birren and Cunningham 1985, p. 4). "Ageing" is viewed as consisting of three components: (a) the process of *biological ageing*, resulting in increased vulnerability or "senescing"; (b) *social age* or "eldering", i.e. the process of adapting social roles that are appropriate to the expectations of society; (c) psychological ageing, or "geronting", defined as the self-regulation which an individual exercises by making decisions and choices in adapting to the processes of senescing and "eldering" (the terms are from Schroots and Birren 1980, cited in Birren and Cunningham 1985).

In sum, "age" − or rather the stage that an individual has reached in his/her life-course, "age" merely being a proxy − is a powerful determinant for behaviour (or for attitude, feelings or opinions).

- **Sex:** The effect is weak, but women appear to have a less negative opinion of the rising number of elderly persons than men do. This is not surprising to the extent that women (continue to) occupy different positions in society than men (different career opportunities) and within the family (where they are the primary caregivers for children and for elderly parents).
- **Marital status & children:** The developments of the second demographic transition (low fertility, fewer marriages, higher divorce rates ...) are usually associated with increased individualism (Lesthaeghe 1983). To the extent that individualistic lifestyles were interpreted as egoistic behaviour, this should be reflected in a more negative attitude towards the role of the elderly in society.[6]

---

[5] The subject matter of ontogenetic psychology is the organisation of behaviour from conception to death.

[6] Lesthaeghe (1983) describes the individualistic lifestyle as follows (p. 429): "The underlying dimension of this shift [decline in marital fertility and nuptiality, changes in family formation and procreation] is the increasing centrality of individual goal attainment, that is, the individual's right and freedom of defining both goals and the means of achieving them."

- **Educational level:** Citizens with a higher level of education have different career opportunities than those who are less well educated. They are likely to view older workers as being less competitive, and therefore to pose less of a threat to their own future.
- **Employment:** It is assumed that unemployed citizens will distrust the idea of keeping older workers in the work force as long as possible. For them, older people must be a direct threat.

10.2 The Results

Before presenting the results of the GLM analyses, we discuss the frequency distribution of the OAP index on a country-by-country basis. The GLM results are divided into two parts: first those of the model with country effects, then those of separate analyses by country.

10.2.1 "Attitude" by Country

Figure 10.4 (Appendix, p. 212–213) presents the frequency distribution of the OAP index by country. In addition to the country-specific distribution, each panel also shows the "all country" distribution (see Fig. 10.3 in Appendix, p. 208).

There are unambiguous country-by-country differences. By and large, all countries show a bimodal distribution; however, some countries show a very different percentage for the peak values. Estonia, Lithuania and Slovenia show a much smaller percentage for the value of "6", and hence the most positive attitude (of 1.0%–3.8% compared to 6.5%); Austria on the other hand shows a much larger percentage in this most positive assessment than the "all country" distribution (12.8%). Lithuania, Poland and Slovenia show a much higher peak value around the median (of 16.2% and more, compared to 13.4%), whereas Austria, the Czech Republic and Estonia show a much lower percentage (less than 10.5%). The two "countries" (here regions) that follow the "all country" distribution most closely are Western and Eastern Germany.

Both phenomena are nicely summarised by the median (T50). A ranking from high to low closely corresponds to the apparent ranking from the country with the lowest number of citizens with a positive attitude to the country with the highest number: Estonia (median of 12.6), Slovenia (12.2), Lithuania (12.0), Western Germany (11.6), Eastern Germany and Poland (*ex aequo* with 11.1), the Czech Republic (10.9) and Austria (10.6).

10.2.2 Results of a GLM Analysis with Country-by-country Effects

Table 10.1 (Appendix, p. 218) gives the results of a GLM analysis in which "country" has been included as a covariate. As could be expected – were it to have been

Covariate	Importance of effect			
	Very strong	Strong	Weak	Very weak
Country	Austria Czech Republic Eastern Germany Poland	Western Germany	Estonia* Lithuania*	
Sex		male		
Marital status			married/cohabitating*	never married* separated/divorced*
Children		no children		
Employment				not employed
Education			below upper sec* upper secondary	
Age	20-29	30-49		

* = effect insignificant

Fig. 10.2 Ranking of the categorical effects according to their importance

otherwise, there would have been a need to reconsider the analysis – the results in Table 10.1 confirm those observed earlier: Estonia, Lithuania and Slovenia (associated with small negative or positive B coefficients) are the countries with the lowest number of citizens showing a positive attitude. On the other hand, Austria and Poland (associated with relatively large negative effects) are the countries with the highest number of citizens showing a positive attitude.[7]

Also, most effects of the other covariates are in line with the assumptions. For example, citizens in older age groups show a more positive attitude towards the elderly than citizens in younger age groups. And citizens without children look less favourably upon the elderly (which does not yet mean that childlessness is "proof" of an individualistic and egoistic attitude).

While "never married" may perhaps be interpreted as indicating a more individualistic lifestyle, this is certainly not the case for "widowed" and "separated/divorced". In both cases, the latter need rather to be associated with misfortune (widowed) or failure in a relationship (separated/divorced).[8] The pattern points to an assumption that attitudes would indeed be the result of personal experiences. The observation that the effects for "never married" and "separated/divorced" are not significant moreover indicates that the importance depends on the precise nature of the experience. Not only may "widowhood" be perceived to be a more traumatic experience, but there is also the likelihood that it occurred later in life, which increases the probability of not being able to cope with the future.

Another way of looking at the results is by ranking the categorical effects according to their importance (based on absolute value). The results of this exercise are given in a second diagram (Fig. 10.2):[9]

---

[7] The fact that Slovenia has been taken as a reference category is a statistical constraint imposed by the procedure used, but has no substantive meaning.

[8] For many divorcees also the term "failure" is possibly too strong.

[9] The categories "very strong", "strong", "weak" and "very weak" have been obtained with EDA techniques (Tukey 1977), classifying effects on the basis of median values.

Quite clearly, "country" is a strong determinant. The only two countries showing a weak effect are Estonia and Lithuania, and in both cases the effect is insignificant.[10] The other covariates with very strong and strong effects are "sex", "children" and "age". All categories for "marital status" are weak to very weak. What is more, they are statistically insignificant. The effect of being without employment is very weak (although significant); citizens who are not employed tend to have a more positive attitude toward older persons.[11] This finding is in contradiction with the assumption put forward. A possible explanation could be that older persons are not immediately seen as older *workers*. As a result, they are not seen as competitors (on the labour market) by unemployed persons.

Educational level does not appear to be a major determining factor in attitudes toward elderly. Citizens who completed their upper secondary schooling would show the most positive attitude (more so than those with a higher qualification). Those with a lower school-leaving qualification would show a less positive attitude, but the effect is statistically insignificant.

As has been said, "age" is one of the covariates with an apparently important effect. The effects are however not constant over all age groups. Based on the B coefficients, the strongest effect would be with age group 20–29 (0.972), and the weakest with age group 30–49 (0.580). However, another way is to look at the relative differences between the estimated values. These are 13.452, 13.061, and 12.408 for the age groups 20–29, 30–49, and 50–64, respectively.[12] As such, the relative change between ages 20–29 and 30–49 is –2.91% and –4.31% between ages 30–49 and 50–64. In other words, the empathy which citizens feel towards the elderly is not a gradual process. The GLM results rather suggest that the process intensifies when citizens approach the age which they (personally) consider to constitute being "old".

A next step in the analysis is to investigate the cross-country differences. One possible way is by introducing interaction terms in the GLM analysis. However, interaction terms are always complicated to interpret. It was therefore decided to opt for separate analyses for each country. The results are presented in Table 10.2 (Appendix, p. 219–220).

10.2.3 Results of Separate GLM Analyses by Country

"Sex" and "age" are the only covariates with a systematic pattern in the effects over all countries. Men show a less positive attitude toward the elderly, and also in all countries older citizens show a more positive attitude than younger ones. In

---

[10] This strictly speaking implies that the results for Estonia and Lithuania are statistically not different from those for Slovenia (reference category).

[11] The covariate can only be taken as a proxy for employment since it refers to the current situation only; the data do not permit the construction of a variable that would reflect respondents' employment history.

[12] Calculated as follows: $13.4516 = 12.4800 + 0.9716$; $13.0605 = 12.4800 + 0.5804$; and 12.4800 being equal to the intercept, age group 50–64 corresponding to the reference category.

addition, the effects of both covariates are statistically significant in all countries except one.[13]

The global importance of these two covariates appeared to be a good reason for taking a closer look at the frequency distribution of the OAP index by age and sex. This is done in Fig. 10.5 (Appendix, p. 214).

At first sight, the differences (between "age" on the one hand and "sex" on the other) are merely the result of shifting the distribution alongside the x axis. In all cases, the highest peak in the frequencies is observed at a value of 12. Age group 50–64 shows higher frequencies before the peak value, and lower ones thereafter; in the case of "sex", women show (slightly) higher values before the peak frequency and (slightly) lower ones thereafter. A closer look at the distributions by age group however reveals that the most important differences are between ages 50–64 and ages 30–49 (greater than between 30–49 and 20–29). The pattern is in line with the earlier assumption that the effect of age is not a gradual process.

The other quasi-systematic pattern concerns the effect of "employment". The effect is insignificant in all but one country (Czech Republic). The effects are however consistent with the results already observed from the analysis "all countries", i.e. that citizens who are jobless show a (somewhat) more positive attitude toward the elderly.

The most important conclusion to be drawn from the results is however that the effects vary widely between countries as to the sheer scale, to the direction of the effect (negative or positive), and to whether or not the effect is statistically significant. Both could be best clarified on the basis of the estimated values. This is the subject of Fig. 10.6.

10.2.4 Estimated Effects by Country

Figure 10.6 (Appendix, p. 215–216) presents the estimated values by DIALOG country. The estimates by age group and sex are shown for each country. The figures clearly show the systematic pattern that can be observed between all countries in the effects by age group and by sex. This does not imply that the effects are also constant, in fact the contrary is true. For "age group", the overall effect[14] varies between 0.60 (for Poland) and 2.83 (for Estonia). For "sex", the strongest overall effect is observed for the Czech Republic (0.73) and the weakest for Western Germany (0.03).

In addition to the effects for "age" and "sex", Fig. 10.6 shows the effects for "marital status", "children" and "education". The figure does not show all categori-

---

[13] Effect for age group 30–49 in the Czech Republic (significance = 0.131).

[14] "Overall" effect means the most important effect (in absolute terms) between all categories for a specific variable (here: "age").

cal effects, but only the overall effect for each covariate as can be derived from the B coefficients that are statistically significant.[15]

Austria is the only country where, in addition to "age" and "sex", also the three other covariates clearly determine attitudes toward the elderly. On the other hand, only "age" and "sex" appear to be of any importance for the Czech Republic. For all other countries one needs to take into account the effects of either one or two additional covariates.

The effects of "marital status" appear important for both Austria and Estonia. The overall effect is strongly negative in both countries. In Austria, however, the strongest effect (1.73) is associated with "never married", while in Estonia the strongest effect (1.79) is associated with "separated/divorced" (closely followed by the effect of "never married": –1.72).

Educational level plays a role in Austria, Eastern Germany, Lithuania and Poland. The effect is strongest in Eastern Germany (0.87), and weakest in Poland (0.41). The overall effect stems from the category "below upper secondary" in all countries. It is however worth noting that the effect of a lower educational level is positive in Eastern Germany, Lithuania and Poland (indicating a less positive attitude), whereas it is negative in Austria (indicating a more positive attitude).

In four countries (Austria, Western Germany, Lithuania and Slovenia) the fact of not having children would produce a less positive attitude (effects comprised between 0.53 and 0.79).

To conclude the discussion on the effects of the covariates, let us take a closer look at the "age" effect. On the basis of the results of the GLM analysis, with "country" as a covariate, it was already suggested that the empathy which citizens have toward the elderly increases with age, but that this is not a gradual process. However, can the pattern be observed for all countries? It can already be assumed from Fig. 10.4 (Appendix, p. 212–213) that countries must differ in this respect. Figure 10.7 (Appendix, p.217) facilitates a more detailed investigation.

Figure 10.7 presents the relative differences (in %) between the estimates[16] of the successive age groups. In 5 (out of the total of 8) DIALOG countries (Austria, Eastern and Western Germany, Lithuania and Slovenia) included in the present analysis, one does indeed observe a relatively greater change between age groups 30–49 and 50–64 than between 20–29 and 30–49. In one country (Poland) relative differences are nearly the same (in other words, Poland is the only country where age indeed has a gradual effect on attitudes toward the elderly). The pattern is reversed in two countries (the Czech Republic and Estonia), meaning that one observes a greater "jump" from ages 20–29 to 30–49 than from 30–49 to 50–64. Moreover, both countries show a major change between age groups 20–29 and 30–49, which is between two- and four-times bigger than in the other countries.

---

[15] The effect of "employment" has not been included as it is insignificant in every country but one (see above).

[16] Cf. calculation in footnote 12, but here based on the B coefficients of Table 10.2.

Appendix

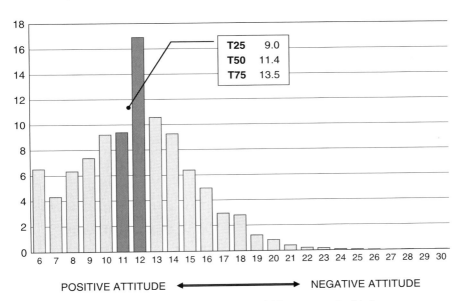

T25	9.0
T50	11.4
T75	13.5

POSITIVE ATTITUDE ←————————→ NEGATIVE ATTITUDE

Fig. 10.3 Relative frequency distribution (in %) of the "old-age perception" index
Notes: Weighted results all countries, ages 20–64[26]

---

[26] The age restriction stems from the fact that the age range differs between PPAS DIALOG partner countries.

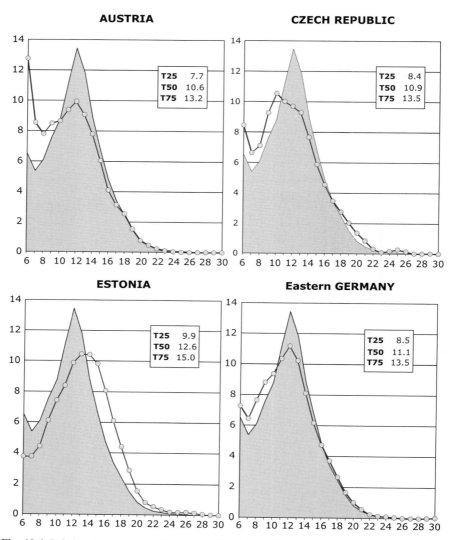

Fig. 10.4 Relative frequency distribution (in %) of the "old-age perception" index, by country (Results ages 20–64; ● Smoothed values; shaded curve corresponds to result "all countries")

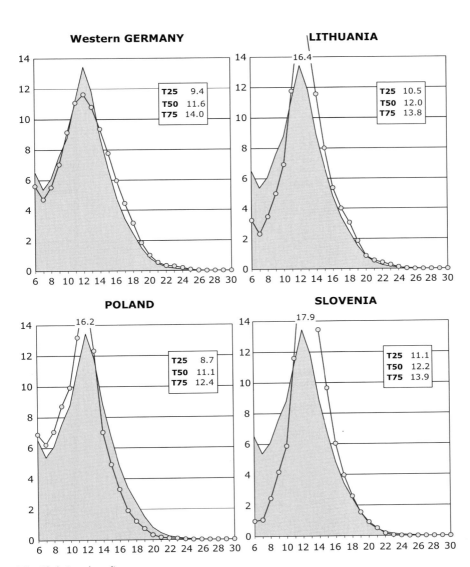

Fig. 10.4 (continued)

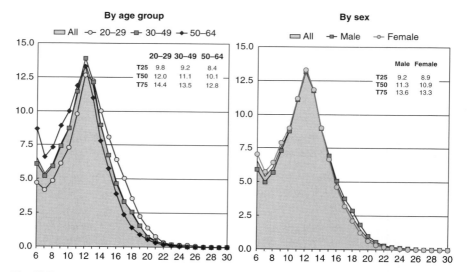

Fig. 10.5 Relative frequency distribution (in %) of the "old-age perception" index, by age group and by sex

Notes: Weighted results for all countries, ages 20–64

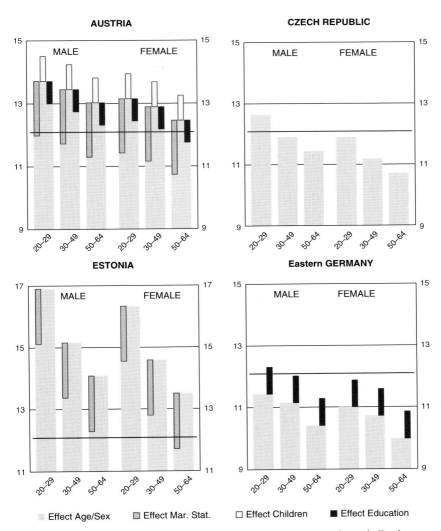

Fig. 10.6 Estimates for the "old-age perception" index by age group and sex, indicating overall effect of "marital status" (bar on the left), "having (no) children" (middle) and "educational level" (right). Results of GLM analyses by country

Notes: Horizontal line corresponds to the median value (of 12.09) between intercepts of separate analyses (see Table 10.2); see notes Table 10.2; same scale used except for Estonia

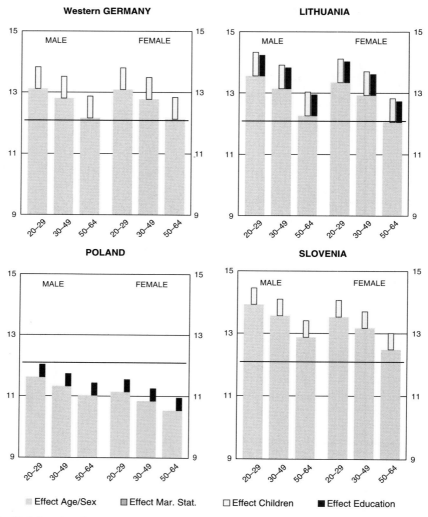

Fig. 10.6 (continued)

Chapter 11
Activating Older Workers: Policies Versus Opinions and Expectations

Janina Jóźwiak, Irena E. Kotowska, and Anita Abramowska

Abstract The main aim of the article is to confront older-worker oriented policies, as well as reforms in pension systems in Europe, with individual preferences and expectations towards transition to retirement, economic activity after retirement and governmental policies aimed at making pension systems sustainable. This comparative analysis is supplemented with experts' views on active ageing (obtained in the Delphi study). Recent trends in labour force participation of persons aged 55+ in Europe are examined. Special emphasis is placed on retirement policies and on pension system reforms. Comparative analyses of individuals' opinions on retirement age, economic activity of the elderly and transition to retirement, as well as on changes in the pension system, are carried out using descriptive methods and logistic regression models in which basic characteristics of respondents such as age, sex and education were taken into account. Respondents' expectations and preferences are compared both with experts' views, and with policies implemented in the countries under study.

Keywords: Pension system reforms · Statutory retirement age · Transition to retirement · Older workers

11.1 Introduction

The new demography of Europe, resulting from the Second Demographic Transition and becoming an all-European phenomenon, leads not only to rapid ageing of the population, but also to considerable changes in the labour force. Recent UN population projections (2003), as well as labour force projections by Eurostat and the OECD (Burniaux et al. 2004), clearly show that population ageing, i.e. the shrinking and ageing of the working-age population, are unavoidable characteristics of the Europe of the future. The decline in the working-age population will already take place in most countries in 2005–2015, and will culminate around 2025–2035.

J. Jóźwiak
Institute of Statistics and Demography, Warsaw School of Economics, Warsaw, Poland
e-mail: ninaj@sgh.waw.pl

C. Höhn et al. (eds.), *People, Population Change and Policies: Vol. 2: Demographic Knowledge – Gender – Ageing*, © Springer Science+Business Media B.V. 2008

Changes in the size and age structure of the working-age population are accompanied by a decline in the labour force participation of significant population groups, in particular older male workers. An unmistakeable trend towards lower labour force participation of persons aged 55 and over has been observed over a period of years in European countries with developed market economies. During the last decade, similar changes have taken place in countries of Central and Eastern Europe.

These two factors, demographic and labour market changes, are decisive for widespread concerns about the financial viability of public pension systems, predominantly funded on a pay-as-you-go basis. The different interventions taking place in a rising number of countries in the 1990s illustrate the importance attached by governments to keeping people on the labour market for longer.

However, populations do not necessarily approve of pension reforms. Moreover, the citizens' perspective is underrepresented in debates on necessary adaptations to population ageing. Especially, a cross-country perspective is missing. The IPPAS database provides a unique opportunity to study people's opinions on retirement policies. In addition, the perceptions of reforms differ between the population and experts/politicians. Therefore, comparisons between the individual perspective on retirement and suggested policy measures with experts' views in that respect give added value to discussions on how to influence people's awareness about needed adaptations to population ageing and the shrinking labour force.

Our attention is given below to changes on the labour market. The chapter continues with remarks on trends towards lower labour force participation of persons aged 55 and over. Since older worker-oriented policies have been dominated by pension and welfare reforms to date, a brief overview of the pension reforms which are underway in Europe is provided in Section 11.3. Sections 11.2 and 11.3 provide the background for a cross-country empirical analysis. The two subsequent sections present results of the IPPAS-based analyses. Firstly, in Section 11.4, citizens' opinions on retirement age and transitions to retirement are presented by making use of data on preferred and expected retirement age, as well as of ways to combine (or not combine) work and retirement. Here, consequently, a cross-country perspective is used which refers to descriptive comparisons and logistic modelling results. Secondly, in Section 11.5, experts' views of relevant policy measures are described which were found under the policy Delphi study. In the final Section 11.6 conclusions drawn from our analyses are placed in the perspective of the Lisbon Strategy.

11.2 Changes in the Labour Force Participation Rates of Persons Aged 55 and over[1]

Changes in the labour force participation of persons aged 55 and over, which have been taking place since the mid-1970s, will be among major developments in the

---

[1] This section makes use of study results presented in the paper by Kotowska (2005) "Older workers in the labour market and social policies" for the Council of Europe, published in Population Studies no. 50.

economic activity of the EU-15 Member States. They can be summarised as follows (Kotowska 2005):

- The past three decades have brought about considerable changes on the labour market: an increase in female employment, declining economic activity of males, with regard to the youngest and to older workers. Later entrance into the labour force and the early exit affect the individual time spent in employment. This has been becoming shorter despite the rising life expectancy. Cross-country differences in economic activity can be attributed to differences in the labour force participation of women, young people and older workers, while the economic activity of males aged 25–54 shows a universal pattern. As has been demonstrated by Burniaux et al. (2004) for the OECD countries, participation rates of prime-age males vary little from one country to another, while those of older workers reveal the greatest disparities, followed by young people (15–24 years old) and prime-age women (Burniaux et al. 2004, 86–87);
- The general downward trend in the labour force participation rates (LFPRs) of persons aged 55 and more is also markedly differentiated by countries. Despite the fact that in most countries the statutory retirement age for males, being at least 65 years in the 1970s (Greece and Italy are exceptions), was relatively stable over time, in 1990 economic activity rates of males aged 55–59 ranged from 54% (Luxembourg) to 84% (Sweden and Denmark) and those of males aged 60–64 from 14% (Austria) to 64% (Norway and Sweden). In 2003, the range for economic activity rates of males aged 55–59 remained as in 1990, while for males aged 60–64 the lowest values shifted to higher levels of 18–19% (Austria and France).

The general downward trend in economic activity of persons aged 55 and over is a subject of concern, all the more so when referring to the anticipated shrinking of the labour force and its ongoing ageing in addition to population ageing. There are some signs, however, that this tendency stopped at EU-15 level at the end of 1990s. Employment rates of older males in the majority of EU-15 Member States were higher in 2003 than in 1992, except for Italy, Portugal and Sweden (see Figs. 11.1 and 11.2).

In contradistinction to males, the economic activity of females aged 55–64 at the EU-15 level revealed a more consistent increase during the period from 1992 to 2003. However, a more detailed look at the year-by-year changes across countries showed that these changes were not uniform. A steady increase in female economic activity occurred only in Ireland and the Netherlands. The rise began in other countries in the second half of the 1990s. The relevant rates have been increasing in all countries since 2002. Labour force participation of older females in all EU-15 countries was higher in 2003 than in 1992 (in terms of labour force participation rates as well as employment rates). The increase was greater than for older males. Despite this, economic activity indicators remain low (around 20%) in Austria, Belgium, Italy and Luxembourg. Sweden is again located at the top of the list, with employment rates exceeding 65%, followed by Denmark with rates around that level.

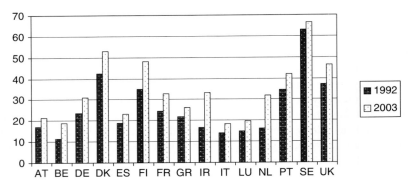

Fig. 11.1 Changes in employment rates of females aged 55–64, 1992–2003, EU-15
Source: Employment in Europe 2004, Recent Trends and Prospects, European Commission, Employment and Social Affairs, Brussels

Centrally-planned economies had, by European standards, a high level of economic activity for both males and females. These countries were almost uniform in terms of LFPRs of males and slightly differentiated in terms of females' rates.[2] Labour force participation changed drastically in the 1990s. The LFPRs, available from labour force surveys, fell in all countries, most visibly in Bulgaria, Hungary and Poland. In 2003, only the Slovak Republic had an activity rate above the EU level (76.7% vs. 70%); the Baltic states and the Czech Republic kept the economic activity rate close to the EU level, and the other "transition" countries were well below the EU level (the lowest rate of 63.9% was in Poland).

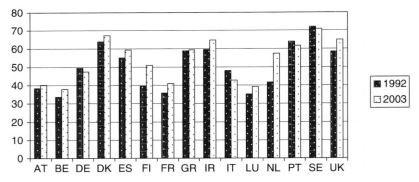

Fig. 11.2 Changes in employment rates of males aged 55–64, 1992–2003
Source: Employment in Europe 2004, Recent Trends and Prospects, European Commission, Employment and Social Affairs, Brussels

---

[2] In fact, that measure can be compared with employment rates for the developed market economies, given the full-employment principle and a lack of open unemployment before the 1990s.

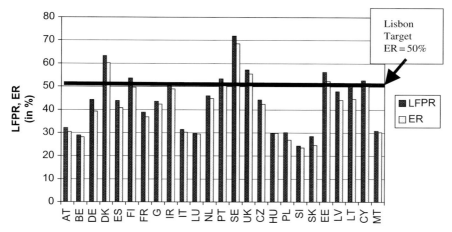

Fig. 11.3 Economic activity of older workers, 2003, EU-25
Source: Employment in Europe 2004, Recent Trends and Prospects, European Commission,
Employment and Social Affairs, Brussels

To deal with rising unemployment, governments of countries in Central and Eastern Europe liberalised disability and early retirement provisions. As a result, economic activity of persons aged 55–64 dropped considerably. The relatively rapid changes of employment of older workers in "transition" countries led to male employment rates being considerably lower when compared to the developed economies (in Hungary, Poland and Slovenia the activity rates of males were well below 40% in 2003; in other countries they ranged between 48% in the Slovak Republic and 64% in Estonia). Figure 11.3 demonstrates cross-country differences of economic activity indicators of older workers (both males and females) in the EU Members States and the degree to which they fall short of the Lisbon target defined by the employment rate of 50% to be reached in 2010.

However, it should be noted that the statutory retirement age in the CEE countries is, for both males and females, lower than in the EU-15 countries – on average 60 years for males and 57 for females. It is also important to remember that in the EU-15 countries the trend in the labour force participation of older workers up to the second half of the 1990s resulted mainly from declining economic activity of males, while in the CEE countries declines in both male and female labour force participation in the 1990s contributed to the observed change.

11.3 Reforms of Old-Age Pension Systems

Changes in the size and age structure of the working-age population, accompanied by a decline in the labour market participation of older workers, give rise to serious concerns as to the financial viability of public pension systems. There has therefore been extensive study of determinants of the labour market conduct of older workers.

Their results markedly contributed to the reasoning behind pension system reforms, which had debated since the 1990s and have already been implemented in many European countries.

The declining labour force participation of older workers is most commonly attributed to three main factors: increased living standards among the population, incentives embedded in social security systems, and labour market structures (for example Blöndal and Scarpetta 1998, 1999; Gruber and Wise 1999; Disney and Whitehouse 1999a,b; OECD 1995a,b; Scherer 2001; Casey et al. 2003; Duval 2003). The intensity of changes across age groups is also affected by the statutory retirement ages, which differ from one country to another.

Labour market-related effects and institutional factors are highlighted as the main determinants in empirical studies on changes in the economic activity of older workers. Most commonly, both the demand effects (structure of the economy, high and persistent unemployment, technological progress), and the supply effects (the size and age composition of the labour force, old-age pensions and other non-employment-related benefits) are analysed. However, the studies refer almost entirely to the OECD countries, excluding "transition" countries. The main findings of comparative studies on retirement decisions of male workers for OECD countries, directly referred to here, can be summarised as follows (Blöndal and Scarpetta 1998; Casey et al. 2003; Duval 2003):[3]

- There is a close correlation between the average effective retirement age and continued work;
- Pension wealth accrual and unemployment-related benefits have a strong impact on decisions to retire;
- The availability of generous non-employment benefits seems to be a prerequisite for labour market variables to influence activity rates of older workers;
- Implicit tax rates on continued work embedded in old-age pension systems and other social transfer programmes, widely dispersed across OECD countries, affect older male workers' retirement decisions;
- Labour market variables play a significant role in explaining cross-country and time variations in the economic activity of older men: The increase in the prime-age unemployment rate influences the drop in the labour force participation rate; changes in the size and the age composition of the working-age population appear to exert considerable pressure on older male workers towards early withdrawal;
- Incentives to retire vary across age groups. For the age group of 55–59 years they result from a number of social transfer programmes, which in fact have been used

---

[3] The study on determinants of changes in the labour force participation rates of older men aged 55–64 countries by Blöndal and Scarpetta (1998) is based on panel data on fifteen OECD countries from 1971–1995. Duval (2003) has separately analysed economic activity of males aged 55–59, 60–64 and 65 and over by using panel data relating to 22 OECD countries over the years 1967–1999. The paper by Casey et al. (2003) makes use of the dataset for fifteen OECD countries, which provides an assessment of the incentives to retire in current systems for single individuals aged from 55 to 70 at various levels of income.

as early retirement schemes. Eligibility ages also appear to have a specific impact for the 60–64 and 65+ age groups;

- Other institutional factors such as different bargaining systems (the level of centralisation/co-ordination of wage negotiations) and the degree of unionisation (the share of trade union members) play direct and indirect roles.

The main conclusion is that labour market and institutional factors go a long way towards explaining the cross-country and time-series differences in the labour force participation rates of older workers; however, a large part of the cross-country variation remains unexplained.

Another study on changes in economic activity rates in the EU-15 by Vlasblom and Nekkers (2001),[4] in which both the labour supply and labour demand factors were represented along with institutional variables, allows for the following synthesis:

- Higher-educated persons tend to stay on the labour market for longer;
- The higher the statutory retirement age, the higher the activity rates;
- The possibility to defer pensions increases the activity rates;
- The possibility of early retirement lowers the activity rates of males younger than 65, and increases the rates of males older than 65;
- A similar effect has been noted regarding the possibility to draw a part pension.

The studies referred to here confirm that the majority of the differences in labour force participation rates between countries stem from differences in the country-specific labour force behaviour (behaviour and work attitudes) and from institutional and policy factors affecting labour supply decisions, i.e. they confirm the relevance of contextual factors.

The decline in economic activity of persons aged 55 and over in the Central and Eastern European countries could also be related to both the demand and supply sides. The demand for labour has been strongly influenced by the transformation processes: institutional changes linked to the establishment of a labour market and the restructuring of the economy and employment structures. Economic reforms imposed a fundamental reconstruction of labour market control mechanisms aimed at the more effective management of the workforce, a rise in labour productivity and an improvement in the quality of work. Demand for labour changed drastically in quantitative (a strong decline) and qualitative terms (skills, mobility and flexibility of workers). The supply of labour was influenced by the increase in the working-age population and by its ageing, as well as by the declining spatial mobility of the population. Moreover, the fact that the overwhelming majority of older workers were low-skilled significantly reduced their capacity to avoid skill mismatches. Demand-supply imbalances led to rising unemployment in most countries on a large and unanticipated scale. In addition, the strategy to re-allocate some groups of the population from work to outside the labour market was frequently used to limit the labour

---

[4] Labour force participation rates of both females and males aged 55–74 at the national and regional (NUTS-II) levels have been analysed for the period 1992–1997.

supply (for example liberalising entitlements to early retirement and implementing non-employment-related benefits). And despite recent reforms aimed at reducing early withdrawal from the labour market, the economic activity of older workers in the new EU Member States is significantly lower that in the EU-15, except for the Baltic states and Cyprus.

A great deal of policy initiatives have been undertaken since the 1990s, and since the second half of the decade in particular, to consolidate funding arrangements for pension systems. The commonly listed goals of pension reforms are:

- to establish a closer link between contributions and benefits;
- to reduce pension generosity;
- to remove financial incentives to early retirement;
- to increase the adequacy of pension benefit levels;
- to increase the share of the population covered by pension arrangements;
- to promote private pension schemes, and
- to achieve greater coherence between existing public and private pension schemes.

Among different measures implemented under pension reforms that are underway in Europe, those promoting the economic activity of older workers have been a special focus. Increases in the statutory retirement age, especially with regard to women's ages, have been a key measure (see Table 11.1).[5]

Other relatively frequent measures counteracting early retirement concern mostly:

- extending the contribution period (Italy, Belgium, Greece, Portugal and France),
- increasing the minimum age (Italy, Finland and Germany),
- restricting access to early retirement schemes (Austria, Finland, Germany, Italy, Sweden and the Netherlands), and
- improving the actuarial fairness of the system (Austria, Finland, France, Germany, Italy, Portugal, Sweden, the United Kingdom and the Netherlands).

Pension reforms have also been implemented in a number of countries in Central and Eastern Europe (Latvia, Estonia Lithuania, Hungary, Poland, Bulgaria, Romania and Lithuania). Only Poland and Latvia replaced the "pay-as-you-go" (PAYG) schemes with the notional defined contribution schemes.[6] Others implemented multi-pillar systems with the public mandatory pillar based on significantly-modified PAYG

---

[5] For a comprehensive overview of reforms to pensions systems in the OECD countries since the early 1990s see Casey et al. (2003), Burniaux et al. (2004); a review of reforms in Europe accounting for two main strategies i.e. parametric and paradigmatic approaches, is given by Holzman et al. (2003).

[6] Two types of pension schemes can exist under the public defined-benefit pension systems: the flat-rate basic pension scheme and the earnings-related pension scheme. The former aims to guarantee a minimum income for the elderly, while the latter scheme provides income to retirees. Public defined-benefit systems are predominantly based on contributions and tax revenues from the current working population (PAYG basis). A notionally-defined contribution pension scheme is based on workers' individual accounts. Accumulated contributions are credited at a special rate related to growth in the aggregate wage. Individual old-age pensions depend on the amount accumulated and the average life expectancy at retirement age.

Table 11.1 Statutory retirement age and its changes in the EU-25+2 since 1999*

Country	Males	Females
Austria	65	60 (to 65 in 2019–2028)
Belgium	65	62 (to 65 by 2009)
Denmark	67	67
Finland	65	65
France	60	60
Germany	65	65
Greece	62 (65 for those entering the labour force post-1992)	57 (65 for those entering the labour force post-1992)
Ireland	66	66
Italy	60 (to 65 by 2008)	60 (65 for those entering the labour force post-1995)
Luxembourg	65	65
Netherlands	65	65
Norway	67	67
Portugal	65	65
Spain	65	65
Sweden	67	67
Switzerland	65	62 (to 64 by 2005)
United Kingdom	65	60 (to 65 by 2020)
Czech Republic	60 (to 62 by 2006)	53–57** (increase to 57–61 by 2007)
Hungary	62	57 (increase to 62 by 2009)
Poland	65	60
Romania	60 (increase to 65 by 2013)	57 (increase to 60 by 2013)
Slovak Republic	60	53–56**
Estonia	62.5 (increase to 63 by 2001)	57.5 (increase to 63 by 2016)
Latvia	60 (increase to 62 by 2003)	57 (increase to 62 by 2005)
Lithuania	61 (increase to 62.5 by 2009)	57 (increase to 60 by 2009)
Slovenia	60 (increase to 63)	53–58** (increase to 58–61)

*Malta and Cyprus are omitted
**The retirement age depends on the number of children
Source: Kotowska 2005, p. 147

schemes. The changes concern: increases in the statutory retirement age (see Table 11.1), reduced accrual rates (Bulgaria, Hungary and Estonia), adjustments to individual contribution (Poland and Latvia) and lower indexation of pension benefits in all countries, which kept their increases below rises in wages (Chłoń-Domińczak 2004). The indexation of pensions was defined in such terms as to limit their increase: pensions increased slower than wages.

11.4 People's Opinions on Transition to Retirement

The citizens' perspective is underrepresented in debates on economic and social adaptations to population changes. Very little is known about individual opinions on these issues and on attitudes towards suggested policies, especially in a cross-country perspective. That knowledge seems to be essential to gain public understanding and support for pension reforms and for any efforts to activate older workers.

The following PPAS questions will be used to analyse people's preferences and expectations as to retirement age and their opinions on retirement policies: The expected and preferred retirement age (questions A7 and A8 respectively), people's preferences regarding policy measures aimed at the sustainability of the pension systems (question A6a about the first preference), and opinions on the transition to retirement (question A16) and on working arrangements for retirees who want to work (question A17) (the detailed description of questions is given in the Appendix). Our analyses on retirement age refer to different population groups: respondents aged 20–64 are to be studied to learn about general opinions in society; persons aged 55–64, as well as the employed aged 20–64, make up the "target" groups relevant of policy reforms. Additionally, employed persons aged 55–64, i.e. older workers, are considered when opinions on defined policy measures are analysed.

11.4.1 Preferences and Expectations Towards Retirement Age and Early Retirement

We will start by looking at basic distributions of answers to questions regarding preferred and expected retirement ages by respondents' age and sex. The main finding obtained when comparing Figs. 11.4 and 11.5, which refer to respondents aged 20–64, is that all respondents in all countries, except Estonia, would prefer to retire below 65 years of age. At the same time, it was possible to observe that preferences

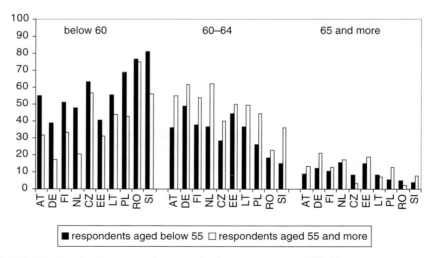

Fig. 11.4 Preferred retirement age by respondent's age, persons aged 20–64
Source: IPPAS; own calculations

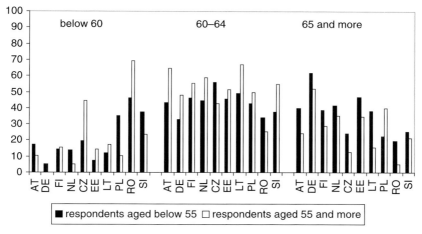

Fig. 11.5 Expected retirement age by age of respondent, persons aged 20–64
Source: IPPAS; own calculations

and expectations with regard to retirement age depended heavily on respondents' ages, which might suggest that they change as individuals' biographies progress. A visible tendency, common to all countries, was that younger respondents preferred a lower retirement age, and especially that they would prefer to retire below 60.

Preferences for a lower retirement age were more frequent in Central and Eastern European countries, which might be related to the fact that both statutory and actual retirement ages were indeed lower on average in these countries than in Western Europe.

When comparing preferences towards the retirement age with the expected age, it appeared that – apparently due to confrontation of preferences with real conditions and constraints – respondents in all countries expected to retire at an older age than they prefer. They expected most frequently to retire at an age higher than 60 years (especially 60–64). Younger respondents (below 55) expected more frequently to retire at an age higher than 65 as compared to older respondents. This means that discrepancies between preferences and expectations are more significant among respondents younger than 55 years. Especially in the case of Germany, about 60% of respondents aged under 55 did not expect to retire before 65, while only around ten percent preferred such a retirement age.

The above discrepancy appears to stem from public discussions on necessary reforms in pension systems, including increases in the retirement age, and regulations which have already been implemented in several countries. Consequently, one can conclude that respondents have become aware that they will have to work longer than they would like to.

As we noted above, preferences and expectations change as respondents age. Figures 11.4 and 11.5 present the distribution of answers among all respondents. Next, our focus is on the sub-set of respondents at their pre-retirement age (55–64),

and the analyses relate to preferences and expectations as to the statutory retirement
age. Comparisons of preferences and expectations on retirement age with the statutory retirement age situate respondents' opinions in the actual situation in a specific
country.

Figure 11.6 shows that regardless of the country both men and women aged
55–64 would prefer to retire at an age below the statutory retirement age. In all
cases (except Austrian females), proportions of those who prefer to retire earlier
than at the statutory age equal at least 70%, and in the extreme case of women in
the Czech Republic this percentage is almost one hundred.

Similar to all respondents, preferences towards earlier retirement were more popular in Central and Eastern Europe than in the Western countries, although differences between various regions of Europe were less evident. What is more, with the
exceptions of Austria, Lithuania, Poland and Slovenia, the proportions of women
preferring earlier retirement were higher than of men. Almost equal proportions
of women and men preferring earlier retirement were observed in Finland and the
Netherlands. No clear relationship between preferences by sex and the statutory retirement age of women and men can be noted, although it seems justified to assume
that differences in opinions of women and men on their preferred retirement age
might result from the statutory age in the country, as well as from the difference
in the statutory retirement age of women and men. For instance, in Finland and
the Netherlands, where the statutory retirement age is the same for both sexes,
preferences of men and women do not differ significantly. This is not the case,
however, in Germany where the difference is evident.[7] In Austria and Poland, where
fewer women than men preferred early retirement, there is a wide gender difference
between the statutory retirement age (5 years), and at the same time the statutory

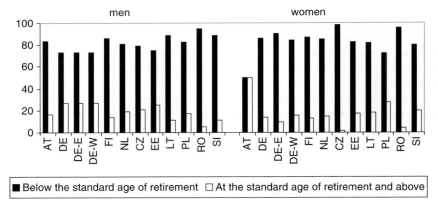

Fig. 11.6 Persons aged 55–64 years by preferred retirement age
Source: IPPAS; own calculations

---

[7] While in Germany there is no gender difference in the statutory retirement age, most early retirement schemes did offer women the opportunity to retire earlier than men.

retirement age of men is relatively high (65 years). In the two countries with a similar relation between men's and women's preferences (Lithuania and Slovenia), the statutory retirement age of men is low (61 and 60 years, respectively), and the age of women is lower by 4 years (Lithuania) and 2–7 years (Slovenia). By contrast, in the Czech Republic, which has the same statutory retirement ages for both sexes as Slovenia, the proportion of women preferring early retirement is much higher than that of men. Estonia, with a not particularly high statutory age for men (62.5 year) and a rather wide gender gap between the statutory retirement ages (5 years) can be characterised by different preferences related to early retirement of men and women. Finally, Romania, with a low statutory retirement age of men (60 years), and a narrower gap in the statutory age between sexes (3 years), has the smallest difference between preferences of women and men. Although this case seems to be similar to Finland and the Netherlands, the proportion of those who would prefer to retire below the statutory age is much higher in Romania than in the latter countries.

In summary, no clear relation has been found between preferences and legal regulations on the statutory retirement age in specific countries. However, one can conclude, although with some reservations, that these preferences are – at least to some extent – influenced simultaneously by statutory retirement ages of men and women; differences between them; as well as by the stage of implementation of pension reforms in a country considered (see Table 11.1). It is also most probable that the preferences, such as reforms (see Section 11.3), are determined by the labour market situation, including access to early retirement schemes, economic activity of older workers and the actual (average) retirement age in a country.

There is no doubt that the macro-economic context plays a significant role in forming preferences and expectations as regards retirement. Individual characteristics, however, seem to be even more important for preferences and expectations towards retirement age. That supposition has been tested by using a logistic model for preferred and expected retirement ages in ten countries. Tables 11.2 and 11.3 display the results of the estimated models, which account for employed respondents aged 20–64 years and three basic individual characteristics of respondents: age (20–29, 30–39, 40–49, 50–59, 60–64), sex, and education (primary and lower secondary, higher secondary, post-secondary). The research question we seek to answer is as follows: To what extent do these characteristics differentiate employees' preferences and expectations about retirement age.

We can conclude from the estimates presented in Table 11.2 that the level of respondents' education is the most important variable to significantly determine preferences related to retirement age in all countries with the exception of Poland. In all cases, the increasing level of education explicitly reduces the relative probability that an individual would prefer to retire earlier than at the statutory retirement age.

The same relationship is valid for the expected retirement age: The higher the level of education, the lower the relative probability of a person expecting to retire earlier (see Table 11.3).

The results of modelling confirm indirectly that preferences (see Table 11.2) and expectations (see Table 11.3) depend on an individual's position on the labour

Table 11.2 Estimates of the logistic model[8] for the preferred retirement age (1- below the statutory retirement age, 0-at the statutory retirement age and above), employed aged 20–64 years*

Country	Age group		Sex		Educational level	
	B_1	$Exp(B_1)$	B_2	$Exp(B_2)$	B_3	$Exp(B_3)$
AT (N=1137)	–	–	–1.215	0.297	–0.629	0.533
CZ (N=658)	–	–	1.328	3.774	–0.708	0.493
DE (N=2489)	–0.214	0.807	0.924	2.520	–0.466	0.628
EE (N=702)	–	–	1.434	4.197	–0.701	0.496
FI (N=2177)	–0.112	0.894	0.392	1.480	–0.532	0.587
LT (N=684)	0.260	1.296	–0.795	0.452	–0.665	0.514
NL (N=1094)	–	–	0.295	1.343	–0.368	0.692
PL (N=1063)	–	–	–0.328	0.721	–	–
RO (N=516)	0.410	1.508	–	–	–0.790	0.454
SI (N=951)	–	–	1.060	2.885	–1.491	0.225

*All estimates are significant at the 10% level – Non-significant estimates
Notes: Age-group: 10-year age group (1 = 20–29, 2 = 30–39, 3 = 40–49, 4 = 50–59, 5 = 60–64);
Sex: 1 = male, 2 = female; Educational level: 1 = primary or lower secondary education, 2 = higher secondary education, 3 = post-secondary education
Source: IPPAS

market, something which is very much influenced by education. Persons with a higher level of education are usually in a better situation in terms of better jobs, higher salaries and more opportunities to choose a job, less physical strain, etc. Hence, early retirement is less attractive to them than to less well-educated persons.

Table 11.3 Estimates of the logistic model for the expected retirement age (1- below statutory retirement age, 0-at the statutory retirement age and above), employed aged 20–64 years*

Country	Age group		Sex		Educational level	
	B_1	$Exp(B_1)$	B_2	$Exp(B_2)$	B_3	$Exp(B_3)$
AT (N=1152)	0.393	1.481	–0.786	0.455	–0.610	0.544
CZ (N=661)	–	–	1.982	7.256	–0.427	0.653
DE (N=2480)	0.191	1.211	1.013	2.753	–0.378	0.685
EE (N=697)	–0.130	0.878	0.959	2.608	–0.400	0.670
FI (N=2178)	0.147	1.158	0.177	1.193	–0.212	0.809
LT (N=669)	–0.384	0.681	–0.899	0.407	–	–
NL (N=1094)	–	–	–	–	–0.205	0.815
PL (N=778)	–	–	–0.332	0.717	–	–
RO (N=507)	–	–	–0.473	0.623	–0.237	0.789
SI (N=950)	0.277	1.319	1.154	3.171	–0.920	0.399

*All estimates are significant at the 10% level – Non-significant estimates
Notes: Age group: 10-year age group (1 = 20–29, 2 = 30–39, 3 = 40–49, 4 = 50–59, 5 = 60–64);
Sex: 1 = male, 2 = female; Educational level: 1 = primary or lower secondary education, 2 = higher secondary education, 3 = post-secondary education
Source: IPPAS

---

[8] $P(Y=1) = \frac{e^{B_1 AGE + B_2 SEX + B_3 EDUCATION + B_0}}{1 + e^{B_1 AGE + B_2 SEX + B_3 EDUCATION + B_0}}.$

An impact of the second characteristic – the sex of an individual – on the relative probability that a person prefers to retire below the statutory retirement age is ambiguous, although this variable is statistically significant in all countries under study except Romania (see Table 11.2). In Austria, Lithuania and Poland, women prefer less frequently than men to retire earlier, while quite the opposite holds in the other countries under study: The probability of this preference is lower for men than for women. In other words, in the Czech Republic, Germany, Estonia, Finland, the Netherlands and Slovenia, being a man reduces the relative probability of preferring early retirement. This result is consistent with observations concerning differences between women and men in their labour force participation. It also reflects the influence of a big gender difference in the statutory retirement age on opinions of women and men, as has been commented on earlier.

Estimates of the models of the expected retirement age (which may be understood as a result of confronting preferences and real constraints), reveal that the relationships between sex and preferences are maintained for the probability of an expectation to retire before reaching the statutory retirement age in specific countries (see Table 11.3). However in the models for expected retirement age, individuals' sex became a significant characteristic for Romania, whilst not being significant for the Netherlands.

As regards age, estimates confirm that it does not play a very important role in defining preferences among employed respondents (see Table 11.2). Only in the models of four countries (Germany, Finland, Lithuania and Romania), is respondents' age significant. However, the way in which age influences preferences is quite opposite in Germany and Finland as compared to Lithuania and Romania. In the former countries, belonging to older age groups reduces the relative probability of preferring early retirement, whilst more advanced age increases this probability in the latter.

It is interesting to note that in the countries where the statutory retirement age is relatively low (Lithuania and Romania) preferences for early retirement increase with age. The situation is diametrically opposed in Germany and Finland, where the statutory retirement age is much higher, the probability of preferring early retirement falls with respondents' advancing age (see Table 11.2). There are two possible explanations for this phenomenon: different working conditions in the two groups of countries, and early retirement schemes (or opportunities) which are probably more attractive to older workers in Lithuania and Romania than in Finland and Germany.

Surprisingly, age changed its influence in the models for the expected retirement age (see Table 11.3). First of all, in the models for the countries where age was the significant variable for preferences, estimates in the models for expectations have opposite signs. Additionally, age became the significant variable for expectations in Austria, Estonia and Slovenia, while age was not significant in Romania in the model for the expected retirement age, and replaced sex as the significant characteristic. The differences between estimates for age in the models for the preferred and the expected retirement age of employed respondents in countries under study reflect the previous observation for all respondents on differences between these ages.

In the most common pattern observed in the countries considered, younger respondents in particular expressed a preference to retire earlier, whilst at the same time expecting to work longer. This discrepancy most likely reflects a shared awareness of a necessity to remain economically active for a longer period of time in the future due to changes in the macro-economic and social context and unavoidable reforms of the old-age pension systems.

Concluding this part of the analysis, one can state as follows:

- Although respondents' preferences and expectations related to their age at retirement change during biographies and seem to depend on the current stage in their lives, age does not play a very important role in determining preferences and expectations. Also, no major differences were observed between groups of respondents (all aged 20–64, aged 55–64, employees) in their prevailing preferences as regards early retirement;
- Obvious differences in preferences and expectations between the sexes can be found in most countries under study. These differences can be related to regulations on the statutory retirement age of women and men in these countries;
- Education is the most important characteristic influencing individuals' propensity (preferences and expectations) to retire earlier, and the higher the level of education, the lower is this propensity;
- Preferences and expectations as to retirement age seem to be influenced by the actual situation on the labour market and by the retirement (especially, early retirement) schemes available in a country;
- Preferences to retire earlier are more frequently expressed in the Central and Eastern European countries despite their lower statutory retirement age.

11.4.2 Preferences and Opinions on the Transition to Retirement and Policy Measures

From an individual perspective, both (statutory and actual) retirement ages, and a way of transition to retirement are relevant: People want to know not only "when" but also "how" they will retire. Questions on policy measures concerning the transition from work to retirement (A16) and the desirable scheme of work for retired persons wanting to work (A17) provide an opportunity to analyse individuals' opinions in that respect. Moreover, by confronting policies already implemented in the countries under study with people's opinions, preferences for certain policy measures aimed at the sustainability of the pension system (A6a) can be studied.

Table 11.4 displays the opinions of three sub-groups of respondents on possible variants of the transition from work to retirement: younger respondents (aged 20–54 years), older respondents (aged 55–64 years) and older workers (employed persons aged 55–64 years). We have introduced this division in order to capture possible differences in opinions of respondents with different experience in their professional life. In the upper panel of Table 11.4, we compare the younger and the older age

Table 11.4 Opinions on policies concerning the transition from work to retirement (age groups 20–54 and 55–64 years)

Country	Forced to stop working altogether	Combine retirement and work	Gradually diminishing work	Forced to stop working altogether	Combine retirement and work	Gradually diminishing work
	Up to 54			55–64 years		
DE	16.4	32.5	51.1	18.0	34.6	47.4
DE-E	25.9	33.5	40.5	24.2	36.8	39.0
DE-W	14.0	32.2	53.8	16.2	34.0	49.7
EE	5.4	18.3	76.3	5.3	16.0	78.7
LT	22.3	45.7	32.0	17.5	52.9	29.6
PL	37.7	42.9	19.4	36.5	44.4	19.1
RO	33.0	43.7	23.3	32.3	45.6	22.1
	55–64 years			Older workers		
DE	18.0	34.6	47.4	16.4	32.2	51.4
DE-E	24.2	36.8	39.0	18.3	36.6	45.1
DE-W	16.2	34.0	49.7	15.9	31.3	52.7
EE	5.3	16.0	78.7	2.2	11.7	86.1
LT	17.5	52.9	29.6	11.1	63.9	25.0
PL	36.5	44.4	19.1	30.2	46.7	23.1
RO	32.3	45.6	22.1	38.9	33.3	27.8

Source: IPPAS

groups, and in the lower panel the entire older age group is compared with older workers. However, available data limit this study to five countries only (plus Eastern and Western Germany).

Both younger and older respondents considered stopping work altogether as the least attractive way of transition to retirement in all countries. This choice was even less popular for older respondents than for younger ones (with the exception of Western Germany[9]). In case of the two remaining modes, opinions are not so unanimous. In Germany (both Eastern and Western), and in Estonia, gradually diminishing work was the most commonly preferred method of transition to retirement for both younger and older respondents. Combining retirement and work was the most frequently selected option in Lithuania, Poland and Romania. This preference was even higher for older respondents. Also in Estonia, a gradual transition from work to retirement was more popular among older respondents. In Eastern and Western Germany a redistribution of opinions from gradually diminishing work towards combining retirement and work occurred among older respondents. One can conclude that older Germans would prefer to have more opportunities and scope for individual decisions in their transition to retirement.

Older workers formulated similar preferences to those expressed by older respondents, and the choices are even clearer. The only and somewhat surprising exception is Romania, where in the group of older workers the distribution of opinions between

---

[9] Therefore also for Germany, since four-fifths of the population live in the West.

these three options is much more uniform with the option to stop working altogether in the first place. In the other countries this model was the least commonly favoured by older workers.

Except the last case, the main conclusion drawn from the analysis is that regardless of age and employment status respondents in the countries under study prefer a "smooth" transition from work to retirement and, moreover, they would like to have a possibility to choose a proper model of this transition.

Similar attitudes are displayed in preferable schemes of work for persons who would like to work after retirement: The clearly prevailing option is to have a choice between full- and part-time work (cf. Question A17). This option is dominant in all countries considered, among younger and older respondents, as well as among older workers.

Next, preferences about governmental measures to safeguard old-age benefits in the future have been analysed. Tables 11.5 and 11.6 show the first preference of various groups of respondents in ten countries under study.

Actually, these preferences also express respondents' convictions about the necessity of policy measures to be undertaken by the government to keep the pension system sustainable, as well as their knowledge of the existing and proposed system itself, and not only respondents' preferences with regard to the measures.

The general conclusion which can be drawn from data contained in Tables 11.5 and 11.6 is that according to respondents' opinions in almost all countries the most appropriate measure that should be undertaken by their governments aiming to safeguard the financial stability of the pension system is to raise monthly taxes or (less often) to abolish early retirement programmes. Only in a few cases were other measures indicated: raising the retirement age (more frequently among older workers

Table 11.5 First preference as to governmental measures to safeguard old-age benefits in the future, workers 20–64 years (population 20–64 years)

Country	To raise the retirement age	To raise monthly taxes	To lower monthly benefit payments to pensioners	To force children to support their parents	To abolish early retirement programmes	To make old-age benefits dependent on the number of children
BE-2	7.5 (9.2)	27.0 (26.5)	6.1 (5.3)	3.3 (3.2)	45.2 (45.2)	10.9 (10.7)
DE	15.9 (15.1)	11.8 (11.9)	8.4 (8.9)	2.4 (2.8)	33.8 (33.3)	20.2 (20.7)
FI	24.3 (26.5)	42.2 (40.5)	5.9 (5.6)	3.0 (3.8)	16.8 (15.5)	7.8 (8.1)
NL	13.8 (14.3)	41.7 (40.9)	5.9 (4.9)	1.2 (1.4)	33.3 (33.7)	4.2 (4.8)
CZ	11.3 (11.4)	27.1 (27.0)	3.3 (2.7)	8.5 (7.2)	30.0 (30.7)	19.8 (21.1)
EE	18.2 (19.1)	15.6 (17.2)	3.8 (3.6)	9.5 (9.3)	27.9 (25.7)	25.0 (25.1)
LT	10.1 (9.5)	28.4 (28.6)	1.7 (2.0)	5.4 (6.8)	27.9 (24.8)	26.4 (28.3)
PL	8.7 (9.1)	39.6 (39.1)	2.8 (2.5)	7.9 (7.8)	21.5 (20.5)	19.6 (21.0)
RO	25.0 (26.2)	31.0 (30.6)	4.3 (4.0)	8.8 (10.6)	20.5 (17.1)	10.5 (11.4)
SI	11.3 (10.9)	38.8 (38.7)	5.5 (5.3)	2.4 (2.6)	24.7 (24.3)	17.2 (18.3)

Source: IPPAS; figures in bold mean the two most frequently selected measures

Table 11.6 First preference as to governmental measures to safeguard old-age benefits in the future, older workers (55–64 years) (population 55–64 years)

Country	To raise the retirement age	To raise monthly taxes or social premiums on income	To lower monthly benefit payments to pensioners	To force children to support their parents	To abolish early re-tirement pro-grammes	To make old-age benefits dependent on the number of children
BE-2	11.6 (12.5)	24.0 (24.6)	1.3 (1.5)	2.7 (2.4)	52.4 (52.1)	8.0 (6.8)
DE	13.0 (13.7)	13.0 (12.7)	8.2 (8.2)	3.1 (3.5)	42.0 (38.1)	14.3 (17.5)
FI	31.8 (35.9)	45.6 (41.6)	5.8 (4.8)	1.5 (1.8)	12.8 (12.9)	2.6 (2.9)
NL	15.2 (18.6)	48.9 (39.7)	0.0 (1.7)	0.0 0.0	34.8 (38.0)	1.1 (2.1)
CZ	12.7 (12.3)	22.5 (26.3)	2.8 (1.8)	11.3 (5.8)	33.8 (32.7)	16.9 (21.1)
EE	20.8 (21.3)	17.7 (20.4)	0.8 (1.3)	7.7 (7.1)	37.7 (34.2)	15.4 (15.6)
LT	11.1 (10.3)	37.0 (37.9)	1.9 (1.4)	5.6 (6.9)	25.9 (18.6)	18.5 (24.8)
PL	7.0 (7.4)	37.3 (39.5)	3.2 (2.0)	10.1 (9.9)	25.9 (20.8)	16.5 (20.3)
RO	13.3 (31.1)	66.7 (30.4)	20.0 (5.4)	0.0 (10.1)	0.0 (14.9)	0.0 (8.1)
SI	19.4 (14.6)	38.9 (39.3)	2.8 (2.5)	5.6 (2.9)	19.4 (24.7)	13.9 (15.9)

Source: IPPAS

and respondents aged 55–64) or relating old-age benefits to the number of children (more often among all respondents).

It is striking that the option of increasing the retirement age is indicated (as the second most appropriate measure) in Finland, where the retirement age is relatively high and in Romania where, in stark contrast, it is relatively low. This result may suggest in the first instance acceptance by Finnish people of their government's policy in this respect. The latter case may suggest that Romanian respondents are conscious that an increase in the retirement age in their country is necessary and approve of their government's recent decision to increase this age (see Table 11.1). Another striking result concerns older workers in Romania who more often selected the option to lower monthly benefit payment to pensioners than raising the retirement age. The first solution may have been perceived as related to persons already retired, while the second was internalised, i.e. it was understood as related to their own situation.

Generally, however, increasing the retirement age is not commonly accepted or preferred by respondents in the countries considered. This may be interpreted such that opinions expressed by respondents are rather against one of the important measures of necessary reforms of pension systems in their countries. On the other hand, abolishment of early retirement programmes – which seems to be the other side of the same coin – is the most common first preference when it comes to governmental measures to safeguard old-age benefits in the future. One should remember, however, that the former case (increasing the retirement age) may be understood as a change or cancellation of existing rights, while the latter case (abolishment of early retirement) means resignation from privileges.

To sum up, two findings should be emphasised:

• Older workers as well as other respondents would like to remain on the labour market after retirement, but they would like to be able to choose between different options both as to the style of transition from work to retirement, and to the type of economic activity exercised after retirement.

Measures implemented or discussed to keep the pension system sustainable are not always fully supported by respondents who express their own preferences in this respect. This concerns increasing retirement age. At the same time, opinions and preferences reveal that there is strong support for the other measures being implemented in the countries considered, and that these preferences are consistent with reforms which have been brought into effect in these countries. Consolidation of the pension systems, consisting first of all of the abolishment of the early retirement schemes, is commonly accepted.

11.5 Experts' View of Active Ageing[10]

The policy-Delphi study, carried out under the DIALOG project, aimed to formulate demographic and societal scenarios up to 2030. The policy-Delphi method is particularly useful to obtain a consensus on complex issues by a group of experts who work independently. This presents experts' opinions on responses to population ageing.

The policy objectives most frequently selected by the experts were: safeguarding retirement provision and adapting old-age pension systems to socio-demographic changes, as well as improving the quality of life of the elderly. And eleven out of fifteen DIALOG countries participating in the Delphi study consequently included policy priorities related to active ageing in their final policy scenarios. These priorities also covered objectives relevant to older workers' participation in the labour force: to make retirement flexible (Switzerland), to support employment of the elderly (i.e. persons aged at least 60 years and more) (Austria, Italy and the Netherlands), to promote active ageing (the Czech Republic, Lithuania, the Netherlands, Poland and Slovenia).

Active ageing was considered to be composed of five elements: involvement in paid work, life-long learning, voluntary work, leisure and health. As regards paid work of the elderly, experts suggested to implement the following measures: promoting part-time work, introducing innovative forms of part-time work, reducing work-load, continuation of work after retirement, removing old-age barriers from the labour market, vertical job-sharing, tax-exemption for hiring retired persons and

---

[10] That section is based on the research report entitled Work Package 3, Delphi-Study. Comparative Delphi Report, Summary Policy Implications of the Delphi Study, prepared by the Research Institute of Population and Social Policy in Rome. DIALOG Programme: Work Package No. 3, Deliverables D11 & D12, 2005.

the adoption of leave during work biographies as a form of anticipated retirement during a working lifetime. Life-long learning was also recommended as a tool to sustain active ageing.

That the old-age pension issue is highly relevant is reflected by the fact that all countries included different objectives related to pension systems in their final policy scenarios. Adjusting a social security system to the ageing population and increasing intergenerational solidarity was selected by the majority of countries (except for the Czech Republic, Estonia, the Netherlands, Poland and Switzerland). Five countries defined safeguarding the sustainability of pension systems as a policy objective (Belgium (Flanders), the Czech Republic, Estonia, Italy and Switzerland).

The policies suggested by experts to attain these goals may be grouped as follows:

- innovation and flexibility of work models and pension systems proposed by all countries,
- better investment in health improvement and life-long learning (Finland, Hungary, Lithuania and Estonia),
- intergenerational solidarity and rejuvenation of society (Lithuania, Romania, Slovenia and Italy),
- gender balance in the work environment and new immigrants' work schemes (Austria, Germany and Italy).

Among the first group of policies, an increase in the retirement age was the measure most commonly recommended to safeguard the financial sustainability of pension systems. However, experts from six countries did not select that solution as a priority for 2030 (the Czech Republic, Italy, Lithuania, Poland, Slovenia and Romania). The second option for experts was the expansion of private retirement schemes, while the flexible and gradual retirement and work after retirement ranked third and fourth respectively in terms of their capability to assist in reforming pension systems.

As illustrated, adjusting a social security system to the ageing population is considered as a highly important and complex issue, but relevant policy measures to be implemented differ across countries. That reflects a variety of ways to tackle the problem. However, within the broad scope of possible solutions those related to changes in working patterns and pension systems were most commonly suggested. And raising the retirement age received a high degree of recognition from experts in that respect.

11.6 Concluding Remarks

Our study of PPAS results clearly shows strong preferences to withdraw from the labour market earlier, i.e. to retire either before 60 or before 65. Expectations were more realistic, but still reveal early retirement attitudes. These discrepancies between preferences and expectations may suggest that public discussions on necessary reforms of pension systems which included increases of the retirement age, solutions already implemented in several countries, affect respondents' perceptions in that respect. They have become aware that they would have to work longer than they would prefer. But in their opinion, it would be a better result of consolidation of existing regulations on transition to retirement than increases in the compulsory, statutory retirement age, the latter being the most popular measure recommended by experts and suggested in debates on pension scheme reforms.

Individual views showed some consistency with the experts' opinions about flexible and gradual retirement and work after retirement. However, that option depends heavily on both employees' ability to stay on the labour market, and on employers' attitudes to keep them employed. And that perspective is adopted in the revised European Employment Strategy, approved by the European Council in Thessalonica in June 2003. To achieve three overarching objectives: full employment, quality and productivity at work, social cohesion, and an inclusive labour market, four key strategies were recommended:

- increasing adaptability of workers and enterprises;
- attracting more people to the labour market;
- investing more effectively in human capital; and
- ensuring effective implementation of reforms through better governance.

Putting the emphasis on labour supply would appear to reflect a viewpoint that rapid ageing is calling into question Europe's ability to achieve the defined strategic goals, in particular higher employment and productivity rates. Interventions to improve the adaptability of the labour force for a dynamic and highly competitive labour market are therefore strongly recommended. In particular, actions towards older workers require radical policies and a culture shift away from early retirement, which we have proved to still be predominant in the countries under study.

Increasing participation by older workers, along with higher participation of women and other groups of the population which are underrepresented in the labour force, are considered fundamental to meet the goals of increasing economic growth, improving competitiveness and achieving greater social cohesion. In order to achieve this, both institutional and cultural adaptations are required, and reforming the old-age pension systems is a component of a more comprehensive approach to prolonging the length of time people remain on the labour market.

Also the Green Paper on "Confronting demographic change: a new solidarity between generations", published by the European Commission in March 2005, identifies measures to activate older workers as key solutions to respond to financial and economic challenges with which European countries are faced.

Therefore, not only measures aimed at removing disincentives for workers to work longer and to discourage early retirement should be discussed, but also policies which stimulate lifelong learning should be examined besides those oriented towards improving working conditions and encouraging employers to retain and retrain older workers. In that respect our results give some optimistic indications: Education is the most important characteristic influencing an individual's propensity (preferences and expectations) to retire earlier or to continue being economically active.

Appendix

A6a. First preference about the Government's way to safeguard old-age benefits in the future?

People's preferences regarding policy measures to be implemented in order to safeguard the financial stability of the old-age pension system might be evaluated by analysing respondents' opinions on the following measures:

- to raise the retirement age,
- to increase monthly taxes or social premiums on income,
- to lower the monthly benefit payment to pensioners,
- to force children to support their parents,
- to abolish early retirement programmes,
- to make old-age benefits dependent on the number of children: the more children one has, the higher the benefit.
- other.

  Data for A6a are not available for Austria, Cyprus, Hungary or Italy.

  A7. Expected retirement age

  A8. Preferred retirement age

  Data for A7 and A8 are not available for Belgium, Cyprus, Hungary or Italy.

  A16. Opinion on policy concerning transition from work to retirement

- forced to stop working altogether
- combine retirement and work
- gradually diminishing work

  Data for A16 are available for Estonia, Germany, Lithuania, Poland and Romania only.

Chapter 12
Only Fools Rush In?

On Transition to Retirement

Lucie Vidovićová, Beatrice Elena Manea, and Ladislav Rabušic

Abstract Age at retirement and age of exit from the labour market have become an important issue in ageing European societies. This paper deals with the perspective that people aged 45–64 have towards the timing of their retirement. We examine the question of the preferred and expected ages at retirement and introduce the concept of "desire to retire early". Using the results of the PPAS, the paper uncovers the paradox of early retirement. Our respondents know that their societies are ageing and that their own lives are going to be longer, resulting in a higher proportion of old-age pensioners. Today's old-age pension systems in many cases have quite a substantial impact on the standard of living of new retirees. However, our respondents indicate a considerable desire to retire early no matter these facts and regardless of their country of residence, gender and other factors. This desire to retire early does not seem to have a strong influence on whether they favour various policy measures.

Keywords: Transition to retirement · Retirement age · Preferences · Pension policy · Early retirement

12.1 Introduction

European populations are ageing, and some are experiencing economic recession. In this context, pension reforms have become hot political, economic and social issues in most European countries. The main objective of the reforms is to stop the trends towards early retirement and to empower individuals by increasing individual involvement in their own old-age provision. Retirement age has become a crucial issue within these reforms. In this paper, we will focus on the role of retirement age in the whole process of transition from work to retirement.

L. Vidovićová
Faculty of Social Studies, Masaryk University, Brno, Czech Rep.
email: lucie.vidovic@seznam.cz

C. Höhn et al. (eds.), *People, Population Change and Policies: Vol. 2: Demographic Knowledge – Gender – Ageing*, © Springer Science+Business Media B.V. 2008

Statutory retirement age represents just one side of the phenomenon, while the actual retirement age is the other side of it. In most European countries, where many people "race out of the workforce at the earliest affordable opportunity" (The Economist 2004, 13), the average exit age from the labour force and the average age of effective retirement is lower than the statutory retirement age. One of the main causes is the early retirement process. Early retirement was widely used as a policy instrument to make room for younger workers whose interest in the labour market was given higher priority in a certain period of time when unemployment was rapidly increasing, mainly in the 1970s and 1980s. By that time, in order to ensure the success of early retirement schemes for older workers, early exits needed to be "a financial opportunity not to be missed" for the worker, and easy to manage by firms (Guillemard and van Gunsteren 1991). This led not only to their success, at least in terms of pushing older workers from the labour market, but also to a sharp increase in their costs. Even today, a large proportion of the cost of early retirement is covered from public funds and does not represent a major challenge to firms' redundancy policies in most cases, except when labour force shortages become an issue.

The success of this measure was only partial, and these schemes were very short-sighted. Samorodov (1999) offers the examples of France, where only about half of the vacancies in specific sectors created by early retirement were filled, and the Netherlands, where the total number of unemployed people who found jobs thanks to the early retirement system was smaller than the number of people aged 60–64 years who actually left the labour market. Furthermore, this approach towards older workers started a vicious circle of early exits from which it is now difficult to escape, when prolonged labour force participation is needed on the part of all ages.

Early exits, among which early retirements constitute a special case, influence the overall decrease in labour force participation, as well as the out-flow of the labour force from declining sectors, while new recruitment is concentrated in key expanding areas. This second feature is one of the reasons why some specific sectors are continuing to "grow older" (e.g. agriculture).

The incentives for retirement are linked to older workers' income, and usually are/were appealing enough to persuade workers to retire "voluntarily". However, Samorodov (1999) argues that the very fact that a big share of those who are/were enjoying early retirement were unemployed or with some kind of disability suggests that this kind of retirement is not truly voluntary, but that workers are actually channelled in that direction. Disability, unemployment, long service and arduous working conditions are among major (legal) qualifying conditions for early retirement. Thus, unemployment and/or disability benefits bridge those periods of time without a job until the worker becomes eligible for a pension (Guillemard and van Gunsteren 1991). Even though Herbertson (2003) argues that the real causes are rooted more in economic policy and structure than in cultural and environmental factors, it should be said that changing attitudes and behaviour at the workplace also played a major role. There is greater pressure within the workplace, such as increased job dissatisfaction, longer working hours, greater stress and a wide range of lifestyle choices that value personal autonomy over higher living standards.

Individual decisions are made within the preferences and structural constraints one encounters. All these factors both strengthen and bring about an exit from the labour market, generating a new focus on early retirement lifestyles, especially among those from white-collar, managerial and professional occupations. Early exit has become part of workers' normal biographies, and expectations of early exit determine employees' life course and strategic choices in many cases (Phillipson 2002).

Early exit is a multifaceted issue with a variety of causes and outcomes. However, the most striking is the fiscal one: "regardless of its causes, the withdrawal of older workers from the labour force leads to an increase in unused production capacity, a reduced tax base, and a heavier load on pension and fiscal systems" (Herbertson 2003, 4). According to Herbertson (2003), some European countries lost from 10 to 12% of their potential GDP due to early retirement in 1998. This wastage could potentially grow further, and it is something that ageing countries cannot afford. We are therefore witnessing a major shift in the discourse, as well as in the policy efforts to deal with this situation. From a historical point of view, European social old-age protection is now making a major U-turn, from lowering the age of eligibility via support for early retirement towards today's increase in the retirement age (factual or if necessary, statutory) and closing down the early retirement gateways.

In this chapter, we will take a closer look at one specific feature which is of enormous importance within this complex system: the individual actor. What perspective on the timing of their retirement do people have? Do they support the U-turn of social policy, or do they represent a serious obstacle to it?

12.2 The Paradox of Early Retirement

We will develop our argument along the lines of the so-called (Czech) *early retirement paradox*. This retirement paradox is based on a series of arguments developed by Rabušic (2004) in the context of Czech society, and is based on its citizens' retirement behaviour. We will try to apply it to the broader context of ten DIALOG countries: Austria, the Czech Republic, Germany, Estonia, Finland, Lithuania, the Netherlands, Poland, Romania and Slovenia.

Rabušic (2004) departs from the following presuppositions in his paper: Retirement has become a significant element in the life cycle of the individual in contemporary modern societies. Research indicates that views towards retirement are positive on the whole (Atchley 2000), and that the popularity of retirement, and early retirement in particular, is growing (Quadango and Hardy 1996). With respect to the main subject of this paper, i.e. the timing of retirement, it has become clear that "retirement decisions are shaped by individual preferences, but [that] the individual choices are made relative to the opportunities and constraints that workers encounter" (Quadango and Hardy 1996, 326). These opportunities and constraints may take the form of a kind of chain, which, when connected, creates the previously-mentioned *paradox of early retirement*. There are five distinct links in this chain:

(a) Life expectancies in selected DIALOG countries are quite high, or are rising. Although individuals are living longer, the statutory retirement age is relatively low. Thus the period of life spent in retirement is relatively long, especially for those, and for women in particular, who in many countries are both living longer and traditionally leave the labour market earlier.

(b) Even though the number of pensioners is expected to increase according to demographic projections, and the increasing statutory retirement age should have kept numbers in check to a certain degree, the number of pensioners has been growing faster than expected. The cause of this phenomenon is the continuing popularity of early retirement.

(c) Although the European population should be well informed about the negative effects of population ageing on the current pension systems, and in spite of the fact that they are aware of a need to further increase the statutory retirement age, the overwhelming majority of the populations in the DIALOG countries would like to retire before reaching the statutory retirement age. If their wishes were to be fulfilled, there would be a further extension of the period of time spent in retirement.

(d) There is a tendency to take early retirement in spite of the fact that the majority of people in pre-retirement age should be aware that their pensions will be much lower than their previous income, and that their standard of living will drop considerably in some cases.

(e) However, some data show that people like to work and that there is some additional value of work, which they miss later. One could even conclude that many of those who have already retired may admit that they did not really want to retire.

These distinct points will be illustrated in the following sub-chapters.

12.2.1 Methodology

We use the IPPAS database (version September 2005) in order to illustrate the previous points. Due to data availability restrictions, we will provide the analysis only for ten selected countries: Austria (AT), the Czech Republic (CZ), Germany (DE), Estonia (EE), Finland (FI), Lithuania (LI), the Netherlands (NL), Poland (PL), Romania (RO) and Slovenia (SL), unless stated otherwise. Some of the results are available for an even smaller number of countries. We have chosen for our analyses a sub-sample of respondents aged 45–64 (not including retirees) because we consider responses given by younger respondents with regard to their preferred retirement age as irrelevant for the purposes of this paper. All the presented results are therefore valid for this age group only. Data were weighted by internal weight only. SPSS PC+ and STATA programs were used for the analysis.

The aggregated data presented, and other information, are given for the years of the PPA national surveys or to the closest year, respectively. Therefore, they do not mirror the latest developments in ageing and retirement policies, or trends in life expectancy or further rising retirement age.

12.2.2 Life Expectancy vs. Effective Retirement Age (A)

The combination of early exit (and retirement) and longer life expectancy results in a much longer span of inactivity. Male life expectancy at birth ranges from 65.3 (EE) to 76 (NL) years, and for women it ranges from 74.8 (RO) to 81.7 (AT) years in the selected DIALOG countries. When we take into consideration the average exit age from the labour force in the given countries, which varies from 57.1 (FI) to 62.6 years (NL) for men, and from 55.4 (SL) to 61.9 years (NL) for women, we can approximate how long retirees can expect to live in retirement – if we assume today's mortality rates to apply to future pensioners. When we calculate the difference between life expectancy and average exit from the labour market, we reach an average of 11.8 years for males and 20.6 for females. However, even here major differences among the countries included in the analysis can be observed (see Fig. 12.2.2).

We can distinguish three groups of countries both for the male and female population. With regard to men, the lowest expectancy of time spent in retirement (up to 10 years) is found in Estonia, Romania and Lithuania; medium expectancy (11–15

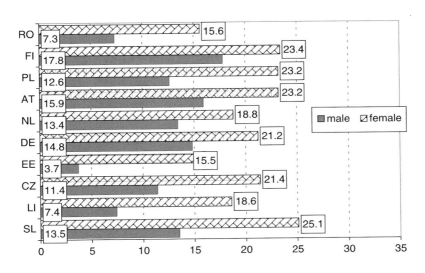

Fig. 12.1 Quasi life-in-retirement expectancy for men and women by country (in years)
Notes: Quasi life-in-retirement expectancy was obtained as the difference between life expectancy at birth and average exit age from the labour market
Source: Kontula and Miettinen (2005)

years) in the Czech Republic, Poland, the Netherlands, Slovenia and Germany; the longest life in retirement (more than 15 years) can be expected by males in Austria and Finland. In the case of women, time spent in retirement is even higher: up to 20 years in EE, RO, LI and NL; 21–25 years in DE, CZ, PL, AT, FI; the longest life in retirement is experienced by women in Slovenia – 25.1 years.

These estimations seem to be relatively high. Especially in those societies that are still very strongly work (occupation)-oriented and where insufficient acceptable activities/functions for retirement time have so far been developed. Attempts to fulfil retirement time with leisure, lifelong education, involvement in community activities and care responsibilities are witnessing only partial success since there are great objective (health, income, policy priorities, etc.) as well as subjective (personal value system, etc.) barriers to practise them. On the other side "... connection to the work process... is decisive in the fight against involuntary social exclusion. Work brings with it various kinds of benefits for a number of reasons: aside from income, it gives people the feeling of stability and a direction in life, and creates wealth for the entire society" (Giddens 2001, 95[1]).

According to scholars who focus on such issues, cf. for example Ryder (1975), Uhlenberg (1987) or Day (1988), life expectancy is one of the factors from which a more or less rational model of retirement age could be derived. These authors suggest that retirement age should be set at a level that would allow for life expectancy in retirement of either 10 or 15 years. If we take the second of the two norms – 15 years of retired life – as standard, we may conclude that there is a high possibility, at least theoretically, for a large part of Europe and especially for the female population – who live longer and experience earlier withdrawal from the labour market – to extend their working lives and still enjoy an entirely sufficient amount of retirement time.

12.2.3 The Numbers of Pensioners are Increasing (B)

According to the UN data sheet 2002, all selected DIALOG countries were among the oldest countries in the world (based on the share of population 60+). Since all these countries are also struggling with low fertility rates and the ageing of the baby boom cohorts, one can be almost sure that they will maintain their positions for at least the next 30 years. The number of old (65+) and oldest old (80+) people is increasing in these countries, and will continue to do so. Our respondents are well aware of this. Although when asked in the survey, they did not know the exact share of older people in their countries, there are however clear indications that they are aware of the fact that something "major" is about to happen. An average of 89% of respondents overestimated the share of people aged 65+ by more than ten percent points.

---

[1] Re-translated from the Czech version.

We have already shown that people under a certain (and relatively low) age are leaving the labour market and entering one type of economic inactivity or another. Another way to look at this phenomenon is to show the falling employment rates in higher age groups. The employment rate in the age group 60–64 (employed persons among all persons in the age group) was quite low in all DIALOG countries. The male employment rate averaged 29%, and it varied from 15% (in AT) to 50% (in EE). The female employment rate averaged 16%, and it varied from 6% (in AT) to 36% (in EE). The greatest gender difference was found in Romania (22p.p), and the lowest in Finland (5p.p.). In other words, an average of 70% of men and 84% of women in this age group is outside the labour market. If nothing changes, there will be not only a further increase in the share and number of older people, but also in the number of inactive older and old people.

Governments have started to take steps to reverse these trends on the labour market, as higher employment rates would mean spreading the burden of funding pensions among a greater number of people. Moreover, one year's increase in the effective retirement age would absorb about 20% of the average expected increase in pension expenditure in 2050 (European Council 2003). Two main policies were introduced to achieve higher employment rates in the majority of countries in focus: Generous early retirement schemes are phased out or restricted with permanent reductions of the benefits, and the statutory retirement age has increased after the year when the data were gathered in six of the countries analyzed (i.e. AT, CZ, EE, LI, RO and SL).

12.2.4 Desire to Retire Early (C)

Policies and reforms to tackle the economic effect of ageing took a lot of political bargaining, and the public was heavily involved in their preparations. Thus, one could expect that people should be well informed about the possible financial burden of ageing on society as a whole, and that they should be aware that this type of reform is needed in greater numbers in the near future. However, being informed about the political and economic situation is one thing, while individual conduct and insight into such information may be another. This fact will be illustrated further.

In the PPAS we asked a question: *"When do you expect to retire?"*. We received the following opinions about *expected retirement age:* For respondents aged 45–64 years, it was an average of 62 years for men and 59.5 years for women, which is very close to the statutory retirement age of 63 for men and 60.3 for women in the average of all the countries in focus (UN 2002). The mean difference between the statutory and expected ages is about 0.65 years for women and 1.2 years for men. We can thus conclude here that the level of awareness of the legislation concerning pensions is quite high. Differences among the countries analyzed exist with regard to the above-described issue (see Fig. 12.2).

Figure 12.2 illustrates the differences between the statutory legal retirement age and the average expected age for different sexes in each country. If the expected retirement age is higher than the current statutory age (resulting in negative values

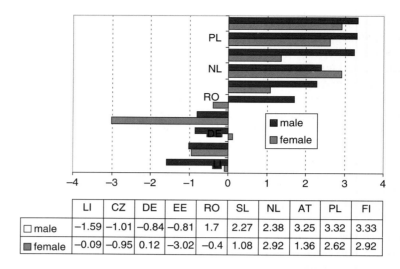

	LI	CZ	DE	EE	RO	SL	NL	AT	PL	FI
□ male	−1.59	−1.01	−0.84	−0.81	1.7	2.27	2.38	3.25	3.32	3.33
■ female	−0.09	−0.95	0.12	−3.02	−0.4	1.08	2.92	1.36	2.62	2.92

Fig. 12.2 Statutory legal retirement age (UN 2002) minus average expected age of retirement by sex of respondent (in years)

as a result of calculation), it is because of respondents' anticipation of postponement of exit from the labour market planned by the new legislation, as is case in CZ, LI, DE and EE. However, such legislative change could also be expected in AT and RO, but the current statutory retirement age in these two countries is somewhat higher than the retirement age expected by respondents. We can thus see in these two cases that the preferences for early exit seem to be stronger than the pressure coming from the public debate about the need for prolonged labour force participation and the corresponding retirement legislation.

Apart from the question on expected retirement age, the survey also asked a question on *preferred retirement age*. We consider the information on preferred retirement age to be more important than the expected retirement age because the latter is usually more or less in line with the statutory age. The question was phrased as follows: "*If you could decide, when you would like to retire?*".

Average preferred retirement age for the analyzed countries and sub-sample of respondents aged 45–64 years was 58.7 for men and 56.3 for women. When compared with the real average exit age from the labour force, the differences are not too big: The average exit age was 59.9 for men and 58.7 years for women around the year 2002 (D 13 Report 2003). One can thus conclude that significant changes in the retirement behaviour of these respondents cannot be expected, since their preferred retirement age is very close to the retirement age now effective, when older workers are actually leaving the labour market. Since the statutory retirement age is considerably higher than the average exit age, the differences between preferred and statutory retirement age are also greater – it is an average of 3.9 years for women and 4.5 years for men. In other words, women in the IPPAS countries would like to retire an average of 3.9 years earlier than the average statutory retirement age. Men would like to retire even earlier – 4.5 years.

In order to compare expected and preferred retirement ages, we introduce the concept of *desire to retire early (DRE)*. The *DRE* indicates the level of desired early retirement, expressed in number of years, calculated as the difference between the *expected* retirement age (probably understood by respondents as actually planned according to expected legislation) and *preferred* retirement age. This concept offers slightly different information than the plain *preference* for early retirement because it does not take into account only a respondent's wish to leave the labour market earlier than the statutory retirement age would suggest, but also his/her actual plan to leave earlier, expressed here as an *expectation*. We believe that this combination is a more powerful predictor of actual behaviour than the information of the two separate variables. The intensity of the desire to retire early is depicted in Fig. 12.3, in which a higher position of the bar indicates a greater willingness to rush into retirement if able to do so.

As the figure suggests, the countries can be clustered into three groups. The first and biggest one is represented by CZ, RO, AT, FI and NL, where the average difference between the expected and the preferred retirement age is less than three years. Then we have the second group of two countries with about 3.5 years of difference (PL and DE). Finally, there is the group of three countries (EE, SL and LI) with the greatest desire to retire early – on average around four years before the expected retirement age.

Desire to retire early may be understood in two slightly different ways: First, since there is some correlation between the expected age and the statutory

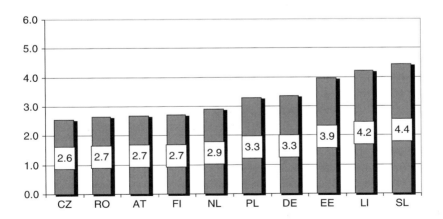

Fig. 12.3 Average desire to retire early in years, by country
Source: IPPAS

retirement age,[2] the *DRE* can be understood literally as a preference for early exit as opposed to the legislative threshold. Secondly, the *DRE* can be used as an indicator of consistency of respondents' wishes and behaviour. In such a case the *DRE* is close to zero.

The preference theory, initially established by Hakim in the field of reconciliation of work and family (2002) and applied in the field of occupational activity in advanced age by Vidovicova (2005), might help us to understand the meaning and significance of such preference-behaviour consistency. According to Hakim (2002), work plans were significant predictors of actual work behaviour, and it can be expected that it might be the case of retirement plans too. We are unfortunately not able to test this hypothesis with our IPPAS data. However, the results presented below strongly support the need for further exploration of this idea in future research.[3]

From Table 12.1 it seems that those deciding to follow their preferences comply with the statutory retirement age only in the Czech Republic and Lithuania, although this also applies to men in Germany and women in Romania. All other groups would like to exercise preferences which fall short of the statutory retirement age, with the

Table 12.1 Statutory retirement age (UN 2002 data) and average expected retirement age for sub-population of those respondents who do not claim a difference between preferred and expected time of retirement (in years, by sex and country (total N = 1.592))

	Statutory retirement age (UN 2002)		Expected age of those where preference equals expectation	
	M	F	M	F
Austria	65	60	60.5	58.3
Czech Rep.	61	55–59*	60.9	57.1
Estonia	63	59	62.3	60.6
Finland	65	65	60.8	61.3
Germany	63	63	63.3	61.4
Lithuania	62	60	62.3	60.0
Netherlands	65	65	62.5	60.3
Poland	65	60	60.8	56.3
Romania	60	55	55.4	54.4
Slovenia	63	58	60.4	56.9

*Depends on number of children, age 57 would be a modal case of two children
Notes: According to the D13 Dialog report, Slovenia had a statutory retirement age in 2002 of 58 for men and 53 for women, and Germany claims to have 65 as a statutory age limit, while age 63 better reflects the real/actual retirement age. (See D13 Report for further details)

---

[2] Pearson r. = 37, sig. = 0.00. Correlation obtained from aggregated data set consisting of information from ten analyzed countries.

[3] For more on the preference model of activity in advanced age (retirement-oriented, work-oriented and adaptive types of older workers) and value systems influencing the level of activity, see project website http://ivris.fss.muni.cz or Vidovicova (2005).

interesting exception of Estonian women, who on average would like to stay at work for longer.

We can claim that all the DIALOG countries observed have to some extent a lower average preferred retirement age than the expected retirement age, and that the latter more closely approximates to the statutory retirement age laid down by the legislation of the respective country. However, the preference for early exit is rather pronounced, and we may suspect that this preference is going to translate into real early exits.

One may wonder whether the desire to retire early is really a question of preferences, or whether it is dependent on socio-demographic, economic or maybe welfare-state conditions. We will take a closer look at the impact of respondents' sex, since transition to retirement is usually understood as a highly gendered experience. Age may also play a role since individual perception of retirement may change as people approach the actual beginning of retirement, and when more and more peers share their experience of life after retirement. Attained level of education may serve as a proxy variable for job quality and level of the workload, especially in a physical sense. While those with a lower educational level may be more likely to perform more manual and physically-demanding jobs, and therefore seek to exit the labour market early, those with higher education may not need to "rush" into retirement, since the service sectors are more favourable for older workers (Reday-Mulvey 2005). Further, we will look at the respondents' labour force partic-

Table 12.2 Description of variables

Desire to retire early	*Dependent variable* that equals 1 if the respondent prefers early retirement and 0 if the respondent's preference and expectation as to retirement age are equal.
Labour force participation	*Independent variable* that equals 0 if the respondent is not working (not employed) and 1 if the respondent works (full-time or part-time).
Sex	*Independent variable* that equals 1 for a man and 0 for a woman.
Age of respondent	*Independent variable* with four dummy variables for each age category: 45–49, 50–54, 55–59 and 60–64 years of age.
Attained level of education	*Independent variable* indicating three levels of education and three dummy variables for each level: lower secondary education, higher secondary education and university education.
Region *(applies only to Germany)*	*Independent variable* indicating regional separation for Germany – Western Germany versus Eastern Germany.

ipation because those who are already outside the labour market (but not yet retired) may see early retirement as an especially appealing "safe harbour".

We chose desire for early retirement as dependent variable, while labour force participation, sex, age of respondent, attained level of education and region are independent variables. The dependent variable was dichotomized into two categories: (1) Preferred retirement age is higher than expected, and (2) Preferred and expected retirement age are equal. Logistic regression analysis will allow us to estimate the effects of a characteristic on the probability of desire for early retirement while holding constant the effects of other variables. A more detailed description of the variables used in the analysis is contained in Table 12.2.

The results of the analysis are reported in Table 12.3, separately for each country. There were some statistically-significant differences between respondents with regard to the characteristics included in the models, though these differences were relatively minor on the whole. We used the odds ratio in order to explain the effect of individual characteristics on the probability of preference for early retirement.

Some of the individual characteristics in the Czech Republic, Germany and Slovenia seem to be significant determinants in explaining the preference for early retirement. Although we assumed that there are differences in preferences between men and women with regard to the desire to retire early, the analysis showed no statistically-significant difference. Respondents living in the Czech Republic and Slovenia and participating in the labour force are more likely to prefer early retirement as compared to respondents who do not work. This would suggest that

Table 12.3 Determinants of the desire to retire early, based on the logistic regression analysis estimated for population in the age group 45–64 (odds ratio)

	Czech Rep.	Germany	Poland	Romania	Slovenia
Gender					
Male (vs. female)	0.57	0.98	0.96	0.67	1.19
Labour force participation					
Working (vs. not working)	3.80***	1.29	0.71	2.43	2.01*
Level of education					
Higher secondary education (vs. lower secondary education)	0.90	0.98	0.98	0.88	0.77
University education (vs. lower secondary education)	0.32	0.69	0.53	0.75	0.28**
Age of respondent					
50–54 (vs. 45–49)	1.36	0.84	0.87	0.53	0.97
55–59 (vs. 45–49)	0.61	0.57***	0.63	0.75	0.48
60–64 (vs. 45–49)	0.33	0.45***	1.24	0.17	1.82
Region					
Western Germany (vs. Eastern Germany)	–	0.79	–	–	–
BIC	6.849	25.108	33.785	26.782	21.579

*significant for $p <= 0.05$; **significant for $p <= 0.01$;***significant for $p <= 0.00$

Notes: Reference variable in brackets; data weighted by internal weight; Austria, Belgium (Flanders), Estonia, Hungary, Italy, Lithuania, The Netherlands and Cyprus had to be excluded from the analysis because of the missing relevant variables

those who actually experience life outside the labour market see its disadvantages more clearly. The desire to retire early depends on the level of education attained only in Slovenia, where people with a university degree are more likely to want to retire early than those with a lower educational qualification, once other variables are excluded. It is surprising that the level of education is not a significant determinant in all the other countries included in the analysis. Respondents in the age groups 55–59 and 60–64 living in Germany are more likely to want to retire early as compared to respondents in the younger age categories. There are no significant differences between the Eastern and Western regions of Germany with regard to the desire to retire early.

The desire to retire early does not depend on age, gender, level of education and labour force participation in Romania and Poland.

These results of logistic regression, indicating in many instances the statistical insignificance of the impact of independent variables, underpin the idea that work-retirement decisions are not based on commonly-analysed socio-demographic variables.

12.2.5 Pensions Offer Much Less Money than the Income Prior to Retirement Does (D)

Literature on retirement upholds the idea that the decision to retire is related to the financial incentives offered by the labour market and the pension system. It is to be expected that a person's decision regarding whether or not to retire is based on a rational choice: a comparison of one's anticipated financial needs in retirement with the anticipated financial resources. Having said that, people also compare how satisfied they are in their current employment with how satisfied they expect to be in retirement. In the event that satisfaction in the latter case is expected to be higher, a person may decide to make a trade-off between being more satisfied and having a lower level of pension income (Atchley 2000). Let us have a closer look at the first part of the argument. According to the information offered by the OECD, the individual average pension entitlement as a percentage of individual pre-retirement gross earnings varies between 78.3% in Austria and 44.4% in the Czech Republic (Pensions 2005). There is therefore a substantial drop in objective terms in the income when a person's source of income shifts from the labour market to the social security system. Moreover, there is more at stake if one's pre-retirement income is above average. In Table 12.4, which gives an overview of the redistribution practice within the old-age pension systems, we can see that the higher income groups are disadvantaged by the redistribution in half of the countries for which data are available. For example, in the Czech Republic, if the pre-retirement income of a male is only half of the mean Czech income, then his pension is 1.58 times higher than his pre-retirement earnings. However, if a Czech male earns two times the average, his pension is only 57% of his earnings.

Table 12.4 Level of redistribution within pension systems – percentage of gross replacement rate by individual earnings (average = 100%), mandatory pensions, men only

	Multiple of average income	
	Half	Double
Austria	100	82
Czech Republic	158	57
Finland	120	100
Germany	103	82
Netherlands	101	100
Poland	100	100

Notes: In the case of Austria and Poland the replacement rates differ for women, otherwise relevant to both sexes
Source: OECD (Pensions...2005), own calculation

12.2.6 However, Early Retirement is not Something to be Looked Forward to (E)

Coming to the other part of the argument offered above at (D), people – future pensioners, are highly aware of the fact that their level of income will decrease after retirement in many cases. When we asked in the IPPAS survey what they think they would miss most from the world of work when they retire, the answer was clear: the difference between salary and pension (46%). Other possibilities as "being busy with duties" (21.9%), "feeling of being useful" (16.2%) and "contacts with co-workers/customers and business partners" (13.2%/2.8%) were also important, but to a lesser extent. Here we have an illustration of one of the paradoxes in the chain: Even though the respondents know about the financial disadvantage of being retired, they still opt for an early exit – those who think that they may miss the financial resources would wish to retire 3.7 years earlier. On the other hand, those who are afraid of loosing the feeling of usefulness are not in such a hurry to retire; their wish to retire earlier only makes a difference of 2.7 years. One may speculate that it is connected to the satisfaction which a job may actually provide. While money can be earned "elsewhere", it may be more difficult to feel useful once retired. These work-related values are usually gender-specific (see Fig. 12.4). Although the differences are not too big, it seems that the social features of work may play a larger role for women in preventing early exit than for men.

Bearing this in mind, we have made only a small step towards answering the key question as to why do so many Europeans look forward to or even rush into retirement when they are aware of its implications. We can present other speculative explanations of this phenomenon. A number of studies have been carried out into satisfaction after exit from the labour market. McGoldrick and Cooper (1988) or Vickerstaff et al. (2004) provide a long list of possible factors impacting satisfaction after early retirement, including retirement type, age, time since retiring, financial provisions, work after retirement, health factors, employers' policies, voluntary vs. involuntary early exit, etc. Other authors state that "the two most important factors

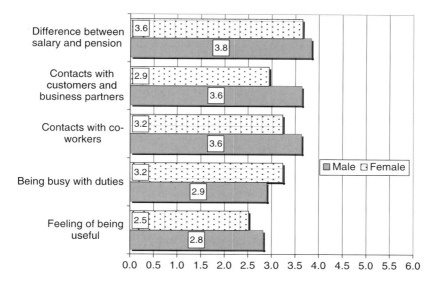

Fig. 12.4 Desire to retire early by the expected lack of work features (in years, by sex)
Source: IPPAS
Notes: The high value of the DRE indicator means that a respondent has a strong preference for
early retirement; Data available for CZ, LT, NL, PL, RO and SL only

[for achievement of satisfaction in retirement] are an accurate preconception of retirement and a favourable pre-retirement attitude toward retirement" (Harris and
Cole 1980, 254). Our data unfortunately do not permit us to evaluate the relevance
of these important factors since we do not have the relevant variables. However, we
can use as a proxy overall satisfaction with the standard of living, present work and
available time for doing things, and see if it makes any difference to the level of
desire to exit the labour force early (Fig. 12.5).

It seems that the level of reported satisfaction makes a major difference: For
instance, those who are not at all satisfied with their work would like to retire
5.3 years earlier, while those who are highly satisfied wish to retire 2.1 years
earlier – quite a substantial difference (3.2 years). Similarly, a high level of satisfaction with the standard of living – as we have seen earlier, a type of satisfaction
seriously threatened by (early) retirement – reduces the desire for early retirement
by 2.1 years. Respondents' satisfaction with their time for doing things suggests a
slightly different interpretation. We may speculate that those with a subjectively
insufficient amount of time to be invested in their preferred activities are more
probably those with "second careers", rushing out of the labour market to exercise
another type of activity. One can almost hear: "I am not satisfied with the amount
of time I have now for the things I would like to do, therefore I would like to retire
early and have more time for doing things which I like".

Fig. 12.5 Desire to retire early (in years) by level of satisfaction with standard of living, present work and available time for doing things
Note: Question "Are you satisfied ... with your current situation with regard to the following ...?"
Data available for AT, CZ, LT and SL only
Source: IPPAS

Another influential feature that we may explore in the IPPAS database is the opinion as to how the transition between work and retirement should be organised. McGoldrick and Cooper (1988) propose that those who have been somehow pushed out of the labour market and forced into retirement seem to be less satisfied with their life after early retirement. Rabušic (2004) also showed in the Czech environment that many retirees actually claimed that they did not want to retire, and that they were also dissatisfied with their decision.

We can see in Fig. 12.6 the level of desire to retire early, broken down by opinions as to the best method of transition to retirement for older workers.

We can derive two different conclusions from Fig. 12.6. On the one hand, those who support gradually diminishing work, i.e. more flexible work-retirement arrangements, are less likely to want to retire earlier than those who prefer being forced to stop working altogether. On the other hand, those who are very keen to retire would like to stop working at once. This fact underpins the idea introduced above as to the possible application of preference theory to work-retirement decisions, since this type of respondent seems to be coherent in their preferences and only strongly oriented towards retirement. One could however also consider it to be somewhat paradoxical to prefer to be forced to stop working altogether (including being dismissed or fired, followed by being unemployed) as early as possible.

Table 12.5 Average desire to retire early (in years) by support for selected sustainable pension-related policies by country

	SL	EE	PL	LI	NL	DE	RO	FI	CZ
To raise the retirement age	4.6	3.7	2.4	1.8	0.5	1.6	1.4	1.7	2.1
To abolish early retirement	4.5	4.3	3.5	3.5	3.3	3.3	2.6	2.3	2.0

Notes: Data not available for AT
Source: IPPAS

How does this personal desire, which can be observed *en masse*, influence policy-making in the societies in focus? With regard to this aspect, we can have a look at the preference for two policy measures in the analysed countries (see Table 12.5).

Both policy measures quoted in Table 12.5 aim to increase the employment rates of older workers by closing down the early exit routes from the labour force. When we tested the impact of the preference for such measures on respondents' own desire to retire early, we obtained quite surprising results once again, since some major differences can be found within the countries. In Finland, the Netherlands, Germany, Romania and Lithuania, those respondents who tend to support the idea of rising the retirement age are also less keen on retiring early themselves. In other countries such as the Czech Republic, Poland, Estonia, and most notably

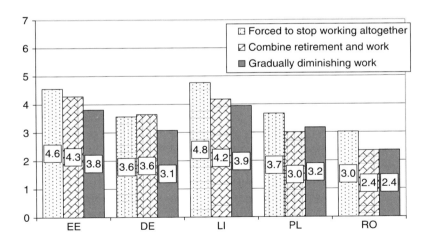

Fig. 12.6 Wish to retire earlier (in years) by opinions as to how the transition into retirement should be structured
Note: Data available for EE, DE, LI, Pl and RO only
Source: IPPAS

Slovenia, the expressed support for this policy is not accompanied by low desire for early exit. The lack of consistency between attitudes and preferences seems rather paradoxical, rather as if people would like to *cut the branch on which they are sitting*.

Secondly, Table 12.5 shows us that there seems to be a conviction in the Czech Republic and Slovenia that outcomes of rising retirement age and abolishing early retirement schemes are pretty much similar, at least in terms of differences in expected and preferred retirement age. However, in the Netherlands, Germany or Lithuania, those respondents who support the abolishment of early retirement are much more likely to want to retire early themselves than those respondents who support the idea of rising the retirement age. The reasons for such intercultural differences are very interesting, but rather complex, and may form the inspiration for wider discussion of further research, as we cannot provide an explanation from our IPPAS data sets.

12.3 Discussion

It seems that we have observed not just one but several retirement paradoxes based on the results presented above. Firstly, despite the fact that citizens seem to be aware that societies are ageing and cannot really afford to see their labour forces shrink or to exacerbate the public debts of the pension schemes, people do not tend to behave accordingly, and they would like to leave the labour market as soon as possible. They feel this way even though they are aware of the serious losses, both financial and social, that they might witness as retirees. Secondly, it seems that awareness of possible dissatisfaction with life after leaving the labour market does not prevent their wanting to retire early. Last but not least, respondents' personal preferences for early retirement do not prevent them from supporting the policies of closing down early exit pathways by increasing the statutory retirement age.

Schoenmaeckers and Vanderleyden (2005) also talk about a *paradox* in connection with the obvious discrepancy between preferred and expected retirement age. They refer to recent research in which this phenomenon is explained by older workers' "reluctance" to work longer if "others exit the labour force at a younger age" (2005, 56). This explanation indicates that retirement in modern societies is socially constructed. And it is clear that there is much more at stake than just a question of wanting to retire early. Guillemard and van Gunsteren (1991) talk about an across-the-board reorganisation of the life course when considering redrawing the boundary between working life and retirement. These authors argue that early exit is not a matter of merely rescheduling the three-box life-cycle model, but that it is part and parcel of the process of transformation of the relationship between the welfare system and the life course, part of flexibilization and individualization, as it represents a challenge for the definite connection (equation) between old age, retirement, and non-occupational activity. Definitive withdrawal from the labour market is no longer defined by the old-age pension system, but by different early exit pathways, often not connected to old age at all. Those who go directly from a job into retirement are becoming a minority, and only a shrinking share of people leaves at the normal retirement age. Old-age retirement is being substituted by other institutional arrangements, such as disability or unemployment schemes, albeit these are less generous. Given that disability insurance rarely applies strict age-related criteria, we can conclude that reaching a certain qualifying age is being supplemented by functional criteria when it comes to marking the end of people's careers (Guillemard and van Gunsteren 1991).

The results of the IPPAS presented here support the idea that the age of exit from the labour market is becoming more and more blurred. People in many European countries have different preferences and expectations about the age of retirement, and these differ to a certain degree from the legal "ideal". To what extent this almost universally-expressed desire to retire early will actually influence the situation on the labour market, in policy-making and individual life courses of our respondents can be questions to be addressed in further research.

Part V
Policy Implications and Conclusions

Chapter 13
The Need to Adapt and Reform Social Policy: Setting the Stage for Effective Population-friendly Policies

Dragana Avramov and Robert Cliquet

Abstract Family life and working conditions, gender relations and intergenerational solidarity, the three broad domains on which citizens and policy stakeholders of 14 European countries reported their experiences, attitudes and expectations in the Population Policy Acceptance Study (DIALOG), and in particular the findings from the International Population Policy Acceptance database (IPPAS), are central to several European Union social, economic and political challenges.

We first give a policy insight into the processes of standard setting at the European level. Then we report on the key scientific insight from the DIALOG study on desired fertility and the scope for fertility enhancement, women's aspirations towards employment, the desire for early retirement among both men and women, and preferred living arrangements at advanced age, as well as the impact of income on behaviour and attitudes. For each research question we identify specific policy challenges, and in the last part we draw general conclusions about the need to adapt and reform policy.

Keywords: Social policy · Population policy · Social cohesion · Family life · Desired fertility · Quality of work · Ageing

13.1 Introduction

At the beginning of the 21st century, European societies are struggling to adapt to the global economy while having to adapt to population changes. The public policy debate, and more particularly as it relates to social protection, is clearly changing. People's expectations towards public support in all phases of the life course are persistently in line with the very high value which they attach to what has become known as the European social model.

D. Avramov
Population and Social Policy Consultants (PSPC), Brussels, Belgium
e-mail: avramov@avramov.org

C. Höhn et al. (eds.), *People, Population Change and Policies: Vol. 2: Demographic Knowledge – Gender – Ageing*, © Springer Science+Business Media B.V. 2008

The main pillar of the European social model enshrined in the welfare states in the last decades of the 20th century has been the widespread distribution of prosperity throughout the population by means of legal measures and the redistribution of resources. We observed a marked acceleration in the development of welfare functions in most European countries in the 1960s and 1970s. Public policies evolved towards the enlargement of the domains of protection, the increase in the number of beneficiaries and the transformation of parts of needs-based assistance into a set of social rights. We have seen the emergence of social rights which are not work-related, such as minimum non-contributory benefits. These trends can be seen in the evolution of the costs of social protection, the development of a broad range of collective social services, and the assertion and strengthening of fundamental social rights that are protected by law.

Today, the mainstream social policy discourse is shifting away from "passive" protection as a matter of individual rights, and is moving towards "active" policies. Action is oriented towards economic growth and job creation, open and competitive markets inside Europe, getting people back to work, longer working lives, maintaining employability of older workers by life-long education, greater flexibility for enterprises, and adaptability of workers to labour market requirements.

The fear that globalisation and demography are going to drag down the potential growth rates in Europe is clearly articulated in the Communication from the President of the European Commission Barroso to the Spring European Council (2005). In view of the current and expected pressure on the pension and other functions of the social security system, which is associated with demographic ageing, the quest to modernize public policies is encapsulated in the objective "to give people jobs and make sure they remain in work or education throughout their lives".

Whereas it is the prerogative of elected or appointed politicians to make the political decisions on directions and priorities for action, the role of researchers is limited to the sphere of the identification of challenges to social cohesion, analyses of policy options and implications of policy choices. With regard to the priorities for action with a view to addressing population challenges in increasingly competitive economies and at least preserving social cohesion, if not reinforcing it, the study of the implications of policy choices inherently needs to include the identification of the requirements for their effectiveness.

Here we will address some of the main requirements or key success factors for policies, namely the policy insight and the knowledge-based involvement of citizens as actors in shaping their own future.

13.2 The Policy Insight

Family life and working conditions, gender relations and intergenerational solidarity, the three broad domains on which citizens and policy stakeholders of 14

European countries reported their experiences, attitudes and expectations in the Population Policy Acceptance Study (DIALOG), and in particular the findings from the International Population Policy Acceptance database (IPPAS), are central to several European Union social, economic and political challenges.

In accordance with the subsidiarity principle, European institutions have no formal competence to act directly on family life in any stage of the life course. This implies that it is first and foremost the responsibility of Member States to devise appropriate responses to the social needs and to develop policies and measures relevant for the country. National governments determine the conceptual and normative frameworks for social and population-related policies and are responsible for their financing, organization and implementation.

Ever since the Amsterdam Treaty of 1997 and the development of a "co-ordinated strategy for employment", the strong EU focus is on the employment and unemployment dimensions of policy priorities. Whereas the achievement of economic goals remains central, in recent years the themes of quality of work and family well-being are increasingly emerging and interweaving in various documents. The emphasis of several Community policies, in particular regarding employment and unemployment, funding and reforming the pension schemes, provision of care services in view of reconciliation of work and family life, promotion of gender equality, active ageing, health and long-term care for the elderly, and welfare and social cohesion, are among the key priority areas that are shaping the European social model and impinging on people's family lives.

The aspirational principles of "Social Europe" are summarized in the strategic goals set at the Lisbon European Council (2000). The Lisbon Strategy seeks to create "the most competitive and dynamic knowledge-based economy in the world, capable of sustainable economic growth with more and better jobs and greater social cohesion". Improved co-ordination between the Member States in the areas of economic, employment and social policies by means of the open method of co-ordination builds on an agreement by governments on common objectives to be achieved by 2010 and a monitoring procedure to progressively develop a framework for the analysis of achievements and future action.

The comparative analyses of the International Population Policy Acceptance Survey (IPPAS) regarding family matters that cuts across age groups and generations provide abundant information on how well countries are performing with regard to their proclaimed policy aims and to the expectations of their citizens. The results of the DIALOG analyses that pitch so well into a monitoring procedure set out by the open method are culture-sensitive and built on the analysis of the country-specific history of the development of values and norms underpinning public policies and individual behaviour in family matters. Consequently, the study enhances the depth of the learning process at the European level that goes far beyond the champion league approach and ranking of countries according to selected indicators of social progress.

With the accession of ten Member States in 2004, the cohesion policies increased in importance. The reduction of disparities between rich and poorer regions enshrined in the Amsterdam Treaty and of the fall in excessive social disparities achieved by means of the integration of social policy dimensions, especially through the Broad Economic Policy Guidelines and European Social Policy Agenda, reinforces the inter- and intra-country solidarity. The Population Policy Acceptance Study provides rich material for the understanding of the way in which the socio-economic and political transformation in the Eastern and Central European Member States and one candidate country, notably in the Czech Republic, Estonia, Lithuania, Hungary, Poland, Slovenia, and Romania, impact people's family and working conditions, and in which direction policies need to evolve to meet citizens' needs and expectations.

Diversity is no doubt a feature of the social protection systems and population-related policies. There are however communalities – more particularly when the prospective framework conditions associated with demographic development and greater economic integration are taken aboard. This horizon of universality is reflected in the communication from the Commission's Green Paper (March 2005) "Confronting demographic challenge: a new solidarity between generations". The Paper stresses that the Community must take demographic changes into account for modernizing social protection systems, especially pensions, and for improving the quality of jobs available to elderly people.

In view of the magnitude of the increase of the elderly population, Ambient Assisted Living for the ageing societies to extend the time during which elderly people can live independently in their preferred environment with the support of information and communication technologies, is also a high policy priority (Commission of the European Communities 2006).

A strong Community political commitment to the realization of the modernization of social protection systems and enhancement of citizens' quality of life, under conditions of population ageing and the globalisation of the economy, may need to be underpinned by a strong public awareness of the issues at stake, acceptance of proposed reforms and future actions, but also by acknowledgement of gaps in the proposed policy platforms.

Today, it is generally acknowledged at the European Union level, as well as by national governments, that demography needs to be considered for developing adaptive policy choices (Avramov 2002; Höhn 2005). This need stems from demographic ageing, due to low fertility and increased longevity. But is low fertility, which is the principal push factor for accelerated ageing of European populations, our inevitable destiny?

13.3 The Scientific Insight on Fertility from the IPPAS

Low fertility is a demographic challenge, but the need for policy adaptation does not stem only from the demographic consequences. The need for public policy originates today first and foremost from the insight that people would like to have more children than they eventually have. The realization of a smaller-than-desired family size is a result of adaptive strategies on the part of individuals and couples that may be both the result and cause of stress and a feeling of dissatisfaction and regret.

13.3.1 *How many Children and Which Family Policies do Europeans Want?*

Fertility is below replacement level in all Member States. However, the IPPAS data show that people would like to have more children in the 14 countries studied. In Germany, Belgium (Flanders), Finland and the Netherlands, the total number of children respondents expect to have over their life course is slightly higher than the present total fertility rate. In all the Eastern European countries, and in Austria, Italy and Cyprus, the expected number lies considerably above the present fertility levels in the country (Fig. 13.1).

Desired fertility is even higher than the expected number of children. In Estonia, for example, the total fertility rate stands at 1.37 children per woman, and is thus 35% below replacement level. If people actually had the number of children they would like to have, the total fertility rate would be comfortably above replacement level.

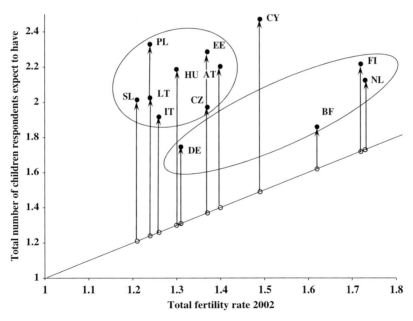

Fig. 13.1 The relation between the total fertility rate and the total number of children respondents expect to have during their life course, by country
Source: IPPAS database (Avramov and Cliquet 2006)

Whether these fertility expectations and desires will be realized or not depends on two sets of circumstances: the scope and intensity of societal support, and life course obstacles that individuals encounter.

With regard to the policy measures that were put on the table in the Population Policy Acceptance Survey respondents were confronted both with a range of standard measures that already exist but may need further improvement, and new measures that are perceived as desirable.

Five policy areas are considered:

- Labour market conditions;
- Services to assist (working) parents;
- Income support or income replacement;
- Tax rebates; and
- Access to low-cost housing and education.

Labour market conditions (more and better part-time work and flexible working hours) are the top priority in Austria, Belgium, Finland, Germany, Italy and the Netherlands. Financial benefits in the form of direct transfer payments to parents (bonus at birth, bonus for families with children) are seen as the first priority by most respondents in the Czech Republic, Lithuania and Poland. Indirect benefits (lower taxes) appeal to the majority as the first priority in Romania and Cyprus. General social protection functions (housing, education) are the first preference of the majority in Hungary and Estonia.

Whereas there are some intra-country differences in the choice of the first preferred measures, in 14 countries eight out of every 10 respondents on average are in favour of each one of the family measures they were asked to comment on.

The specific family policy measures evaluated and favoured by the overwhelming majority of Europeans with regard to fertility intentions are:

- Improved parental leave;
- Lower income tax with dependent children;
- Better day-care for children <3;
- Better day-care for children >3;
- Income-dependent child allowance;
- Allowance at childbirth;
- Allowance for care-giving parents;
- Substantial rise in child allowance;
- Childcare for school-going children;
- Flexible working hours;
- More opportunities for part-time work;
- Substantial decrease in costs for education;
- Better housing for families with children.

These results reflect the experience and awareness of the significance of public policies to enable families to bear and rear children. The issues at stake are obviously people's quality of life, and the realization of their expectations about the timing of parenthood and the number of children they would like to have. For the majority,

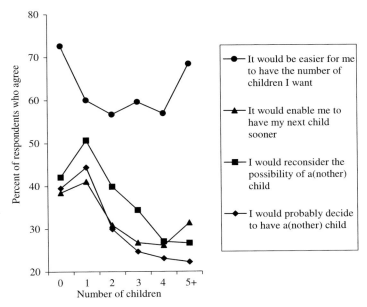

Fig. 13.2 Expected consequences of desired family policy measures, by number of children (pooled and weighted data)
Source: IPPAS database (Avramov and Cliquet 2006)

the family-friendly measures would make it easier to have the number of children they would like to have. For an important proportion of people, policies would also lead to reconsidering the possibility of having a(nother) child or would enable them to have a(nother) child sooner (Fig. 13.2).

If all the measures favoured by the citizens were implemented would that have any effect on fertility levels in the country?

There seems to be potential for a modest, albeit not negligible, positive effect on fertility levels.

We have analysed the possible consequences of the implementation of desired family policy measures for: facilitating the realization of the number of children the respondent would like to have; enabling the respondent to have their next child sooner; encouraging a respondent to reconsider the possibility of a(nother) child; and encouraging a respondent to probably decide to have a(nother) child.

In order to analyse the possible effects of the selected family policy measures on fertility, an investigation is carried out not only of the relations between measures and possible consequences, but also of the relations between the measures and the total number of children people expect to have. In general, positive relations are found between the individual policy measures considered and the possible consequences on future childbirth. The strength of the relation, however, varies according to the measure considered. The correlation between the family policy measures considered and the possible consequences on future fertility is positive but quite low

($r = 0.17$). Also, the correlation between the composite variable on policy measures and the expected number of children is low ($r = 0.14$). A somewhat stronger association is found between the composite variable on policy measures and the number of additionally expected children ($r = 0.23$), but the correlation with the expected number of children is much lower ($r = 0.09$). This analysis on pooled and weighted data shows that some positive effect may be expected, but that we cannot expect the eleven proposed measures to contribute to a substantial increase in the fertility level.

How much exactly might those measures boost fertility? On the basis of the number of respondents who originally didn't know whether they would have a(nother) child and those who declared that they did not want a(nother) child, but who stated that they would probably decide to have a(nother) child were the desired family policy measures to be implemented, it can be calculated for the pooled PPAS data that the effect of policy measures would increase the average number of children by approximately 7%. This is, however, a minimal estimate. This result may underestimate the potential for a real increase because respondents who intend to have a(nother) child might also further increase their intentions upon implementation of specific family policy measures. A maximum estimate can be obtained if all respondents are considered who would probably decide to have a(nother) child were the desired policy measures to be implemented. In that case, the effect of policy measures would be an increase by approximately 15%. It can be concluded that the effect of desired family policy measures has the potential for increasing fertility levels within the estimated range between 7 and 15%.

However, the number of children people expect to have and additional children they might want to have providing that the desired policy support is obtained needs to be revisited in view of obstacles which people do not currently perceive or acknowledge. Indeed, research shows that people realign their intentions with regard to the number of children they want in view of their personal life-course experience, which is lived in a dynamic family and general societal context. Postponement of childbearing or the decision not to have (another) child may be associated with health problems, sub-fecundity, relational problems (no partner, disruption of a relation such as divorce or bad relationship), various forms of social exclusion (unemployment, precarious employment and poor access to social protection), as well as lifestyle choices made over the life-course.

Data on the total number of children people expect to have as the sum of children they already have and the expressed intention to have additional children, as recorded in the IPPAS, used for the calculation of expected fertility levels, need to take into account life course events that result both in deficit and excess fertility, i.e. realised fertility that lies below or above the level intended.

Fertility surveys undertaken at regular time intervals in the past decades have shown that excess fertility has become a minor problem due to the generalised use of modern contraceptives and the availability of induced abortion. Deficit fertility (i.e. the difference between larger desired and smaller realized number of children) is still a considerable problem.

The rationale for taking into account deficit fertility in evaluating and correcting expressed fertility intentions is based on two major sources of information, namely the results of earlier investigations on reproductive behaviour and the knowledge about recent societal trends with respect to family life. On the basis of the two last Belgian (Flemish) fertility surveys (1982 and 1991) in which information was gathered on the degree of and the reasons for deficit fertility, this phenomenon may be estimated to be around 20% (Cliquet et al. 1983; Cliquet and Callens 1993). Contrary to what is often thought, the major reasons for deficit fertility in developed countries are not so much of a simple economic nature, but have mainly to do with socio-biological factors (in particular sub-fecundity at higher ages), relational problems (e.g. no partner, divorce), and socio-psychological factors (various lifestyle choices which result in low fertility). The major societal trends which can be expected to have a depressing effect on reproductive behaviour under the prevailing labour market conditions, welfare models and value shifts towards ever-increasing secularisation in the DIALOG countries are: decreasing employment security, increasing female employment, increase of alternative living arrangements, and increase of divorce and dissolution of unions. In the former socialist countries, economic factors associated with the transition play a particularly important role in the birth deficit. Nevertheless, here too alternative living arrangements and union instability are on the rise and may become, as in the West, the more predominant determinants of deficit fertility than income.

When we apply the survey-based Belgian (Flemish) correction factor to the pooled PPAS data, the expected number of children for the youngest age group (20–24), decreases from 2.00 to 1.75 children. The effect, however, varies quite substantially according to country. For example, in Western Germany the expected number of children corrected for deficit fertility decreases from 1.9 to 1.5, whereas in Finland it decreases from 2.4 to 1.9.

13.3.2 Conclusions About the Possible Effect of Policy Measures on Fertility

The general conclusion is that the family policy measures considered in PPAS would have a modest positive effect on completed fertility. The overall impact of the eleven proposed policy measures on increasing the number of children (taking into account both the desired policy support and possible life-course obstacles) may be estimated at between 6 and 14%. Our analysis does, however, indicate that the modest increase resulting from a comprehensive basket of measures that combines enhancement of family-friendly employment with family-friendly support services and direct and indirect financial support to parents of dependent children, would bring fertility levels close to or even above replacement level in many countries. This could be the case in Estonia at the higher end of the scale, Cyprus, Finland, Poland, Lithuania, Slovenia, Austria, the Czech Republic, the Netherlands and Hungary, at the lower end. Consequently, these countries would be much better placed

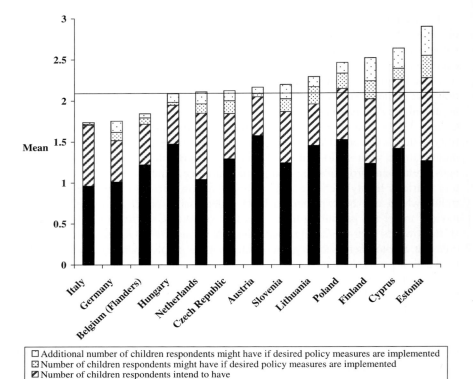

Fig. 13.3 Positive effect on fertility of desired policies, taking into account expectations and possible life-course obstacles, by country
Source: IPPAS database (Avramov and Cliquet 2006)

to deal with the negative impact of population ageing. However, in Germany, Italy and Belgium, the population expects much more than the eleven measures studied under the DIALOG project to bring fertility close to replacement level (see Fig. 13.3).

The general scientific insight leads us to a conclusion that more substantial and sustainable effects of policy measures to enable people to have the number of children they wish in all the countries can only be expected to ensue from comprehensive changes in the labour market conditions and a concomitant enhancement of opportunities for individuals to manage their life course in innovative ways. An important asset over which people have relatively little control, up until retirement age, is time. The prolongation of education, sometimes lengthy periods of unemployment, a successful career, delayed parenthood, first birth in the late 20s and/or experience of sub-fecundity in mid-30s, excessive pressure on time in mid-life, and long years of inactivity in retirement, are factors of the malfunctioning of the "economics of time" in our modern societies. The future fertility levels may be

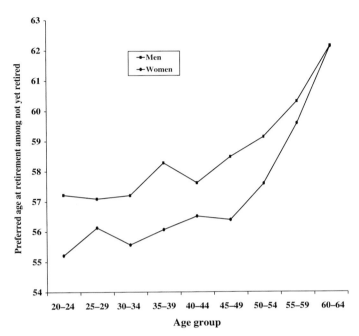

Fig. 13.7 Preferred age at retirement among not yet retired
Notes: Pooled weighted data for: the Czech Republic, Estonia, Germany, Lithuania, the Netherlands, Austria, Poland, Romania, Slovenia and Finland
Source: IPPAS database (Avramov and Cliquet 2006)

policies that affect labour market conditions in general and into age-friendly work policies in particular.

Whereas younger elderly people may have to recalibrate their expectations for long years of leisure following early retirement, considerable adaptations will also be necessary at very high age with regard to independent living. Our study shows that living at home is the preferred environment even when age-related ailments set in and the elderly need help from others (Table 13.2). Almost eight out of every ten people would like to continue living in their own homes with the help of professionals, or of professionals assisted by their own children. The caring capacity of the existing social support infrastructure will come under considerable and ever-increasing strain as numbers of the elderly, especially the oldest old (80+), continue to increase.

The number of children matters for living arrangement preferences. The higher the number of children, the higher are expectations towards children to provide regular help to their parents who wish to remain in their own homes (Fig. 13.8).

Table 13.2 Preferred living arrangements as an old person in need of help

Preferred living arrangement as an old person in need of help	%
At home, but with professional help	19.0
A home, but with regular help of children and family	36.2
At home, but with regular help of professionals and children	21.7
In a home for the elderly or in the room of a boarding house	8.9
Other	14.2
N (absolute number = 100%)	23,587

Pooled weighted data for: the Czech Republic, Estonia, Germany, Lithuania, Austria, Poland, Romania and Slovenia
Source: IPPAS database (Avramov and Cliquet 2006)

In the Population Policy Acceptance Survey, we did not ask people about their attitudes towards information and communication technology (ICT) to enhance options for the elderly to communicate, increase mobility, enhance independent living, allow for health monitoring and decrease the sense of social isolation. However, if tomorrow's elderly are to realise their preference for independent living in their preferred environment, namely their own home, the assistance from professionals,

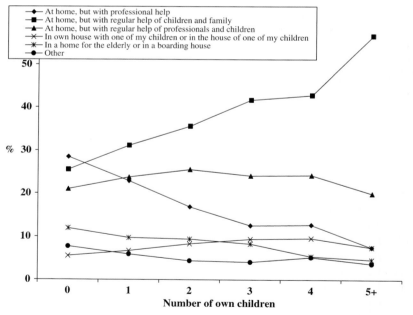

Fig. 13.8 Preferred living arrangements as an old person in need of help, by number of own children
Notes: Pooled weighted data for: the Czech Republic, Estonia, Germany, Lithuania, Austria, Poland, Romania and Slovenia
Source: IPPAS database (Avramov and Cliquet 2006)

who are already in a short supply, and children, who will be in the workforce, will
need to be complemented by acceptable, affordable ICT-based solutions.

13.6 Does Income Matter?

In order to analyse the effects of income on behaviour and attitudes under study,
we have constructed the "equivalised household income" variable. The equivalence
scale is used to adjust incomes for the varying size and composition of households.
The equivalised income is thus the income per adult equivalent. The first adult in
a household is given a weight of one, other adults a weight of 0.5 and each child
below the age of 16 a weight of 0.3.

The Population Policy Acceptance Study confirms that the cross-country
differences in household income in the early 2000s – that is at the time of the
surveys – are more pronounced between Western and Eastern European countries
(Table 13.3).

We measure poverty here in relative terms. This means that poor households are
defined as households with less then 60% of the equalised median income of the
country in which they live.

The most important intra-country differentiation in income levels is according to
educational level (gamma = 0.35). In our survey, we did not find that poverty risks
are associated with age ($r = 0.03$).

With regard to household composition, the best-off are couples without children
and the worst-off are single mothers. This finding is identical to conclusions from
other surveys (Avramov 2002).

Both the current number of children and the total expected number of children
are negatively related to the equivalised household income in all countries. This
means that those on a higher income have and intend to have fewer children than
the poor (Fig. 13.9). Regarding the reasons for not wanting a(nother) child, among
the better-off the financial cost is less important than the desire for more leisur time.

Table 13.3 Equivalised household income in Euro, by country in the early 2000s

Country	Median income per adult equivalent in Euro	Year of the IPPAS survey	Number of respondents
Netherlands	1,163	2002	1,853
Western Germany	1,083	2003	1,337
Belgium (Flanders)	1,000	2003	3,670
Finland	920	2002	2,831
Austria	920	2001	1,535
Eastern Germany	916	2003	1,478
Slovenia	306	2000	1,349
Czech Republic	208	2001	820
Hungary	127	2000	2,269
Romania	41	2001	1,331

Source: IPPAS database (Avramov and Cliquet 2006)

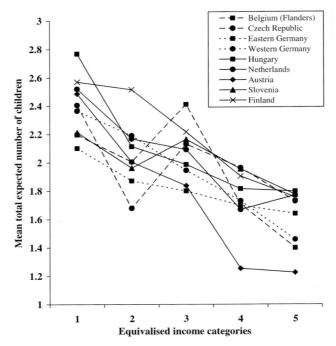

Fig. 13.9 Total expected number of children by equivalised income and country
Source: IPPAS database (Avramov and Cliquet 2006)

On the basis of a multiple classification analysis, the negative relation between
the equivalised income and the total expected number of children is maintained
when controlled for country, age, sex, education and employment status.

The significance of children for their parents is experienced slightly differently
by the poor and the better-off. The poor attach somewhat more importance to having
children and are somewhat more child-oriented than higher income groups.

Regarding the perception of governmental responsibility for family-related policies, higher income groups have lower expectations than low income groups.

Five questions in the Population Policy Acceptance Survey addressed satisfaction
in various domains. The analysis shows that income levels impact satisfaction in
all domains. The higher the income, the greater is the level of satisfaction with
the financial situation, standard of living, dwelling, present work, and available
leisure time.

Whereas financial incentives, be it via tax rebates or direct transfer payments
to parents, are welcomed by the overwhelming majority, both among the poor
and the non-poor, these measures alone cannot be expected to produce a fertility-
enhancement effect. Financial aid to parents is a typical welfare measure that contributes to reducing social disparities, rather than influencing fertility levels.

Furthermore, in view of the fact that the overwhelming majority of the population
are not poor (on average eight out of every ten respondents have a household income

which is above the poverty threshold in the country in which they live), the demographic effects may be expected only from measures that positively affect also this broad population base. Consequently, a mix of legislative measures – a combination of tax regimes, direct transfer payments, childcare facilities, flexible working hours coupled with greater social security, improved education and housing policies could potentially contribute to boosting birth rates.

13.7 Conclusions About the Need to Adapt and Reform Policy

The key challenges for effective future policies as they stem from the Population Policy Acceptance Survey are associated with the following findings:

- Young people, especially women, wish to have more children than they expect to eventually have – they perceive and experience societal obstacles to the realization of their parenthood aspirations;
- Young people would prefer to retire even earlier than their parents, who are causing social concern because they are retiring too early;
- People wish to continue living in their own home at a high age and to receive assistance from professionals and children in their preferred environment – a desire that will result in increasing pressure on the social support infrastructure.

People's perception of disadvantages and risks underpinning choices about parenthood, paid work, and preferred living arrangements, have an impact on the intergenerational transfer of financial resources, services and care provision.

Parenthood and inter-generational solidarity have a great deal to do with social cohesion and the dynamic nature of the human experience of well-being, in particular regarding work and work-free hours, days and years, family dynamics, health, care-giving and care-receiving practices and expectations, and the feeling of security that the social protection system is a reliable source of support when a person is less competitive or unable to perform in the regular labour market.

The key lessons learnt from the IPPAS that need to be taken aboard in public policy formulation and implementation are: There is a need for governments to adapt policies and develop measures and services to meet the needs and expectations of citizens in the early stages of the family cycle and as people grow old; and there is a need for governments to identify requirements and develop instruments to facilitate response shifts among citizens which will be necessary in view of the labour market changes and long-term sustainability of social security and needs for care at high age.

If individuals are to be available on the labour market throughout their lives, the standard life course sequence of events: education→work→ inactivity, is to be changed not only in terms of the timing of events and shortening the duration of retirement years, but also in the centrality of competitive work in people's lives at all ages.

Reconciling life-long education and life-long work, in view of being part of a highly-skilled, adaptable, mobile workforce, with having children, in view of achieving self-fulfilment and intergenerational continuity, requires even more fundamental response shifts.

In order to embark on reforms of the social security systems, there is a considerable need for governments to adapt social institutions and public policies with a view to enhancing the quality of life and well-being of people over their life courses. And there is a major need for the response shifts so that individuals realign their lifestyles and expectations in a competitive, flexible labour market and in an ageing social environment.

Old age is a phase in individuals' life course. The living circumstances depend largely on the individual's history, which is a mix of chances and choices regarding health, education, work, family life, personality features and socio-cultural environment in which opportunities have been enhanced or limited. Thus, more effective ways are needed of spreading the risks associated with competition in the labour market, the low-income/high needs nexus for young parents, stress at work, and high demands on time in the workplace and family over the entire life-course. This challenge may require both adaptive measures and substantive policy reforms.

The need for rethinking social policy choices made in the past about the future obviously goes hand-in-hand with the necessity for palliate measures. The two policy dimensions are complementary. More and better child-care to assist working parents are a must, but will not suffice to address long-term challenges of low fertility and related accelerated demographic ageing. Improving the funding and reforming the pension schemes are necessary, but will not solve many of the social challenges associated with intergenerational solidarity, special needs of elderly workers, and need of a social support infrastructure and assistive technology for ageing populations.

We will go as far as to conclude that **the key success factor** for addressing parenthood choices and population ageing challenges are underpinned by the current and future public policy choices that impinge the paid work in general and family-friendly and age-friendly **working conditions** in particular. The working conditions may be considered as the key to enabling people to have as many children as they wish. They create the framework conditions that enhance the sense of security which may in turn enhance the wish for more than one or two children, and for activating policies on the elderly so that people also live a healthier and more productive life at advanced age.

With regard to the ageing of individuals in ageing societies, ICT has the potential for improving working conditions by partly compensating for age-related fragilization, disabilities and health conditions, thus making elderly workers more competitive in the labour market.

In view of the expected unprecedented increase in numbers of the oldest old, and the desire of people to continue living in their preferred home environments when they become frail at advanced age, the elderly will need assistive technologies that help them, and their family and informal care providers, as well as social care and health care institutions.

Chapter 14
Conclusions

Charlotte Höhn

Abstract This closing chapter aims at synthesising the manifold results of the articles presented in the two volumes. It structures and subsumes the findings into both policy implications and lessons learned for further research from the Population Policy Acceptance Study. Policy implications cover family-friendly policies and policies related to ageing. Family-friendly policies should mainly respond to the rather strong request to reconcile family and paid work. At least in the Central and Eastern European DIALOG countries there is a noticeable difference between actual and desired number of children and political opportunities to help realise fertility intentions by offering financial and childcare support as well as jobs to (potential) parents. Ageing-related policies will have to deal with restructuring social security systems and employment opportunities in view of the still strong desire to retire early. Since the majority of respondents wish to live at home in old age both informal family care and professional services need to be maintained and strengthened. As to research findings a critical reflection of the results, as well as the description of methodological problems and an outlook on the questions still to be answered is proposed. This aspect addresses the scientific community as user of the IPPAS database, which is provided with these books.

Keywords: Family-friendly policies · Policies related to population ageing · Implications for population research

14.1 Objectives at the Outset of the Dialog-project

14.1.1 Contribution and Relevance to the Development of Policy

At the policy level, a systematic comparative analysis of the acceptance of existing population policy measures and expectations regarding future development of

C. Höhn
Federal Institute for Population Research, Wiesbaden, Germany
e-mail: charlotte.hoehn@destatis.de

policy was supposed to provide informed basis for the development of integrated population policies through active participation of citizens. Comparative analysis of the international database of 14 national Population Policy Acceptance surveys (IPPAS) contributed to this objective. Organising and analysing dialog between policy actors, citizens' associations and individuals was performed with policy Delphi studies.

Section 14.2 brings together what policy conclusions authors of these volumes proposed. Section 14.2.1 illustrates demographic change as a challenge as seen by the Delphi panellists and the interviewed citizens as well as the congruence of their views. Section 14.2.2 presents conclusions for family-friendly policies and Section 14.2.3 conclusions for policies related to population ageing.

14.1.2 Scientific Benefits

Scientific benefits should include broadening of the theoretical knowledge about the impact of population policies on individual behaviour and the interaction between attitudes, expectations and behaviour regarding family building, partner relations and care functions, and one's own old age.

The benefits were intended to relate both to empirical concerns and impetus for the verification and construction of theories concerning the inter-relationship between fertility behaviour, within-family transfers of resources and care, gender equity and public policies.

Section 14.3 highlights research implications. It starts with challenges of data harmonisation (Section 14.3.1), recommends Delphi study as a demographic tool (Section 14.3.2), provides examples of the scientific value of opinions, attitudes and expectations and turns to the broadening of the theoretical knowledge (Section 14.3.4). Section 14.4 covers contributions to typologies of welfare, family and gender policies and to theories ranging from low fertility over consequences of population ageing to gender equity and demographic behaviour.

As coordinator of the DIALOG project it was my intention to enhance joint research across national borders. I would like to mention that 6 chapters in these two volumes have been prepared by authors from different countries (Van Peer and Rabušic; Miettinen, Esveldt and Fokkema; Esveldt, Fokkema and Miettinen; Stropnik, Sambt and Kocourková in volume 1/Schoenmaeckers, Vanderleyden, Vidovićová and Callens; Manea, Rabušic and Vidovićová in volume 2). Also the three editors of these volumes live and work in three different countries. Not only email made such joint research across national borders possible but also good use of the few meetings of the DIALOG group and mainly the creation of the international data base.

In order to let this joint research shine I deliberately will offer many direct quotes to substantiate my conclusions.

14.2 Policy Implications

14.2.1 Demographic Change as a Challenge

Both policy actors and stakeholders participating in the policy Delphi and citizens in the PPA surveys were asked to evaluate different features of demographic change, such as population increase or decrease, fertility trends, age at first motherhood, female labour force participation, population ageing. We will first portray the view of Delphi panellists, second of interviewed citizens and then try to see whether there is congruence between their views and policy options.

14.2.1.1 The View of Policy Actors

The policy Delphi had the aim to design population and society scenarios up to 2030.

In their assessment of policy Delphis carried out in the 14 DIALOG countries Palomba and Dell' Anno state: "Overall, Europe in 2030 is a socio-political and economic arena within which stake-holders dream of better quality of life on behalf of citizens. If we consider the arena as a complex system, we can assume on the basis of the results provided within the scenarios that the system will outperform itself if all stakeholders remain actively involved: not only in laying the basement 'bricks', but also in designing its architecture. There are no sectorial priorities: Overall system performance is the priority. This is due to the strong interconnections existing between economic growth and social development." (Palomba and Dell' Anno, Vol. 2, 5, p. 106.)

More action-oriented and also considering demographic change Delphi panellists conclude: "Europe's development should be promoted considering national specificity, even though the path should unavoidably take into consideration work, family and free-time." (Palomba and Dell' Anno, Vol. 2, 5, p. 107.)

Each policy Delphi was conducted over four rounds of interviews, meaning that the panels of experts were called four times to express their opinions, wishes and points of view. The same happened for the section aiming at expressing desired future population trends. These desired trends do not correspond to a demographic forecasting logic, but – in line with the overall methodology applied – are the results of wishful thinking based on current opinions of the status quo as well as results from the national PPA survey. Panellists desire the following demographic trends:

"Number of inhabitants: This trend shows two major positions, namely those countries which wish to see a population increase in the years to come, and those which hope to see the number of inhabitants maintained at current levels. Those countries which are aiming at an increase are proposing a slight growth of the curve (Germany, Lithuania, Poland and Slovenia), while higher growth is suggested in Italy. ... Remarkably, nobody wishes the population to decline, nor do panellists believe that it will do so.

Fertility: All in all, 2030 is a time of desired fertility increase, albeit with different levels being recorded in the various countries. In fact, while in Austria, Germany and Italy the [desired] fertility increase is close to replacement level, in Belgium (Flanders), Estonia, Poland and Switzerland the future 25 years are desired to be characterised by more than two children per woman. Between these two expectations are positioned those of Lithuania, the Netherlands, Romania and Slovenia, showing a desire for growth in line with the current situation. Last but not least, the panellists in Hungary dreamed of an increase in the birth rate, which they however regarded as '*questionable*'. With this, the Hungarian panellists are the most realistic dreamers." (Palomba and Dell' Anno, Vol. 2, 5, p. 105.; square brackets my addition)

"*Age at first motherhood:* The common tendency in Europe is to postpone the founding of a family, and the age of women at first birth is continuously rising as a consequence. The anticipated trend shows a progression toward the higher part of the scale in all the countries investigated. It remains a mystery how the fertility increase which panellists dream of would materialise.

Female labour force participation: ... Somewhat sustained growth in female participation in the labour market has been observed in most countries in the recent past, with the exception of some of Eastern European ones. The recent increase has narrowed country differences, bringing about homogeneity amongst European regions and shaping a less heterogeneous labour market, at least from a gender perspective. The trends coming out of the policy Delphi highlight European-wide agreement amongst the panels to sustain higher female participation and to increase wealth production via their higher participation in the labour market. The only exception in this commonly-shared trend is Hungary, where a moderate decrease in the trend has been mentioned." (Palomba and Dell' Anno, Vol. 2, 5, p. 106)

Also Bertschinger as well as Menniti and Misiti note the strong focus of Delphi panellists on female labour force participation. "The panellists react to high female labour force participation with a strong focus on gender issues. ... A low female employment rate creates a strong demand for governmental activities." (Bertschinger, Vol. 2, 6, p. 129)

"We have seen a clear convergence of opinions and attitudes mainly towards the need for an increase in women's participation in the labour market, a consensus that confirms and validates EU strategies regarding female employment." (Menniti and Misiti, Vol. 2, 7, p. 148)

While Delphi panellists show a remarkable consensus as to increasing female labour force participation as a goal in itself they are much less vocal and concerned about low fertility and a need to address this demographic change politically. This is reflected in the overall summary of Palomba and Dell' Anno already quoted above as well as by Menniti and Misiti and Bertschinger who analysed the Delphi findings as well in this monograph.

Menniti and Misiti find: "Beyond its main role of enhancing the work-life balance, the promotion of part-time working has also been considered in a number of countries to be a key tool to attain other important policy goals, such as support for an increase in the fertility rate." (Menniti and Misiti, Vol. 2, 7, p. 148). Bertschinger writes: "There is evidence that the focus on a certain motive for family policy is influenced by contextual factors." (Bertschinger, Vol. 2, 6, p. 129). Such contextual factors Bertschinger rather finds in the central and eastern European countries:

"Strong economic performance in a country (western countries) leads to a lower focus on families." (Bertschinger, Vol. 2, 6, p. 129)

Another source for assessing the preferred population-related policies of governments in the DIALOG countries are information gathered in all participating countries in work package 4 on which Kontula and Söderling draw in their paper. "According to the country reports, none of the DIALOG countries had specific programs for addressing population policy, such as low fertility. In contrast, in most of the CEE countries current governmental population policy attitudes seemed to be very passive and mostly more restrictive. In some of these countries, pro-natal policies had been pursued prior to transition, and the contrast between the past and the present was clear. Individual freedom and choice appear to be highly valued in all countries." (Kontula and Söderling, Vol. 2, 1, p. 18) It should however be noted that these country reports were supposed to refer to the year before the survey was taken in the participating country in order to reflect the knowledge of the interviewed citizens. Information in most cases was taken from the UN Inquiry on population-related policies as assessed around 2000. Delphi panellists were interviewed at a later stage of the DIALOG project and they were encouraged to give their personal "dreams" up to the year 2030. At least in their expectations and/or hopes panellists wished a fertility increase up to replacement level or above.

14.2.1.2 The View of Citizens

Demographic change and its consequences are no longer being discussed only among population researchers, but have reached a broad public. This is shown by the fact that at least in some respects the population has relatively precise knowledge of the demographic processes and makes a differentiated evaluation of low fertility and the increasing number of elderly.

Van Peer and Rabušic show "that the declining number of births is perceived negatively in all countries by substantial numbers of respondents (about 75% on average), except for Estonia and the Netherlands whose populations seemingly do not regard low fertility as a problem. On the other hand, almost all Hungarians, Slovenians and Lithuanians do." (Van Peer and Rabušic, Vol. 1, 10, p. 218) They also observe that "the lower the TFR, the higher the share of people who regard the declining number of births as a bad thing" (Van Peer and Rabušic, Vol. 1, 10, p. 218).

While citizens have a rather negative view on low fertility they have a rather modernised and differentiated attitude on marriage. "The consequences drawn: 'if partnership, then marriage' and 'if children, then marriage' appear to be dissolving, while by contrast the consequence 'if children, then partnership' continues. The distant stance towards marriage cannot however be regarded as constituting such a stance towards the family. In the opinion of the respondents, marriage is no longer regarded as being necessary for family formation, but family, for which marriage is not absolutely necessary, is still categorised as a children-friendly institution" (Dorbritz, Vol. 2, 2, p. 44). In this respect, however "differences in evaluation can still be found between the western and the former Socialist countries. A distant stance towards the classical family model can be found more often in the western and northern countries of Europe. It can be presumed that those orientations which date back to the Socialist era have been conserved and are changing only gradually." (Dorbritz, Vol. 2, 2, p. 44)

Citizens too desire an increase in female labour force participation. "Strong preferences for families with women in either full- or part-time employment, revealed by the analyses, as well as the impacts had by preferences on the work-family life arrangements practised, allow one to conclude that there is potential for further increases in female labour force participation, especially of more well-educated women." (Kotowska and Matysiak, Vol. 1, 14, p. 317)

14.2.1.3 The Congruence of Policy Options

Both Bertschinger and Menniti/Misiti looked into congruence of concerns of Delphi panellists and experts on the one hand side and of citizens on the other hand side. "Moreover, it was shown that the populace reacts differently, and that their appreciation of a particular issue is based on different assumptions. There is a divergence between these two groups; one can speak of a culture of experts, which does not often match the people's opinion" (Bertschinger, Vol. 2, 6, p. 130). This mismatch particularly concerns the evaluation of low fertility. Citizens and experts, however, largely agree in considering undesired consequences of demographic ageing as a challenge for policy-makers. They also share a high esteem of gainful employment of women.

"On the other hand, the promotion of female work – if successful – may exacerbate existing problems related to the reconciliation between work and family, mostly for mothers. A possible solution could be to support part-time job opportunities for women; in fact this is a view that is broadly shared by both the population and the Delphi panellists." (Menniti and Misiti, Vol. 2, 7, p. 148)

"This issue represents the core of the dilemma as it forces citizens, panellists and policy-makers to face all the conflicts that European women have to deal with in trying to reconcile work and family. All Delphi panellists considered this problem a priority to be solved in the future. In contrast to the panellists, citizens seem to hold more diverse and ambiguous opinions: While equity between men and women is a consolidated and broadly-shared concept, there also exist deeply rooted values, linked to traditional women's roles regarding motherhood, family tasks, or gendered social roles. Moreover, one of the most frequently-debated measures proposed to empower women in the labour market, so-called 'quotas', still remains controversial in every Delphi study (except in Finland)." (Menniti and Misiti, Vol. 2, 7, p. 148)

14.2.2 Family-friendly Policies

14.2.2.1 The Relevance of Fertility Intentions

Fertility is low in the DIALOG countries ranging (in 2002) from 1.2 children per woman in Slovenia to nearly 1.8 in the Netherlands and Finland. Fertility expectations also vary considerably. A good overview is provided in Fig. 13.1 by Avramov and Cliquet (Vol. 2, 13, p. 271).

In this figure, there are two obvious clusters: the central and eastern European DIALOG countries joined by Italy, Austria and Cyprus where the difference between actual fertility and desired fertility is large and the other western European DIALOG countries with a moderate to small difference. At the outset we may conclude that the margin for political action is larger where the difference between expected and achieved number of children is larger. In principle one may also conclude that "Young people, especially women, wish to have more children than they expect to eventually have – they perceive and experience societal obstacles to the realization of their parenthood aspirations" (Avramov and Cliquet, Vol. 2, 13, p. 285). In any case there are not only remarkable differences in this gap between expected and achieved fertility by countries but also within countries by being childless or already a parent, by education, by value orientations, by expectations as to certain family-friendly policies and by the possible way to react to an implementation of personally preferred policy measures.

We will start with a few findings on *childlessness*. Sobotka and Testa "found in every country a significant proportion of childless respondents who intend to remain childless or are uncertain about parenthood," and "Germany stands out for the high overall level of both intended childlessness and uncertainty" (Sobotka and Testa, Vol. 1, 9, p. 204). "Parenthood frequently competes with other options and opportunities in people's lives. Respondents not only weight different advantages and disadvantages of parenthood, but they may also consider childlessness as a possible option." (Sobotka and Testa, Vol. 1, 9, p. 202)

"Respondents in Belgium (Flanders) and the Netherlands show generally the most positive attitudes towards childlessness, whereas relatively traditional attitudes prevail in the post-communist societies of Central and Eastern Europe, as well as in Austria and 'familistic' Italy. Childbearing is often seen in these countries as a duty towards society; childless people are commonly considered as unhappy and respondents strongly accentuate the value of happy family life with children. This finding supports part of our first hypothesis, which envisioned that the low childlessness levels recorded until recently in all Central and Eastern European societies will continue to shape people's generally negative attitudes towards voluntary childlessness." (Sobotka and Testa, Vol. 1, 9, p. 204)

What can be found on the influence of the *level of education*? The multivariate analysis performed by Van Peer and Rabušic shows "that higher education no longer prevents women from wanting large families" and that lower educated women encounter obstacles to realise their desired fertility. This result is to "put in relation to the labour market opportunities for this segment of the active population" (van Peer and Rabušic, Vol. 1, 10, p. 240). The three-child family "is already popular among the more highly educated". If those people can be seen as "trendsetter" this could lead to higher fertility (van Peer and Rabušic, Vol. 1, 10, p. 239).

Value orientations obviously matter in considering to form a family or to have a second or third child. Fokkema and Esveldt as well as Kowalska and Wróblewska find that in all DIALOG countries the value of children is high – although the fertility is low in all these countries. The value of children is specially seen as a source of parental and family joy and not so often considered to enhance personal happiness or as a responsibility towards the society (Fokkema and Esveldt, Vol. 1, 7, p. 154). Child-related values are particularly important in the CEE countries (Kowalska and Wróblewska, Vol. 1, 8, p. 174).

However, younger people show less altruistic attitudes and are less interested in family life and children. While "they still consider children to be substantial for parents' lives and for family life, the value of children has been declining as compared with" older people. (Kowalska and Wróblewska, Vol. 1, 8, p. 174) "A further link can be established between attitudes towards childbearing and intentions: Our study found a relatively strong correlation between a respondent's very positive attitude towards family life with children and his or her intentions towards childbearing." (Sobotka and Testa, Vol. 1, 9, p. 205)

Ruckdeschel distinguishes two groups of women with different value orientations, the work-centred and the home-centred type. "The work-centred type, which is younger, less frequently married and less well educated, concentrating on achieving self-realisation and independence by means of their own careers... want fewer children and show a wider gap between desired and achieved fertility than home-centred women." (Ruckdeschel, Vol. 2, 9, p. 189f) "The work-centred type, on the other hand, never reaches two children with its intended fertility, the only exception being Cyprus." (Ruckdeschel, Vol. 2, 9, p. 190)

"Home-centred women have the highest expectations, averaging more than two children, with Cyprus at the top. In the post-socialist countries, the intended number of children of the home-centred type exceeds two children as well." (Ruckdeschel, Vol. 2, 9, p. 190) "In seven out of nine countries, the home-centred type is the one with the highest fertility intentions and the highest achieved fertility." (Ruckdeschel, Vol. 2, 9, p. 190)

Expectations towards family-friendly policies are very large in all DIALOG countries. Unfortunately not all citizens prefer the same measure or the same mix of measures.

"Expectations were not confirmed that fertility intentions would be higher within the welfare regime which is the most supportive of reconciliation of work and family (Belgium (Flanders), Finland and Slovenia), i.e. characterised by the lowest incompatibility between family and work, than in other institutional settings." (Kotowska and Matysiak, Vol. 1, 14, p. 318)

The **impact of preferred policy measures on fertility** behaviour is quite revealing to policy-makers though this is a double virtual assessment including opinions on personal (or couple) behaviour and the anticipated effect of a political measure. Esveldt, Miettinen and Fokkema examine this issue among the two groups with the highest intention to have a(nother) child: childless people and one-child parents. "If we take desired fertility into account (no intentions, uncertain, intentions), the percentages still range from eight percent of childless people with no desired fertility and living in LFCs[1] (1.3–1.5) who believe that they would probably decide to have a child if new or improved policies were to be implemented, up to 84%

---

[1] LFCs: low fertility countries with a total fertility rate between 1.3–1.5 children per woman.

of one-child parents in LFCs who are still not sure whether they would like to have more children, and who say that they would reconsider having another child." (Esveldt et al., Vol. 1, 17, p. 385)

"Furthermore, we found that parents generally seem to be slightly more sensitive to the impact of policies than childless people. (...) Parents, having had the experience of needs, can define exactly which policies they miss which might persuade them to speed up the timing of childbearing or to have another child." (Esveldt et al., Vol. 1, 17, p. 386)

"Childless people who intend to have children more often think that family policies might support them in having the number of children they would like to have than those who are still uncertain as to whether or not to start a family." (Esveldt et al., Vol. 1, 17, p. 386)

The possible impact of preferred family policies on deciding to have a(nother) child is also analysed by Avramov and Cliquet. Their conclusion is "that the family policy measures considered in PPAS would have a modest positive effect on completed fertility. The overall impact of the eleven proposed policy measures on increasing the number of children (taking into account both the desired policy support and possible life-course obstacles) may be estimated at between 6 and 14%." (Avramov and Cliquet, Vol. 2, 13, p. 275)

As to the ***impact of changing values on fertility*** the assessment of authors to these volumes is not uniform. On the basis of values and intentions studied, Van Peer and Rabušic found indications of a possible end to lowest low fertility, even near to replacement level. In CEE countries, they believe, the fertility level seems to recover, whilst the German speaking countries transform from medium to low fertility. Van Peer and Rabušic suggest that the fertility in those countries will remain below European average. Desired childlessness is most widespread in Western Germany and in Austria small families are preferred. Families without children or only one child are now an alternative for the two-child family in Austria and Germany (Van Peer and Rabušic, Vol. 1, 10, p. 239). In this respect they corroborate the assessment of Avramov and Cliquet.

Other arguments are presented by Kotowska and Matysiak and by Ruckdeschel. "Preferences for one child are visibly stronger within welfare regimes which offer hardly any public support for work and family reconciliation, i.e. in countries with the lowest fertility in Europe (the Czech Republic, Estonia, Hungary, Italy, Lithuania and Poland). This observation confirms the expectation that fertility will remain low in this region." (Kotowska and Matysiak, Vol. 1, 14, p. 318)

"A substantial shift in preferences [from home-centred to work-centred] in those countries could lead to lower intended fertility, and indeed to lower achieved fertility in the future." (Ruckdeschel, Vol. 2, 9, p. 190)

What matters more in the decision to have no children at all or to live in a family, values or family policy, is impossible to say. It is only fair to remind policy-makers that also value orientations play a role when it comes to have a small or a larger family. As it seems more "traditional" or rather family-centred values support the decision to have children, particularly if preferred (valued?) family policy measures are in place.

14.2.2.2 The Relevance of Living Arrangements

Living arrangements cover the wide range from living alone, having a partner, being married or not, having children, living with old parents, living with parents and children in a three-generation household. Here we are mainly interested in the relevance of living arrangements on having a(nother) child.

"Respondents who prefer arrangements with a low level of commitment, such as single-living or living-apart-together relationship, also express a high degree of preference for childlessness. Living arrangement preferences and intentions to remain childless obviously constitute two sides of one coin and reveal underlying values, life-style preferences and personality traits." (Sobotka and Testa, Vol. 1, 9, p. 205)

"Having a partner does not constitute an influence for childless people when it comes to the number of children, but it clearly enlarges their belief in the impact of policies regarding the timing of childbearing and a more general belief in the supportive role of policies in having the number of children they would like to have." (Esveldt et al., Vol. 1, 17, p. 386)

"In particular, we do not find convincing evidence that cohabiting persons have more modern attitudes than married or single persons. The findings indicate that the number of children correlates negatively with an increase in modern gender attitudes." (Philipov, Vol. 2, 8, p. 174)

"Parents with a partner believe more strongly that policies might persuade them to decide to have a second child after all." (Esveldt et al., Vol. 1, 17, p. 386)

"We found home-centred women to be married more often, less well educated on average and older than other women. They have high fertility intentions, and also high achieved fertility in comparison to the other types." (Ruckdeschel, Vol. 2, 9, p. 189)

As in the discussion of findings on fertility intentions we again meet the importance of values. It is to be noted that particularly in western European countries more individualistic living arrangements (living alone and LAT) as well as cohabitation and single parents are on the rise while "traditional" marriage or the "classical" family are loosing ground. Shifts towards such diversification of living arrangements are to be expected for CEE countries as well. Marriage, family orientation or less modern gender roles are however confirmed to support both higher fertility intentions and a family with two or more children.

14.2.2.3 Institutional or Financial Measures

The PPAS questionnaire contained a long battery of possible family policy measures. They can be grouped into institutional and financial measures plus housing. The question is whether "time" or "money" is more preferred.

"The difficulty in combining preferences and needs is evident in people's answers to questions regarding policy actions: when asked to choose options related to policy measures for the family, most respondents expressed a wide range of preferences, including an increase in part-time work opportunities, but also in childminding facilities and financial support." (Menniti and Misiti, Vol. 2, 7, p. 149)

Miettinen, Esveldt and Fokkema summarise their findings as follows: "The results show that socio-demographic characteristics explain some of the differences in acceptance of financial and institutional measures. The family phase is reflected in the attitudes, and parenthood particularly increases support for financial measures. In general, age tends to decrease support for financial measures particularly among parents. As could be expected, institutional policy measures in particular are more appealing to women than to men, implying that family issues are still 'women's issues' in many countries. The impact of education is not as straightforward as might be expected. Increasing educational level tends to decrease support for financial measures, but its relation to institutional measures varies. In the lowest-low-fertility countries [CEE countries], economic problems related to childbearing and child upbringing affect all population groups, and the impact of education on attitudes is therefore less visible. In low-fertility countries [Austria, Cyprus, Germany, Italy], education increases support for institutional measures only among parents, and among childless persons in moderate-fertility countries [Belgium/Flanders, Finland, Netherlands]." (Miettinen et al., Vol. 1, 16, p. 366; square brackets my addition)

"Family orientation, or the idea of the number of children one wishes to have, also appears to impact attitudes. The impact is more visible among childless persons than among parents. In general, increasing expected family size tends to increase acceptance of both financial and institutional measures. However, when the family size exceeds two, particularly the preference towards improvements in institutional measures diminishes." (Miettinen et al., Vol. 1, 16, p. 366)

Kocourková, Sambt and Stropnik study one selected institutional measure (parental leave) and one financial (child allowance). "It may be concluded that Europeans on the whole want to have an option of parental leave lasting 2–3 years." (Stropnik et al., Vol. 1, 18, p. 410) "In the countries observed, people are mostly satisfied with the current mode(s) of taking parental leave." (Stropnik et al., Vol. 1, 18, p. 410) "There is a high preference for ... granting the child allowance. It is however interesting that in most of the countries the majority favours child allowances with elements of (income-dependent) social assistance." (Stropnik et al., Vol. 1, 18, p. 410) "People obviously want all children to receive a child allowance, but the level of benefit should take account of the financial situation of the family." (Stropnik et al., Vol. 1, 18, p. 410) "Preferences regarding the dependence of child allowance on the age of the child strongly correlate with actual arrangements, meaning that the majority supports child allowance independent of the age of the child." (Stropnik et al., Vol. 1, 18, p. 410)

We may conclude that preferences are not only influenced by the measures available and familiar but also by the factual situation of the person or family. There is a difference between the anticipated needs of support by family policy of the childless persons and the objective needs of parents. In addition the age and the number of children as well as the employment situation of father and mother matter in shaping preferences for more "time" or more "money".

14.2.2.4 Paid Professional Work or Unpaid Family Work

When discussing demographic challenges as seen by Delphi panellists and citizens in Section 14.2.1, we already noted the dominant interest in female paid professional work and the high demand to better reconcile paid and unpaid work.

This is also the dominant change when comparing the DIALOG PPAS results with PPA 1-surveys taken a decade ago (cf Palomba and Moors 1998), an analysis carried out by Dorbritz for this monograph. "Probably the most important change of attitude ascertained in the European PPAS countries is the trend towards reconciling family and work. (...)Firstly, the proportion of women has increased who consider it ideal to reconcile family and work. Secondly, those measures have become more significant among possible, future measures of family policy which make it easier to reconcile family and work." (Dorbritz, Vol. 2, 4, p. 88)

Cernič Istenič and Kveder provide more detailed insight distinguishing full-time versus part-time work also with a view to have or to desire children and family. Their general finding is that "respondents who were more oriented towards children wished to participate in the labour market less actively." (Cernič Istenič and Kveder, Vol. 1, 13, p. 295)

"Women preferring to work full-time had considerably fewer children than those who either preferred to work part-time or not to work at all. Although women aged 36–49 and satisfied with their full-time employment reported that they had fewer children, they also would have liked to have more children. They represent an important share of women who would like to have more children, together with young women who do not work and are dissatisfied with their work status." Cernič Istenič and Kveder, Vol. 1, 13, p. 295)

Esveldt, Fokkema and Miettinen study the reception of family policy by work and family status. "Having a paid job or being inactive is virtually insignificant for the parents' attitude, but plays a decisive role for childless people. The anticipated effects of policies are greater for inactive people, both as to the timing of childbearing, and to the reconsideration or decision to have children after all. Their stronger conviction of the impact of policies on their fertility behaviour might suggest that they lack the means to have a child at this moment, or to have a child at all, and certain policy measures might help them to start a family at an earlier date or to reconsider their decision as regards children. This is supported by the fact that (childless) young people in particular face a less secure economic position. They cannot afford to start a family, or are afraid to shoulder the financial risk." (Esveldt et al., Vol. 1, 17, p. 386)

Philipov tries to gain an understanding of gender issues related to unpaid work in the family and to gainful employment. "Women not in work are more traditional than those who do work, whether full-time or part-time" (Philipov, Vol. 2, 8, p. 174). In addition, Philipov finds that modern gender attitudes have "an inverse effect on men's and women's intentions to become parents. While its effect on women is as expected, i.e. modern attitudes correlate with lower intentions to become parents, the inverse correlation is observed for men" (Philipov, Vol. 2, 8, p. 174).

In this reverse correlation one might suspect a source of disagreement among partners in having children.

While Kotowska and Matysiak see room for further increases of female labour force participation being silent about fertility implications, Ruckdeschel sees at least the ideal of staying at home in a number of countries and not uniformly the preference for paid work. "Strong preferences for families with women in either full- or part-time employment, revealed by the analyses, as well as the impacts had by preferences on the work-family life arrangements practised, allow one to conclude that there is potential for further increases in female labour force participation, especially of more well-educated women" (Kotowska and Matysiak, Vol. 1, 14, p. 317). "The most prevalent type is constituted by home-centred women. They are very important in all of the post-socialist countries, but also in Austria and Cyprus. A clear polarisation between the home-centred and work-centred types can be found in the Western region of Germany, whereas the Eastern part is the only region where the double performer ideal predominates. The Netherlands are the only country where the work-centred type clearly predominates." (Ruckdeschel, Vol. 2, 9, p. 189)

As we already said before, the home-centred women have more children but they become a minority in most countries. Women's aspirations are directed towards own gainful employment. Ways to reconcile paid work and unpaid family work are sought. One possible avenue is part-time work or a temporary retreat from the labour market in the form of parental leave.

14.2.2.5 Conclusions for Family-friendly Policies

The authors to this monograph offered a number of conclusions for policy-makers in general, for family-friendly policies in different settings, for better ways to reconcile gainful employment and having children, and, last but not least for prospects to close the gap between the actual and the desired number of children.

Conclusions for Policy-makers in General

"The contribution of the IPPAS to the knowledge base [of policy-makers]... consists to a great extent in highlighting the increasing role of culture and the significance of an attitudinal dimension." (Katus et al., Vol. 1, 15, p. 343; square bracket my addition)

"It seems that family size expectations and family orientation influence perceptions of policies, and therefore would require more attention from the government." (Miettinen et al., Vol. 1, 16, p. 367)

"The DIALOG countries form a very heterogeneous group in terms of family policy provisions and models. While attitudes among the population are in many cases in agreement with the family policy situation in the country, variety between countries cannot always be related to differences in adopted policies." (Miettinen et al., Vol. 1, 16, p. 367)

"These findings suggest that country-specific cultural and social norms and practices, as well as general expectations towards the government's role in family matters, must be taken into consideration when designing future family policies." (Miettinen et al., Vol. 1, 16, p. 367)

"Europe's development should be promoted considering national specificity, even though the path should unavoidably take into consideration work, family and free-time." (Palomba and Dell' Anno, Vol. 2, 5, p. 107)

Conclusions for Family-friendly Policies

"Our findings show that people believe that policies might influence their fertility behaviour, which suggests that there is scope for new and better policies, which may eventually lead to higher fertility. This impact is especially significant in the lowest-fertility countries (where TFR is 1.3 or below), all of which are CEE countries." (Esveldt et al., Vol. 1, 17, p. 387)

"Family policy regimes have been found to be associated with public opinion on family-related issues and family policies. Respondents in 'Imposed home care'[2] regimes attached much greater value to marriage, children and home care of children than respondents of the other policy regimes. They also strongly supported family benefits provided by governments. Paradoxically, governments were unable to meet these expectations of their citizens. That gap between citizens' expectations and limitations in government support for families contributes to low fertility in these countries." (Kontula and Söderling, Vol. 2, 1, p. 17)

"Respondents' expectations and actual public policy are better matched in the 'Day care service'[3] and 'Labour market'[4] regimes. Respondents of the former regime relied on and valued day care more than the others. Respondents of the latter regime disregarded childbearing as a societal duty, and valued the individual freedom to have children. They like, however, to take care of children by themselves. It is difficult to judge whether public opinion had an impact on public policies, or vice versa. Be that as it may, the fertility rates were higher in these countries than in the two other groups." (Kontula and Söderling, Vol. 2, 1, p. 17)

"We succeeded in showing that the Mediterranean policy model, where the emphasis lies on the private networks and traditional gender roles, does have a negative impact on the gap between intended and achieved fertility. More important, we succeeded in showing an independent positive impact of child oriented preferences on the closing of this gap which could be interpreted as the prevalence of individual orientations over structural opportunities." (Ruckdeschel, Vol. 2, 9, p. 190)

---

[2] CEE countries in transition which closed down many public childcare institutions thus, according to the typology of Kontula and Söderling, "imposing" home care.

[3] Finland and Slovenia according to the typology of Kontula and Söderling.

[4] Netherlands, Switzerland and Cyprus according to the typology of Kontula and Söderling.

typically become different during the second demographic transition. More and more families risk to age and eventually die out. The last persons of a family will necessarily depend on professional care at home or on institutions. Intergenerational solidarity among multigenerational families very likely will continue.

14.2.3.4 The Issue of Early Retirement

Manea, Rabušic and Vidovićová present the "paradox of early retirement": "Firstly, despite the fact that citizens seem to be aware that societies are ageing and cannot really afford to see their labour forces shrink or to exacerbate the public debts of the pension schemes, people do not tend to behave accordingly, and they would like to leave the labour market as soon as possible … Secondly, it seems that awareness of possible dissatisfaction with life after leaving the labour market does not prevent their wanting to retire early. Last but not least, respondents' personal preferences for early retirement do not prevent them from supporting the policies of closing down early exit pathways by increasing the statutory retirement age." (Vidovićová et al., Vol. 2, 12, p. 262)

This key challenge for policies intended to adapt the pension system to demographic changing is likewise stated by Avramov and Cliquet (Vol. 2, 13) and Jóźwiak et al. (Vol. 2, 11).

Particularly in the Central and Eastern European countries the discrepancy between the preferred (traditionally) low age at retirement and the expected age is quite large. Respondents have become aware that increases in the compulsory, statutory retirement age are "the most popular measure recommended by experts and suggested in debates on pension scheme reforms." (Jóźwiak et al., Vol. 2, 11, p. 242)

Jóźwiak et al. also explore attitudes towards more flexible options. "Individual views showed some consistency with the experts' opinions about flexible and gradual retirement and work after retirement. However, that option depends heavily on both employees' ability to stay on the labour market, and on employers' attitudes to keep them employed." (Jóźwiak et al., Vol. 2, 11, p. 242)

The issue of preference for early retirement requires particular attention of policy-makers. Even in Western countries where citizens at least expect to work longer than the current elderly they still feel this is against their preferred.

14.2.3.5 Conclusions for Policies Related to Population Ageing

Theoretically, population ageing could be overcome by increasing fertility, and shortages on the labour market to be expected in the next decades could be mitigated by immigration. In the DIALOG project citizens were not asked their opinion on immigration. Also Delphi panellists did neither advocate immigration nor increasing fertility.

"Concerning *pro-natal orientation*, the people's disapproval of the decline in fertility is stronger compared to the panellists" (Bertschinger, Vol. 2, 6, p. 129). As we already concluded in the section on family-friendly policies these are most welcome with a general focus on reconciling work and family life. Avramov and Cliquet remind that demographic "solutions" alone cannot replace policies adapting to population ageing. "More and better child-care to assist working parents are a must, but will not suffice to address long-term challenges of low fertility and related accelerated demographic ageing. Improving the funding and reforming the pension schemes are necessary" (Avramov and Cliquet, Vol. 2, 13, p. 286), but the agenda of adaptation and change is longer. A new culture to ensure the best possible adaptation to the unavoidable population ageing through transforming diffuse fears and encouraging active ageing involves raising awareness, considering adequate living arrangements, and enabling people to like to work longer.

Raising awareness: "There is a need for governments to identify requirements and develop instruments to facilitate response shifts among citizens which will be necessary in view of the labour market changes and long-term sustainability of social security and needs for care at high age." (Avramov and Cliquet, Vol. 2, 13, p. 286)

"European societies are now facing the task of building bridges between generations and stages of life. At the individual level, life-course thinking should assume a greater role, while the role of the strategies oriented towards short-term goals and values should diminish" (Katus et al., Vol. 1, 11, p. 257). Raising awareness of the need to cope with population ageing hence should emanate from governments and ideally be also transmitted by the media. With that individuals will become aware that ageing concerns them personally in the future and that it is less a threat than an opportunity. Since healthy longevity is not just increasing but is a "great triumph of civilization", as the late great demographer Frank Notestein said, people must learn to prepare themselves for a successful ageing. The young old of today (60–79 years) already realize that their "felt" age is much lower, and that they are indeed mentally and physically younger than their parents were at the same age. This experience of retarded ageing should be communicated to those still younger and that they should develop healthy lifestyles to remain active probably even longer. People should not be afraid of becoming old but rather enjoy the prospect of prolonged activity, of active ageing.

Living arrangements of the oldest old: However, there remains the issue of the oldest old, an age that today involves persons aged 80 years and more. "In view of the expected unprecedented increase in numbers of the oldest old, and the desire of people to continue living in their preferred home environments when they become frail at advanced age, the elderly will need assistive technologies that help them, and their family and informal care providers, as well as social care and health care institutions" (Avramov and Cliquet, Vol. 2, 13, p. 286). It might well be that this age where an increasing percentage of people need assistance in daily activities or become dependent of long-term care might shift to the age of 85 or 90. Nonetheless, an increasing number of oldest old will require assistance. Preferences are clear to wish to remain at home as long as possible. Spouses and children (who increasingly will be over 60 years themselves when they become care-providers of their parents or parents in law) are assuring family care today. They should be supported in this task. Frail persons without a partner or own children have to rely on more expensive and less personal professional care. With changing family structures there is a risk that the group of the "single" oldest population boosts care-related costs. For persons with individualised life-course it should be recommended to build up informal networks of friends and neighbours early in life so that this network remains sustainable for staying at home in case of needing care. Those preferring institutional arrangements are well advised to join senior villages or multi-generational houses.

Working longer: Reforms towards a demographically sustainable pension system include the need to raise the factual age at retirement. Promoting the concept of active ageing and overcoming the still dominant preferences for early retirement are important preconditions. But such pension system reforms are not feasible without employment opportunities for older workers. "Therefore, not only measures aimed at removing disincentives for workers to work longer and to discourage early retirement should be discussed, but also policies which stimulate lifelong learning should be examined besides those oriented towards improving working conditions and encouraging employers to retain and retrain older workers. In that respect our results give some optimistic indications: Education is the most important characteristic influencing an individual's propensity (preferences and expectations) to retire earlier or to continue being economically active." Jóźwiak et al., Vol. 2, 11, p. 242)

In passing Schoenmaeckers et al. remind that "analysis shows that the negative effect of an older population structure on the number of people in working age in society may indeed be largely compensated for by increased employment. The validity of these results at political level might however be questioned to the extent that its successful implementation will depend on the availability of jobs, an unlikely prospect when the unemployment rate is around or above 10% (as is the case for Belgium (8%), the Czech Republic (8.2%), Finland (8.8%), France (9.7%), Germany (9.6%), Greece (10.2%), Italy (8%), Poland (18.4%), the Slovak Republic (17.1%) and Spain (10.5%); source: OECD statistics 2004)." (Schoenmaeckers et al., Vol. 2, 10, p. 206, footnote 20)

"We will go as far as to conclude that **the key success factor** for addressing parenthood choices and population ageing challenges are underpinned by the current and future public policy choices that impinge the paid work in general and family-friendly and age-friendly **working conditions** in particular." (Avramov and Cliquet, Vol. 2, 13, p. 286)

Indeed, the challenges of population ageing can be best overcome by lifelong learning, by remaining active in the labour force and at home, by considering individual ageing as a part of life. A mayor obstacle is unemployment that hits older workers hardest. The prospect of a longer and healthier life should convince older workers that it is better to continue working for pay and not to retire as early as possible. Employers should appreciate the experience of older workers and they should learn that younger workers will become rarer than today or in the past. With more and longer employment the costs of financing pensions and expenditures for health and long-term care will be more easily covered.

14.3 Research Implications

14.3.1 Challenges of Data Harmonisation

In their methodological chapter on setting up the international database IPPAS Avramov and Cliquet (Vol. 1, 2) mention a number of challenges that had to be overcome or accepted whenever nationally taken surveys have to be harmonized in order to be internationally comparable:

- Some countries eliminated entire modules or questions or dropped one or more sub-items of particular question sections. The possibility for comparison between countries has thus been reduced.

"There are many reasons for the country deviations. In addition to the lack of a formal obligation to comply with the core questionnaire and all the modules, several other factors contributed to the variation in the composition of the national survey questionnaires and results obtained. In some cases, some of the modules were not included because the national institute recently undertook a specific survey on the topic of the module (e.g. ageing/elderly in Belgium, Italy, Hungary, and the Netherlands). In other cases, the national institute chose not to include a particular topic (e.g. gender in Belgium, Finland, and Slovenia; values in Austria, Belgium and the Netherlands). In one case, in Italy, the survey methodology (telephone survey) did not allow for a lengthy interview. In another case, in the Netherlands, the survey was done by a computer aided personal interview sent over the Internet. In some countries the available financial resources were too limited to cover all of the PPAS subjects (e.g. Cyprus and Romania). In some cases, several of these factors cumulated, resulting in relatively weaker contributions to the overall international endeavour." (Avramov and Cliquet, Vol. 1, 2, p. 39f)

- Difference in the definition of concepts, such as level of education, living apart together (LAT), even of 'child' had to be harmonized.

"Most countries did not apply an age limit to the notion of children, but some did, e.g. Belgium recorded as children in the household only those below 19 years of age. Some variation occurred in the definition of 'own children': some considered only 'own' biological children, others included step-, adopted and foster children, and sometimes even children already deceased. For most analyses, the inter-country variation in the definition of children will have little effect on the trends or associations observed, but the construction of the variables in the international database and the comparative analysis would have been easier and more pertinent if stringent conceptual rules had been followed." (Avramov and Cliquet, Vol. 1, 2, p. 43)

- The sample size was sufficient, that is nationally representative, for most purposes.
- Specific population sub-groups usually are quite small in the PPAS national survey samples. Here the pooling of data is proposed.

"The pooled database, hence, makes it possible ... to compare ... many small social sub-populations that often require special policy concern and care. In the field of demography, well-known minority or problem groups are one-parent families, large families, divorcees, widow(er)s, reconstituted families, childless couples, retired people and immigrants." (Avramov and Cliquet, Vol. 1, 2, p. 38)

- Some countries took a Population Policy Acceptance Survey a second time. The opportunity to make comparisons over time was and could not be fully grasped. Only Dorbritz (Vol. 2, 4) undertook this exercise covering the topics of evaluation of demographic ageing, attitudes towards marriage, family and children, desired fertility, evaluation of family policy measures, preferred forms of reconciliation of family and work, and general value systems for up to 8 countries respective regions. Obstacles included changes in the wording and scales of questions, deletion of questions from the first round, and differing age brackets.

"All this makes it more difficult, but not impossible, to compare the two surveys, whilst explaining why in some cases there are only four or five countries for which it was possible to carry out the comparative analyses." (Dorbritz, Vol. 2, 4, p. 67)

Though the research teams intended to contribute their national data to an international comparison (before the analysis within the DIALOG Project was graciously funded by the European Commission) and cooperated to develop the common research goals, the questionnaire, including variable design, and survey methodology the agreed guidelines for the core questionnaire and the modules could not be strictly followed for various reasons. The dominating reason is that national Population Policy Acceptance Surveys were funded from domestic resources.

In my capacity as coordinator of the DIALOG project and based on cumbersome experience with earlier international survey exercises I fully agree with the conclusion of Avramov and Cliquet: "The availability of international funds from the very outset of the study for the development of the survey tools as well would undoubtedly have enhanced the potential for more comprehensive comparability of PPAS data." (Avramov and Cliquet, Vol. 1, 2, p. 44)

- Multilevel analysis would require 10 or more countries. Since this was rarely the case in the project analysis of covariance or separate regressions were the recommended by Callens (Vol. 1, 3)

"However, neither analysis of covariance nor separate regressions will be able to give an answer to the quest in quantitative cross-national research: to replace the name of nations with the names of country-level variables". (Callens, Vol. 1, 3, p. 57)

- The cross-sectional character of the IPPAS dataset, finally, does not allow for exploration of past or future attitudes of the respondents. Changes in attitudes and their impact on factual behaviour can only be studied in a panel design.

14.3.2 Delphi Study as a Demographic Tool

Demographers traditionally rely on the analysis of official population statistics and of survey data. Most of the analyses presented in these two volumes indeed follow this quantitative liking. Conducting a policy Delphi (Palomba and Dell' Anno, Vol. 2, 5) is to be recommended.

It is most illuminating to learn more about the opinions (and even "dreams") of stakeholders concerning population issues on national and European level. One would have expected that concerns about low fertility or about reforming the social security systems would be much more prominent. Dominant were the enhancement of female employment opportunities and of social cohesion.

Perhaps one should consider Bertschinger's observation that "the study stands on 'sandy' ground concerning the selectivity of the panels, the small number of countries considered and the selection of the explanatory variables, there is evidence that political actors react to contextual factors." (Bertschinger, Vol. 2, 6, p. 130) It is the charm of qualitative interviews such as a policy Delphi to get insight into the evaluation of population issues from those responsible to deal with it in politics, media and social partners. Therefore the critical remarks do not prevent Bertschinger from concluding: "This study did not provide robust results, but constituted an attempt to explore the interaction between experts and the environment. Further studies are needed to confirm the evidence" (Bertschinger, Vol. 2, 6, p. 130). I gladly recommend colleague demographers to venture upon a policy Delphi in order to further explore whether citizens' and stakeholders' views diverges or converge.

14.3.3 The Scientific Value of Opinions, Attitudes and Expectations

It seems to be a moot point to underscore the scientific value of opinions, attitudes and expectations having analysed 35,000 interviews. And yet, we wish to present a few encouraging examples to continue dealing with "soft" survey questions in population studies.

The interplay of public policy and citizens' opinions is also a theme of Kontula and Söderling who analyse IPPAS data against contextual data on family policies in place before the period of survey taking. "Respondents' expectations and actual public policy are better matched in the 'Day care service' and 'Labour market' regimes. Respondents of the former regime relied on and valued day care more than the others. Respondents of the latter regime disregarded childbearing as a societal duty, and valued the individual freedom to have children. They like, however, to take care of children by themselves. It is difficult to judge whether public opinion had an impact on public policies, or vice versa. Be that as it may, the fertility rates were higher in these countries than in the two other groups ['Income transfer' and 'Imposed home care' countries]. This finding could entail some political implications for population policies." (Kontula and Söderling, Vol. 2, 1, p. 17; square brackets my addition)

Concerning the attitudes towards the pluralisation of living arrangements, Pongracz and Spéder diagnose ambivalence: On the one hand the analysis of attitudes shows that a majority does not consider marriage as the superior living arrangement anymore. On the other hand a majority sees marriage as a personally desirable union form. The same holds true with cohabitation: Most people accept and tolerate cohabitation but it as not their ultimately desired living arrangement. The authors suggest having an "in-depth survey" concerning this issue, to explain this ambivalence (Pongracz and Spéder, Vol. 1, 5, p. 112).

Desired number of children still is a favourite topic of demographers. There still is much to do. The issue whether answers expressing uncertainty, like "perhaps" or "don't know" should be omitted or classified as "no (further) child requires additional studies as well as the question if and how family policies influence the decision to have a child. "Childless people who intend to have children more often think that family policies might support them in having the number of children they would like to have than those who are still uncertain as to whether or not to start a family" (Esveldt et al., Vol. 1, 17, p. 386). It seems worthwhile to give more thought to the undecided. This is one of the questions where the category "don't know" makes sense. Otherwise people give rather clear positive or negative opinions. They have high expectations towards policies and consider most of them "very important" so that rarely one single favourite measure comes to the fore. When asking for first, second and third preferred measure or just one among possible proposed measures one risks missing the complexity of expectations.

Repeated surveys with the same questions allow analysing general trends in opinions; they do not yield insight into individual changes in values and situations. From his comparison of two cross-sectional PPA surveys in 8 countries Dorbritz concludes: "The change in demographically-relevant attitudes and values in comparison to the situation found at the beginning of the nineties encompasses several general trends, as well as country-specific developments which ran in completely different directions. It even appears that different trends in the individual countries of the PPAS are more noticeable than joint development directions." (Dorbritz, Vol. 2, 4, p. 88)

Some authors combined several items of one or more questions to an index or composite variable. Philipov constructed three composite variables which he called "dimensions". "The results of our analysis suggest that the 'gender ideology' dimension is the one that provides the most information as regards the attitudes of men and women towards gender roles, as against the 'family consequences' and 'economic consequences' dimensions" (Philipov, Vol. 2, 8, p. 173). Schoenmaeckers et al. developed the 'old-age perception index' (or OAP index) out of seven variables measuring citizens' attitudes toward older persons. "By and large the seven statements cover two domains. Statements (A), (B), (C) and (G) would be associated with the social or emotional sphere, while statements (D), (E) and (F) would be associated rather with the economic sphere. From the inception of the analysis it was decided to transform these seven 'attitude' variables into one single index variable. The main argument was that within each domain there must be a considerable overlap between each of the statements. The attitude of each respondent would not be measured on the basis of one single statement, but would reflect an overall attitude based on several statements. Also, there would be the extra attraction that attitude would be measured over a wider range." (Schoenmaeckers et al., Vol. 2, 10, p. 197)

These illustrations of the value of opinions, attitudes and expectations should suffice to join Bertschinger in his conclusion that "(t)here is a need for further population policy acceptance studies to better understand the people's expectations and attitudes and to transmit the results into the political system." (Bertschinger, Vol. 2, 6, p. 130)

14.3.4 Broadening of the Theoretical Knowledge

14.3.4.1 Typologies of Welfare, Family and Gender Policies

Fux had been entrusted the task to develop a typology of welfare policies to better analyse the DIALOG data. He starts with a broad theoretical concept. "Our conclusions are based on the hypothesis that modernisation is something like a 'basso continuo' structuring the development of European countries. The welfare state is obviously an important midwife in the birth of modernisation. However, in contrast to structural-functionalist modernisation theories, as formulated in the 1970s, we assume that there are distinct trajectories of modernisation, and by consequence also distinct welfare regimes." (Fux, Vol. 1, 4, p. 81)

After discussing available typologies and analysing both macro and IPPAS data of almost all European countries, mainly with factor analyses, Fux "attempted to carve out nine country groups which differ mainly in their cultural legacies, as well as with regard to their social-structural prerequisites. In a subsequent step, we reduced the number of groups based on the hypothesis that there are three trajectories which on the one hand are based, in turn, on different focal values (equality, freedom of choice and security), and on the other on the focal actors, which could be either the state, lower-level institutions and particularly the family, and finally the individual." (Fux, Vol. 1, 4, p. 81)

Fux summarizes his findings as follows: "First, we find a relatively dense cluster following the etatistic trajectory. These are the Nordic states. Secondly, there is also a 'family of nations' (Castles and Mitchell 1993) in the Eastern hemisphere where the late transition countries are characterized by the persistence of rather traditional structures which stand, however, in opposition to secularization due to their communist legacy. The two other clusters are much wider, and show marked internal differences. These are first and foremost the countries with a Catholic history. These can be subdivided into those which became secular and developed strong welfare systems based on the concept of subsidiarity. Secondly, we find the non-secularized countries (Counter Reformation countries), which permit one to observe much weaker welfare systems. These prioritize the family as an important actor in this respect. Mutual self-help within the family is partly a substitute for the welfare state. Both sub-groups can be seen as variants of a familialistic trajectory of modernisation." (Fux, Vol. 1, 4, p. 83)

As to a typology for the DIALOG countries, Fux proposes to put *Finland* to the Nordic cluster and the **etatistic trajectory**. "If one takes a look at the Eastern European countries participating in the DIALOG project, one can find that etatistic elements are still relevant in *Estonia*, as well as in *eastern Germany* (former GDR)." (Fux, Vol. 1, 4, p. 84; bolds and italics my addition)

The *Netherlands* and *Switzerland* follow the **individualistic trajectory**. "Again, modern values are wide-spread in both countries. Nevertheless, welfare state residualism leads to behavioural outcomes often including conservative elements." (Fux, Vol. 1, 4, p. 83)

Belgium, Austria, Western Germany, and *Italy* belong to the **familialistic trajectory**. "While the former combined this [family] resource with modern welfare systems, the welfare state is less well established in Italy. By consequence, the impact of the family is much more prominent." (Fux, Vol. 1, 4, p. 83; square brackets my addition)

"*Poland, Lithuania, Hungary* and *Slovenia*, as well as *Cyprus*, permit one to observe something like a double-bind situation in the sense that familialistic structures are as relevant as their communist legacy [etatistic trajectory]. It seems that particularly Slovenia and Cyprus adjusted their welfare systems more quickly to the direction of the Southern European countries. There are many indicators which permit one to assume that the three other countries will follow this path [towards the **familialistic trajectory**]." (Fux, Vol. 1, 4, p. 84; square brackets my addition; bolds and italics my addition)

"Although familialistic structures are also pertinent in the *Czech Republic*, one can assume that due to this country's early secularisation, it will combine this resource with **etatistic, and/or individualistic** elements. Finally, *Romania* is characterised by the ongoing process of economic and social transformation, which still hampers the adjustment of the welfare state." (Fux, Vol. 1, 4, p. 84; bolds and italics my addition)

Fux offers a theoretically founded typology to analyse DIALOG data. In the following articles a few, more specialised typologies are proposed.

More Specialised Typologies

Kontula and Söderling develop a typology of family policies: "The DIALOG countries were grouped into four family policy regimes, based mainly on the generousness of public support to families. These regimes can be ordered as follows in terms of their level of generosity in family support: 'Day care service' model, 'Income transfer' model, 'Labour market' model, and 'Imposed home care' model. These groups were found to overlap closely with the clusters that were formulated by use of socio-economic, demographic and gender equity contextual variables." (Kontula and Söderling, Vol. 2, 1, p. 17) It is interesting to note that Kontula and Söderling cluster all CEE countries, except Slovenia, in the 'Imposed home care' model.

This makes sense in grouping family policies; indeed family policy measures in communist times were generous, but largely collapsed after 1990. Slovenia (the economically most successful country in transition) obviously can afford to maintain childcare services. Slovenia therefore joins Finland as a second member of the 'Day care service' model. It is not the aim of Kontula and Söderling to analyse whether the CEE countries will remain in the 'Imposed home care' model for ever or towards which of the other three proposed models they might tend.

In order to study gender-related aspects of the IPPAS data, both Philipov (Vol. 2, 8) and Ruckdeschel propose special typologies not exclusively targeted at grouping countries but also at sub-populations. Philipov distinguishes three dimensions (gender ideology; family consequences; economic consequences) while Ruckdeschel works with the dichotonomy of home-centred versus work-centred women.

Eastern and Western European Patterns

From the many findings that point to remarkable East-West differences in attitudes, values and behaviour let us choose a few examples.

In comparing the first and second round results of PPA surveys Dorbritz refers to Fux's terminology. "Whilst a relatively high level of constancy in attitudes was found for Hungary, a change of attitude is afoot in the Czech Republic. Contradictory trends in evaluation can also be found in the "western" countries. One may almost speak of re-traditionalisation in the Netherlands. The very high tolerance towards the decline in the significance of marriage and change in the family measured at the beginning of the nineties has considerably weakened. The contrary trend was observed for Italy. The highly familialistic attitudes in the first round of the PPAS have given way to broad tolerance towards unmarried developments." (Dorbritz, Vol. 2, 4, p. 89)

Philipov states less modern gender roles in the CEE countries. "A descriptive analysis of the data indicates that modern gender roles, as described in the 'gender ideology' dimension, are considerably less prevalent in the CEE countries than in Western European countries. Moreover, mean values of the composite variables indicate that gender role ideology in the CEE countries is more traditional than modern on average, while in the Western countries it is more modern than traditional." (Philipov, Vol. 2, 8, p. 173)

Also Ruckdeschel confirms a high degree of preference for the less progressive gender role, particularly in the East. "The most prevalent type is constituted by home-centred women. They are very important in all of the post-socialist countries, but also in Austria and Cyprus." (Ruckdeschel, Vol. 2, 9, p. 189)

14.3.4.2 Theories of Low Fertility

This is not the place to reiterate available theories of fertility decline. What we want to contribute, based on working with DIALOG opportunities, are additional findings that might enlarge theoretical approaches. There are three fields which in my mind deserve to be mentioned: the impact of value change, the shift in structure by level of education and the determinants to delay family formation. We will start with underscoring that the search for one most important determinant of fertility behaviour is naive. "Most respondents cite several reasons for opting for not intending to have a child. Thus, intended childlessness cannot be frequently explained by a single 'reason', but by a mixture of lifestyle choices and different constraints or adverse personal circumstances." (Sobotka and Testa, Vol. 1, 9, p. 201)

If there were one single determinant and if this were apt to be influenced by policy the efficacy of intended pronatal policies would be higher. The issue of efficacy of policies will be the final point of this section.

The Impact of Value Change

Value change is not easily influenced by political measures. Perhaps authentic, trustworthy politicians or VIPs might be able to redirect (undesirable) value change; but this would require longer periods of reorientation. Measuring value change is not a favourite of most demographers. From our studies we present a few findings that enlarge the range of determinants of low fertility.

"Our analysis ... shows that, paradoxically, the highest values of children are found in those countries with currently the lowest total fertility rates." (Fokkema and Esveldt, Vol. 1, 7, p. 154) These are the CEE countries and Italy.

Both Fokkema/Esveldt (Vol. 1, 7, p. 154) and Van Peer/Rabušic (Vol. 1, 10, p. 239) found that being already or planning to become a parent has a positive impact on the value-of-children. Fokkema and Esveldt however find a negative assessment of the value of children among the determined childless.

"Surprisingly, as raising children costs a lot of money, people who consider materialistic values as very important in their life show the highest scores on the value of children, with Estonia as the exception. In addition, no significant, universal relationship is found between the central nature of post-materialistic values on the one hand and having children on the other. Only Finns, Western Germans and Hungarians are less enthusiastic about children when they highly strive for post-materialistic goals." (Fokkema and Esveldt, Vol. 1, 7, p. 155) The shift to more post-materialistic values, particularly in Western Europe, seems to jeopardise the value of children. Post-materialistic values include self-realisation, leisure time and job orientation, while materialistic values include not only income but also 'a spacious house'. If one adds in the dichotomy of Ruckdeschel of work-centred versus home-centred women the value orientation gains additional weight. Value change should be systematically considered and shifts in the percentage of population groups with values favouring or discouraging to have children carefully monitored.

Diminishing groups with strong (Christian) religious values also contribute to low fertility. "The strongest and most uniform findings refer to the effect of education and religiosity: lower values of children are observed among more highly-educated people and among those to whom religion is less important in their lives." (Fokkema and Esveldt, Vol. 1, 7, p. 153) The impact of education is discussed in the next section.

Shift in Structure by Level of Education

The level of education is rising in Europe. Among the younger cohorts particularly women are catching up with men of their age, and in many countries women
with higher education are relatively more numerous than men of equivalent age. As
Fokkema and Esveldt (Vol. 1, 7, p. 142) found the effect of education belongs to the
strongest on the value of children and hence for fertility. Here are a few pertinent
explanations from our studies.

"Prolonged education delays the transition to a steady job, and hence to economic independence, but it also influences the timing of parenthood in a number of
indirect ways, through a less traditional or family-centred value orientation. Other
factors that are commonly identified as the main determinants of first birth postponement are the conflict between employment and motherhood, the individual
and societal impacts of uncertainty, the widespread adoption of the contraceptive
pill, and profound changes in the character of intimate relations (Sobotka 2004)."
(Kontula, Vol. 1, 12, p. 273)

"Education made a difference to age at first birth in all DIALOG countries.
Highly-educated women have been having their first child roughly three years later
than less well-educated women." (Kontula, Vol. 1, 12, p. 272)

"The multivariate analysis showed that higher education no longer prevents
women from wanting large families, as it did in previous decades. This is a positive evolution. But nowadays, the less-educated seem to encounter impediments for
realizing their desired number of children. This finding must be put in relation to
the labour market opportunities for this segment of the active population." (van Peer
and Rabušic, Vol. 1, 10, p. 240) Here we have another example that it is never just
one determinant that influences the decision to have a(nother) child. It is even not
fixed that the much discussed determinant "higher education" is fertility depressing.
Other conditions, such as job opportunities versus the risk of being unemployed after
finishing university, and the availability of day-care facilities, as well as preferred
lifestyles or family-centred values have to be understood.

Determinants to Delay Family Formation

Age at first birth is increasing in Europe. Whether this delay in family formation also
implies a lower final family size depends on future behaviour to remain childless, to
have one child or the earlier desired number of children.

Kontula struggles with the still low though since the 1990s increasing age at first
birth in the CEE countries. "The assumption that there is necessarily an interrelation
between early births and higher fertility rates was contradicted by the finding that the
early births had been associated with very low fertility rates in Central and Eastern
European countries. It had become very common to strictly limit the number of
children in these countries after an (early) first birth." (Kontula, Vol. 1, 12, p. 271)
The currently observed low fertility in the CEE countries is hence more a non-
recuperation, the waiting for more opportune conditions to have more than one child.
Low age at first birth indeed is not the only and most important determinant of
"higher" fertility.

Van Peer and Rabušic discuss low factual and desired fertility in Austria, Belgium, Germany and Italy. They suppose that a part for an explanation for low fertility are to be found in postponement on completed fertility, what seems to be result from lower female labour participation compared to males (van Peer and Rabušic, Vol. 1, 10, p. 239).

On the Efficacy of Pronatal Policies

In addition to conclusions on family-friendly policies in Section 14.2.2.5 here are a few more scientific findings.

"Looking at the opinions of the population, it seems that there is some scope for family policy. The potential impact on fertility behaviour of the implementation of people's *preferred* family policy measures is certainly not negligible. The lowest percentage that we found is still 18% of childless people living in the [low fertility countries] LFCs (1.3–1.5) saying that they would probably decide to have a child if the government introduced their *preferred* policy measures; the highest percentage is 75 in case of one-child parents living in the [lowest fertility countries] LSFCs (≤ 1.3) who think that implementing the *policies chosen by them* would make it easier for them to have the number of children they want." (Esveldt et al., Vol. 1, 17, p. 376; square brackets and underscoring my additions)

Also Van Peer and: Rabušic discuss the question whether expectations will be realized and they illustrate the broad range of policy implications. "Our results are more or less scenarios for the future. Whether they become reality will depend on conditions in the family policy context (good parental leave, extensive day care, family allowances), but also on the European labour market, the availability of (part-time) jobs, the gender equity system, changes in family values, congruency between partners. Alleviating the burden for young mothers is the necessary precondition for women to realize their desired fertility – and we did find evidence of a demand for better policies at least in the low-fertility countries. ... The varying country results pertaining to the labour market situation of people showed us that improving conditions on the labour market remains an important field of action for social policies; such policies should aim to allow people to combine both work and a family, by offering high-quality, flexible jobs. In this way, family strategies need not counteract employment strategies and vice versa. In countries that offer high-quality part-time jobs, good parental leave, crèches, family allowances, and in countries having a gender balance in labour participation and household task division, fertility is ultimately generally higher." (van Peer and Rabušic, Vol. 1, 10, p. 241)

If it were possible to meet the differing preferences of population groups, couples and individuals such encompassing family-friendly measures might have an impact. And yet the desired number of children remains the limit.

Finally, van Peer and Rabušic remind us "that, without the policies that have already been implemented in the past decades in the field of gender equality, creating more opportunities for women to reconcile motherhood with gainful employment, financial support for families with small children and leave schemes for young parents, fertility might even have been lower." (van Peer and Rabušic, Vol. 1, 10, p. 241)

14.3.4.3 Theories of Marriage and the Family

Family structures and living arrangements change rapidly in Europe. While fertility and nuptiality are declining non-marital and individual living arrangements increase. On overview is provided by Pongracz and Spéder (Vol. 1, 5). From our studies we contribute information on the attitudes towards marriage and cohabitation, prevailing differences in this regard between Western and Eastern Europe and the internal differences in the CEE countries.

Attitudes Towards Marriage, Cohabitation and the Family

"The consequences drawn: 'if partnership, then marriage' and 'if children, then marriage' appear to be dissolving, while by contrast the consequence 'if children, then partnership' continues. The distant stance towards marriage cannot however be regarded as constituting such a stance towards the family. In the opinion of the respondents, marriage is no longer regarded as being necessary for family formation, but family, for which marriage is not absolutely necessary, is still categorised as a children-friendly institution." (Dorbritz, Vol. 2, 2, p. 44) In his comparison of the PPA survey from the 1990s and the recent PPAS Dorbritz confirms the change over the last decade and he adds: "This result of the PPAS is of considerable importance for family policy. Wherever married people are the primary addressees of family policy measures, the impact of family policy will be restricted." (Dorbritz, Vol. 2, 2, p. 88)

Pongracz and Spéder are puzzled by the dualism and even ambivalence of attitudes versus preferred lifestyles with regard to marriage and cohabitation. "On the one hand, statements expressing superiority of marriage are commonly rejected (married people are happier, marriage is the only acceptable way of living together), but on the other hand the overwhelming majority deems marriage to be a desirable, not outdated, and indeed even preferred lifestyle. Even though public opinion fundamentally tolerates cohabitation with no intention to marry, the proportion of those who prefer cohabitation as a permanent lifestyle is fairly low among young and older people alike. We believe that ambivalence of opinions would deserve an in-depth analysis and a thorough survey, and only a few of the potential components are mentioned here." (Pongracz and Spéder, Vol. 1, 5, p. 112) They explain the acceptance of marriage against the demographic facts with "marriage's deep social roots as a prevailing lifestyle which has developed over the centuries." (Pongracz and Spéder, Vol. 1, 5, p. 112)

Differences Between Western and Eastern Europe

"The trend is for more traditional stances towards marriage and family to be found in eastern Europe than in western Europe." (Dorbritz, Vol. 2, 4, p. 89) Dorbritz presumes that these more traditional attitudes "which date back to the Socialist era have been conserved and are changing only gradually." (Dorbritz, Vol. 2, 2, p. 44)

"The different attitudes on marriage and family between the western and former Socialist countries have not disappeared. Even in the reunified Germany, different evaluation patterns have been retained." (Dorbritz, Vol. 2, 4, p. 89)

Internal Differences in the CEE Countries

In general, one of the main findings is that there is not an identical development of family changes in the region of the CEE countries. This regards the start, velocity and the achieved level of family changes. "According to the demographic trends, the changes started earliest in Eastern Germany and Slovenia (the first indications of the changes were manifested in the 1960s–1970s), slightly later in the Czech Republic and Hungary (in the 1970s–1980s), and latest in Lithuania and Poland (in the 1990s). The demographic developments are echoed in attitudes towards the family changes: They are usually best accepted, and attitudes towards them are less negative, where they started earliest and are most advanced, and vice versa." (Stankuniene and Maslauskaite, Vol. 1, 6, p. 135).

Stankuniene and Maslauskaite found variables, which have an impact on the attitudes: "Firstly, attitudes vary in terms of an assessment of the different attributes of the family changes. In general, changes in the family formation pattern (de-institutionalisation of the family) receive greater social approval (and a lesser degree of disapproval), while the significant decrease in fertility is the object of greater disapproval. ... Secondly, attitudes towards changes in the family formation pattern are conditioned not only by their timing, but also by the power of the ideational factors associated with the [Second Demographic Transition] SDT (individualisation, secularisation and emancipation)." (Stankuniene and Maslauskaite, Vol. 1, 6, p. 135).

Stankuniene and Maslauskaite (Vol. 1, 6, p. 135) range the CEE DIALOG countries between "two poles" of countries: Eastern Germany and the Czech Republic on the one side with the most advanced demographic family formation changes together with the most positive assessment and on the other side Poland and Hungary with the most conservative attitudes and a strong familistic tradition. Lithuania and Slovenia are between those two poles.

"The eastern European countries appear to form a less homogeneous group today than was the case at the beginning of the nineties." (Dorbritz, Vol. 2, 4, p. 89)

14.3.4.4 Theories on the Consequences of Population Ageing

It is interesting for further research on the consequences of population ageing to note the need to develop a methodological approach to study intergenerational solidarity and to disentangle the three paradoxes found, namely on the evaluation of the elderly versus population ageing, on familial versus societal responsibility to care for the elderly and on preferred versus expected age at retirement.

The Concept of Intergenerational Solidarity

" 'Intergenerational solidarity' is a difficult concept to measure. One single instrument, such as an index of attitudes toward the elderly, is hardly sufficient to measure its presence in society. ... [I]ndividuals will rarely refer to the generation to which they belong, or see their current situation in a life course perspective." (Schoenmaeckers et al., Vol. 2, 10, p. 208) Schoenmaeckers et al. indeed just discuss one set of items by defining on "Old-age perception index" (OAP) (Vol. 2, 10, p. 196) and by using "a mix of 'visual exploration' and of the application of a multivariate technique (GLM). The results show quite major differences between countries. Moreover, GLM estimates indicate that the most important individual characteristics are age and sex. As such, the results point to the importance of a 'life course strategy' for enhancing true intergenerational solidarity." (Schoenmaeckers et al., Vol. 2, 10, p. 196) Demographers of course know that age and sex are the classic differentials in population studies. But Schoenmaeckers et al. indeed explore a whole array of other variables as well among which age and sex appear as the most salient ones.

"The much-needed intergenerational solidarity will not become a reality without across-the-board public support. ... [T]his will not take place without the dissemination of the adequate information." (Schoenmaeckers et al., Vol. 2, 10, p. 209) Information from research on their concept or even a theoretical approach on intergenerational then tested with empirical data is a gap to be closed.

The Evaluation of the Elderly versus Population Ageing

As already mentioned in our policy conclusions (Section 14.2.3.2) citizens generally take a rather positive attitude with respect to the role and situation of the elderly in society. "This runs counter to the earlier finding (Schoenmaeckers et al., forthcoming) that some 70% of citizens regard the rising number of older persons as 'bad' or 'very bad'. One first conclusion is therefore that both statements must cover quite different issues. Citizens' negative views of the increasing number of older people do not mean that the elderly are not respected, or that their qualities are ignored. A more correct conclusion is that a vast majority of citizens is simply worried by the demographic evolution. One underlying reason is likely to be that its societal implications and the potential impact of the latter on the individual are largely unknown; never before in the history of Europe (or of the world) has there been a situation in which more than 25% of its citizens were aged 65 and over. This alone justifies a sense of wariness." (Schoenmaeckers et al., Vol. 2, 10, p. 206) A neat distinction between opinions and the way respondents might understand certain questions related to "ageing" are warranted. Population ageing, individual ageing and the image of the elderly obviously are not the same. Each aspect deserves a pertinent question to avoid "paradoxes" in interpreting findings.

Care for the Elderly: Family versus the State

Concerning the issue who should care for the elderly it also matters whether one asks for government's responsibility (which relates probably more for health care systems and adequate institutions) or directly asks whether elderly should be looked after by family members and/or professionals or admitted to old-age homes. "It is evident that citizens from the countries under study see an overall high level of responsibility for governments in different areas which affect private life and especially care for old people. However, even that does not mean that they prefer care to be organised by institutions – the preference as to "who should care" does not appear to cohere with the responsibility attribution." (Mai et al., Vol. 2, 3, p. 62)

Although Mai et al. state that "[i]n general, institutional care is preferred to familial care" (Mai et al., Vol. 2, 3, p. 63) this would be a quote out of context. This particular finding is due to the structural effect inherent to their analysis of the bulk of respondents with typically high expectations to the state in comparison to those few with low expectations combined with their personal preferences. The above quote alone would be misleading, and indeed not the central finding of Mai et al. who "conclude that the attribution of governments' responsibility or expectations of the welfare state cannot be used as an explanatory variable for the question of 'who should care'." (Mai et al., Vol. 2, 3, p. 63) Looking at the distribution of respondents' opinions who should provide care and where and how they would like to be cared for in need of help the overwhelming majority wants to stay at home with the help of family members and/or professionals. Institutions are personally or for own parents much less desired. This is another example that mixing too diverse levels and types of opinions might create artificial paradoxes.

Preferred versus Expected Age at Retirement

"Schoenmaeckers and Vanderleyden (2005) also talk about a *paradox* in connection with the obvious discrepancy between preferred and expected retirement age. They refer to recent research in which this phenomenon is explained by older workers' 'reluctance' to work longer if 'others exit the labour force at a younger age' (2005:56). This explanation indicates that retirement in modern societies is socially constructed." (Vidovićová et al., Vol. 2, 12, p. 262)

"The results of the IPPAS presented here support the idea that the age of exit from the labour market is becoming more and more blurred. People in many European countries have different preferences and expectations about the age of retirement, and these differ to a certain degree from the legal "ideal". To what extent this almost universally-expressed desire to retire early will actually influence the situation on the labour market, in policy-making and individual life courses of our respondents, may be questions to be addressed in further research." (Vidovićová et al., Vol. 2, 12, p. 263)

Possibly our third paradox found is more a challenge, for policy-makers to convince people that working beyond the age of 55 is gratifying in view of their expertise and good health, for researchers to find determinants, characteristics and conditions of those who prefer to work as long as they can or are allowed.

14.3.4.5 Theories on Gender and Demographic Behaviour

Demographers usually analyse data by age and sex but only recently consider attitudes of women and men on gender roles. The DIALOG project contained only a
small module on gender roles focussing on gender, work and family. In his capacity
as a demographer studying gender Philipov was surprised "that age and marital
status are not as depictive as it could be expected." (Philipov, Vol. 2, 8, p. 174) His
finding, that "[w]omen are more orientated towards modern gender roles than men",
was of course to be expected (Philipov, Vol. 2, 4.1, p. 173).

In the following we will present a few more results that might contribute to further research on gender and demographic behaviour, starting with value orientations
over the desired number of children, reconciling work and family to the elderly.

Gender and Value Orientation

"Decreasing religiosity relates positively with the increase in the modern orientation
of gender attitudes, and this is mostly observed in the case of the family consequences dimension, but also in the ideology dimension. The same holds for the
increase in education." (Philipov, Vol. 2, 8, p. 174)

"Women not in work are more traditional than those who do work, whether full-
time or part-time." (Philipov, Vol. 2, 8, p. 174)

East-West differences deserve to be mentioned as well: "Female emancipation,
which was and remains a crucial factor for the family transformation in "Western"
DIALOG countries, shapes attitudes toward the family formation changes in the
CEE region differently (with the exception of Eastern Germany). Positive attitudes
towards female emancipation are not directly interconnected with social acceptance
of the family formation changes, so that female emancipation was and is developing
along with the preservation of the traditional family formation pattern." (Stankuniene and Maslauskaite, Vol. 1, 6, p. 135)

Gender and Desired Number of Children

"The gender ideology has an inverse effect on men's and women's intentions to
become parents. While its effect on women is as expected, i.e. modern attitudes
correlate with lower intentions to become parents, the inverse correlation is observed
for men." (Philipov, Vol. 2, 8, p. 174) Fokkema and Esveldt (Vol. 1, 7, p. 155) specify
that in the Netherlands, Belgium (Flanders), Finland and Lithuania women value
children less than men.

"Men turned out to be quite distinct from women as regards their working-hours
preferences and the number of children they have. They also showed a less uniform
pattern since the men with the most children were either in full-time employment,
or were aged 36–49 and not working. However, young men dissatisfied with their
non-working status wished to have more children in the future. In addition, men who
were employed full-time also expressed similar preferences for additional children."
(Cernič Istenič and Kveder, Vol. 1, 13, p. 295)

"Surprisingly, men and women have the same attitudes towards the impact of policies. ... Also, age does not appear to be a major factor. It is only the highest age group that has less confidence in the fertility effects of policies." (Esveldt et al., Vol. 1, 17, p. 386)

Gender, Family and Work

"It has also been established that gender, age and education are important factors associated with the respondents' actual and preferred working arrangements." (Cernič Istenič and Kveder, Vol. 1, 13, p. 295)
"The acceptance of segregated gender roles between men and women proved to be related to lower female workforce participation and a greater prevalence of the traditional breadwinner model. Support for more symmetrical roles of men and women was reflected in the stronger attachment of women to the labour force and the higher frequency of the dual-earner or modernised breadwinner models." (Katus et al., Vol. 1, 15, p. 341)

Gender and the Elderly

"[I]n all countries women show a more positive attitude toward the elderly than men" Schoenmaeckers et al. (Vol. 2, 10, p. 207) report and they explain: "Women's more positive attitudes do seem to be consistent with what psychologists refer to as 'social age' and 'psychological ageing'. ... [W]omen are still considered – and most likely consider *themselves* – as society's primary care-givers. Much of their more positive attitude toward the elderly could emanate from the way in which they project their future role as an older person – as likely to find themselves caring for grandchildren and giving care to elderly persons who are in less good health than themselves. This can be regarded as an indication of the existence of different values (between men and women); however, more than anything, it could be a 'strategy' for ensuring – or maintaining – a place in society." (Schoenmaeckers et al. Vol. 2, 10, p. 207)

14.3.5 A Few Final Remarks

It would be boring to reiterate the many findings and innovative aspects of the DIALOG project. Here only a few striking communalities have to be reminded.

- The comparative Delphi study among policy makers and other stakeholders revealed a remarkable divergence to the evaluations of citizens.
- Citizens, policy-makers and researchers, however, converge in their evaluation to reconcile work and family. Work seems to gain priority over having a family.
- It is of course the basic right of couples and individuals to decide freely informed and responsibly on the number of children. Making use of the right to opt against children is increasing.

- Values matter much more than usually considered by demographers. The traditional, family-oriented values are more important in the decision to have (more than one) children.
- Since people with such "traditional" values become less numerous in progressive societies the fertility depressing effect is structural.
- The expectations to both family and ageing-related policies are enormous. Since they are also very diverse it seems difficult to serve all. The most important policy is to create jobs for the young as well as the elderly.
- As to unavoidable population ageing the image of the elderly is much better than presumed. The attitudes to care for the elderly who wish to stay in their homes are positive. It remains to be seen whether the increasing number of childless elderly will build up informal networks while still young.
- The discrepancy between preferred, expected and legal age at retirement should encourage efforts to convince people that working beyond the age of 55 is gratifying.
- Promoting a new attitude to the life course might include having children earlier in life, starting a career when the child/ren go to school, developing a healthy lifestyle, maintain good family relations or informal networks, remain active on the labour market or in family or voluntary work and enjoy the prospect of living a long and healthy life.

References

Abuladze, L., 2004, *Final Delphi Report – Estonia*, unpublished report prepared for the Workpackage 3, DIALOG Project, Institute for Economics Research, Tallin.

Atchley, R. C., 2000, *Social Forces and Aging,* 9th ed., Wadsworth, Belmont, CA.

Avramov, D., 2002, *People, Demography and Social Exclusion*, Council of Europe Publishing, Strasbourg.

Avramov, D., and Cliquet, R., 2003a, Economy of time and population policy: Rethinking the 20th century life course paradigm, *Zeitschrift für Bevölkerungswissenschaft.* **28**(2–4): 369–402.

Avramov, D., and Cliquet, R., 2003b, Economy of time and population policy: Rethinking the 20th century life course paradigm in the light of below-replacement fertility, *Zeitschrift für Bevölkerungswissenschaft.* **28**(2–4):905–938.

Avramov, D., and Cliquet, R., 2005, *Integrated Policies on Gender Relations, Ageing and Migration in Europe. Lessons from the Network for Integrated European Population Studies,* CBGS Publications, Brussels.

Avramov, D., and Cliquet, R., 2006*, Manual, Questionnaire, Codebook and Database of the International Population Policy Acceptance Study (IPPAS),* BiB-Materialien, Bundesinstitut für Bevölkerungsforschung, Wiesbaden.

Avramov, D., and Maskova, M., 2003a, *Active Ageing in Europe*, European Population Paper Series no. 12, Council of Europe, Strasbourg.

Avramov, D., and Maskova, M., 2003b, Active ageing in Europe*, Population Studies.* **41**.

Baccaïni, B., and Gani, L., 1997, Connaissances et représentations de la population chez les lycéens de terminale, *Population et Sociétés.* **324**.

Becker, G. S., 1981, *A Treatise on the Family*, Harvard University Press, Cambridge (Mass).

Billari, F. C., Frejka, T., Hobcraft, J., Macura, M., and van de Kaa, D., 2004, Discussion of paper "Explanations of the fertility crisis in modern societies: A search for commonalities", *Population Studies.* **58**(1):77–92.

Binder, H.-M., and Kübler, D., 2003, *Analysis about the Condition of Family Policy on a Cantonal and Communal Level*, Interface Politikstudien, Luzern/Zürich.

Birren, J. E., and Cunningham, W. R., 1985, Research on the psychology of aging: Principles, concepts and theory. In: *Handbook of the Psychology of Aging*, J. E. Birren, and K. W. Schaie, eds., 2nd ed., Van Nostrand Reinhold Company, New York.

Blekesaune, M., and Quadagno, J., 2005, Public attitudes toward welfare state policies, *European Sociological Review.* **19**(59):415–427.

Blöndal, S., and Scarpetta, S., 1998, *The Retirement Decisions in OECD Countries*, Economics department working paper no. 202, OECD, Paris.

Blöndal, S., and Scarpetta, S., 1999, *Early Retirement in OECD Countries: The Role of Social Security Systems*, OECD Economic studies no. 29, 1997/II, Paris.

Bongaarts, J., 2001, Fertility and reproductive preferences in post-transitional societies, *Population and Development Review* (Supplement). **27**:260–281.

Börsch-Supan, A., et al., 2004, *Akzeptanzprobleme bei Rentenreformen*, Dt. Institut für Altersvorsorge, Köln.

Braun, M., 2004, Gender-role attitudes (ISSP 1994). In: *ZUMA-Informationssystem. Elektronisches Handbuch Sozialwissenschaftlicher Erhebungs-instrumente*, Gloeckner-Rist, Hrsg., ZIS Version 8.00., Zentrum fuer Umfragen, Methoden und Analysen, Mannheim, www.gesis.org/en/methods_consultation/ZIS/index.htm.

Braun, M., Scott, J., and Alwin, D., 1994, Economic necessity or self-actualisation? Attitudes toward women's labour-force participation in East and West Germany, *European Sociological Review*. **10**(1):29–48.

Burniaux, J.-M., Duval, R., Jaumotte, F., 2004, *Coping with Ageing: A Dynamic Approach to quantify the Impact of Alternative Policy Options on Future Labour Supply in OECD Countries*, Economics department working paper no. 371, OECD, Paris.

Callens, M., 2004, *Regression Modelling of Cross-National Data*, Paper presented at the consortium meeting in Bled.

Callens, M., 2005, *Regression Modelling of Cross-National Data with an Application based on the Population Policy Acceptance Survey*, BiB-Materialien, Bundesinstitut für Bevölkerungsforschung, Wiesbaden.

Casey, B., Oxley, H., Whitehouse, E., Antolin, P., Duval, R., and Leibfritz, W., 2003, *Policies for an Ageing Society: Recent Measures and Areas for further Reform*, Economics department working paper no. 369, OECD, Paris.

Castles, F. G., and Mitchell, D., 1993, Worlds of welfare and families of nations, in: *The Development of the Dutch Welfare State, F. G. Castles and R. H. Cox, eds.*, University of Pittsburgh Press, Pittsburgh, pp. 93–128.

Chłoń-Domińczak, A., 2004, Evaluation of reform experiences in Eastern Europe. In: *Pension Reforms: Results and Challenges*, FIAP, Santiago, pp. 145–237.

Cliquet, R. L., and Callens, M., eds., 1993, *Gezinsvorming in Vlaanderen: hoe en wanneer? Resultaten van de Enquête Gezinsontwikkeling 1991 (NEGO V)*, CBGS-Monografie, 1993, 1, Centrum voor Bevolkings- en Gezinsstudiën, Ministerie van de Vlaamse Gemeenschap, Brussel.

Cliquet, R. L., Debusschere, R., Deven, F., Delmotte, G., van Maele, C., and Wijewickrema, S., 1983, *Gezinsvorming in Vlaanderen, Resultaten van de Nationale Enquête Gezinsontwikkeling 1975–1976 (NEGO-III)*, C.B.G.S. Rapport 58, Brussel.

Coleman, D., 2005, Facing the 21st Century: New developments, continuing problems. In: *The New Demographic Regime. Population Challenges and Policy Responses*, M. Macura, A. MacDonald, and W. Haug, eds., United Nations, New York and Geneva, pp. 11–44.

Commission of the European Communities, 1999, Communication from the Commission: Towards a Europe for all ages. Promoting prosperity and intergenerational solidarity, COM (1999) 221 final, Commission of the European Communities, Brussels.

Commission of the European Communities, 2000, The future evolution of social protection from a long-term point of view: Safe and sustainable pensions, COM (2000) 622 final, Commission of the European Communities, Brussels.

Commission of the European Communities, 2001, Communication from the Commission to the Council and the European Parliament on an open method of coordination for the community immigration policy, COM (2001) 387, Commission of the European Communities, Brussels.

Commission of the European Communities, 2002, Report from the Commission to the Council, the European Parliament, the Economic and Social Committee and the Committee of the Regions: Report requested by Stockholm European Council: *Increasing Labour Force Participation and Promoting Active Ageing*, COM (2002) 9 final, Commission of the European Communities, Brussels.

Commission of the European Communities, 2004, *Third Report on Economic and Social Cohesion*, COM (2004) 107 final, Commission Communication, Commission of the European Communities, Brussels.

Commission of the European Communities, 2005a, Commission staff working paper "*Working Together for Growth and Jobs. Next Steps in Implementing the Revised Lisbon Strategy*", Commission of the European Communities, Brussels.

Commission of the European Communities, 2005b, Green Paper "*Confronting Demographic Change: A New Solidarity between the Generations*", Commission of the European Communities, Brussels, 27 p.

Commission of the European Communities, 2005c, Working together for growth and jobs: A new start for the Lisbon strategy, Communication from the President Barroso in agreement with Vice-President Verheugen, COM (2005) 24, Commission of the European Communities, Brussels.

Commission of the European Communities, 2006, *i2010 – First Annual Report on the European Information Society,* Communication from the Commission to the Council, the European Parliament, the European Economic and Social Committee and the Committee of the Regions, Brussels.

Cooperrider, D., and Srivastra, S., 1987, Appreciative inquiry in organisational life, *Research in organisational change and development,* Vol. 1, 129–169, JAI press, Greenwich CT.

Council of Europe, 2004, *Recent Demographic Developments in Europe 2004*, Council of Europe Publishing, Strasbourg.

Courbage, Y., 2003, Immigration and integration of migrants from Maghreb in some european countries – challenges for the future research. In: *The Second Workshop on Demographic and Cultural Specificity and Integration of Migrants*, I. Söderling, ed., workshop held in Helsinki, 21–23, March 2002, Solicited Papers, pp. 63–84.

Dalla Zuanna, G., and Micheli, G. A., 2005, *Strong Family and Low Fertility: A Paradox?* Kluwer Academic Publishers, Dordrecht.

Day, L. H., 1988, Numerical declines and older age structures in European populations: An alternative proposal, *Family Planning Perspectives.* 20:139–143.

Dell'Anno, P., Forcellini, A., Menniti, A., Misiti, M., Palomba, R., and Tintori, A., 2005, *Comparative Delphi Report and Summary Policy Implications of Delphi Study*, Workpackage 3, DIALOG Project, Istituto di Ricerche sulla popolazione e le politiche sociali, Rome.

Demographic Research Centre, 2004, *Final Delphi Report – Lithuania*, unpublished report prepared for the Workpackage 3, DIALOG Project, Demographic Research Centre, Vilnius.

Department of Sociology–School of Social Studies, 2004, *Final Delphi Report – Czech Republic*, unpublished report prepared for the Workpackage 3, DIALOG Project, Masaryk University, Department of Sociology–School of Social Studies, Brno.

Disney, R. F., and Whitehouse, E. R., 1999a, *Retirement: The Demand Side*, Social protection discussion paper, World Bank, Washington, D.C.

Disney, R. F., and Whitehouse, E. R., 1999b, *Pensions Plans and Retirement Incentives*, Social protection discussion paper, World Bank, Washington, D.C.

Dorbritz, J., Fux, B., 1997, eds., Einstellungen zur Familienpolitik in Europa. Ergebnisse eines vergleichenden Surveys in den Ländern des „European Comparative Survey on Population Policy Acceptance (PPA)". Schriftenreihe des Bundesinstituts für Bevölkerungsforschung, Bd. 24, Munich: Boldt im Oldenburg Verlag.

Dorbritz, J., 2006, Kinderlosigkeit in Deutschland und Europa – Daten, Trends und Einstellungen, *Zeitschrift für Bevölkerungswissenschaft.* 30(4), 339–407.

Duval, R., 2003, *The Retirement Effects of Old-age Pension and Early Retirement Schemes in OECD Countries*, Economics department working paper no. 370, OECD, Paris.

Eisen, R., 1999, Alternativen der Pflegeversicherung. In: *Alternative Konzeptionen der sozialen Sicherung*, R. Hauser, ed., Berlin, pp. 94–119.

Esping-Andersen, G., 1990, *The Three Worlds of Welfare Capitalism*, Cambridge Polity Press, Cambridge.

Esping-Andersen, G., 1999, *Social Foundations of Postindustrial Economies*, Oxford University Press, Oxford.

Esping-Andersen, G. (2002), A Child-Centred Social Investment Strategy, Chapter 2 in: *Why We Need a New Welfare State,* Oxford University Press, Oxford.

Esveldt, I., 2004, *Country Report the Netherlands,* unpublished.

Esveldt, I., and Fokkema, T., 2006, *Child-friendly Policies,* DIALOG paper Series No.7, Wiesbaden.

European Commission, 1996, *Social Europe, the Outlook on Supplementary Pensions, in the Context of Demographic, Economic and Social Change,* Directorate General for Employment and Social Affairs, Office for Official Publications of the European Communities, Luxembourg.

European Commission, 1999, *New Paradigm in Ageing Policy,* (online); http://europa.eu.int./comm/employment_social/soc-rot/ageing/news/paradigm_en.htm.

European Commission, 2002, *Scoreboard on Implementing the Social Policy Agenda,* COM (2002) 89 final, 2002b, Brussels.

European Commission, 2005a, *Confronting Demographic Change: A New Solidarity Between the Generations,* Communication from the Commission, Green Paper 2005/94, Brussels.

European Commission, 2005b, *Integrated Guidelines for Growth and Jobs,* http://europa.eu.int/comm/employment_social/news/2005/apr/com_2005_141_en.pdf.

European Council, 2003, *Joint Report by the Commission and the Council on Adequate and Sustainable Pensions,* (EPSCO/Ecofin), 7165/03, (March 10), Council of the European Union, Brussels.

European Foundation for the Improvement of Living and Working Conditions, 2002, *Quality of Women's Work and Employment–Tools for Change,* Foundation paper NO. 3, December, Dublin.

European Parliament, Committee on Employment and Social Affairs, 2002, *Report on the Communication from the Commission to the Council, the European Parliament, the Economic and Social Committee and the Committee of the Regions on taking Stocks of Five Years of the European Employment Strategy,* (2002/2152(INI) A5-0301/2002 final), Brussels.

Eurostat, 2004, *How Europeans spend Their Time – Everyday Life of Women and Men–Data 1998–2002,* Luxembourg.

Evers, A., 1993, The welfare mix approach. In: *Balancing Pluralism,* A. Evers, and I. Svetlik, eds., European Centre for Social Welfare Policy and Research, Vienna, pp. 3–31.

Evers, A., and Leichsenring, K., 1994, Paying for informal care, *Ageing International.* **3**:29–40.

Fagan, C., 2003, *Working-time Preferences and Work-life Balance in the EU: Some Policy Considerations for Enhancing the Quality of Life,* European Foundation for the Improvement of Living and Working Conditions; http://www.eurofound.eu.int/publications/files/EF0342EN.pdf.

Fahey, T., and Spéder, Z., 2004, *Fertility and Family Issues in an Enlarged Europe,* European Foundation for the Improvement of Living and Working Conditions, Dublin.

Flora, P., 2000, *Stein Rokkan: State, Nation and Democracy in Europe,* Suhrkamp, Frankfurt am Main.

Fux, B., Bösch, A., Gisler, P., and Baumgartner, D., 1997, *Population and a Pinch of Policy,* Seismo, Zürich.

Fux, B., 2002, Which models of the family are en- or discouraged by different family policies? In: *Family Life and Family Policies in Europe, Vol. 2: Problems and Issues in Comparative Perspective,* F.-X. Kaufmann, A. Kuijsten, H.-J. Schulze, and K. P. Strohmeier, eds., Clarendon Press, Oxford, pp. 363–418.

Fux, B., 2004, *Presentation of the Theoretical Concept,* unpublished presentation in DIALOG meeting, September 29, in Bled, Slovenia.

Fux B., Bertschinger A., 2004, *Final Delphi Report –Switzerland,* unpublished report prepared for the Workpackage 3, DIALOG Project, Soziologisches Institut der Universität Zürich, Zurich.

Fux, B., 2008, Pathways of Welfare and Population-related Policies, in: People, Population Change and Policies. Lessons from the Population Policy Acceptance Study, Vol. 1: Family Change, C. Höhn, D. Avramov, and I. E. Kotowska, eds., Springer.

Gauthier, A. H., 1996, *The State and the Family, a Comparative Analysis of Family Policies in Industrialized Countries,* Clarendon Press, Oxford.

Gauthier, A., 2002, Family Policies in Industrialized Countries: Is There Convergence? Population (English Edition), Vol. 57, No. 3 (May, 2002), Paris, pp. 447–474.

Geist, C., 2005, The Welfare State and the Home: Regime Differences in the Domestic Division of Labour, European Sociological Review, Oxford, Vol. 21, N.1, pp. 23–42.

Gelissen, J., 2002, *Worlds of Welfare, Worlds of Consent? Public Opinion on the Welfare State*, Brill, Leiden–Boston, Köln.

Giddens, A., 2001, *Treti cesta. Obnova sociální demokracie, (The Third Way)*, Mladá Fronta, Prague.

Glatzer, W., and Mohr, H.-M., 1987, Quality of life: Concepts and measurement, *Social Indicator Research*. **19**(1):15–24.

Glenn, E. N., 1994, Social constructions of mothering: A thematic overview. In: *Mothering: Ideology, Experience, and Agency*, E. N. Glenn, G. Chang, and L. R. Forcey, eds., Routledge, New York, London.

Gornick, J. and M. Meyers, 2003, *Families that work: policies for reconciling parenthood and employment*. New York: Russel Sage.

Grant, J., Hoorens, S., Sivadasan, S., van Het Loo, M., DaVanzo, J., Hale, L., Gibson, S., and Butz, W., 2004, *Low Fertility and Population Ageing: Causes, Consequences, and Policy Options*, Rand Europe, Brussels.

Greene, W., 2000, *Econometric Analysis*, 4th ed., Prentice Hall, New York.

Gruber, J., and Wise, D. A., 1999, Social Security Programs and Retirement around the World, University of Chicago Press for National Bureau of Economic Research.

Guillemard, A., and van Gunsteren, H., 1991, Pathways and their prospects: A comparative interpretation of the meaning of early exit. In: *Time for Retirement*, M. Kholi, et al., eds., Cambridge University Press, Cambridge.

Hakim, C., 1999, Models of the family, women's role and social policy, a new perspective from preference theory, *European Societies*. **1**(1):33–58.

Hakim, C., 2001, Alternative European models of women's roles in the family and the labour market. In: *The Making of the European Union, Contributions of the Social Sciences*, M. Haller, ed., Springer, Berlin, pp. 265–286.

Hakim, C., 2002, Lifestyle preferences as determinants of women's differentiated labour market careers, *Work and Occupations*. **29**(4):428–459.

Hantrais, L., 2000, From Equal Pay to Reconciliation of Employment and Family Life. In: Hantrais, L. (ed.): Gendered Policies in Europe. Reconciling Employment and Family Life. Macmillan Press, London, 1–26.

Hantrais, L., 2004, *Family Policy Matters: Responding to Family Change in Europe*, The Policy Press, University of Bristol, Bristol.

Harris, D. K., and Cole, W. E., 1980, *Sociology of Aging*, Houghton Mifflin Comp, Boston.

Hautaniemi, P., 2004, *Final Delphi Report–Finland*, unpublished report prepared for the Workpackage 3, DIALOG Project, The Population Research Institute, Family Federation of Finland, Helsinki.

HCSO Demographic Research Institute, 2004, *Final Delphi Report–Hungary*, unpublished report prepared for the Workpackage 3, DIALOG Project, Demographic Research Institute, Budapest.

Herbertson, T. T., 2003, International perspectives on early retirement, *Generations Review*. **13**(1):4–9.

Herwartz-Emden, L., 1995, *Mutterschaft und weibliches Selbstkonzept. Eine interkulturell vergleichende Untersuchung,* Juventa, Weinheim, München.

Hoem, J. M., 2000, Social policy and recent fertility change in Sweden, *Population and Development Review*. **16**(4):735–48.

Höhn, C., 2005, Demographic challenges for social cohesion: A review and analysis of the work of the European Population Committee 2001–2004, Study prepared for the European Population Conference 2005, *Population Studies*. **48**.

Holzmann, R., Mackellar, L., and Rutkowski, M., 2003, Accelerating the European pension reform agenda: Need, progress, and conceptual underpinnings. In: *Pension Reform in Europe:*

Process and Progress, R. Holzmann, M. Orenstein, and M. Rutkowski, eds., The World Bank, Washington, D.C.

Hörl, Josef; Schimany, Peter: Gewalt gegen pflegebedürftige alte Menschen in der Familie. In: Zeitschrift für Familienforschung, 2/2004, 194–215.

Hrynkiewicz, J., 1993, A shift towards a welfare mix – for innovation or for survival. In: *Balancing Pluralism*, A. Evers, and I. Svetlik, eds., Vienna, pp. 217–230.

Huf, S., 1998, *Welfare State and Modernity*, Duncker & Humblot, Berlin, pp. 37–66.

ILO, 1997, Part-time work: Solution or trap? *International Labour Review Perspectives.* **136**(4), 557–579.

IMF, 2004, *World Economic Outlook*, Sept. 2004, World Economic and Financial Surveys, Washington.

Inglehart, R., 1997, *Modernization and Postmodernization: Cultural, Economic and Political Change in 43 Societies,* Princeton University Press, Princeton.

Intercollege, 2004, *Final Delphi Report – Cyprus*, unpublished report prepared for the Workpackage 3, DIALOG Project, Intercollege, Nicosia.

Jahnert, G., Gohrisch, J., Hahn, D., Nickei, H., Peini, I., and Schäfgen, K., 2001, *Gender in Transition in Eastern and Central Europe: Proceedings*, Trafo Verlag, Berlin.

Jaumotte, F., 2003, *Female Labour Force Participation: Past Trends and Main Determinants in OECD countries*, OECD Economics Department Working Paper No 376, OECD Publishing, Paris.

Joshi, H., 2002, Production, Reproduction, and Education: Women, Children, and Work in a British Perspective, *Population and Devolpment Review,* **28**(3), NewYork, pp. 445–474.

Kamerman, S., Neuman, M., Waldfogel, J., and Brooks-Gunn, J., 2003, *Social Policies, Family Types, and Child Outcomes in Selected OECD Countries,* OECD Social, Employment, and Migration Working Papers No. 6, Paris.

Kaufmann, F.-X., 2002, Politics and policies towards the family in Europe. In: *Family Life and Family Policies in Europe*, Vol. 2, F.-X. Kaufmann et al., eds., University Press, Oxford, pp. 419–490.

Kaufmann, F.-X., 2005, *Social Policy and the Welfare State: Sociological Analysis*, VS Verlag für Sozialwissenschaften, Wiesbaden.

Klie, T., and Blinkert, B., 2002, Pflegekulturelle Orientierungen. In: *Gerontologie und Sozialpolitik*, C. Tesch-Römer, ed., Kohlhammer, Stuttgart, pp. 197–218.

Kohl, J., 2002, Einstellungen der Bürger zur sozialen Sicherung, insbesondere zur Alterssicherung, *Deutsche Rentenversicherung.* **9–10**:477–493.

Kontula, O., and Miettinen, A., 2005, *Synthesis Report on Demographic Behaviour, Existing Population Related Policies and Expectations Men and Women Have Concerning the State*, Working Papers E19/2005, The Population Research Institute, Family Federation of Finland, Helsinki.

Kontula, O., Miettinen, A., 2005, *General Population Related Policies and Attitudes*, DIALOG paper series No.4, Wiesbaden.

Korpi, W., 1989, Power, politics, and state autonomy in the development of social citizenship, *American Sociological Review.* **54**:309–328.

Korpi, W., 2000, *Faces of Inequality: Gender, Class, and Patterns of Inequalities in Different Types of Welfare States*, Social Politics, Summer 2000, Oxford University Press, Oxford.

Kotowska, I. E., Matysiak, A., Domaradzka, A., 2004, *Final Delphi Report – Poland*, unpublished report prepared for the Workpackage 3, DIALOG Project, Institute of Statistics and Demography – Warsaw School of Economics, Warsaw.

Kotowska, I. E., 2005, Older workers in the labour market and social policies, *Population Studies.* **50**:117–168.

Kotowska, I. E., Matysiak, A., Muszyńska, M., Abramowska, A., 2006, *Work and Parenthood*, DIALOG paper series No.6, Wiesbaden.

Kuijsten, A. C., 1996, Changing family patterns in Europe: The case of divergence? *European Journal of Population.* **12**(2):115–143.

Lamura, G., 2003, *Supporting Careers of Older People in Europe, Ancona 2003*, INRCA, 11th European Social Services Conference, July 2–4, Venice.

Leisering, L., and Berner, F., 2001, *Vom produzierenden zum regulierenden Wohlfahrtsstaat*, Regina-Arbeitspapiere 1, Bielefeld.

Lesthaeghe, R., 1983, A century of demographic and cultural change in Western Europe: An exploration of underlying dimensions, *Population and Development Review*. **9**(3): 411–436.

Lesthaeghe, R., 1995, The second demographic transition in Western countries: An interpretation. In: *Gender and Family Change in Industrialized Countries*, K. O. Mason, and A.-M. Jensen, eds., Clarendon Press, Oxford, pp. 17–62.

Lesthaeghe, R., and Surkyn, J., 2002, *New Forms of Household Formation in Central and Eastern Europe: Are they Related to Newly Emerging Value Orientations?* IPD-WP 2002-2, Vrije Universiteit Brussel.

Lesthaeghe, R., and Surkyn, J., 2004, When History Moves on: The Foundations and Diffusion of a Second Demographic Transition, Interface Demography, Free University of Brussels, Brussels.

Lewin-Epstein, N., Stier, H., Braun, M., and Langfeldt, B., 2000, Family policy and public attitudes in Germany and Israel, *European Sociological Review*. **16**(4):385–401.

Linstone, H. A., Turoff, M., 1975, *The Delphi Method: Techniques and Applications*, Addison-Wesley Pub. Co., Reading.

Lisbon European Council, 2000, Presidency Conclusions, http://www.europarl.europa.eu/summits/lis1_en.htm

Lohkamp-Himmighofen, M., Dienel, C., 2000, Reconciliation Policies from a Comparative Perspective. In: Hantrais, L. (eds.): Gendered Policies in Europe. Reconciling Employment and Family Life. Macmillan Press, London, 49–67.

Manea, B. E., 2004, *Final Delphi Report –Romania*, unpublished report prepared for the Workpackage 3, DIALOG Project, Masaryk University Department of Sociology – School of Social Studies, Brno

McDonald, P., 2000a, Gender equity and theories of fertility transition, *Population and Development Review*. **26**(3):427–439.

McDonald, P., 2000b, Gender equity, social institutions and the future of fertility, *Journal of Population Research*. **17**(1):1–16.

McGoldrick, A. E., and Cooper, C. L., 1988, *Early Retirement*, Gower, Hants.

Moors, G., 2004, Facts and artefacts in the comparison of attitudes among ethnic minorities, A multigroup latent class structure model with adjustment for response style behavior, *European Sociological Review*. **20**(4):303–320.

Moors, H., and Palomba, R., eds., 1995, *Population, Family, and Welfare. A Comparative Survey of European Attitudes*, Vol. 1, Clarendon Press, Oxford.

NIDI, 2005, Comparative Report on Children and Child-friendly Policies and Summary Policy Implications Regarding Children and Child-friendly Policies, Workpackage 7, DIALOG Project, Netherlands Interdisciplinary Demographic Institute, The Hague.

Noro, A., 1998, *Long-term Institutional Care among Finnish Elderly Population*, Stakes, Helsinki.

Notestein, F., 1954, *Some Demographic Aspects of Aging*, Proceedings of the American Philosophical Society, Talk first read before the American Philosophical Society on April 23, 1953, in the Symposium on Social and Economic Problems of Aging. **98**:38–46.

OECD, 1995a, *The Transition from Work to Retirement*, Social policy studies no.16, Paris.

OECD, 1995b, *The Labour Market and Older Workers*, Social policy studies no.17, Paris.

OECD, 2001, *Citizens as Partners: Information, Consultation and Public Participation in Policymaking*, OECD Publishing, Paris.

OECD, 2005, *Pensions at a Glance: Public Policies Across OECD Countries*; www.oecd.org/els/social/ageing/PAG.

Oppenheim-Mason, K., and Jensen, A.-M., eds., 1995(2003), *Gender and Family Change in Industrialised Countries*, Clarendon Press, Oxford.

O'Reilly, J., 1996, Theoretical considerations in cross-national employment research, *Sociological Research Online.* **1**(1), http://www.socresonline.org.uk/1/1/2.html.

Ostner, I., and Lewis, J., 1995, Gender and evolution of European social policies. In: *European Social Policy: Between Fragmentation and Integration*, S. Liebfreid, and P. Pierson, eds., Brookings Institute, Washington D.C., pp. 159–194.

Palomba, R. ed., 2005, *Delphi Study*, DIALOG paper Series No.3, Wiesbaden.

Palomba, R., and Moors, H., eds., 1998, *Population, Family and Welfare, A Comparative Survey of European Attitudes*, Clarendon Press, Oxford, Vol. 2, p. 287.

Palomba, R., et al., 2005, *Comparative Delphi Report: Summary Policy Implications of Delphi Study*, D11/12, submitted to the European Commission.

Philipov, D., 2006, *Gender Issues*, DIALOG paper series No.5, Wiesbaden.

Philipov, D., and Dorbritz, J., 2003, Demographic consequences of economic transition in countries of Central and Eastern Europe, *Population Studies.* **39**:151–164.

Phillipson, C., 2002, *Transitions from Work to Retirement: Developing a New Social Contract*, The Policy Press, Bristol.

Pinnelli, A., 2001, Determinants of fertility in Europe, *Population Studies.* **35**:47–182.

Quadango, J., and Hardy, M., 1996, Work and retirement. In: *Handbook of Aging and the Social Sciences*, R. H. Binstock, and L. K. George, eds., 4th ed., Academic Press, San Diego, pp. 235–345.

Rabušic, L., 2004, Why are they all so eager to retire? *Sociologický časopis/Czech Sociological Review.* **40**(3):319–342.

Ragin, C. C., 1987, *The Comparative Method*, University of California Press, Berkley/Los Angeles.

Reday-Mulvey, G., 2005, *Working beyond 60, Key Policies and Practices in Europe*, Palgrave, Macmillan, New York.

Riley, M. W., 1987, On the significance of age in sociology, American Sociological Association, 1986 presidential address, *American Sociological Review.* **52**:1–14.

Riley, M. W., Johnson, M., and Foner, A., 1972, *Aging and Society, Vol. 3: A Sociology of Age Stratification*, Russell Sage Foundation, New York.

Rindfuss, R. R., Brewster, K., and Kavee, A., 1996, Women, work, and children: Behavioral and attitudinal changes in the United States, *Population and Development Review.* 22(3):457–482.

Rosenfeld, R., Trappe, H., and Gornick, J., 2004, Gender and work in Germany, Before and after reunification, *Annual Review of Sociology.* **30**:103–124.

Rosenmayr, L., 1985, Changing values and positions of aging in western culture. In: *Handbook of the Psychology of Aging,* J. E. Birren, and K. W. Schaie, eds., 2nd ed., Van Nostrand Reinhold Company, New York.

Ryder, N. B., 1972, Notes on the concept of a population. In: *Aging and Society, Vol. 3: A Sociology of Age Stratification,* M. W. Riley, M. Johnson, and A. Foner, eds., Russell Sage Foundation, New York, pp. 91–111.

Ryder, N. B., 1975, Notes on stationary populations, *Population Index.* **41**:3–27.

Sabatier, P. A., and Jenkins-Smith, H. C., 1993, *Policy Change and Learning: An Advocacy Coalition Approach*, Westview Press, Boulder/San Francisco/Oxford.

Sabatier, P. A., and Jenkins-Smith, H. C., 1999, The advocacy coalition framework: An assessment. In: *Theories of the Policy Process*, P. A. Sabatier, ed., Westview Press, Oxford/Colorado, pp. 117–156.

Safilios-Rothschild, C., 1970, Toward a cross-cultural conceptualization of family modernity, *Journal of Comparative Family Studies.* **1**:17–25.

Sainsbury, D., 1996, *Gender, Equality and Welfare States*, Cambridge University Press, Cambridge.

Samorodov, A., 1999, Ageing and labour markets for older workers, International Labour office, Geneva.

Schenk, Herrad, 1988, Die feministische Herausforderung : 150 Jahre Frauenbewegung in Deutschland, Beck, Munich.

Scherer, P., 2001, *Age of Withdrawal from the Labour Force in OECD Countries*, OECD Labour Market and Social Policy Occasional Papers No 49.

Schlager, E., 1999, A comparison of frameworks, theories, and models of policy processes. In: *Theories of the Policy Process*, P. A. Sabatier, ed., Westview Press, Oxford/Colorado, pp. 233–260.

Schneider, N. F., 1994, *Familie und Private Lebensführung in West- und Ostdeutschland*, Enke.

Schoenmaeckers, R. C., 2005, Population ageing and its economic and financial implications, *Population Studies*. **50**, Council of Europe Publishing, Strasbourg.

Schoenmaeckers, R. C., and Vanderleyden, L., 2005, Intergenerational solidarity, the elderly and ageing: Main results. In: *Studia Demograficzne* **148**(2), Kotowska, I., ed., Warsaw, pp. 100–113.

Schoenmaeckers, R. C., Vanderleyden, L., and Vidovićová, L., 2006, Intergenerational Solidarity, the Elderly and Ageing, DIALOG paper series No.8, Wiesbaden.

Schroots, J. J. F., and Birren, J. E., 1980, *A Psychological Point of View towards Human Aging and Adaptability, Adaptability and Aging*, Proceedings of the 9th International Conference of Social Gerontology, Quebec, Canada, pp. 43–54.

Schütze, Y., 1991, Die gute Mutter. Zur Geschichte des normativen Musters „Mutterliebe". Bielefeld: Kleine Verlag.

Schwartz, P., 1996, *The Art of the Long View: Planning for the Future in an Uncertain World*, Currency-Doubleday, New York.

Shorter, E., 1975, The Making of the Modern Family. New York: Basic Books.

Skuban, R., 2004, *Pflegesicherung in Europa*, Verlag für Sozialwissenschaften, Wiesbaden.

Snijders, T. A. B., and Bosker, R. J., 1999, *Multilevel Analysis, An Introduction to Basic and Advanced Multilevel Modeling*, Sage, London.

Sobotka, T., 2004, *Postponement of Childbearing and Low Fertility in Europe,* Dutch University Press, Amsterdam.

Söderling, I., and Laitalainen, E., 2005, *Summary of Demographic Trends and Policy Implications*, The Population Research Institute, Väestöliitto, Working Papers E 20/2005, Helsinki.

SPSS, 2003, *SPSS Advanced Models 12.0*, Spss Inc., Chicago.

StataCorp, 2003, *Stata Statistical Software: Release 8.0*, College Station, Stata Corporation, TX.

Stropnik, N., 2004, *Final Delphi Report – Slovenia*, unpublished report prepared for the Workpackage 3, DIALOG Project, Institute for Economic Research, Ljubljana.

Taqi, A., 2002, Older people, work and equal opportunity, *International Social Security Review.* **55**(1):107–124.

Tárkányi, A., 2004, *Country Report Hungary*, unpublished.

The Economist, 2004, *A Survey of Retirement*, March 27.

Tukey, J. W., 1977, *Exploratory Data Analysis*, Addison-Wesley, Reading, Massachusetts.

Uhlenberg, P., 1987, How old is "Old Age"? *The Public Interest.* **82**:67–78.

UN, 1994, Programme of action, adapted at the International Conference on Population and Development. Cairo, 5–13 September 1994.

UN, 1995, *Programme of Action of the World Summit for Social Development*, Copenhagen, March 6–2.

UN, 2002, *Report of the Second World Assembly on Ageing: Madrid Political Declaration and International Plan of Action 2002*, Second World Assembly on Ageing, Madrid, April 8–12.

UN, 2003, *World Population Prospects: The 2002 Revision*, ESA/P/WP.180, Department of Economic and Social Affairs, Population Division, United Nations, New York.

UN, 2005, *Population Prospects, The 2004 Revision*, Department of Economic and Social Affairs, Population Division, United Nations, New York.

UN data sheet, 2002, www.un.org.

van de Kaa, D. J., 2001, Postmodern fertility preferences: From changing value orientation to new behaviour, *Population and Development Review* (Supplement). **27**:290–331.

van Dongen, W., Malfait, D., and Pauwels, K., 1995, *De dagelijkse puzzel "gezin en arbeid"*, *Feiten, wensen en problemen inzake de combinatie van beroeps- en gezinsarbeid in Vlaanderen*, CBGS Monografie 2, Centrum voor Bevolkings- en Gezinsstudie, Brussel.

van Peer, C., Desmet, B., 2004, *Final Report on the Flemish Delphi*, unpublished report prepared for the Workpackage 3, DIALOG Project, Population and Family Study Centre, Brussels.

Vanderleyden, L., and Vanden Boer, L., 2003, Ouderen en de Tweede Demografische Transitie, Een signalement vanuit het LeefsituatieOnderzoek Vlaamse Ouderen (LOVO-1), *Bevolking en Gezin.* **1**:45–64.

Veenhoven, R., 2002, Why social policy needs subjective indicators, *Social Indicators Research.* **58**:33–45.

Vickerstaff, S., Baldock, J., Cox, J., and Keen, L., 2004, *Happy Retirement? The Impact of Employers' Policies and Practice on the Process of Retirement,* The Policy Press, Bristol.

Vidovicova, L., 2005, *To be active or not to be active, that is the Question, Rethinking Age and Employment according to the New Preference Model of Activity in Advanced Age,* Paper presented on ESA Conference, Toruń, Poland, September 9–13.

Vienna Institute for Demography, 2004, *Final Delphi Report – Austria,* unpublished report prepared for the Workpackage 3, DIALOG Project, Vienna Institute for Demography, Vienna.

Vlasblom, J. D., and Nekkers, G., 2001, *Regional Differences in Labour Force Activity Rates of Persons aged 55+ within European Union,* Eurostat working papers: Population and Social Conditions 3/2001/E/no.6.

Weick, S., 2002, Subjektive Bewertung der sozialen Sicherung im Zeitverlauf mit besonderer Berücksichtigung der Alterssicherung, *Deutsche Rentenversicherung.* **9–10**:494–509.

WHO, 2001, *Health and Ageing,* A discussion paper prepared by P. Edwards, WHO, Geneva.

Wielink, G., and Huijsman, R., 1999, The relationship between attitudes towards care and care preferences of elderly community residents in the Netherlands, *Canadian Journal on Aging.* **18**(4):493–512.

Index

European Studies of Population

1. J.-P. Gonnot, N. Keilman and C. Prinz: *Social Security, Household, and Family Dynamics in Ageing Societies.* 1995 ISBN 0-7923-3395-0
2. H. van den Brekel and E Deven (eds.): *Population and Family in the Low Countries 1994.* Selected Current Issues. 1995 ISBN 0-7923-3396-9
3. R. Cliquet and C. Thienpont: *Population and Development.* A Message from the Cairo Conference. 1995 ISBN 0-7923-3763-8
4. H. van den Brekel and F. Deven (eds.): *Population and Family in the Low Countries 1995.* Selected Current Issues. 1996 ISBN 0-7923-3945-2
5. H.A. de Gans: *Population Forecasting 1895-1945.* The Transition to Modernity. 1999 ISBN 0-7923-5537-7
6. D. van de Kaa, H. Leridon, G. Gesano and M. Okólski (eds.): *European Populations: Unity in Diversity.* 1999 ISBN 0-7923-5838-4 (HB)
7. J. de Beer and L. van Wissen (eds.): *Europe: One Continent, Different Worlds.* Population Scenarios for the 21st Century. 1999 ISBN 0-7923-5840-6 (HB)
8. J. de Beer and F. Deven (eds.): *Diversity in Family Formation.* The 2nd Demographic Transition in Belgium and The Netherlands. 2000 ISBN 0-7923-6461-9
9. E. Tabeau, A. van den Berg Jeths and C. Heathcote (eds.): *Forecasting Mortality in Developed Countries: Insight from a Statistical, Demographic and Epidemiological Perspective.* 2001 ISBN 0-7923-6833-9
10. M. Corijn and E. Klijzing (eds.): *Transitions to Adulthood in Europe.* 2001 ISBN 0-7923-6965-3
11. G. Wunsch, M. Mouchart and J. Duchêne (eds.): *The Life Table.* Modelling Survival and Death. 2002 ISBN 1-4020-0638-1
12. H.-P. Blossfeld and A. Timm (eds.): *Who Marries Whom?* Educational Systems as Marriage Markets in Modem Societies. 2003 ISBN 1-4020-1682-4
13. T. Frejka and J.-P. Sardon: *Childbearing Trends and Prospects in Low-Fertility Countries.* A Cohort Analysis. 2004 ISBN 1-4020-2457-6
14. G. Dalla Zuanna and G.A. Micheli (eds.): *Strong Family and Low Fertility: A Paradox?* New Perspectives in Interpreting Contemporary Family and Reproductive Behaviour. 2004 ISBN 1-4020-2836-9
15. S. Gustafsson and A. Kalwij (eds.): *Education and Postponement of Maternity.* 2006 ISBN 1-4020-47 15-0
16. C. Höhn, D. Avramov and I.E. Kotowska (eds.): *People, Population Change and Policies: Vol. 2: Demographic Knowledge – Gender – Ageing.* 2008 ISBN 978-1-4020-6610-8